STILW

KEY TO E

🕭 Children welcome (from age shown in brackets, if specified)

P Off-street car parking (number of places shown in brackets)

✂ No smoking

TV Television (either in every room or in a TV lounge)

🐾 Pets accepted (by prior arrangement)

✕ Evening meal available (by prior arrangement)

V Special diets catered for (by prior arrangement - please check with owner to see if your particular requirements are catered for)

▥ Central heating throughout

accessible to wheelchair user travelling independently; 2 means accessible to wheelchair user travelling with assistance; 3 means accessible to person with limited mobility able to walk a few paces/up maximum three steps

�֎ Christmas breaks a speciality

☕ Coffee/tea making facilities

cc Credit cards accepted

Use the **National Grid** reference with Ordnance Survey maps and any atlas that uses the British National Grid. The letters refer to a 100 kilometre grid square. The first two numbers refer to a North/South grid line and the last two numbers refer to an East/West grid line. The grid reference indicates their intersection point.

The **location heading** – every hamlet, village, town and city listed in this directory is represented on the local county map at the head of each section.

Local pubs – these are the names of nearby pubs that serve food in the evening, as suggested by local B&Bs.

Kirkwhimsey

HX2096 🍺 *Highland Hotel, Macleod's*

Tallstorey House, *Reverie Road, Kirkwhimsey, Nonesuch, KH10 0QT.*

C18th former rectory, lovely garden. Situated in beautiful lowland village.

Open: All Year

Grades: STB 3 Star B&B

01631 730309 Mrs Macdonald

moorland@netcomuk.co.uk

D: £17.00–£20.00 **S:** £20.00–£22.00

Beds: 1F 1D 1T

Baths: 1 Pr 2 Sh

🕭 (4) **P** (2) ✂ **TV** 🐾 ✕ ▥ **V** �֎ ☕ ♿2 **cc**

Bedrooms
F = Family
D = Double
T = Twin
S = Single

Bathrooms
En = Ensuite
Pr = Private
Sh = Shared

D: **Price range** *per person sharing* in a *double room*.
S: **Price range** for a single person in a room.

Scottish Tourist Board (**STB**) grades have two parts: the Star rating is for quality (**1 Star** to **5 Star**, highest), the other part designates the type of establishment, e.g. **B&B**, Guest House (**GH**), Country House (**CH**) etc. Ask at Tourist Information Centres for further information on this grading system. The Automobile Association (**AA**) and Royal Automobile Club (**RAC**) both grade B&Bs for quality in Diamonds (**1 Diamond** to **5 Diamond**, highest) and hotels in Stars (**1 Star** to **5 Star**).

Currency Converter

Here is a quick dollar/sterling conversion table for our American readers, based on rates as we went to press in November 2000 ($10 = £7.01 or £10 = $14.27). On these terms, the average starting double rate per person per night in this book is $27.

$20 = £14.02	£15 = $21.41
$30 = £21.03	£20 = $28.55
$40 = £28.04	£25 = $35.68
$50 = £35.06	£30 = $42.82

Please note: while it may be fine in some States to make advance bookings with several B&Bs for the same date, only to choose the final one later, it is certainly not acceptable practice in Britain. Owners who suffer at the hands of 'double-bookers' in this way are entitled to sue for compensation.

SCOTLAND BED & BREAKFAST 2001

Publisher **Tim Stilwell**

Editor **Martin Dowling**

STILWELL
Publishing Ltd

Distributed in Great Britain, Ireland and the Commonwealth by Orca Book Services,
Stanley House, 3 Fleets Lane, Poole, Dorset BH15 3AJ (Tel: 01202 665432);
and in the USA by Seven Hills Distributors, 49 Central Avenue, Cincinatti, OH 45202
(Tel: 513 381 3881).
Available from all good bookshops.

ISBN 1-900861-23-2

Published by Stilwell Publishing Ltd,
59 Charlotte Road, Shoreditch, London, EC2A 3QW.
Tel: 020 7739 7179.

Publisher: Tim Stilwell
Editor: Martin Dowling
Design and Maps: Space Design and Production Services Ltd
Front Cover Design: Crush Design Associates

Printed in the Channel Islands by the Guernsey Press Company Ltd, Guernsey.

Contents

Introduction & Regional Map	vi-ix
Aberdeenshire & Moray	2-20
Angus	21-26
Argyll & Bute	27-42
Ayrshire & Arran	43-53
Borders & Berwickshire	54-65
Dumfries & Galloway	66-83
Fife	84-92
Glasgow & District	94-99
Highland	100-141
Inner Hebrides	142-155
Lanarkshire	156-159
Lothian & Falkirk	160-175
Orkney	176-179
Perthshire & Kinross	180-190
Shetland	191-193
Stirling & the Trossachs	194-205
Western Isles	206-211
Index	213-216

Introduction

This directory is really very straightforward. It sets out simply to list as many B&Bs in as many places in Scotland as possible, so that wherever you go, you know there is one nearby.

A few years ago my wife and I visited Scotland and decided to use B&Bs for accommodation on our trip. Like most visitors, our knowledge of Scotland's geography was reasonable but not brilliant. We had the Tourist Board's accommodation lists, but found it hard to match the listings to our road atlas - indeed, some places were impossible to find on any map, while others were miles away from the heading they were listed under. In the end, we just stayed in the big towns, missing out on the choice offered by the hundreds of B&Bs dotted all over the countryside.

We had had similar experiences in England as well. In 1993, I decided to set up a company devoted to publishing information about good, low-cost accommodation right across Britain, illustrated with proper maps and arranged in a way that everyone could understand without having to peer down narrow columns or interpret obscure symbols. The eighth edition of the British book appears this year. This is the sixth edition of the book for Scotland alone.

This is therefore a book to save the reader time and money: it suits anyone who wishes to plan a trip in Scotland, who appreciates good value and who is open to ideas. The directory is quite deliberately not a guidebook. Its aim is that of any directory in any field: to be comprehensive, to offer the widest choice. By this definition, *Stilwell's Scotland: Bed & Breakfast* outstrips any guidebook - we publish by far and away the largest number of B&Bs listed anywhere outside the Tourist Board's lists. What we don't do is make up the reader's mind for them. There are plenty of other B&B books that push their particular premises as 'exclusive' or 'special'. We think that a simple glance over the salient details on any page and the reader will be his or her own guide.

We have two kinds of reader in mind. The first knows exactly where to go but not where to stay. The nearest B&B is the best solution; a quick look at the right regional map gives the answer. The other reader is not so sure where to go. As they browse the pages, the short descriptions provide good ideas. All information here has been supplied by the B&B owners themselves. All are bona fide B&Bs; all are on the books of the local Tourist Board. We should make it clear that inclusion in these pages does not imply personal recommendation. We have not visited them all individually; all we have done is write to them. The directory lists over 1,300 entries in 600 locations throughout Scotland. The vast majority were included because they offered B&B for under £27.50 per person per night (in fact the average starting double rate per person per night in this book is £18.00).

Owners were canvassed in the summer of 2000 and responded by the end of October. They were asked to provide their lowest rates per person per night for 2001. The rates are thus forecasts and are in any case always subject to seasonal fluctuation in demand. Some information may, of course, be out of date already. Grades may go up or down, or be removed altogether. The telephone company may alter exchange numbers. Proprietors may decide to sell up and move out of the business altogether. This is why the directory has to be a yearbook; in general, though, the information published here will be accurate, pertinent and useful for many a year. The pink highlight boxes are advertisements - the B&B has paid for some extra wordage and for their entry to stand out from the page a little more.

The main aim has been to provide details that are concise and easy to understand. The only symbols used are some conventional tourist symbols. There are some abbreviations, but it should be clear what they stand for without having to refer to the key on the first page. The grades are perhaps more difficult - each inspecting organisation has its own classification system with its own definition of merit. Once again, though, the reader will soon pick out the exceptional establishments - many have high grades from each organisation. The general rule is that more facilities mean higher prices. Do not be misled into thinking that an ungraded establishment is inferior. Many B&B owners are locally registered but never apply for grades or do not wish to pay for one. They thrive on business from guests who return again and again because the hospitality is excellent. My advice is: ring around. A simple telephone call and some judicious questions will give you an impression of your host very effectively. Your own tastes and preferences will do the rest.

We have deliberately arranged the book by administrative region in alphabetical order. We also hope to delight the hearts of many who take pride in their native or adopted counties. From April 1996, our government saw fit to rename administrative regions and revise many local government boundaries. Out went many of the the 1975 creations of the Heath government - Strathclyde, Grampian, Central and Tayside. In came older and much loved names, such as Argyll & Bute, Ayrshire and Lanarkshire. While this has undoubtedly served to make many people happier (hatred of the 1975 regions was quite intense), it has proved rather a headache for travel book publishers. Many of the new Scottish regions are too small to merit their own chapter and so we have merged them into neighbouring regions - hence 'Lothian & Falkirk' or 'Stirling & the Trossachs' (which includes Clackmannanshire). The Glasgow chapter mixes six new unitary authorities. The reason for the reorganisation is to remove 'two-tier' authorities. We are told that this will cost the tax payer less. In perusing the map the dispassionate observer sees other, more cynical reasons.

The major boundary changes occur along the Clyde and seem calculated to neuter power in traditional Labour heartlands. In the end, the savings to be made in administrating these unitary authorities will, hopefully, outweigh any confusion caused to tourists with limited knowledge of Scottish geography. Was that a pig in the sky outside my window?

Another feature of the book is that we insist on using the proper postal address. Many entries thus carry a county name different from the region they are listed under or a 'post town' that is some miles from the village. These oddities arise from the Royal Mail's distribution system. They should not, under any circumstances, be used as a directional guide. In one case the village of Durness in the North-West Highlands is 69 miles from Lairg, its quoted 'post town' - not a journey to make in error. Used on a letter though, it does speed the mail up. If you need directions to a B&B (especially if you are travelling at night), the best solution is to telephone the owner and ask the way.

The regional maps are intended to act as a general reference. They present only the locations of each entry in the directory. For a more accurate idea of the location of a B&B, use the six-figure National Grid Reference published under each location's name. Used in tandem with an Ordnance Survey map (such as the excellent Landranger series) or any atlas that uses the National Grid, these numbers provide first-class route-planning references. The pubs that appear beneath each location heading are included on the recommendation of B&Bs themselves. The tankard symbol shows that they are local pubs where one can get a decent evening meal at a reasonable price.

Throughout the book you will find boxes offering peremptory advice to readers. These may seem of little consequence; some may even annoy. We are sorry for intruding upon your sensibilities like this but the boxes actually neaten the page. Those that request courtesy and care for the customs of your hosts need no apology, however. Opening your home to strangers, albeit for payment, requires a leap of faith for most people; B&B owners are no exception. We simply ask everyone to observe the usual house rules. In this way, other guests will continue to meet with a welcome when they, too, pass through.

The Publisher,
Stoke Newington, December 2000

Scotland – *Regions*

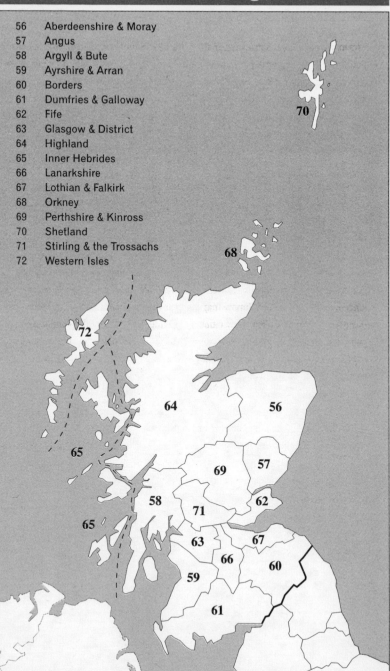

56   Aberdeenshire & Moray
57   Angus
58   Argyll & Bute
59   Ayrshire & Arran
60   Borders
61   Dumfries & Galloway
62   Fife
63   Glasgow & District
64   Highland
65   Inner Hebrides
66   Lanarkshire
67   Lothian & Falkirk
68   Orkney
69   Perthshire & Kinross
70   Shetland
71   Stirling & the Trossachs
72   Western Isles

Aberdeenshire & Moray

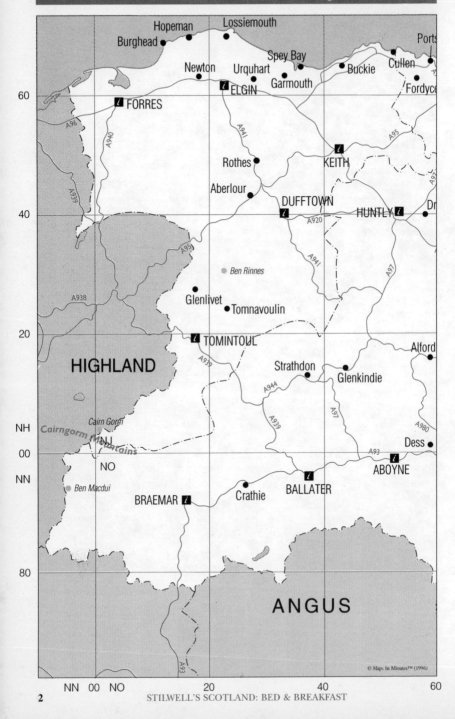

STILWELL'S SCOTLAND: BED & BREAKFAST

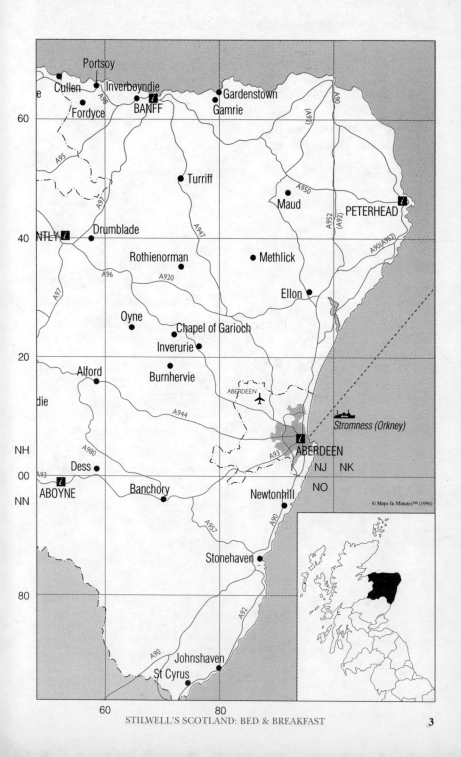

AIRPORTS ⊕
Aberdeen Airport, tel. 01224 722331.

AIR SERVICES & AIRLINES ✈
British Airways, *Aberdeen to Birmingham, Bristol, Glasgow, Kirkwall (Orkney), London (Gatwick & Heathrow), Manchester, Newcastle, Plymouth, Sumburgh (Shetland)*, tel. (local rate) 0345 222111.

KLM UK, *Aberdeen to Humberside, London (Stansted), Norwich, Teesside*, tel. (local rate) 0870 5074074.

BUS 🚌
Scottish Citylink, tel. 08705 505050.
National Express, tel. 0141 226 4826.

RAIL ⇌
For rail information, telephone the National Rail Enquiries line on 08457 484950.
For the Minicom service for the deaf and hard of hearing, tel. 0845 605 0600.

FERRIES ⛴
P&O Scottish Ferries, *Aberdeen to Lerwick (Shetland)* 14 hrs/20 hrs.

Aberdeen to Stromness (Orkney) 8 hrs/14 hrs. Tel. 01224 589111.

TOURIST INFORMATION OFFICES 🄸
St Nicholas House, Broad Street, **Aberdeen**, AB9 1GZ, 01224 632727.

Railway Museum, Station Yard, **Alford**, Aberdeenshire, AB33 8AD, 01975 562052 (Easter to Oct).

Station Square, **Ballater**, Aberdeenshire, AB35 5QB, 01339 755306 (Easter to Oct).

Bridge Street, **Banchory**, Kincardineshire, AB35 5SX, 01330 82200.

Collie Lodge, Low Street, **Banff**, AB45 1AU, 01261 812419 (Easter to Oct).

The Mews, Mar Road, **Braemar**, Ballater, Aberdeenshire, AB35 5YE, 01339 741600 (Easter to Oct).

Car Park, **Crathie**, Ballater, Aberdeenshire, AB35 5TT, 01339 742414 (Easter to Oct).

The Clock Tower, The Square, **Dufftown**, Keith, Banffshire, AB55 4AD, 01340 820501 (Easter to Oct).

17 High Street, **Elgin**, Moray, IV30 1EE, 01343 542666.

116 High Street, **Forres**, Moray, IV36 0PH, 01309 672938 (Easter to Oct).

Saltoun Square, **Fraserburgh**, Aberdeenshire, AB43 5DB, 01346 518315 (Easter to Oct).

7a The Square, **Huntly**, Aberdeenshire, AB54 5AE, 01466 792255 (Easter to Oct).

18 High Street, **Inverurie**, Aberdeenshire, AB54 5AE, 01467 625800 (Easter to Oct).

66 Allardice Street, **Stonehaven**, Kincardineshire, AB3 2AA, 01569 762806 (Easter to Oct).

The Square, **Tomintoul**, Ballindalloch, Banffshire, AB37 9ET, 01807 580285 (Easter to Oct).

Aberdeen

NJ9306 ◀ *Star & Garter, Goldies, Cafe D'Ag, Gates, Gillie's Lair, Inn at Park, Gerards, The Abergeldie, Club House, Brentwood Hotel, Flare & Firkin, Highland Hotel, Gerards, Ferryhill House Hotel*

Dunrovin Guest House, *168 Bon Accord Street, Aberdeen, AB1 2TX.*
Open: All Year
Grades: STB 3 Star
01224 586081
Mrs Dellanzo
dellanzo@hotmail.com
D: £17.50–£30.00 **S:** £20.00–£30.00
Beds: 1F 1D 3T 3S **Baths:** 2 En 2 Sh
ⵗ⌇⧖🐾🏚🚶
Family-run C19th guest house set in a tree-lined street approximately 1000 yards to city centre and also park and river. Rail and bus stations are both only a 10-minute walk and there is easy parking. Surgery across road. Satellite TV throughout.

Beeches Private Hotel, *193 Great Western Road, Aberdeen, AB10 6PS.*
Victoria detached property residential area close to the city centre.
Open: All Year (not Xmas)
Grades: STB 3 Star
01224 586413
Mr Sandison
Fax: 01224 596919
beeches-hotel@talk21.com
D: £18.00–£22.50 **S:** £22.00–£32.00
Beds: 2F 3D 2T 3S **Baths:** 7 En 2 Sh
🅿 (13) ⌇🖵🐾🏚🚶 cc

Roselodge Guest House, *3 Springbank Terrace, Aberdeen, AB11 6LS.*
Quiet city centre location, convenient for all amenities. Private parking.
Open: All Year (not Xmas)
Grades: STB 2 Star
01224 586794 (also fax)
Mrs Wink
marywink@roseguest.freeserve.co.uk
D: £15.00–£18.00 **S:** £18.00–£20.00
Beds: 3F 2T 1S **Baths:** 2 Sh
ⵗ🅿 (3) 🖵🏚🚶

Aberdeen Springbank Guest House, *6 Springbank Terrace, Aberdeen, AB11 6LS.*
Comfortable family-run Victorian terraced house, non-smoking, 5 minutes from city centre.
Open: All Year
Grades: STB 2 Star
01224 592048 (also fax)
Mr & Mrs Robertson
D: £16.00–£20.00 **S:** £21.00–£26.00
Beds: 3F 4D 3T 4S **Baths:** 12 En 4 Sh
ⵗ⌇🖵🏚🚶

The Ferndale Private Hotel, *62 Bon-Accord Street, Aberdeen, AB11 6EL.*
City centre, easy walk to station, shopping, clubs, etc.
Open: All Year (not Xmas/New Year)
01224 584835
A Noble
Fax: 01224 584724
ferndale@elbon.u-net.com
D: £17.00–£20.00 **S:** £20.00–£25.00
Beds: 7F 2T 2S **Baths:** 6 Sh
ⵗ 🅿 (4) 🖵🚶 cc

Crown Private Hotel, *10 Spring Bank Terrace, Aberdeen, AB1 2LS.*
Small, central, family-run private hotel.
Open: All Year
Grades: STB 2 Star
01224 586842
Mr Buthlay
Fax: 01224 573787
crown_hotel@yahoo.co.uk
D: £18.00–£22.00 **S:** £16.00–£28.00
Beds: 2F 2D 2T 3S **Baths:** 7 En 1 Sh
ⵗ🖵🐾🏚🚶

Cairnvale B&B, *5 Cairnvale Crescent, Kincorth, Aberdeen, AB1 5JB.*
Homely accommodation. Personal attention. Easy access to Royal Deeside, city centre.
Open: All Year
Grades: STB 3 Star
01224 874163 (also fax)
Mrs Miller
D: £15.00–£18.00 **S:** £16.00–£18.00
Beds: 1D 1S 3F
⌇🖵🐾🏚🚶

St Elmo, *64 Hilton Drive, Aberdeen, AB24 4NP.*
Traditional granite family home, near historic
university and city centre.
Open: All Year
Grades: STB 3 Star
01224 483065
Mrs Watt
stelmobandb@aol.com
D: £16.00–£17.00 **S:** £20.00–£24.00
Beds: 1D 2T **Baths:** 1 Sh
🛏 (1) 🅿 (2) ⌇ 📺 🛏, ♨

Aaran Central Guest House, *27 Jasmine
Terrace, Aberdeen, AB24 5LA.*
By beach, Links Golf Course,
fitness/swimming complex, city centre.
Open: All Year
01224 641410
G Reid
D: £14.00–£17.00 **S:** £16.00–£20.00
Beds: 2F 1D 5T 4S **Baths:** 3 Sh
🛏 (12) ⌇ 📺 🛏, ❋ ♨

Roselea Private Hotel, *12 Springbank
Terrace, Aberdeen, AB11 6LS.*
Friendly family-run hotel in city centre of
Aberdeen.
Open: All Year
Grades: STB 2 Star GH
01224 583060 (also fax)
candfmoore@roseleahotel.demon.co.uk
D: £16.00–£20.00
S: £21.00–£27.00
Beds: 2F 3D 1T **Baths:** 1 En 2 Sh
🛏 ⌇ 📺 🐾 🛏, �V ♨ cc

Corner House Hotel, *385 Great Western
Road, Aberdeen, AB1 6NY.*
Elegant West End hotel, offering good food
with friendly service.
Open: All Year (not Xmas/New Year)
Grades: STB 3 Star, AA 3 Diamond
01224 313063 (also fax)
Mrs Heras
cornerhouse.hotel@virgin.net
D: £25.00–£30.00
S: £38.00–£48.00
Beds: 2F 6D 3T 6S **Baths:** 17 En
🛏 🅿 (8) 📺 🐾 ✗ 🛏, �V ♨ ⚕ cc

The Noble Guest House, *376 Great
Western Road, Aberdeen, AB10 6PH.*
Family-run guest house, convenient for city
centre and Deeside.
Open: All Year
Grades: STB 3 Star
01224 313678
H Noble
Fax: 01224 326981
D: £20.00–£27.00 **S:** £20.00–£27.00
Beds: 1F 1D 3S **Baths:** 3 En 2 Sh
🛏 🅿 (3) 📺 ✗ 🛏, �V ♨ cc

Bon Accord Guest House, *162 Bon
Accord Street, Aberdeen, AB1 2TX.*
Family-run, quiet, central. Bus-rail-ferry
terminals, shopping, museums.
Open: All Year (not Xmas/New Year)
01224 594764 (also fax)
lorraine@bonaccordguesthouse.fsnet.co.uk
D: £16.00–£20.00 **S:** £20.00–£30.00
Beds: 3F 2T 1D 4S **Baths:** 2 En 2 Pr 6 Sh
🛏 🅿 (2) ⌇ 📺 🛏, �V ♨

Arden Guest House, *61 Dee Street,
Aberdeen, AB1 2EE.*
3 Star STB guest house in the heart of the
city centre.
Open: All Year (not Xmas/New Year)
Grades: STB 3 Star
01224 580700 (also fax)
Mr Kelly
ann@ardenguesthouse.co.uk
D: £20.00–£24.00 **S:** £25.00–£40.00
Beds: 1F 2D 3T 5S **Baths:** 2 En 4 Sh
🛏 📺 🛏, �V ♨ cc

Jurayne Guest House, *272 Holburn
Street, Aberdeen, AB1 6DD.*
Friendly guest house. Close to town, park
and pubs.
Open: All Year
01224 575601 Mr Ingram
D: £18.00–£20.00 **S:** £20.00–£22.00
Beds: 1F 2T 2S 2D **Baths:** 2 Sh
🛏 (3) 📺 🐾 🛏, ♨ ⚕ ♿

Planning a longer stay?
Always ask for any special rates

BATHROOMS
Pr - Private

Sh - Shared

En - Ensuite

Adelphi Guest House, *8 Whinhill Road, Aberdeen, AB11 7XH.*
Family-run guest house, close to Duthie Park city centre. **Open:** All Year
Grades: STB 3 Star
01224 583078 Fax: 01224 585434
stay@adelphiguesthouse.com
D: £17.50–£20.00 **S:** £22.50–£27.50
Beds: 3F 1D 1T 1S **Baths:** 3 En 1 Sh
ॐ 🖵 🛏 🕮. Ⅴ 🕯 cc

81 Leggart Avenue, *Aberdeen, AB12 5UP.*
Open: All Year
Grades: STB 2 Star
01224 872898 Mr & Mrs McIlraith
D: £17.50 **S:** £25.00
Beds: 1T **Baths:** 1 Pr
ॐ (7) 🄿 (1) ⅍ 🖵 🕮. 🕯
Convenient Royal, Deeside, Stonehaven, Altens, Tullos. Private parking, non-smoking.

Stewart Lodge Guest House, *89 Bon Accord Street, Aberdeen, AB11 6ED.*
Centrally situated, family-run, clean and friendly, near local amenities.
Open: All Year
01224 573823 (also fax) Mrs Wann
D: £15.00–£19.00 **S:** £20.00–£23.00
Beds: 1F 3T 3S **Baths:** 3 Sh
ॐ 🄿 (3) 🖵 🛏 🕮. 🕯 cc

Haven Guest House, *62 Albergeldie Road, Aberdeen, AB1 6EN.*
Victorian house, quiet location. Warm, friendly atmosphere with personal attention.
Open: All Year (not Xmas)
01224 585659 Mrs Hay
Fax: 01224 585672
albert.hay@tjrp.net
D: £14.00–£25.00 **S:** £16.00–£20.00
Beds: 1F 1D 2T 1S **Baths:** 2 Sh
ॐ ⅍ 🖵 🛏 🕮. Ⅴ 🕯

Butler's Islander Guest House, *122 Crown Street, Aberdeen, AB11 6HJ.*
Comfortable central Georgian town house convenient for all transport.
Open: All Year (not Xmas)
01224 212411 (also fax)
Mr Butler
bookings@butlerigh.demon.co.uk
D: £18.00–£22.00 **S:** £25.00–£35.00
Beds: 3D 3T 1S **Baths:** 2 En 2 Sh
ॐ ⅍ 🖵 🕮. Ⅴ 🕯 cc

Lillian Cottage, *442 King Street, Aberdeen, AB2 3BS.*
Situated only 15 min walk from Aberdeen centre. Very comfortable accommodation.
Open: All Year
01224 636947 (also fax)
lilliancottage.demon.co.uk
D: £18.00–£25.00 **S:** £23.00–£30.00
Beds: 1F 2D 1T 2S **Baths:** 1 En 2 Sh
ॐ 🄿 (6) ⅍ 🖵 🛏 ✕ 🕮. Ⅴ 🕯 cc

The Angel Islington Guesthouse, *191 Bon Accord Street, Aberdeen, AB1 2UA.*
Centrally located family-run business with satellite television in all rooms.
Open: All Year
01224 587043
D: £18.00–£22.50 **S:** £20.00–£30.00
Beds: 4F 3D 2T 2S **Baths:** 11 En
ॐ 🄿 (1) ⅍ 🖵 🛏 🕮. Ⅴ 🕯

Roselynd House, *27 Kings Gate, Aberdeen, AB15 4EL.*
Elegant Victoria town house, situated in the West End, 20 mins' walk city centre.
Open: All Year
01224 640942 Mrs Neyedli
roselynd27@aol.com
D: £17.00 **S:** £23.00
Beds: 1F 2D 1T 1S **Baths:** 3 En 1 Sh
🄿 (3) ⅍ 🖵 🕮. Ⅴ 🕯

High season, bank holidays
and special events mean low
availability anywhere

Aberlour

NJ2642   🏨 *Aberlour Hotel*

83 High Street, *Aberlour, Banffshire,*
AB38 9QB.
The heart of a village famous for whisky and
shortbread.
Open: All Year
01340 871000 Miss Gammack
ruth@resolute.fsnet.co.uk
D: £15.00–£16.00 **S:** £15.00–£16.00
Beds: 1T 2D **Baths:** 2 Sh
🛇 🄿 (2) ⅍ 📺 🛏 🖳 📼 🛆 cc

Aboyne

NO5298   🏨 *Boat Inn*

Struan Hall, *Ballater Road, Aboyne,*
Aberdeenshire, AB34 5HY.
We are quietly situated in 2 acres of
woodland garden.
Open: Mar to Oct
Grades: STB 5 Star
013398 87241 (also fax)
Mrs Ingham
struanhall@zetnet.co.uk
D: £26.00–£28.50 **S:** £26.00–£34.00
Beds: 1D 2T 1S **Baths:** 3 En 1 Pr
🛇 (7) 🄿 (6) ⅍ 📺 🛏 🖳 📼 🛆 cc

Birkwood Lodge, *Gordon Crescent,*
Aboyne, Aberdeenshire, AB34 5HJ.
Beautiful Victorian home. Large garden,
quiet situation, centre small village.
Open: April to Oct
Grades: STB 4 Star
013398 86347 (also fax) Mrs Thorburn
D: £27.50 **S:** £30.00–£35.00
Beds: 1D 2T **Baths:** 2 En 1 Pr
🛇 (6) 🄿 ⅍ 📺 ✕ 🖳 📼 🛆

Charleston Hotel, *Aboyne, Aberdeenshire,*
AB34 5HY.
Warm welcome to breathtaking scenery near
Balmoral Castle. Innumerable outdoor
activities. **Open:** All Year
013398 86475 Fax: 013398 86473
D: £23.00 **S:** £25.00
Beds: 1F 4T 2D 1S **Baths:** 5 En 2 Sh
🛇 🄿 (40) 📺 🛏 ✕ 🖳 📼 ❋ 🛆 ♿

Alford

NJ5716   🏨 *Vale Hotel, Forbes Arms*

Bydand B&B, *18 Balfour Road, Alford,*
Aberdeenshire, AB33 8NF.
Family home. Warm, friendly welcome. Quiet
location near village centre.
Open: All Year **Grades:** STB 3 Star
01975 563613 Mrs Jack
D: £18.00–£20.00 **S:** £18.00–£20.00
Beds: 1D 1T **Baths:** 2 En
🛇 ⅍ 📺 🖳 🛆

Ballater

NO3695   🏨 *Alexandra Hotel, Highlander, Glen Lui,*
Auld Kirk

Morvada Guest House, *Braemar Road,*
Ballater, Aberdeenshire, AB35 5RL.
Open: All Year (not Xmas)
Grades: STB 3 Star
013397 56334 (also fax) Mr Campbell
morvada@aol.com
D: £19.00–£22.00 **S:** £20.00–£25.00
Beds: 5D 1T **Baths:** 6 En
🄿 (6) ⅍ 📺 🛏 🖳 🛆 cc
Allan and Thea Campbell welcome you to
this lovely Victorian villa set in the beautiful
village of Ballater. Excellent rooms, quality
breakfasts, and a prime location for fine
restaurants, Balmoral Castle, the Cairngorm
Mountains, the Whisky and Castle Trails.

Deeside Hotel, *Braemar Road, Ballater,*
Aberdeenshire, AB35 5RQ.
Open: Feb to Dec
Grades: STB 3 Star
013397 55420 Mr Brooker
Fax: 013397 55357
deesidehotel@talk21.com
D: £22.00–£26.00 **S:** £25.00–£30.00
Beds: 1F 4D 4T **Baths:** 9 Pr
🛇 🄿 (15) 📺 🛏 ✕ 🖳 📼 🛆 ♿ cc
Victorian granite villa in quiet location with
large informal garden. Attractive dining,
conservatory and bar areas. Relaxed
breakfast and dinner times. Good central
base for touring NE Scotland's many varied
visitor attractions. 2 ground floor bedrooms.
Taste of Scotland.

Dee Valley, *26 Viewfield Road, Ballater, Aberdeenshire, AB35 5RD.*
Large detached Victorian house. Quiet location. Stair lift. Beautiful countryside.
Open: Apr to Nov
Grades: STB 2 Star
013397 55408 (also fax)
Mrs Gray
D: £17.00–£20.00 **S:** £22.00–£25.00
Beds: 2F 1D 1T **Baths:** 1 En 2 Sh
🛏 (1) 🅿 (3) ⅍ 📺 ▥ ♨

Inverdeen House B&B, *Bridge Square, Ballater, Aberdeenshire, AB35 5QJ.*
Enjoy the warm welcome excellent beds (2 king-size) and generous world class breakfast menu.
Open: All Year
013397 55759 Mr & Mrs Munroe
D: £22.50–£25.00 **S:** £25.00–£50.00
Beds: 1F 2D **Baths:** 2 Sh
🛏 🅿 (3) ⅍ 📺 ▥ ▣ ✳ ♨ cc

Celicall, *3 Braemar Road, Ballater, Aberdeenshire, AB35 5RL.*
Family-run. Central Royal Deeside village. Patio garden front and rear.
Open: Easter to Oct
01339 755699 Mrs Cowie
D: £17.00–£20.00 **S:** £25.00
Beds: 2D 2T **Baths:** 4 En
🅿 (4) ▥ ♨

Morven Lodge, *29 Braemar Road, Ballater, Aberdeenshire, AB35 5RQ.*
Fine Victorian house in renowned village, close to all amenities.
Open: May to Sep
013397 55373 Mrs Henchie
D: £17.50–£18.00 **S:** £18.00
Beds: 1F 1D 1T **Baths:** 1 Pr 2 Sh
🛏 (2) 🅿 (5) 📺 🐾 ▥ ▣ ♨

RATES
D = Price range per person sharing in a double room
S = Price range for a single room

All details shown are as supplied by B&B owners in Autumn 2000

Banchory
NO7095 *Burnett Arms, Scott Skinners*

Dorena, *Strachan, Banchory, Kincardineshire, AB31 6NL.*
Open: All Year (not Xmas/New Year)
Grades: STB 4 Star
01330 822540 (also fax) D Mutch
D: £20.00 **S:** £25.00–£30.00
Beds: 1T 2D **Baths:** 3 En
🅿 (4) ⅍ 📺 ▥ ▣ ♨
Dorena is a modern bungalow with panoramic views over the river Feugh hills and woodlands. Visit castles, historic buildings, gardens and distilleries, and the breathtaking scenery of Royal Deeside. You are assured of a very warm welcome from Doreen and Bill.

Wester Durris Cottage, *Banchory, Kincardineshire, AB31 3BQ.*
Homely accommodation near castle country, Deeside, welcome tea on arrival.
Open: Easter to Oct
01330 844638 Mrs Leslie
D: £16.00–£18.00 **S:** £20.00
Beds: 1F 1T **Baths:** 1 Sh
🛏 (1) 🅿 (4) ⅍ 📺 ▥ ▣ ♨

Banff
NJ6864 *Banff Springs, Banff Links, County Hotel*

Clayfolds Farm, *Banff, AB45 3UD.*
Warm, comfortable accommodation on working farm. 3 miles from Banff.
Open: Easter to Sep
01261 821288
Mrs Eddison
clayfolds@farming.co.uk
D: £15.00 **S:** £15.00
Beds: 1F 1D 1S **Baths:** 1 Sh
🛏 (2) 🅿 (4) 📺 ✕ ▥ ♨

Links Cottage, *Inverboyndie, Banff, AB45 2JJ.*
Picturesque seaside cottage; comfortable
and relaxing. Explore this spectacular
coastline.
Open: Easter to Nov
Grades: STB 4 Star
01261 812223 (also fax)
Mrs Buchan
D: £24.00 **S:** £30.00–£44.00
Beds: 2D 1T **Baths:** 3 En
▣ (6) ⊬ 📺 ▥ Ⓥ 👤 &

The Trinity and Alvah Manse, *21 Castle
Street, Banff, AB45 1DH.*
Trinity Manse is restored and tastefully
decorated to highest standards.
Open: All Year (not Xmas)
Grades: STB 3 Star
01261 812244 (also fax)
Ms Grant
oldmanse@tesco.net
D: £18.00–£20.00 **S:** £18.00–£23.00
Beds: 2D 1T **Baths:** 1 En 2 Pr
🛏 ⊬ 📺 ▥ Ⓥ 👤

Braemar

NO1491 ◀ *Fife Arms, Braemar Lodge, Invercould
Hotel*

Morningside, *Kindrochit Drive, Braemar,
Ballater, Aberdeenshire, AB35 5YQ.*
Cosy house, ideal for walks, skiing and
cycling. Meals on request.
Open: Jan to Oct
013397 41370 Mrs McKellar
D: £16.00–£20.00 **S:** £18.00–£20.00
Beds: 1D 1T **Baths:** 1 Sh
🛏 ▣ (3) ⊬ 📺 🐾 ✕ ▥

Balnellan House, *Braemar, Aberdeenshire,
AB35 5YQ.*
A charming renovated Victorian family home
offering traditional Scottish hospitality.
Open: All Year (not Xmas)
013397 41474 Mrs Sharp
balnellan@hotmail.com
D: £22.00 **S:** £25.00–£30.00
Beds: 2D 1T **Baths:** 3 En
🛏 (1) ▣ (4) ⊬ 📺 🐾 ✕ ▥ Ⓥ

Schiehallion House, *Glenshee Road,
Braemar, Ballater, Aberdeenshire, AB35 5YQ.*
Hearty breakfasts. Friendly courteous
service. Private parking. Village centre 500m.
Open: Dec to Oct **Grades:** STB 3 Star
013397 41679 Mrs Heyes
D: £18.00–£22.00 **S:** £19.00–£21.00
Beds: 2F 3T 3D 1S **Baths:** 5 En 1 Sh
🛏 ▣ (9) ⊬ 📺 🐾 ✕ ▥ Ⓥ ❊ 👤 & CC

Buckie (Spey Bay)

NJ4165

Cluny Hotel, *2 High Street, Buckie,
Banffshire, AB56 1AL.*
Family-run, centrally located hotel
overlooking the Moray Firth.
Open: All Year **Grades:** STB 3 Star
01542 832922
D: £22.00–£28.00 **S:** £26.00–£28.00
Beds: 1F 2D 2T 1S **Baths:** 6 En
🛏 ▣ (40) 📺 🐾 ✕ ▥ Ⓥ 👤 CC

Burghead

NJ1169

Norland, *26 Grary Street, Burghead, Elgin,
Moray, IV30 2UJ.*
Modern bungalow overlooking Burghead
Bay and miles of golden sands.
Open: All Year (not Xmas)
01343 835212 Mrs Smith
D: £15.00 **S:** £15.00
Beds: 1F 1D 2T **Baths:** 2 Sh
🛏 ▣ ⊬ 📺 🐾 ✕ ▥ Ⓥ 👤 &

Burnhervie

NJ7219

Broadsea, *Burnhervie, Inverurie,
Aberdeenshire, AB51 5LB.*
Homely accommodation on a working family
farm. Good home cooking, quiet rural location.
Open: All Year **Grades:** STB 3 Star
01467 681386 Mrs Harper
elizharber@broadsea99.freeserve.co.uk
D: £19.00–£21.00 **S:** £22.00–£26.00
Beds: 1F **Baths:** 1 En
🛏 ▣ ⊬ 📺 🐾 ✕ ▥ Ⓥ 👤 &

Chapel of Garioch

NJ7124

Kirkton Park Bed And Breakfast, *5 Kirkton Park, Chapel of Garioch, Inverurie, AB51 5HF.*
Open: All Year (not Xmas/New Year)
01467 681281 kirkton-park@msn.com
D: £16.00–£22.00 **S:** £16.00–£22.00
Beds: 2T **Baths:** 1 En 1 Pr
🛏 🅿 (4) ⅃ 📺 ✕ 🏳 Ⓥ 🛢
Convenient for Whisky/Castle Trails - close to Bennachie. Good views.

Crathie

NO2695

Inver Hotel, *Crathie, Ballater, Aberdeenshire, AB35 5UL.*
Historic coaching inn dating from 1760, only 50 yards from the river Dee.
Open: All Year
013397 42345 Mr Mathieson
Fax: 013397 42009
D: £15.00–£30.00 **S:** £20.00–£35.00
Beds: 1F 5D 2T 1S **Baths:** 9 En
🛏 🅿 (30) 📺 🐾 ✕ 🏳 Ⓥ ✷ 🛢 cc

Cullen

NJ5167 🍺 *Royal Oak, Waverley Hotel, Three Kings, Grant Arms*

The Elms Guest House, *2 Seafield Place, Cullen, Buckie, Banffshire, AB56 2UU.*
Open: All Year
01542 841271 (also fax) Mr Welford
D: £16.00–£20.00 **S:** £16.00–£20.00
Beds: 1F 2D 2T 1S **Baths:** 1 En 1 Pr 1 Sh
🛏 🅿 (4) 📺 🐾 ✕ 🏳 Ⓥ 🛢 ♿
Family-run guest house offering very comfortable accommodation. Close to Speyside Way, coastal walks and cycle trails, Whisky Trail & Castle Trail. Fishing, sailing, horse riding. 10 golf courses in 18 mile radius.

Bringing children with you?
Always ask for any special rates

Torrach, *147 Seatown, Cullen, Buckie, Banffshire, AB56 4SL.*
Traditional house, near beach and golf course. Warm friendly atmosphere.
Open: Easter to Oct
Grades: STB 3 Star
01542 840724 Mrs Mair
D: £16.00 **S:** £18.00
Beds: 1F 1D **Baths:** 1 Sh
🛏 🅿 (2) 📺 🐾 🏳 Ⓥ 🛢

Waverley Hotel, *12 Blantyre Street, Cullen, Buckie, Banffshire, AB56 4RP.*
Situated near excellent golf courses. Also Whisky and Castle Trails.
Open: All Year
01542 840210 Mrs Finnie
D: £16.00 **S:** £16.00
Beds: 3F 2T 2S **Baths:** 2 Sh
🛏 🅿 (5) 📺 ✕ 🏳 Ⓥ 🛢

Dess

NJ5700 🍺 *Gordon Arms, Boat Inn, Kincardine O'Neill*

Newton of Drumgesk, *Dess, Aboyne, Aberdeenshire, AB34 5BL.*
Comfortable quiet, typical Scottish farmhouse in own acreage. Cot/high chair available. **Open:** Mar to Oct
013398 86203 (also fax)
Mrs Selwyn Bailey
crogerbailey@cs.com
D: £19.50–£25.00 **S:** £19.50–£25.00
Beds: 1T 1D **Baths:** 1 En
🛏 🅿 (6) ⅃ 📺 🐾 🏳 🛢

Drumblade

NJ5840

Annandale House, *Drumblade, Huntly, AB54 6EN.*
Beautifully furnished early Victorian Manse, idyllic location. Ideal for touring.
Open: Mar to Jan **Grades:** STB 4 Star
01466 740233 (also fax) Ms Staunton
susan.staunton@virgin.net
D: £20.00–£27.50 **S:** £20.00–£25.00
Beds: 1T 2D 1S **Baths:** 4 En
🅿 (4) ⅃ 📺 🐾 ✕ 🏳 Ⓥ 🛢 cc

Dufftown

NJ3240 🏨 *Glenfiddich, Fife Arms, Masons' Arms, Croft Inn, Commercial Hotel*

Davaar, *Church Street, Dufftown, Keith, Banffshire, AB55 4AR.*
Nice Victorian house. Some guest rooms overlooking garden at rear.
Open: All Year (not Xmas/New Year)
Grades: STB 3 Star
01340 820464 Mrs Macmillan
D: £16.00–£18.00 **S:** £25.00–£30.00
Beds: 1T 2D **Baths:** 2 En 1 Sh
🛇 🖻 ✕ 🏢 🖻 ☕

Errolbank, *134 Fife Street, Dufftown, Keith, Banffshire, AB55 4DP.*
Friendly local hosts. Scottish breakfasts our speciality. On Whisky Trail.
Open: All Year
01340 820229 Mrs Smart
D: £15.00 **S:** £15.50–£16.00
Beds: 3F 1D 1S **Baths:** 1 Sh
🛇 🅿 (5) 📺 🐾 ✕ 🏢 🖻 ☕

Fife Arms Hotel, *2 The Square, Dufftown, Keith, Banffshire, AB55 4AD.*
Small, modern town centre hotel. Steaks - beef & ostrich our speciality.
Open: All Year
Grades: STB 1 Star, AA 3 Diamond
01340 820220 Mr Widdowson
Fax: 01340 821137
D: £20.00–£25.00 **S:** £22.00–£27.00
Beds: 2F 4T **Baths:** 6 En
🛇 (1) 🅿 (6) 📺 🐾 ✕ 🏢 🖻 ☕ & cc

Nashville, *8a Balvenie Street, Dufftown, Keith, Banffshire, AB55 4AB.*
Relaxed family-run B&B. Whisky Trail - yards from Glenfiddich Distillery. Speyside Way close by.
Open: All Year
01340 820553 (also fax)
Mrs Morrison
nashville@dufftown72.freeserve.co.uk
D: £14.00–£16.00 **S:** £18.00–£20.00
Beds: 1F 1D 1T **Baths:** 1 Sh
🛇 🅿 (2) 📺 🐾 🏢 ☕

Gowanbrae, *19 Church Street, Dufftown, Keith, Banffshire, AB55 4AR.*
Beautiful Edwardian town house, tastefully decorated and modernised.
Open: All Year (not Xmas)
01340 820461 (also fax)
Mr & Mrs Donald
gowanbrae@breathemail.net
D: £18.00–£20.00 **S:** £22.00–£24.00
Beds: 1F 2D 1T **Baths:** 4 En
🛇 📺 🐾 🏢 ☕

Elgin

NJ2162 🏨 *Laichmoray Hotel, Ashvale, Tor House, Royal, Abbey Court, Crooked Inn*

Foresters House, *Newton, Elgin, Moray, IV30 8XW.*
Situated on B9013, 3 miles west of Elgin, near sandy beaches and Whisky Trail.
Open: All Year
Grades: STB 3 Star
01343 552862 Mrs Goodwin
goodwin@forestershouse.fsnet.co.uk
D: £15.00 **S:** £17.00
Beds: 2F **Baths:** 1 Sh
🛇 🅿 (2) 📺 🐾 🏢 🖻 ☕

Woodlea, *38 Academy Street, Elgin, Moray, IV30 1LR.*
Detached villa with garden near city centre and railway station.
Open: All Year
01343 547114 Mrs Mckenzie
muriel@woodlea18.freeserve.co.uk
D: £15.00–£18.00 **S:** £15.00–£18.00
Beds: 1F 2T **Baths:** 1 En 1 Sh
🛇 🅿 (4) ⚡ 📺 🐾 🏢 ☕

Ardgowan, *37 Duff Avenue, Elgin, Moray, IV30 1QS.*
Welcome to our home - a non-smokers delight. Freshly maintained quality accommodation.
Open: Feb to Nov
01343 541993 (also fax)
Mrs McGowan
NonSmokersHaven@tinyworld.co.uk
D: £18.00–£22.00 **S:** £20.00–£30.00
Beds: 1D 1T **Baths:** 1 En 1 Pr
🅿 (2) ⚡ 📺 🏢 ☕ &

Ellon

NJ9530 🍺 *Casa Salvatori, Buchan Hotel, Station Hotel*

58 Station Road, *Ellon, Aberdeenshire, AB4 9AL.*
Victorian house in town centre near Whisky/Castle Trails, cycle routes.
Open: All Year (not Xmas)
01358 720263 Mrs Thomson
D: £16.00–£18.00 **S:** £18.00–£23.00
Beds: 2T **Baths:** 1 Sh
🅿 (4) ⌇ 📺 🛒 Ⓥ ☕

Station Hotel, *Station Brae, Ellon, Aberdeenshire, AB4 9BD.*
Family-run hotel in quiet part of Ellon. Ample parking.
Open: All Year
Grades: STB 2 Star
01358 720209 Mrs Keith
Fax: 01358 722855
stathotel@aol.com
D: £22.50–£25.00 **S:** £20.00–£35.00
Beds: 3F 3D 1T 1S **Baths:** 8 En
🐕 🅿 (40) 📺 🛏 ✕ 🛒 Ⓥ ☕ cc

Cadha-Beag, *14 Turnishaw Hill, Ellon, Aberdeenshire, AB41 8BB.*
Quiet bungalow. Central to Castle and Whisky Trails. Golf.
Open: All Year (not Xmas)
01358 722383 Mrs Stevenson
D: £17.00–£17.50 **S:** £17.00–£17.50
Beds: 1T 1S **Baths:** 1 Sh
⌇ 📺 🛒 ☕

Fordyce

NJ5563

Academy House, *School Road, Fordyce, Portsoy, Banffshire, AB45 2SJ.*
Tastefully decorated and furnished country house. Paintings and pottery throughout.
Open: All Year **Grades:** STB 4 Star
01261 842743 Mrs Leith
academy_house@hotmail.com
D: £20.00–£24.00 **S:** £25.00–£27.00
Beds: 1D 1T **Baths:** 1 En 1 Sh
🐕 🅿 (5) 📺 🛏 ✕ 🛒 Ⓥ ☕

Forres

NJ0358 🍺 *Mossett Tavern, Crown & Anchor, Chimes, Kimberley*

Morven, *Caroline Street, Forres, Moray, IV36 0AN.*
Beautiful house, centre town location. Warm, friendly atmosphere. Private parking. Brochure available.
Open: All Year
Grades: STB 3 Star
01309 673788 (also fax)
Mrs MacDonald
morven2@globalnet.co.uk
D: £18.00–£20.00 **S:** £18.00–£20.00
Beds: 1F 3T 1S **Baths:** 1 Pr 2 Sh
🐕 🅿 (5) ⌇ 📺 🛏 🛒 Ⓥ ☕

Mayfield Guest House, *Victoria Road, Forres, Moray, IV36 3BN.*
Centrally located with spacious rooms and quiet relaxed atmosphere, with restricted smoking areas.
Open: All Year (not Xmas)
Grades: STB 4 Star
01309 676931 W Hercus
bill-hercus@mayfieldghouse.freeserve.co.uk
D: £17.00–£20.00 **S:** £25.00–£30.00
Beds: 1D 2T **Baths:** 2 En 1 Pr
🅿 (4) ⌇ 📺 🛒 ☕ cc

Milton of Grange Farm, *Forres, Moray, IV36 0TR.*
Working arable farm. 1 mile from Forres, close to picturesque Findhorn village.
Open: All Year (not Xmas)
Grades: STB 4 Star
01309 676360 (also fax) Mrs Massie
hildamassie@aol.com
D: £18.00–£25.00 **S:** £20.00–£25.00
Beds: 1F 1D 1T **Baths:** 3 En
🐕 🅿 (4) ⌇ 📺 🛒 Ⓥ ☕

Heather Lodge, *Tytler Street, Forres, Moray, IV36 0EL.*
Situated in quiet area near town.
Open: All Year (not Xmas)
01309 672377 Mr Ross
D: £15.00–£20.00 **S:** £15.00–£20.00
Beds: 1F 2D 2T 3S **Baths:** 8 Pr
🅿 (12) 📺 🛏 🛒 ☕

Gamrie

NJ7965

Roughwards, *Gamrie, Gardenstown, Banff, AB45 3HA.*
Warm comfortable former farmhouse, walking, bird watching, near scenic Gardenstown, Crovie.
Open: All Year (not Xmas)
01261 851758
Mrs Hawick
hawick@btinternet.com
D: £15.00–£17.00 **S:** £15.00–£18.00
Beds: 1D 1T **Baths:** 1 Sh
ゔ (2) **P** (3) ⊡ ⊀ ✕ ▥ ⓥ ♨ ᵭ 1

Gardenstown

NJ8064   ⌑ *Knowes Hotel*

Bankhead Croft, *Gamrie, Banff, Aberdeenshire & Moray, AB45 3HN.*
Modern country cottage, offering high standards of comfort in tranquil surroundings.
Open: All Year
Grades: STB 3 Star
01261 851584 (also fax)
Mrs Smith
lucinda@bankheadcroft.freeserve.co.uk
D: £15.00–£18.00 **S:** £18.00–£20.00
Beds: 1F 1D 1T **Baths:** 1 Pr
ゔ **P** (6) ⊬ ⊡ ⊀ ✕ ▥ ⓥ ✳ ♨ ᵭ

Garmouth

NJ3364   ⌑ *Garmouth Hotel*

Rowan Cottage, *Station Road, Garmouth, Fochabers, Moray, IV32 7LZ.*
C18th cottage & garden in rural village at Spey estuary.
Open: Jan to Nov
01343 870267
Mrs Bingham
Fax: 01343 870621
patricia@pbingham.fsnet.co.uk
D: £15.00 **S:** £15.00–£17.00
Beds: 1D 1T 1S **Baths:** 1 Sh
ゔ **P** (4) ⊬ ⊡ ▥ ♨

Glenkindie

NJ4313

The Smiddy House, *Glenkindie, Alford, Aberdeenshire, AB33 8SS.*
Comfortable house with spacious garden, ideal touring base, home cooking.
Open: All Year (not Xmas)
019756 41216 Mrs Jones
D: £16.00–£17.00 **S:** £16.00–£20.00
Beds: 1D 1T **Baths:** 2 En
ゔ **P** (6) ⊬ ⊡ ⊀ ✕ ▥ ⓥ ♨

Glenlivet

NJ1929   ⌑ *Croft Inn*

Craighed, *Glenlivet, Ballindalloch, Banffshire, AB37 9DR.*
Traditional country house, overlooking beautiful heather hills, pine trees and stream.
Open: All Year (not Xmas)
Grades: STB 3 Star
01807 590436 R Wilson
D: £16.00–£18.00 **S:** £16.00–£18.00
Beds: 1T 1D
P (4) ⊬ ⊡ ✕ ▥ ⓥ cc

Hopeman

NJ1469   ⌑ *Station Hotel*

Millseat, *Inverugie Road, Hopeman, Elgin, Moray, IV30 2SX.*
Comfortable self-contained suite, wonderful coastline, sports, wildlife, castles, whisky.
Open: All Year
01343 830097 Mrs Brooks
D: £14.00–£22.00 **S:** £18.00–£25.00
Beds: 1D 2S **Baths:** 1 En
ゔ **P** (4) ⊬ ⊡ ⊀ ▥ ⓥ ♨ ᵭ

RATES
D = Price range per person sharing in a double room
S = Price range for a single room

Huntly

NJ5240 🍺 *Huntly Hotel, Gordons Arms*

Greenmount, *43 Gordon Street, Huntly, Aberdeenshire, AB54 8EQ.*
Family-run Georgian house. Excellent base for touring NE Scotland.
Open: All Year (not Xmas)
Grades: STB 3 Star
01466 792482 Mr Manson
D: £16.00–£19.00 **S:** £16.00–£25.00
Beds: 2F 4T 2S **Baths:** 4 En 1 Pr 1 Sh
🛏 🅿 (6) ⅙ 📺 ✗ 🎑 ⅎ

Dunedin Guest House, *17 Bogie Street, Huntly, Aberdeenshire, AB54 5DX.*
Dunedin guesthouse. A few minutes walk from town centre. All room ensuite.
Open: All Year
01466 794162 Mrs Keith
dunedin.guesthouse@btinternet.uk
D: £18.50–£23.00 **S:** £18.50–£23.00
Beds: 6F 1D 4T **Baths:** 6 En
🛏 🅿 (8) ⅙ 📺 🎑 ⅎ

Strathlene, *Macdonald Street, Huntly, Aberdeenshire, AB54 8EW.*
Granite house near town centre and railway station. Warm welcome.
Open: All Year (not Xmas)
Grades: STB 3 Star
01466 792664 Mrs Ingram
D: £15.00–£17.50 **S:** £15.00–£16.00
Beds: 1D 1T 1S **Baths:** 1 En 1 Sh
⅙ 📺 🎑 ⅎ

Southview, *Victoria Road, Huntly, Aberdeenshire, AB56 5AH.*
Private house, close to town centre, convenient, castle and whisky trails.
Open: All Year
01466 792456 Mrs Thomson
D: £15.00 **S:** £16.00
Beds: 1F 2D 1T **Baths:** 2 Sh
🛏 🅿 (3) 📺 🐾 🎑 ❀ ⅎ

Planning a longer stay?
Always ask for any special rates

All details shown are as supplied by B&B owners in Autumn 2000

Inverboyndie

NJ6664 🍺 *Banff Links Hotel*

Links Cottage, *Inverboyndie, Banff, AB45 2JJ.*
Picturesque seaside cottage; comfortable and relaxing. Explore this spectacular coastline.
Open: Easter to Nov
Grades: STB 4 Star
01261 812223 (also fax) Mrs Buchan
D: £24.00 **S:** £30.00–£44.00
Beds: 2D 1T **Baths:** 3 En
🅿 (6) ⅙ 📺 🎑 Ⅵ ⅎ 🚻

Inverurie

NJ7721 🍺 *Bugles*

Kingsgait, *3 St. Andrews Gardens, Inverurie, Aberdeenshire, AB51 3XT.*
Friendly family run establishment close to town centre.
Open: All Year
Grades: STB 2 Star
01467 620431 (also fax)
Mrs Christie
muriel@mchrstie25.freeserve.co.uk
D: £18.00–£23.00 **S:** £18.00–£23.00
Beds: 2T 1S **Baths:** 1 En 1 Sh
🛏 (2) 🅿 (3) ⅙ 📺 🐾 🎑 Ⅵ ⅎ

Broadsea, *Burnhervie, Inverurie, Aberdeenshire, AB51 5LB.*
Homely accommodation on a working family farm. Good home cooking, quiet rural location.
Open: All Year
Grades: STB 3 Star
01467 681386 Mrs Harper
elizharber@broadsea99.freeserve.co.uk
D: £19.00–£21.00 **S:** £22.00–£26.00
Beds: 1F **Baths:** 1 En
🛏 🅿 ⅙ 📺 🐾 ✗ 🎑 Ⅵ ⅎ

BATHROOMS
Pr - Private
Sh - Shared
En - Ensuite

Glenburnie Guest House, *Blackhall Road, Inverurie, Aberdeenshire, AB51 9JE.*
Ideal for touring castle trail/archaeological sites in area. Near town centre.
Open: All Year
Grades: STB Listed, Comm
01467 623044 Mrs Christie
D: £15.00–£17.00 **S:** £19.00–£20.00
Beds: 1D 5T 1D **Baths:** 2 Sh
🛏 🅿 (3) ✯ 📺 🐾 ▥ ⚓

Johnshaven

NO7966 ⚓ *Anchor Hotel*

Ellington, *Station Place, Johnshaven, Montrose, DD10 0JD.*
Comfortable modern family home in old fishing village. Ground-floor twin room.
Open: All Year (not Xmas)
Grades: STB 4 Star
01561 362756 Mrs Gibson
ellington13@supanet.com
D: £18.00–£20.00 **S:** £20.00
Beds: 1T 1D **Baths:** 2 En
🅿 (2) 📺 🐾 ▥ ⚓

Keith

NJ4250 ⚓ *Crown, Royal Hotel*

The Haughs, *Keith, Banffshire, AB55 6QN.*
Large comfortable farmhouse. Lovely view from dining room over rolling countryside.
Open: Easter to Oct
Grades: STB 3 Star GH, AA 4 Diamond
01542 882238 (also fax)
Mrs Jackson
jiwjackson@aol.com
D: £18.00–£21.00 **S:** £22.00–£25.00
Beds: 1F 2D 1T **Baths:** 3 En 1 Pr
🛏 (2) 🅿 (6) 📺 ✗ ▥ ⚓

Lossiemouth

NJ2370 ⚓ *Skerrybrae, Laverockbank, Lossie Inn*

Moray View, *1 Seatown Road, Lossiemouth, Moray, IV31 6JL.*
Open: All Year (not Xmas)
Grades: STB 3 Star
01343 813915 Mrs MacKenzie
D: £17.00 **S:** £21.00–£25.00
Beds: 2D 1T **Baths:** 2 Sh
🛏 🐾 ✯ 📺 ▥ ⚓
Moray View is over 350 years old. All rooms have sea views overlooking the Moray Firth. Many of the original beams are still intact. Close to the harbour and shops and sandy beaches.

Skerryhill, *63 Dunbar Street, Lossiemouth, Moray, IV31 6AN.*
Near beaches and golf course. Convenient for Castle & Whisky Trails.
Open: All Year
01343 813035 Mrs Stewart
D: £16.00–£18.00 **S:** £17.00
Beds: 1F 2D 1T **Baths:** 1 Sh
🛏 🅿 📺 🐾 ▥ ⚓

Laburnum, *54 Queen Street, Lossiemouth, Moray, IV31 6PR.*
Family run home close to all amenities, including Beaches.
Open: All Year
01343 813482 (also fax) Mrs Stephen
wistep@tinyworld.co.uk
D: £16.00–£20.00 **S:** £17.00–£20.00
Beds: 1F 1S 1D **Baths:** 1 En 1 Pr 1 Sh
🛏 🅿 (2) 📺 🐾 ▥ ⚓

Lossiemouth House, *33 Clifton Road, Lossiemouth, Moray, IV31 6DP.*
Interesting house picturesque garden pleasant relaxed retreat friendly family atmosphere.
Open: All Year
Grades: STB 3 Star, AA 3 Diamond
01343 813397 (also fax) Ms Reddy
frances@lossiehouse.freeserve.co.uk
D: £15.00–£18.00 **S:** £18.00–£23.00
Beds: 2F 1D 1T **Baths:** 2 En 1 Pr 1 Sh
🛏 🅿 (5) ✯ 📺 ▥ 📺 ⚓

Maud

NJ9248 ◀ *Brucklay Arms*

Pond View, *Brucklay, Maud, Peterhead,*
AB42 4QW.
Quiet house with panoramic view close to
the National Cycle Route.
Open: All Year **Grades:** STB 3 Star
01771 613675 J & M Hepburn
Fax: 01771 613353
mhepburn@lineone.net
D: £20.00 **S:** £22.00–£25.00
Beds: 1T 1D
🅿 (4) ⊬ 📺 🛏.

Methlick

NJ8537 ◀ *Gight House Hotel, Ythanview Hotel*

Sunnybrae Farm, *Gight, Methlick, Ellon,*
Aberdeenshire, AB41 7JA.
Traditional farmhouse; comfort in a peaceful
location with lovely views. **Open:** All Year
01651 806456 Mrs Staff
D: £17.00–£20.00 **S:** £17.00–£20.00
Beds: 1D 1T 1S **Baths:** 2 En
🛏 🅿 📺 🛏 🛏. 🕯

Gight House Hotel, *Sunnybrae, Methlick,*
Ellon, Aberdeenshire, AB41 0BP.
Friendly family-run hotel overlooking large
garden in picturesque village. CAMRA
recommended. **Open:** All Year
01651 806389 Mrs Ross
Fax: 01651 806577
D: £22.50–£25.00 **S:** £27.50–£30.00
Beds: 2D 1T **Baths:** 3 En
🛏 🅿 (30) ⊬ 📺 ✕ 🛏. 🔽 🕯 cc

Newton (Elgin)

NJ1663

5 Forrestry Cottages, *Newton , Elgin, IV30*
8XP.
Family home - providing warm, clean rooms.
Lounge for relaxing with a TV.
Open: All Year **Grades:** STB 2 Star
01343 546702 Ms Whyte
D: £14.00 **S:** £14.00
Beds: 1T 1D **Baths:** 1 Sh
🛏 🅿 (2) 📺 🛏 ✕ 🛏. 🔽 🕯

Newtonhill

NO9193 ◀ *The Quoiters*

3 Greystone Place, *Newtonhill,*
Stonehaven, Kincardineshire, AB39 3UL.
Beautiful coastal village within easy reach
Aberdeen and Royal Deeside.
Open: All Year (not Xmas)
Grades: STB 2 Star
01569 730391 (also fax)
Mrs Allen
patsbb@talk21.com
D: £15.00–£17.00 **S:** £15.00–£18.00
Beds: 1F 1T **Baths:** 2 Sh
🛏 🅿 (2) 📺 🛏 ✕ 🛏. 🔽 🕯

Oyne

NJ6625 ◀ *Cottage Inn*

Old Westhall, *Oyne, Insch, AB52 6QU.*
Friendly family B&B. Old coaching Inn at the
foot of Bennachie.
Open: All Year
Grades: STB 3 Star
01464 851474 P H West
taphwest@aol.com
D: £17.50–£20.00 **S:** £20.00–£25.00
Beds: 1D **Baths:** 1 Pr
🛏 🅿 (4) ⊬ 📺 ✕ 🛏. 🕯

Peterhead

NK1346

Carrick Guest House, *16 Merchant Street,*
Peterhead, Aberdeenshire, AB42 1DU.
Comfortable accommodation, centrally
situated 2 minutes' walk from main shopping
centre, harbour.
Open: All Year
01779 470610 (also fax)
Mrs Mroczek
D: £20.00–£25.00 **S:** £20.00–£25.00
Beds: 2F 3T 1S **Baths:** 6 En
🛏 🅿 (4) 📺 🛏 🛏. 🔽 🕯

Planning a longer stay?
Always ask for any special rates

Portsoy

NJ5866

The Boyne Hotel, *2 North High Street,*
Portsoy, Banff, Aberdeenshire & Moray,
AB45 2PA.
Family run hotel situated 100 yards from
C17th harbour.
Open: All Year
Grades: STB 2 Star
01261 842242
Mr Christie
enquiries@boynehotel.co.uk
D: £20.00–£25.00 **S:** £20.00–£25.00
Beds: 4D 4T 4S **Baths:** 12 En
🛏 🅿 📺 🏕 ✗ 💻 Ⅴ ❋ 👶 cc

Rothes

NJ2749 ◖ *Seafield Arms, Eastbank Hotel*

Seafield Arms Hotel, *73 New Street,*
Rothes, Charlestown of Aberlour, Banffshire,
AB38 7BJ.
Small family hotel friendly atmosphere.
Excellent homecooked meals, fully licensed.
Open: All Year
01340 831587
Fax: 01340 831892
olga@seafieldarmshotel.demon.co.uk
D: £18.00–£20.00 **S:** £18.00–£20.00
Beds: 1F 1D 1T 2S **Baths:** 1 Sh
🛏 🅿 (8) 📺 🏕 ✗ 💻 Ⅴ 👶 cc

Rothienorman

NJ7235 ◖ *Rothie Inn*

Rothie Inn, *Main Street, Rothienorman,*
Inverurie, Aberdeenshire, AB51 8UD.
Family-run village inn in the heart of castle
country.
Open: All Year (not Xmas)
Grades: STB 3 Star
01651 821206 (also fax)
Miss Thomson
rothieinn@accom90.freeserve.co.uk
D: £20.00–£25.00 **S:** £25.00–£30.00
Beds: 1F 1D 1T **Baths:** 3 En
🛏 🅿 (20) ✄ 📺 🏕 ✗ 💻 Ⅴ 👶 cc

Bringing children with you?
Always ask for any special rates

Spey Bay

NJ3565 ◖ *Spey Bay Hotel*

31 The Muir, Bogmoor, *Spey Bay,*
Fochabers, IV32 7PN.
1 Mile from Spey estuary, sighting of
dolphins, seals, osprey.
Open: All Year
01343 820196 J Philpott
D: £15.00–£16.00 **S:** £15.00–£16.00
Beds: 2D
🛏 🅿 ✄ 📺 ✗ 💻 Ⅴ 👶

St Cyrus

NO7464 ◖ *St Cyrus Hotel*

Kirkton, *St Cyrus, Montrose, Angus, DD10*
0BW.
Comfortable non-smoking house near to
beach and nature reserve. Warm welcome.
Open: All Year
01674 850650 Mrs McGuire
D: £18.00–£20.00 **S:** £20.00–£22.00
Beds: 2T **Baths:** 1 En 1 Pr
🛏 (12) 🅿 (2) ✄ 📺 🏕 💻 Ⅴ 👶

Stonehaven

NO8786 ◖ *Ship Inn, Creel Inn, County Hotel,*
Belvedere Hotel, Marine, St Leonard's Hotel

Glencairn, *9 Dunnottar Avenue,*
Stonehaven, AB39 2JD.
Open: All Year
01569 762612 M Sangster
maureen.sangster@virgin.net
D: £18.00–£20.00 **S:** £20.00–£22.00
Beds: 1T 1D 1S **Baths:** 2 En 1 Pr
🛏 🅿 (5) 📺 💻 👶
Coastal location close to open air swimming
pool and picturesque fishing harbour.
Magnificent Dunnottar Castle one kilometre
away. Recently refurbished to a high
standard, all rooms have satellite TV and
video and tea and coffee. Four poster
available. Ensuite.

Arduthie House, *Ann Street, Stonehaven, Kincardineshire, AB3 2DA.*
Elegant detached Victorian guest house with attractive garden, central Stonehaven.
Open: All Year (not Xmas)
Grades: STB 4 Star GH, AA 4 Diamond
01569 762381 Mrs Marr
Fax: 01569 766366
arduthie@talk21.com
D: £24.00–£26.00 **S:** £18.00
Beds: 1F 2D 2T 1S **Baths:** 5 En 1 Pr
ॐ 📺 ✕ 🛏 Ⅴ ♨

Sirdhana, *11 Urie Crescent, Stonehaven, Kincardineshire, AB39 2DY.*
Victorian town house 5 minutes from centre and beach quiet area.
Open: Easter to Sep
Grades: STB 4 Star
01569 763011
sirdhana.stonehaven@virgin.net
D: £20.00
Beds: 1D 1T **Baths:** 2 En
🅿 (2) ✕ 📺 🛏 ♨

Beachgate House, *Beachgate Lane, Stonehaven, Kincardineshire, AB39 2BD.*
Beach front location, private parking, nice walks, central for all amenities.
Open: All Year (not Xmas)
Grades: STB 4 Star
01569 763155 (also fax)
Mrs Malcolm
bill@beachgate13.freeserve.co.uk
D: £20.00 **S:** £22.00–£30.00
Beds: 2D 1T **Baths:** 2 En 1 Pr
🅿 (4) ✕ 📺 🛏 Ⅴ ♨

4 Urie Crescent, *Stonehaven, Kincardineshire, AB3 2DY.*
Granite-built family house, close to town, station and beach.
Open: All Year
Grades: STB 2 Star
01569 762220 Ms Ling
D: £16.00–£18.00 **S:** £18.00–£20.00
Beds: 1F 1D 1S **Baths:** 1 Sh
ॐ 🅿 ✕ 📺 🐾 🛏 ♨

Dunnottar Mains Farm, *Stonehaven, Kincardineshire, AB3 2TL.*
Friendly farmhouse with sea views. Across road from Dunnottar Castle.
Open: Easter to Nov
Grades: STB 4 Star
01569 762621 (also fax)
Mrs Duguid
dunottar@escosse.net
D: £20.00 **S:** £30.00
Beds: 2D **Baths:** 1 En 1 Pr
ॐ (2) 🅿 ✕ 📺 🛏 Ⅴ ♨

Strathdon

NJ3512 🍺 *Glenkindie Arms, Crofters Inn*

Buchaam Farm, *Strathdon, Aberdeenshire, AB36 8TN.*
Open: May to Oct
Grades: STB 3 Star
019756 51238 (also fax)
Mrs Ogg
e.ogg@talk21.com
D: £16.00 **S:** £16.00
Beds: 1F 1D 1T **Baths:** 2 Sh
ॐ 🅿 (3) 📺 🛏
Enjoy Scottish hospitality on our 600 acre family-run farm in an area of unspoilt beauty, ideal for walkers and nature lovers. On Castle Trail and Highland Tourist Route. Central for touring Donside, Royal Deeside and Speyside. Free fishing.

Tomintoul

NJ1618 🍺 *Glenavon Hotel, Richmond Arms*

Bracam House, *32 Main Street, Tomintoul, Ballindalloch, AB37 9EX.*
Enjoy a warm welcome to the Highlands from the Camerons.
Open: All Year
Grades: STB 3 Star
01807 580278 (also fax)
Mr & Mrs Cameron
camerontomintoul@compuserve.com
D: £15.00–£16.00 **S:** £15.00–£16.00
Beds: 1D 1T 1S **Baths:** 1 En 1 Sh
ॐ 🅿 (2) ✕ 📺 🐾 🛏 Ⅴ ♨

Croughly Farm, *Tomintoul, Ballindalloch,*
Banffshire, AB37 9EN.
Farmhouse with breathtaking views of
Cairngorm mountains. Overlooking River
Conglas. **Open:** May to Oct
Grades: STB 2 Star
01807 580476 (also fax) Mrs Shearer
johnannecroughly@tinyworld.co.uk
D: £16.00–£18.00 **S:** £18.00–£20.00
Beds: 1F 1D **Baths:** 1 Pr 1 En
🛏 🅿 (3) 📺 🏕 🛏 ⬚

Findron Farm, *Braemar Road, Tomintoul,*
Ballindalloch, Banffshire, AB37 9ER.
Situated in the Castle and Distillery area.
Open: All Year (not Xmas/New Year)
Grades: STB 3 Star
01807 580382 (also fax) Mrs Turner
elmaturner@talk21.com
D: £15.00–£17.00 **S:** £15.00–£17.00
Beds: 1F 1D 1T **Baths:** 2 En 1 Pr
🛏 🅿 📺 🏕 ✕ ⬚ Ⓥ ❄ ⬚

Tomnavoulin

NJ2126

Roadside Cottage, *Tomnavoulin,*
Glenlivet, Ballindalloch, Banffshire, AB37 9JL.
Warm welcome, cool prices. Total customer
care in glorious countryside.
Open: All Year (not Xmas)
Grades: STB 3 Star, AA 3 Diamond
01807 590486 (also fax) Mrs Marks
D: £16.00–£18.00 **S:** £16.00–£18.00
Beds: 1F 1D 1S **Baths:** 2 Sh
🛏 🅿 (4) 📺 🏕 ✕ ⬚ Ⓥ ⬚

Turriff

NJ7250

Lower Plaidy, *Turriff, Aberdeenshire,*
AB53 5RJ.
A certificate of excellence ensures a warm
welcome and individual attention.
Open: All Year (not Xmas)
01888 551679
Mr & Mrs Daley
lowplaidy@aol.com
D: £18.00–£22.00 **S:** £18.00–£22.00
Beds: 1D 1T 1S **Baths:** 1 Sh
🛏 🅿 (6) ✂ 📺 🏕 ✕ ⬚ Ⓥ ⬚

Urquhart

NJ2862

The Old Church of Urquhart, *Parrandier,*
Meft Road, Urquhart, Elgin, IV30 8NH.
Distinctly different place to explore Malt
Whisky Country, sea and Highlands.
Open: All Year
Grades: STB 4 Star
01343 843063 (also fax)
A Peter
D: £18.00–£27.50 **S:** £23.00–£28.00
Beds: 1F 2T 1D **Baths:** 2 En 1 Pr
🛏 🅿 (5) 📺 🏕 ✕ ⬚ ⬚ cc

Planning a longer stay?
Always ask for any special rates

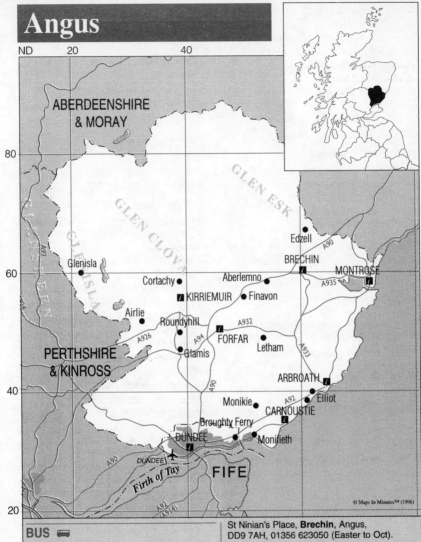

Angus

ND   20   40

ABERDEENSHIRE & MORAY

80

GLEN ESK

GLEN CLOVA

Glenisla

Edzell

BRECHIN

60

Cortachy   Aberlemno   MONTROSE

KIRRIEMUIR   Finavon

A935

Airlie

Roundyhill

FORFAR   Letham

PERTHSHIRE & KINROSS

Glamis

A932

ARBROATH

40

Monikie   Elliot

CARNOUSTIE

Broughty Ferry

Monifieth

DUNDEE

DUNDEE

Firth of Tay   FIFE

© Maps In Minutes™ (1996)

20

BUS 🚌

Scottish Citylink, tel. 08705 505050.
National Express, tel. 0141 226 4826.

RAIL 🚆

For rail information, telephone the National Rail Enquiries line, on 08457 484950. For the Minicom service for the deaf and hard of hearing, tel. 0845 605 0600.

TOURIST INFORMATION OFFICES 🅸

Market Place, **Arbroath**, Angus, DD11 1HR, 01241 872609.

St Ninian's Place, **Brechin**, Angus, DD9 7AH, 01356 623050 (Easter to Oct).

The Library, 1, High Street, **Carnoustie**, Angus, DD7 6AG, 01241 852258 (Easter to Oct).

4 City Square, **Dundee**, DD1 3BA, 01382 434664.

The Library, West High Street, **Forfar**, Angus, DD8 1AA, 01307 467876 (Easter to Oct).

Bank Street, **Kirriemuir**, Angus, DD8 4BE, 01575 574097 (Easter to Oct).

The Library, 214 High Street, **Montrose**, Angus, DD10 8PJ, 01674 672000 (Easter to Oct).

Airlie

NO3150

The Brae Of Airlie Farmhouse, *The Kirkton of Airlie, Airlie, Kirriemuir, Angus, DD8 5NJ.*
Fabulous, relaxing views. Large garden, facilities variable. Telephone for brochures.
Open: All Year
Grades: STB 3 Star
01575 530293 (also fax)
M Gardyne
mamie.gardyne@tesco.net
D: £20.00 **S:** £20.00
Beds: 2T **Baths:** 1 En 1 Sh
🅿 (4) ✕ 📖 📺 ♨ ⅙

Arbroath

NO6441   🍺 *Old Brewhouse*

Inverpark Hotel, *42 Millgate Loan, Arbroath, Angus, DD11 1PQ.*
Small, family-owned hotel renowned and rewarded for quality food.
Open: All Year **Grades:** STB 1 Star
01241 873378 Mr McIntosh
Fax: 01241 874730
D: £17.50–£27.50 **S:** £22.50–£27.50
Beds: 1F 1D 2T 2S **Baths:** 5 En 1 Pr 1 Sh
🐾 🅿 (20) 📺 ✕ 📖 📺 ♨ ⅙ cc

Scurdy Guest House, *33 Marketgate, Arbroath, Angus, DD11 1AU.*
Enjoy friendly warm hospitality and superb breakfast menu. **Open:** All Year
01241 872417 (also fax)
Mr & Mrs Henderson
D: £15.00–£25.00 **S:** £15.00–£30.00
Beds: 3F 2D 4T **Baths:** 4 En 1 Pr 4 Sh
🐾 🅿 (4) 📺 ✕ 📖 📺 ♨ cc

Niaroo, *6 Alexandra Place, Arbroath, Angus, DD11 2BQ.*
Lovely old Victorian villa overlooking sea. Tastefully decorated, smoke free.
Open: All Year (not Xmas)
01241 875660 Mrs Birse
D: £14.00 **S:** £15.00
Beds: 2F 1D 1T **Baths:** 1 Pr 2 Sh
🐾 🅿 ⅙ 📺 ♙ 📖 📺 ⅙

Hilltop, *St Vigeans, Arbroath, Angus, DD11 4RD.*
Pleasantly situated in large gardens. First class accommodation and warm hospitality guaranteed. **Open:** All Year
01241 873200 Mrs Osborne
D: £20.00–£27.50 **S:** £22.50–£27.50
Beds: 1F 1D 1T **Baths:** 2 Pr 1 Sh
🅿 (4) 📺 ♙ ✕ 📖 📺 ♨ ⅙

Broughty Ferry

NO4630   🍺 *Ship Inn, Ferry Inn, Woodlands Hotel*

Dawmara Guest House, *54 Monifieth Road, Broughty Ferry, Dundee, DD5 2RX.*
House is 400 meters from beach and main shopping area.
Open: All Year
Grades: STB 3 Star
01382 477951 Mrs Trainer
D: £20.00 **S:** £20.00
Beds: 2F 2D 2T 2S **Baths:** 3 En 2 Pr 1 Sh
🐾 (1) 🅿 ⅙ 📺 📖 📺 ❀ ♨ ⅙ 3

Invergarth, *79 Camphill Road, Broughty Ferry, Dundee, DD5 2NA.*
Family run in quiet area, close to beach and centre. **Open:** All Year (not Xmas)
Grades: STB 3 Star
01382 736278 Mrs Oakley
jill@oakley79.freeserve.co.uk
D: £17.00–£23.00 **S:** £18.00–£25.00
Beds: 1F 1T **Baths:** 2 Sh
🐾 🅿 (3) ⅙ 📺 📖 ♨

Mossburn, *363 King Street, Broughty Ferry, Dundee, Angus, DD5 2HA.*
Beautiful Victorian house in lovely Broughty Ferry. Many interesting craft shops.
Open: All Year (not Xmas)
01382 477331 Mrs Young
D: £16.00–£18.00 **S:** £20.00
Beds: 1D 1T **Baths:** 2 Sh
🐾 🅿 (2) 📺 ♙ 📖 ♨

All details shown are as supplied by B&B owners in Autumn 2000

Homebank, *9 Ellislea Road, Broughty Ferry, Dundee, DD5 1JH.*
Splendid Victorian mansion house set in beautiful walled gardens in a select area.
Open: All Year
01382 477481 (also fax)
Mrs Moore
D: £22.50–£25.00 **S:** £25.00–£35.00
Beds: 2T 2S **Baths:** 2 En 2 Sh
🅿 (5) 🚭 📺 🛏, 🎿

Carnoustie

NO5634 🍺 *Cairds Hotel, Kinloch Arms*

16 Links Parade, *Carnoustie, Angus, DD7 7JE.*
Stone built villa overlooking 18th fairway of championship golf course.
Open: All Year
01241 852381 (also fax)
Bill & Mary Brand
billbrand@dechmont16.freeserve.co.uk
D: £18.00 **S:** £18.00
Beds: 1D 1T 1S **Baths:** 1 Sh
🅿 🚭 📺 🛏, 🎿

Park House, *Park Avenue, Carnoustie, Angus, DD7 7JA.*
Victorian house, three minutes from championship golf course, sea views.
Open: All Year (not Xmas)
Grades: STB 4 Star, AA 4 Diamond
01241 852101 (also fax)
R Reyner
parkhouse@bbcarnoustie.fsnet.co.uk
D: £25.00 **S:** £25.00
Beds: 1D 1T 2S
🅿 (3) 🚭 📺 🛏, 🎾 🎿 cc

The Two Bs, *13 Queen Street, Carnoustie, Angus, DD7 7AX.*
Established B&B, 2 minutes town centre, 5 minutes golf course.
Open: All Year
Grades: STB 3 Star
01241 852745 Mrs Burgess
Fax: 01241 410493
thetwobs@hotmail.com
D: £20.00 **S:** £20.00
Beds: 2D 1T **Baths:** 2 En 1 Pr
🐾 🅿 (2) 📺 🛏 ✕ 🛏, 🎿

Cortachy

NO3959 🍺 *Drovers Inn, Memus*

Muirhouses Farm, *Cortachy, Kirriemuir, Angus, DD8 4QG.*
Beautiful farmhouse in extensive mature garden on busy farm.
Open: All Year (not Xmas/New Year)
Grades: STB 3 Star
01575 573128 (also fax)
Mrs McLaren
sem8455@aol.com
D: £20.00 **S:** £20.00
Beds: 1F 1D 1S **Baths:** 1 Pr 1 Sh
🐾 🅿 (4) 🚭 📺 🛏, 🎾 🎿

Dundee

NO3632 🍺 *Old Bank Bar, Boar's Rock, Laings Bar, Roseangle, Royal Arch, Russells, Raffles, Hogs Head, Park Hotel, Antonio's, Craigtay Hotel, Ship*

Ardmoy, *359 Arbroath Road, Dundee, Angus, DD4 7SQ.*
Open: All Year
Grades: STB 3 Star
01382 453249
Mrs Taylor
taylord@sol.co.uk
D: £18.00–£25.00 **S:** £18.00–£25.00
Beds: 1F 1D 1T 1S **Baths:** 2 En 1 Sh
🐾 (5) 🅿 (4) 🚭 📺 🛏 ✕ 🛏, 🎾 🎿
Ardmoy is a family run lovely house, overlooking the River Tay. Near city centre, Discovery Point and Broughty Ferry where there are pubs and places to eat on every corner. Mrs Taylor has been serving lovely breakfasts for over 40 years.

Elm Lodge, *49 Seafield Road, Dundee, Angus, DD1 4NW.*
Large Victorian Listed family home. Rooms with river view.
Open: Jan to Dec
Grades: STB 2 Star
01382 228402
Mrs McDowall
D: £18.00–£25.00 **S:** £18.00–£25.00
Beds: 1D 1T 1S **Baths:** 1 Sh
🅿 (4) 📺 🛏 🛏, 🎾 🎿

Ash Villa, *216 Arbroath Road, Dundee,*
Angus, DD4 7RZ.
Home from home. Jim and Jay are waiting
for you.
Open: All Year
Grades: STB 3 Star
01382 450831 Mrs Hill
D: £18.00 **S:** £18.00–£21.00
Beds: 1F 1T 1S **Baths:** 1 Sh 1 Pr
🛏 🅿 (4) ⅙ 📺 🐕 🛏 �*

Errolbank Guest House, *9 Dalgleish*
Road, Dundee, Angus, DD4 7JN.
Spacious detached Victorian house. Family-
run. 1.5 miles city centre.
Open: All Year (not Xmas)
Grades: STB 3 Star
01382 462118 (also fax)
Mr Wilson
D: £22.00–£24.00 **S:** £26.00–£30.00
Beds: 2D 3T 1S **Baths:** 5 En 1 Pr
🛏 🅿 (6) ⅙ 📺 🐕 🛏 🔽 🚱 ♿

Aberlaw Guest House, *230 Broughty*
Ferry Road, Dundee, Angus, DD4 7JP.
Victorian house overlooking River Tay. Warm
welcome from Bruce & Beryl Tyrie.
Open: All Year (not Xmas/New Year)
Grades: STB 3 Star
01382 456929 (also fax)
Mr Tyrie
D: £20.00–£30.00 **S:** £16.00–£30.00
Beds: 1T 2D 2S **Baths:** 1 En 1 Sh
🛏 (12) 🅿 (6) ⅙ 📺 🐕 🛏 🔽 🚱

Craigtay Hotel, *101 Broughty Ferry Road,*
Tayside, Dundee, Angus, DD4 6JE.
Third generation family run hotel. Golfing
and theatre breaks arranged.
Open: All Year
Grades: STB 2 Star
01382 451142
Mr Carson
Fax: 01382 452940
paulshure@aol.uk
D: £24.50–£35.00 **S:** £36.00–£50.00
Beds: 2F 5D 8T 3S **Baths:** 18 En
🛏 🅿 (28) 📺 🐕 ✕ 🔽 🚱 cc

Cloisterbank, *8 Coupar Angus Road,*
Dundee, Angus, DD2 3HN.
Family run friendly accommodation. Near
Country Park 5 minutes to 5 golf courses.
Open: All Year
Grades: STB 1 Star
01382 622181 Mr Black
D: £16.00–£18.00 **S:** £18.50–£25.00
Beds: 1F 5T 1S **Baths:** 2 Sh 1 En
🛏 🅿 (5) 📺 🐕 ✕ 🔽 🚱 ♿

St Leonards Guest House, *22 Albany*
Terrace, Dundee, Angus, DD3 6HR.
Beautiful central town house. Highest rooms
overlooking gardens and river.
Open: All Year
01382 227146 Ms Dunbar
D: £16.00–£18.00 **S:** £25.00
Beds: 1F 2D 2T **Baths:** 2 Sh
🛏 🅿 (2) 📺 🐕 🔽 ❄ 🚱

Edzell

NO6068 🍴 *Glenesk Hotel, Panmure Hotel, Luck*
Inn

Inchcape, *High Street, Edzell, Brechin,*
Angus, DD9 7TF.
Late Victorian house in pretty village.
Open: All Year
01356 647266 Mrs McMurray
D: £16.00–£18.00 **S:** £18.00–£20.00
Beds: 1F 1T 1S **Baths:** 3 En
🛏 🅿 (2) ⅙ 📺 🐕 🔽 🚱

Elliot

NO6139

Five Gables House, *Elliot, Arbroath,*
Angus, DD11 2PE.
Former clubhouse overlooking 18-hole golf
course, panoramic views of coast at
breakfast.
Open: All Year
01241 871632
Fax: 01241 873615
fivegableshouse@yahoo.com
D: £15.00–£25.00 **S:** £20.00–£25.00
Beds: 1F 1D 1T **Baths:** 3 En
🛏 🅿 (20) 📺 🐕 🔽 🚱 ♿ cc

Finavon

NO4957

Finavon Farmhouse, *Finavon, Forfar, Angus, DD8 3PX.*
Located within secluded grounds renowned for quality food and hospitality.
Open: Feb to Oct **Grades:** STB 4 Star
01307 850269 Mrs Rome **Fax: 01307 850380**
jlr@finfarm.freeserve.co.uk
D: £21.00–£22.00 **S:** £21.00–£27.00
Beds: 2D 1T **Baths:** 3 En
ⓗ 🅿 (7) 📺 🍴 ✕ 🎴 Ⓥ 🍵

Forfar

NO4550 ◀ *Castle Club, Plough Inn*

Wemyss Farm, *Montrose Road, Forfar, Angus, DD8 2TB.*
190 acre mixed farm situated 2.5 miles along with a wide variety of animals.
Open: All Year **Grades:** STB 3 Star
01307 462887 (also fax) Mrs Lindsay
wemyssfarm@hotmail.com
D: £17.00–£18.00 **S:** £20.00–£21.00
Beds: 1F 1D **Baths:** 2 Sh
ⓗ 🅿 (6) 📺 🍴 ✕ 🎴 Ⓥ ❀ 🍵 cc

Abbotsford B & B, *39 Westfield Crescent, Forfar, Angus, DD8 1EG.*
Family run B&B close to Queen Mum's ancestral home. **Open:** All Year (not Xmas)
01307 462830 Ms Humphries
abbotsfordbnb@aol.com
D: £16.00 **S:** £32.00
Beds: 1D 2T 1F **Baths:** 2 En 1 Sh
ⓗ 🅿 (4) ⚊ 📺 🍴 ✕ 🎴 Ⓥ 🍵 &

Glamis

NO3846 ◀ *Strathmore Arms*

Arndean, *Linross, Glamis, Forfar, Angus, DD8 1QN.*
Close to Glamis Castle and in ideal walking country. **Open:** All Year (not Xmas)
Grades: STB 2 Star
01307 840535 Mrs Ruffhead
arndean@btinternet.com
D: £16.00 **S:** £16.00–£20.00
Beds: 2T **Baths:** 1 Sh
🅿 (3) 📺 🍴 ✕ 🎴 Ⓥ 🍵

Hatton Of Ogilvy, *Glamis, Forfar, Angus, DD8 1UH.*
Warm welcome awaits at family farm near Glamis Castle and tranquil Angus glens.
Open: Apr to Oct **Grades:** STB 4 Star
01307 840229 (also fax) Mrs Jarron
D: £20.00–£22.00 **S:** £25.00
Beds: 1T **Baths:** 1 En
⚊ 📺 🎴 🍵

Glenisla

NO2160

The Kirkside House Hotel, *11 Conigre Close, Glenisla, Blairgowrie, Perthshire, PH11 8PH.*
Open: All Year
01575 582313 Janice Appleby & Tony Willis
D: £22.50 **S:** £22.50
Beds: 1F 3D 1S **Baths:** 3 En 1 Sh
ⓗ 🅿 (50) ⚊ 📺 🍴 ✕ 🎴 Ⓥ ❀ 🍵 cc
Standing in its own 1.5 acres of garden the Kirkside overlooks the upper River Isla and offers peace, tranquillity, good food and friendly service. Ideal for touring the Central Highlands. Opportunities for hill walking, skiing, fishing, stalking and bird watching.

Kirriemuir

NO3853 ◀ *Glenisla Hotel, Lochside Lodge, Thrums Hotel, Woodville Inn, Park Tavern, Hooks*

Crepto, *Kinnordy Place, Kirriemuir, Forfar, Angus, DD8 4JW.*
10 minutes walk from town centre. Friendly, warm welcome. Comfortable.
Open: All Year **Grades:** STB 2 Star
01575 572746 Mrs Lindsay
D: £22.00–£25.00 **S:** £22.00–£25.00
Beds: 1D 1T 1S **Baths:** 2 Sh
ⓗ 🅿 (3) ⚊ 📺 🎴 🍵

Airlie Arms Hotel, *St Malcolm's Wynd, Kirriemuir, Angus, DD8 4HB.*
Traditional hotel. Listed building, completely refurbished to a high level of comfort.
Open: All Year **Grades:** STB 2 Star
01575 572847 (also fax) Mrs Graham
D: £25.00–£28.00 **S:** £28.00
Beds: 3F 7T **Baths:** 10 En
ⓗ 🅿 (6) ⚊ 📺 🍴 ✕ 🎴 Ⓥ ❀ 🍵 & cc

Woodlands, *2 Lisden Gardens, Kirriemuir, Angus, DD8 4DW.*
Large, modern bungalow with panoramic views over Strathmore Valley, gateway to the Glens. **Open:** All Year (not Xmas)
Grades: STB 4 Star
01575 572582 Mrs Sillence
D: £22.00 **S:** £22.00
Beds: 1D 1T 1S **Baths:** 1 Sh
ॐ ▣ (8) ⅍ TV ⻌ ✕ ▥. Ⅴ ♨

Letham

NO5248 ◖ *Letham Hotel*

Whinney-Knowe, *8 Dundee Street, Letham, Forfar, DD8 2PQ.*
Large semi-detached villa in friendly rural surroundings. Guests lounge.
Open: All Year
Grades: STB 3 Star
01307 818288
E Mann
D: £18.00–£20.00 **S:** £20.00–£25.00
Beds: 1T 2D **Baths:** 1 En 1 Sh
ॐ ▣ (4) TV ⻌ ▥. ♨

Monifieth

NO4932 ◖ *Royal Hotel*

49 Panmure Street, *Monifieth, Dundee, Angus, DD5 4EG.*
Cottage, comfortable beds, good breakfasts. Very near three golf courses.
Open: All Year
01382 535051
Mrs Merchant
Fax: 01382 535205
GeoMerchant@aol.com
D: £18.00–£20.00 **S:** £20.00
Beds: 1T **Baths:** 1 En
ॐ (12) ▣ (4) ⅍ TV Ⅴ

Monikie

NO4938 ◖ *Craigton Coach*

Lindford House, *8 West Hillhead Road, Monikie, Angus, DD5 3QS.*
Deluxe accommodation overlooking country park and close to local amenities.
Open: All Year (not Xmas)
Grades: STB 3 Star B&B
01382 370314 (also fax)
M Milton
D: £18.00–£25.00 **S:** £20.00–£25.00
Beds: 2F 1D **Baths:** 2 Pr
ॐ ▣ (6) TV ▥. Ⅴ ♨

Montrose

NO7157 ◖ *Ferry Den Inn*

Byeways, *11 Rossie Terrace, Ferryden, Montrose, Angus, DD10 9RX.*
Very comfortable, home from home. Turn sharp right past pub.
Open: All Year (not Xmas/New Year)
01674 678510 Mrs Docherty
D: £15.00 **S:** £20.00
Beds: 2D 1T **Baths:** 1 En 2 Pr
▣ (3) ⅍ TV ⻌ ✕ ▥. Ⅴ ♨

Roundyhill

NO3750 ◖ *Strathmore Arms*

The Tollhouse, *Roundyhill, Glamis, Angus, DD8 1QE.*
Enjoy Scottish hospitality and Kiwi informality. C18th tollhouse totally renovated.
Open: All Year (not Xmas)
01307 840436 Fax: 01307 840762
D: £22.00 **S:** £27.00
Beds: 2D 1T **Baths:** 2 En 1 Pr
▣ (4) ⅍ TV ▥. Ⅴ ♨

Argyll & Bute

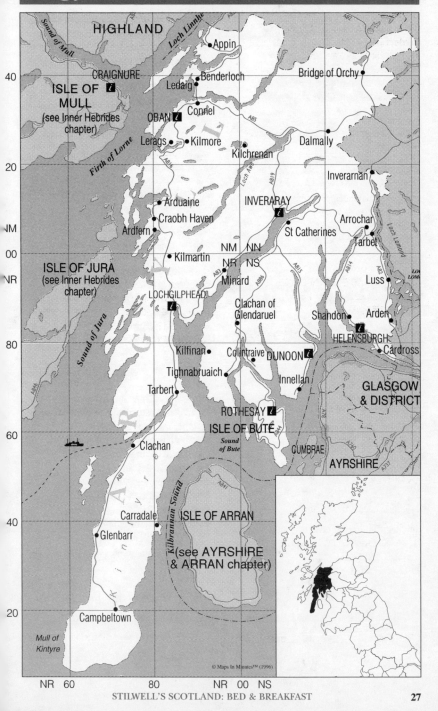

HIGHLAND

Sound of Mull

Loch Linnhe

Appin

CRAIGNURE
40
ISLE OF
MULL
(see Inner Hebrides
chapter)

Ledaig
Benderloch

Bridge of Orchy

OBAN *i*
Connel

20
Lerags
Kilmore
Firth of Lorne
Kilchrenan

Dalmally

Inverarnan

Arduaine
INVERARAY *i*
Craobh Haven
NM
St Catherines
Arrochar

00
Ardfern
NM NN
Tarbet

Kilmartin
NR NS

NR
ISLE OF JURA
(see Inner Hebrides
chapter)
Minard
Luss

LOCHGILPHEAD
Clachan of
Glendaruel
Shandon
Arden

80
Sound of Jura
Kilfinan
Colintraive
DUNOON *i*
HELENSBURGH
Cardross

Tighnabruaich
Innellan
GLASGOW
& DISTRICT

Tarbert
ROTHESAY *i*

60
Clachan
ISLE OF BUTE
Sound
of Bute
CUMBRAE
AYRSHIRE

Carradale
ISLE OF ARRAN

40
Glenbarr
Kilbrannan Sound
(see AYRSHIRE
& ARRAN chapter)

20
Campbeltown

Mull of
Kintyre

© Maps In Minutes™ (1996)

NR 60   80   NR 00 NS

AIRPORTS ⊕

Campbeltown, tel. 01586 552571.
Islay, tel. 01496 302361.

AIR SERVICES & AIRLINES ✈

British Airways for Loganair.
Campbeltown (Mull of Kintyre) to
Glasgow and **Isle of Islay**. **Isle of Islay**
to **Glasgow** and **Campbeltown**,
tel. (local rate) 0345 222111.

RAIL ⇌

For rail information, telephone the National
Rail Enquiries line on 08457 484950. For
the Minicom service for the deaf and hard
of hearing, tel. 0845 605 0600.

BUS 🚌

For services from **Oban**, phone **Scottish
Citylink** on 08705 505050.

FERRIES ⚓

Caledonian MacBrayne: **Oban** to **Mull,
Coll, Colonsay, Tiree, Western Isles.
Tarbert** to **Islay.**
tel. 0990 650000 or 01475 650100.

Western Ferries: **Dunoon** to **Gourock**
tel. 0141 332 9766.

TOURIST INFORMATION OFFICES ℹ

Ardgartan, Arrochar, Argyll, 01301 702432
(Easter to Oct).

Ballachulish, Argyll, PA39 4HP,
01855 811296 (Easter to Oct).

Mackinnon House, The Pier, **Campbeltown**,
Argyll, PA28 6SQ, 01586 552056.

7 Alexandra Parade, **Dunoon**, Argyll,
PA23 8AB, 01369 703785.

The Clock Tower, **Helensburgh**,
Dunbartonshire, G84 7DD, 01436 672642
(Easter to Oct).

Front Street, **Inveraray**, Argyll, PA32 8UY,
01499 302063.

Kilchoan, Acharacle, Argyll, PH36 4LH,
01972 510222 (Easter to Oct).

Lochnell Street, **Lochgilphead**, Argyll,
PA31 8JN, 01546 602344 (Easter to Oct).

Boswell House, Argyll Square, **Oban**, Argyll,
PA34 4AT, 01631 563122.

15 Victoria Street, **Rothesay**, Isle of Bute,
PA20 0AJ, 01700 502151.

Harbour Street, **Tarbert**, Argyll, PA29 6UD,
01880 820429 (Easter to Oct).

Main Street, **Tarbet**, Arrochar,
Dunbartonshire, G83 7DD, 01301 702260
(Easter to Oct).

Appin

NM9346   ⚐ *Duror Hotel, Pierhouse Hotel*

Lurignish Farm, Appin, Argyll, *PA38 4BN*.
Traditional lochside hill farm, good home-
cooking, golf, boating, riding nearby.
Open: May-Sept
Grades: STB 2 Star
01631 730365 Mrs Macleod
lurignish@amserve.net
D: £16.00–£18.50 **S:** £16.50–£19.00
Beds: 1F 1D **Baths:** 1 Sh
🛏 🅿 (4) ⅍ 📺 🐾 ✗ 🎨 Ⅶ ⚓

**High season, bank holidays
and special events mean low
availability anywhere**

Rhngarbh Croft, Appin, Argyll, *PA38 4BA*.
Tranquil lochside croft in beautiful wooded
countryside. Good local food.
Open: All Year
Grades: STB 4 Star
01631 730309 Fax: 01631 730577
welcome@cheesemaking.co.uk
D: £24.00 **S:** £34.00
Beds: 1D 1T **Baths:** 1 En 1 Pr
🛏 🅿 ⅍ 📺 🐾 ✗ 🎨 Ⅶ ⚓ 🔥 cc

RATES

D = Price range per person
sharing in a double room

S = Price range for a
single room

Arden

NS3684

Waters Edge Cottage, *Duck Bay, Arden, Loch Lomond, Dunbartonshire, G83 8QZ.*
Experience our romantic, relaxing ambience and breathtaking views. Charming lochside cottage. **Open:** All Year
01389 850629 Mrs Robertson
watersedge99@hotmail.com
D: £25.00–£30.00 **S:** £40.00–£45.00
Beds: 4D **Baths:** 4 En
🛏 (12) 🅿 (4) ⏣ 📺 🛗 🎔 ✳ ♨ ♿

Polnaberoch, *Arden, Luss, Alexandria, Dunbartonshire, G83 8RQ.*
Charming country cottage in lovely gardens with beautiful surrounding views.
Open: Easter to Nov
01389 850615 (also fax) Mrs McNair
maclomond@sol.co.uk
D: £23.00–£27.00 **S:** £35.00–£40.00
Beds: 1D 1T **Baths:** 2 En
🅿 (3) ⏣ 📺 🛗 ♨

Ardfern

NM8004 ⬤ *Galley Of Lorne, Creels*

Lunga, *Ardfern, Lochgilphead, Argyll, PA31 8QR.*
C17th estate mansion overlooks islands & Firth of Lorne. 3,000 acre private coastal estate. **Open:** All Year
Grades: STB 1 Star B&B
01852 500237 Mr Lindsay-MacDougall
Fax: 01852 500639
colin@lunga.demon.co.uk
D: £19.00–£22.00 **S:** £18.00
Beds: 1F 2D 1T 1S **Baths:** 4 Pr 1 Sh
🛏 🅿 📺 🎔 ✕ 🎔 ♨

Tigh An Innis, *Ardlarach Road, Ardfern, Lochgilphead, Argyll, PA31 8QN.*
Beautiful modern bungalow set near the shores of Loch Craignish.
Open: All Year (not Xmas/New Year)
01852 500682 Mrs Wylie
joan.wylie@tesco.net
D: £18.50–£20.00 **S:** £18.50–£20.00
Beds: 1T 2D **Baths:** 3 En
🛏 🅿 (3) ⏣ 📺 🛗 🎔 ♨ ♿

Arduaine

NM8010 ⬤ *Lord of the Isles*

Asknish Cottage, *Arduaine, Oban, Argyll, PA34 4XQ.*
Open: All Year
01852 200247 Miss Campbell
D: £16.50–£17.50 **S:** £17.00–£22.00
Beds: 2D 1T **Baths:** 1 Sh
🛏 🅿 (3) ⏣ 📺 🎔 🛗 🎔 ♨
Halfway between Oban & Lochgilphead. Warm welcome in hillside cottage overlooking islands Jura to Luing, ideal base for island hopping, Arduaine Gardens, 0.5 miles. Boat trips, birds, castles, walking, etc. nearby. Wild garden, tame owner.

Arrochar

NN2904 ⬤ *Loch Long Hotel, Callum's Bar, Inverberg Inn*

Ferry Cottage, *Ardmay, Arrochar, Dunbartonshire, G83 7AH.*
Open: All Year (not Xmas)
Grades: STB 2 Star
01301 702428 Mrs Bennetton
Fax: 01301 702729
CaroleBennetton@aol.com
D: £17.50–£23.50 **S:** £22.00–£35.00
Beds: 1F 2D 1T **Baths:** 3 En 1 Sh
🛏 (2) 🅿 (6) ⏣ 📺 ✕ 🎔 ♨ cc
Originally the ferryman's cottage some 100 years ago, has now been fully refurbished into our family home. Elevated views overlooking Loch Long and the Cobbler, 5 mins from Loch Lomond. All rooms ensuite. Credit cards accepted, tea/coffee, TV. We are a non-smoking establishment.

Seabank, *Main Road, Arrochar, G83 7AG.*
Open: All Year **Grades:** STB 2 Star
01301 702555 S Smillie
D: £16.00–£20.00 **S:** £20.00–£28.00
Beds: 1F 1D 1T
🛏 (8) 🅿 (6) 📺 🎔 🛗 🎔 ♨
Lovely old house, beautiful views Loch and Arrochar Alps. Great base hill-walking, touring, fishing. Loch Lomond 2 miles, Glasgow 40 miles, historic Stirling 1.5 hours' drive. Walking distance village pub - great food, reasonably priced, warm welcome from Sam and Kathleen.

Oak Bank, *Arrochar, G83 7AA.*
Victorian country house built in 1890 with
stunning views over Loch Long.
Open: All Year (not Xmas)
01301 702400 Mr Nicolson
Fax: 01301 702579
donny400@aol.com
D: £16.00–£25.00 **S:** £20.00–£25.00
Beds: 2F 2D 1T **Baths:** 5 En
🛏 (2) 🅿 (8) 📺 🍖 ✕ 🎢 Ⅴ 👶 ♿ **cc**

Dalkusha House, *Arrochar, Argyll, G83 7AA.*
Detached Victorian villa overlooking Loch
Long and the Arrochar Alps.
Open: All Year (not Xmas)
01301 702234 Mrs Challinor
dalkusha.house@virgin.net
D: £17.50–£20.00 **S:** £22.00
Beds: 2D 1T **Baths:** 2 En 1 Sh
🛏 (6) 🅿 (5) 🍴 📺 Ⅴ 👶 **cc**

Lochside Guest House, *Arrochar,*
Dunbartonshire, G83 7AA.
Located on Loch Long, great for walking,
ornithology, touring, sailing.
Open: All Year
01301 702467 (also fax)
lochsidegh@aol.com
D: £18.00–£25.00 **S:** £20.00–£35.00
Beds: 1F 3D 1T 2S **Baths:** 4 En 1 Pr 1 Sh
🛏 🅿 (10) 🍴 📺 🍖 ✕ 🎢 Ⅴ ❄ 👶 **cc**

Benderloch

NM9038

Hawthorn, *Benderloch, Oban, Argyll, PA37*
1QS.
Open: All Year
Grades: STB 3 Star
01631 720452 Mrs Currile
D: £18.00–£22.00 **S:** £25.00–£30.00
Beds: 1F 1D 1T **Baths:** 2 En 1 Pr
🅿 (5) 📺 ✕ 🎢 Ⅴ 👶 **cc**
A warm welcome awaits you in this
delightful bungalow situated in 20 acres of
farming land. All rooms ensuite, peaceful
accommodation. 9 miles from Oban, the
main ferry terminal for the islands. Ideal
base for touring. Also beach nearby and
family restaurant 50 yds.

Rowantree Cottage, *Keil Farm,*
Benderloch, Oban, Argyll, PA37 1QP.
Peaceful, picturesque location, forest, hill
walks, trails and beach nearby.
Open: Easter to Oct **Grades:** STB 3 Star
01631 720433 Mrs Golding
alan&margiealdwell@email.msn.com
D: £14.00–£16.50 **S:** £19.00–£21.50
Beds: 1F 1D 1T **Baths:** 1 Sh
🛏 🅿 (4) 🍴 📺 🍖 ✕ 🎢 Ⅴ 👶

Bridge of Orchy

NN2939   🍺 *Bridge Of Orchy Hotel*

Glen Orchy Farm, *Glen Orchy, Bridge of*
Orchy, Argyll, PA33 1BD.
Remote sheep farm. Enjoy wildlife,
birdwatching, walking, climbing amongst
beautiful scenery. **Open:** Mar to Nov
01838 200221 Mrs MacLennan
Fax: 01838 200231
D: £16.00–£18.00 **S:** £16.00–£18.00
Beds: 2F **Baths:** 1 Sh
🛏 🅿 📺 ✕ 🎢 Ⅴ 👶

BUTE Rothesay

NS0864   🍺 *Black Bull, Ardmory House, Kettledrum*

Battery Lodge, *25 Battery Place, Rothesay,*
Isle of Bute, PA20 9DU.
Open: All Year **01700 502169** M Leyden
D: £20.00–£22.00 **S:** £18.00–£20.00
Beds: 2F 1T 4D 1S **Baths:** 4 En 2 Pr 1 Sh
🛏 🅿 (7) 📺 ✕ 🎢 Ⅴ 👶 ♿
Built in 1865, Battery Lodge is a splendid
mid-Victorian enjoying spectacular views
across Rothesay Bay to the Argyllshire Hills.
Your hosts Martin and Lorraine offer
attractive bedrooms, most with ensuite
facilities, plus warm Scottish hospitality with
beautiful home cooking.

Alamein House Hotel, *28 Battery Place,*
Rothesay, Isle of Bute, PA20 9DU.
Magnificent views from seafront bedrooms.
Yachting, fishing, riding, cycling closeby.
Open: All Year
01700 502395 J F Hutchings
D: £19.00–£21.00 **S:** £20.00–£22.00
Beds: 1F 3T 3D **Baths:** 3 En 1 Pr 2 Sh
🛏 🅿 (5) 📺 🍖 🎢 Ⅴ 👶 ♿

The Commodore, *12 Battery Place,*
Rothesay, Isle of Bute, PA20 9DP.
Fully modernised seafront guest house,
family run, 'Which?' recommended.
Open: All Year
Grades: STB 3 Star
01700 502178 Mr Spear
Fax: 01700 503492
spearcommodere@aol.com
D: £18.00–£25.00 **S:** £25.00–£35.00
Beds: 2T 4D **Baths:** 6 En
🐕 🅿 📺 🎗 🛏 ▥ 🖂 ⚓

Avion, *16 Argyle Place, Rothesay, Isle of*
Bute, PA20 0BA.
Warm, friendly, family seafront home.
Breakfast to diet for.
Open: All Year
01700 505897 (also fax)
A Smith
avion@compuserve.com
D: £17.00–£22.00 **S:** £17.00–£20.00
Beds: 1F 1T 1S **Baths:** 2 En 1 Pr
🐕 📺 🎗 ▥ 🖂 ⚓

Campbeltown

NR7220 ⚓ Ardshiel Hotel

Homestone Farm, *Campbeltown, Argyll,*
PA28 6RL.
Wonderfully, peaceful location on working
farm/riding centre. Excellent food.
Open: Easter to Oct
01586 552437 L McArthur
lorna@relaxscotland.com
D: £15.00–£17.50 **S:** £15.00–£17.50
Beds: 3D 2S **Baths:** 3 En 1 Sh
🅿 (10) 📺 ✕ ⚓

Sandiway, *Fort Argyll Road, Low Askomil,*
Campbeltown, Argyll, PA28 6SN.
Warm welcome at modern bungalow on
edge of town (lochside).
Open: All Year (not Xmas)
Grades: STB 3 Star
01586 552280 Mrs Bell
106751.1276@compuserve.com
D: £18.00–£20.00 **S:** £23.00–£25.00
Beds: 2T **Baths:** 1 Pr 1 En
🐕 (6) 🅿 (5) ✂ 📺 ✕ ▥ 🖂 ⚓ ♿

Bellfield Farm, *High Askomil,*
Campbeltown, Argyll, PA28 6EN.
Comfortable farmhouse overlooking
Campbeltown and loch; convenient to local
amenities. **Open:** All Year
01586 552646 (also fax) Mrs McLean
D: £15.00–£17.00 **S:** £15.00–£17.00
Beds: 2T 1S **Baths:** 1 Sh
🅿 (4) 📺 🎗 ✕ ▥ ⚓

Cardross

NS3477 ⚓ Muirholm

Glengate Cottage, *Main Road, Cardross,*
Dumbarton, G82 5NZ.
Picturesque village. Minutes from
Helensburgh seaside town. NTS properties
and golf nearby. **Open:** All Year
Grades: STB 2 Star
01389 841737 Miss Mackie
D: £19.00–£21.00 **S:** £17.00
Beds: 2D 1S **Baths:** 1 Pr 1 Sh
🅿 (2) ✂ 📺 ▥ ⚓

Kirkton House, *Darleith Road, Cardross,*
Argyll & Bute, G82 5EZ.
Old farmstead hotel. Tranquil setting. Clyde
views. Wine and dine.
Open: Feb to Nov
Grades: STB 4 Star, AA 5 Diamond,
RAC 5 Diamond
01389 841951 Mr & Mrs Macdonald
Fax: 01389 841868
stil@kirktonhouse.com
D: £30.00–£35.00 **S:** £40.50–£45.00
Beds: 4F 2T **Baths:** 6 En
🐕 🅿 (12) 📺 🎗 ✕ ▥ 🖂 ⚓ ♿ cc

Carradale

NR8138 ⚓ Carradale Hotel, Ashbank Hotel

The Mains Farm, *Carradale, Campbeltown,*
Argyll, PA28 6QG.
Traditional, comfortable farmhouse near
beach, forest walks, fishing, golf, wildlife.
Open: Easter to Oct
01583 431216 Mrs MacCormick
D: £16.50–£17.00 **S:** £16.50–£17.00
Beds: 1F 1D 1S **Baths:** 1 Sh
🐕 🅿 (3) ✂ 📺 🎗 ⚓

Ashbank Hotel, Carradale, Campbeltown, Argyll, PA28 6RY.
Centre of fishing village. Sea views, adjacent to golf course. **Open:** Easter to Oct
01583 431650 Mrs Cook
D: £21.00–£24.50 **S:** £23.00–£24.50
Beds: 1D 2T 1S **Baths:** 3 En 1 Pr
⌂ (1) **P** (5) 🖵 ⊀ ✗ 🔟 ⩔ ⏚

Clachan (Kintyre)
NR7655

The Old Smithy, Clachan, Tarbert, Argyll, PA29 6XL.
Highland hospitality rated excellent by returning guests; home-baking at bedtime.
Open: All Year (not Xmas)
01880 740635 Mrs Moller
moller_kintyre@tesco.net
D: £15.00–£16.00 **S:** £16.00–£17.00
Beds: 1D 1T **Baths:** 1 Sh
⌂ **P** (2) ⊬ 🖵 🔟 ⩔ ⏚ & cc

Clachan of Glendaruel
NS0083

Glendaruel Hotel, Clachan of Glendaruel, Colintraive, Argyll, PA22 3AA.
Charming family run hotel. Ideal for fishing, touring, walking etc.
Open: All Year (not Xmas) **Grades:** STB 2 Star
01369 820274 Fax: 01369 820317
info@glendaruel-hotel.com
D: £30.00–£35.00 **S:** £35.00–£40.00
Beds: 3T 2D 1S **Baths:** 6 En
P (10) 🖵 ⊀ ✗ 🔟 ⩔ ⏚ cc

Colintraive
NS0374

Colintraive Hotel, Colintraive, Argyll, PA22 3AS.
Former Victorian hunting lodge - comfortable and informal family run hotel.
Open: All Year **Grades:** STB 2 Star
01700 841207 Mr Williamson
kyleshotel@aol.com
D: £22.00–£28.00 **S:** £26.00–£30.00
Beds: 1F 1D 1T **Baths:** 4 Pr
⌂ **P** 🖵 ⊀ ✗ 🔟 ⩔ ⏚

Connel
NM9133 ⚓ *Falls of Lora Hotel, Dunstafanage Arms*

Rosebank, Connel, Oban, Argyll, PA37 1PA.
Open: May to Sep **Grades:** STB 1 Star
01631 710316 R L MacKechnie
D: £14.00–£16.00 **S:** £15.00–£17.00
Beds: 1D 1T 1S **Baths:** 1 Sh
⌂ 🖵 ⊀ ⏚
Family house in quiet situation in Connel village overlooking Loch Etive, 5 miles from Oban. Excellent touring centre, large garden at rear. Home made preserves a speciality. Hand-knitted articles for sale. A warm welcome to home and overseas visitors.

Falls Of Lora Hotel, Connel Ferry, Connel, Oban, Argyll, PA37 1PB.
Warm, friendly atmosphere, accommodation to suit everyone, excellent food.
Open: Feb to Dec
Grades: STB 2 Star, AA 2 Star, RAC 2 Star
01631 710483 (also fax) Miss Innes
D: £19.50–£55.50 **S:** £29.50–£53.50
Beds: 4F 6D 14T 6S **Baths:** 30 En
⌂ **P** (40) 🖵 ⊀ ✗ 🔟 ⩔ ⏚ & cc

Ronebhal Guest House, Connel, Oban, Argyll, PA37 1PJ.
Beautiful Victorian villa, speculator sea views. Highest standards and comfort.
Open: All Year (not Xmas/New Year)
Grades: STB 4 Star, AA 4 Diamond, RAC 4 Diamond, Sparkling
01631 710310 (also fax) Mr & Mrs Strachen
ronebhal@btinternet.com
D: £19.00–£28.50 **S:** £18.00–£45.00
Beds: 1F 3D 1T 1S **Baths:** 4 En 2 Pr
⌂ (6) **P** (6) ⊬ 🖵 🔟 ⩔ ⏚ & cc

Ach Na Craig, Grosvenor Crescent, Connel, Oban, Argyll, PA37 1PQ.
Modern house in woodland glade, all rooms ground floor.
Open: Easter to Oct
Grades: STB 2 Star
01631 710588 Mrs Craig
D: £18.00–£19.00 **S:** £25.00–£29.00
Beds: 1D 2T **Baths:** 3 En
P (3) ⊬ 🖵 ⊀ ✗ 🔟 ⩔ ⏚ &

Craobh Haven

NM7907 ◀ *Loch Melfort, Galley Of Lorne*

Buidhe Lodge, *Craobh Haven,*
Lochgilphead, Argyll, PA31 8UA.
Open: All Year (not Xmas)
Grades: STB 3 Star
01852 500291 Mr & Mrs Twinn
D: £23.00–£26.00 **S:** £33.00
Beds: 2D 4T **Baths:** 6 Pr
☎ 🅿 (8) 📺 🏇 ✕ 🛏 ⅴ ♨ ᵈ
Swiss-style lodge located on shores of Loch
Shuna (20 miles from Oban). Near Arduaine
NT Gardens and Historic Kilmartin Valley.
Walk, ride or sail in spectacular West Coast
scenery and return to our lodge to relax,
enjoy good food and company.

Lunga, *Ardfern, Lochgilphead, Argyll,*
PA31 8QR.
C17th estate mansion overlooks islands &
Firth of Lorne. 3,000 acre private coastal
estate.
Open: All Year
Grades: STB 1 Star B&B
01852 500237 Mr Lindsay-MacDougall
Fax: 01852 500639
colin@lunga.demon.co.uk
D: £19.00–£22.00 **S:** £18.00
Beds: 1F 2D 1T 1S **Baths:** 4 Pr 1 Sh
☎ 🅿 📺 🏇 ✕ ⅴ ♨

Dalmally

NN1626 ◀ *Glen Orchy Lodge*

Orchy Bank Guest House, *Dalmally,*
Argyll, PA33 1AS.
Victorian house on the bank of the River
Orchy.
Open: All Year
● **Grades:** STB 2 Star GH
01838 200370 Mr Burke
D: £17.00–£20.00 **S:** £25.00–£28.00
Beds: 2F 2D 2T 2S **Baths:** 4 Sh
☎ 🅿 (8) 📺 🏇 🛏 ⅴ ♨

Craig Villa Guest House, *Dalmally,*
Argyll, PA33 1AX.
Restored farmhouse set amidst breathtaking
mountain scenery. All private suites.
Open: Easter to Oct
01838 200255 (also fax) Mr Cressey
D: £19.00–£23.00 **S:** £25.00
Beds: 2F 2D 2T **Baths:** 6 En
☎ (1) 🅿 (10) 📺 ✕ 🛏 ♨

Dunoon

NS1776 ◀ *Royal Marine Hotel, Hunters Quay*

Moncrieff, *133 Alexandra Parade, Dunoon,*
Argyll, PA23 8AW.
Open: All Year
Grades: STB 2 Star
01369 707945 (also fax) Mrs Peel
willypeel@aol.com
D: £16.00–£20.00 **S:** £19.00–£25.00
Beds: 1T 2D **Baths:** 1 En 2 Sh
☎ 📺 🏇 🛏 ⅴ ♨ ᵈ
Family Tudor style home, panoramic sea
views, private gardens, wheelchair users
catered for. Perfect for walking or cycling in
the Argyll Forest Park. Breathtaking drives
over mountains and through sleepy glens.
Daily sea cruises during the season.

Lyall Cliff Hotel, *Alexandra Parade, East*
Bay, Dunoon, Argyll, PA23 8AW.
Beautifully situated family-run seafront
hotel. 3 ground floor rooms.
Open: Jan to Oct
Grades: STB 3 Star, AA 1 Star
01369 702041 (also fax) Mr & Mrs Norris
lyallcliff@talk21.com
D: £20.00–£30.00 **S:** £22.00–£35.00
Beds: 2F 4D 4T **Baths:** 10 En
☎ 🅿 (10) ⅄ 📺 🏇 ✕ 🛏 ⅴ ♨ ᵈ cc

Craigieburn Hotel, *Alexandra Parade, East*
Bay, Dunoon, Argyll, PA23 8AN.
Friendly family-run private hotel with superb
sea views. **Open:** All Year (not Xmas)
Grades: STB 2 Star
01369 702048 Mrs Hutchinson
dangle@globalnet.co.uk
D: £16.00–£20.00 **S:** £16.00–£20.00
Beds: 3F 2D 2T 2S **Baths:** 3 Sh
☎ 🅿 (5) 📺 🏇 ✕ 🛏 ♨

Milton Tower Hotel, *West Bay, Dunoon,*
Argyll, PA23 7LD.
Small 3 Star family-run hotel with emphasis
on home-cooked meals.
Open: All Year (not Xmas)
01369 705785 (also fax) Mr Fagan
miltontower@ic24.net
D: £18.00–£22.50 **S:** £18.00–£22.50
Beds: 2F 4D 1T 1S **Baths:** 7 En 1 Pr
🛏 🅿 (9) 📺 ✕ ▥ Ⓥ 🍴 cc

Glenbarr

NR6736

Arnicle House, *Glenbarr, Tarbert, Argyll,*
PA29 6UZ.
Beautiful country house situated on working
farm and equitation centre. **Open:** All Year
01583 421208 (also fax) Mrs McArthur
D: £16.00–£20.00 **S:** £20.00
Beds: 1D 2T **Baths:** 1 En 2 Sh
🛏 🅿 (6) 📺 ▥ Ⓥ 🍴

Helensburgh

NS2982   🍴 *Ardencaple Hotel, Toby, Commodore,*
Pinewood, Uppercrust

County Lodge Hotel, *Old Luss Road,*
Helensburgh, Dunbartonshire, G84 7BH.
Open: All Year
01436 672034 Fax: 01436 672033
D: £20.00 **S:** £20.00
Beds: 1F 3D 7T 1S **Baths:** 8 En 2 Sh
🛏 🅿 📺 🍴 ✕ ▥ Ⓥ 🍴 cc
Saviour traditional Scottish hospitality at our
family-run inn style hotel. Ideal location for
Loch Lomond, Trossachs, Clyde area or for
weekends away. Cosy lounge bar with log
fire, entertainment every weekend. Brochure
available, short break discount.

Drumfork Farm, *Helensburgh, G84 7JY.*
Working farm with friendly family, 20
minutes from Loch Lomond.
Open: All Year (not Xmas/New Year)
01436 672329 (also fax) Mrs Howie
drumforkfm@aol.com
D: £20.00–£25.00 **S:** £30.00–£40.00
Beds: 2T 1D **Baths:** 3 En
🛏 🅿 (4) ⌦ 📺 ✕ ▥ Ⓥ 🍴 ⅙ cc

Ravenswood, *32 Suffolk Street,*
Helensburgh, Dunbartonshire, G84 9PA.
Member walkers and cyclists scheme - Silver
Green Tourism Award.
Open: All Year
Grades: STB 3 Star
01436 672112 (also fax)
Mrs Richards
ravenswood@breathemail.net
D: £25.00–£40.00 **S:** £25.00–£50.00
Beds: 2D 1T 1S **Baths:** 2 En 1 Pr 1 Sh
🛏 🅿 (4) ⌦ 📺 ✕ ▥ Ⓥ 🍴

Yetholm, *103 East Princes Street,*
Helensburgh, Dunbartonshire, G84 7DN.
Open: All Year (not Xmas)
Grades: STB 3 Star
01436 673271 Mrs Mackenzie
D: £18.00–£22.00 **S:** £20.00–£22.00
Beds: 1D 1T **Baths:** 1 Pr 1 En
🛏 (5) 🅿 (3) ⌦ 📺 ▥ Ⓥ 🍴
Convenient for an afternoon visit to 'Hill
House' - Rennie Mackintosh. 10 mins drive to
Loch Lomond. Good base for golf, sailing or
touring Trossachs, or day trips to Glasgow,
Oban, Inveraray.

Eastbank, *10 Hanover Street, Helensburgh,*
Dunbartonshire, G84 7AW.
Upper flat of Victorian house 30 minutes
from Glasgow airport.
Open: All Year (not Xmas)
Grades: STB 3 Star B&B
01436 673665 (also fax) Mrs Ross
dorothy-ross@breathemail.net
D: £18.00–£23.00 **S:** £18.00–£20.00
Beds: 1F 1T 1S **Baths:** 1 En 1 Sh
🛏 (3) 🅿 (4) 📺 ▥ Ⓥ 🍴 cc

Arran View, *32 Barclay Drive, Helensburgh,*
Dunbartonshire, G84 9RA.
Panoramic sea views, Convenient NT Hill
House, Loch Lomond, golf.
Open: All Year
Grades: STB 4 Star
01436 673713 Mr & Mrs Sanders
Fax: 01436 672595
arranview@btinternet.com
D: £19.00–£22.00 **S:** £20.00–£25.00
Beds: 1D 1T 2S **Baths:** 2 En 1 Pr 1 Sh
🅿 (5) ⌦ 📺 ▥ Ⓥ 🍴

28 Macleod Drive, *Helensburgh, Dunbartonshire, G84 9QS.*
Stunning views near Loch Lomond, golf, walking and the Highlands.
Open: June to Sept
Grades: STB 3 Star
01436 675206 Mr & Mrs Calder
g.calder@talk21.com
D: £17.00–£19.00 **S:** £18.00–£20.00
Beds: 1F 1T 1S **Baths:** 2 Sh
ॐ **P** (3) ⌖ 📺 ⬛ Ⓥ ♨

4 Redclyffe Gardens, *Helensburgh, Dunbartonshire, G84 9JJ.*
Modern family home; sea views, quiet cul-de-sac, adjacent Mackintosh hill house.
Open: All Year (not Xmas)
Grades: STB 3 Star
01436 677688 (also fax)
Mrs Weston
dweston440@aol.com
D: £21.00–£24.00 **S:** £25.00–£30.00
Beds: 1D 1T **Baths:** 1 Pr 1 En
ॐ **P** (3) ⌖ 📺 ⬛ Ⓥ ♨

Garemount Lodge, *Shandon, Helensburgh, G84 8NP.*
Delightful lochside home; large garden; convenient Loch Lomond, Glasgow, Highlands.
Open: All Year (not Xmas)
Grades: STB 3 Star
01436 820780 (also fax)
Mrs Cowie
nickcowie@compuserve.com
D: £20.00–£23.00 **S:** £28.00–£36.00
Beds: 1F 1D **Baths:** 1 En 1 Pr
ॐ **P** (4) ⌖ 📺 🐕 ⬛ Ⓥ ♨

Maybank, *185 East Clyde Street, Helensburgh, Dunbartonshire, G84 7AG.*
Attractive early Victorian home in a level location.
Open: All Year
Grades: STB 3 Star
01436 672865
Mrs Barella
D: £18.00 **S:** £22.00
Beds: 1F 1D 1T 1S **Baths:** 2 Pr
ॐ **P** 📺 🐕 ⬛ Ⓥ ♨ ♿

Bonniebrae, *80 Sinclair Street, Helensburgh, Dunbartonshire, G84 8TU.*
Stone-built cottage, private garden. 2 mins walk town centre, 10 mins drive Loch Lomond.
Open: All Year
Grades: STB 2 Star
01436 671469
Mrs Kirkpatrick
D: £20.00 **S:** £20.00
Beds: 2F **Baths:** En
ॐ **P** (3) ⌖ 📺 ⬛ ♨

Thorndean, *64 Colquhoun Street, Helensburgh, Dunbartonshire, G84 9NF.*
Warm, spacious Victorian home. 3 nights for price of 2 in off season.
Open: All Year
01436 674922
Mrs Urquhart
Fax: 01436 679913
theurquharts@sol.co.uk
D: £22.00–£26.00 **S:** £22.00–£36.00
Beds: 1F 1D 1T **Baths:** 2 En 1 Pr
ॐ **P** (8) ⌖ 📺 ⬛ Ⓥ ♨ **cc**

Greenpark, *Charlotte Street, Helensburgh, Dunbartonshire, G84 7ST.*
Grade B Listed Art Deco villa set in one acre of park-like grounds.
Open: Apr to Oct
01436 671545 (also fax)
Mrs McNeil
jmcneil@greenpark.swinternet.co.uk
D: £21.00–£24.00
Beds: 1D 1T **Baths:** 1 En 1 Pr
P (3) 📺 🐕 ⬛ ♨

Lethamhill, *20 West Dhuhill Drive, Helensburgh, Dunbartonshire, G84 9AW.*
Delightful villa designed by John Burnet in 1911. Furnished with antiques and memorabilia.
Open: All Year (not Xmas)
01436 676016 (also fax)
Mrs Johnston
D: £25.00–£30.00 **S:** £35.00–£45.00
Beds: 2D 1T **Baths:** 3 En
ॐ **P** (10) ⌖ 📺 ✕ ⬛ Ⓥ ♨

Innellan

NS1469 ◖*Osborne, Braemar*

Ashgrove Guest House, *Wyndham Road, Innellan, Dunoon, Argyll, PA23 7SH.*
Mid-19th century country house in peaceful location, outstanding views.
Open: All Year (not Xmas)
01369 830306 Ms Kohls **Fax: 01369 830776**
kohlsm@netcomuk.co.uk
D: £20.00–£23.00 **S:** £20.00–£23.00
Beds: 1F 1D 1T **Baths:** 3 En
ఠ ⊞ ⊷ ▥ Ⅴ ♨

Inveraray

NN0908 ◖*George Hotel, Fernpoint Hotel*

Claonairigh House, *Bridge of Douglas, Inveraray, Argyll, PA32 8XT.*
Open: All Year (not Xmas)
Grades: STB 3 Star
01499 302160 Fax: 01499 302774
fiona&argyll-scotland.demon.co.uk
D: £16.00–£22.00 **S:** £16.00–£25.00
Beds: 1D 2T **Baths:** 1 En 2 Sh
ఠ ⊡ (8) ⅛ ⊞ ⊷ ✗ ▥ Ⅴ ♨
A historic country house ideally situated for access to the Argyll countryside and coast. Nearby attractions include horse riding, cycling, boat hide, golfing, fishing and walking. We can offer excellent breakfast, beautiful rooms and a warm welcome.

The Old Rectory, *Inveraray, Argyll, PA32 8UH.*
Family-run Georgian house overlooking Loch Fyne. **Open:** All Year (not Xmas)
01499 302280 Mrs Maclaren
D: £15.00–£20.00 **S:** £15.00–£20.00
Beds: 4F 3D 1T 1S **Baths:** 3 Sh
ఠ (3) ⊡ (9) ⅛ ⊞ ▥ Ⅴ

Creag Dhubh, *Inveraray, Argyll, PA32 8XF.*
Family-run bed and breakfast, superbly situated by Loch Fyne. **Open:** Feb to Nov
01499 302430 Mrs MacLugash
creagdhubh@freeuk.com
D: £20.00–£25.00
Beds: 1F 3D 1T **Baths:** 5 En
ఠ ⊡ (6) ⅛ ⊞ ▥ Ⅴ ♨

Inverarnan

NN3118 ◖*Stagger Inn, Drovers Inn*

Rose Cottage, *Inverarnan, Glen Falloch, Arrochar, Dunbartonshire, G83 7DX.*
Renovated C18th cottage on West Highland Way near Loch Lomond.
Open: All Year (not Xmas)
01301 704255 Mr and Mrs Fletcher
D: £19.00–£23.00
Beds: 1F 2T **Baths:** 1 En 1 Sh
ఠ ⊡ (2) ⅛ ✗ ▥ Ⅴ ♨

Kilchrenan

NN0322 ◖*Kilchrenan Inn, Trade Winds*

Innisfree, *Kilchrenan, Taynuilt, Argyll, PA35 1HG.*
Wonderful scenery, modern croft house, quiet, Oban 19 miles, popular destination.
Open: Easter to Sep
01866 833352 Mrs Wright
D: £18.00 **S:** £18.00
Beds: 1D 1T **Baths:** 2 Sh
ఠ ⊡ (4) ⊞ ▥

Kilfinan

NR9378 ◖*Kilfinan Hotel*

Auchnaskeoch Farm House, *Kilfinan, Tighnabruaich, Argyll, PA21 2ER.*
Enjoy unspoiled countryside and magnificent scenery; a warm Scottish welcome awaits you.
Open: All Year (not Xmas)
Grades: STB 3 Star
01700 811397 Mrs Mackay
Fax: 01700 811799
D: £17.50–£20.00 **S:** £18.00–£21.00
Beds: 1D **Baths:** 1 En
⊡ (1) ⊞ ✗ ▥ Ⅴ ♨

BATHROOMS

Pr - Private

Sh - Shared

En - Ensuite

Kilmartin

NR8398

Dunchragaig House, *Kilmartin,*
Lochgilphead, Argyll, PA31 8RG.
Comfortable detached house in large
garden, opposite historic standing stones.
Open: All Year (Not Xmas)
01546 605209 Mrs Norman
Fax: 01546 605300
dunchraig@aol.com
D: £18.00–£22.00
Beds: 1F 2D 2T **Baths:** 5 En
ॐ 🅿 (6) ⅍ 📺 ♠ ✕ ▥ Ⅴ cc

Kilmore

NM8825 🍺 *Barn Bar*

Invercairn, *Musdale Road, Kilmore, Oban,*
Argyll, PA34 4XX.
Open: Easter to Oct
Grades: STB 4 Star
01631 770301 (also fax)
Mrs MacPherson
invercairn.kilmore@virgin.net
D: £20.00–£25.00 **S:** £25.00–£30.00
Beds: 2D 1T **Baths:** 3 En
🅿 (4) ⅍ 📺 ▥ Ⅴ ♨
Beautiful spot, only 10 minute drive from
Oban town centre. Wonderful base for
seeing the splendours of Argyll and the
Isles. Oban, a busy port and local centre,
offers visitors daily excursions to Mull and
Iona. Good food, warm West Highland
hospitality.

Ledaig

NM9037 🍺 *Hawthorn Cottage*

An Struan, *Ledaig, Oban, Argyll, PA37 1QS.*
Large modern bungalow in the picturesque
village of Benderloch, 7 miles north of Oban.
Open: All Year (not Xmas)
Grades: STB 3 Star
01631 720301 Mrs Knowles
Fax: 01631 720734
frankwop@btinternet.com
D: £18.00–£22.00 **S:** £20.00–£25.00
Beds: 2D 1T **Baths:** 1 En 1 Sh
ॐ 🅿 ⅍ 📺 ♠ ✕ ▥ Ⅴ ♿

Lerags

NM8424

Lerags House, *Lerags, Oban, Argyll,*
PA34 4SE.
Enchanting country house in mature
gardens on Loch Feochan shore.
Open: Easter to Oct
Grades: STB 3 Star, AA 4 Diamond
01631 563381
N A Hill
Fax: 01631 563381
leragshouse@supanet.com
D: £22.50–£30.00 **S:** £22.50–£30.00
Beds: 4D 2T 1S **Baths:** 7 En
ॐ (12) 🅿 (7) ⅍ 📺 ✕ ▥ Ⅴ ♨

Lochgilphead

NR8687 🍺 *Stag Hotel, Victoria Hotel*

Corbiere, *Achnabreac, Lochgilphead, Argyll,*
PA31 8SG.
Open: All Year (not Xmas/New Year)
Grades: STB 3 Star
01546 602764
Mrs Sinclair
D: £16.50–£17.50 **S:** £20.00
Beds: 1T 1D **Baths:** 2 Sh
ॐ 🅿 📺 ♠ ▥ Ⅴ ♨
Bedrooms are spacious, comfortable,
thoughtfully equipped. Peaceful, rural
location. Uninterrupted views over meadows
towards Crinan Canal and hills beyond.
Convenient for exploring historic mid-Argyll,
Kintyre Peninsula and Inner Isles. Looking
forward to welcoming you.

Empire Travel Lodge, *Union Street,*
Lochgilphead, Argyll, PA31 8JS.
Former cinema converted to create quality
travel lodge.
Open: All Year (not Xmas)
Grades: STB 3 Star
01546 602381
Mr Haysom
Fax: 01546 606606
D: £23.00 **S:** £23.00
Beds: 2F 5D 2T **Baths:** 9 En
ॐ 🅿 (9) 📺 ▥ Ⅴ ♨ ♿ 1 cc

Kilmory House, *Paterson Street,*
Lochgilphead, Argyll, PA31 8JP.
Lovely house & gardens situated lochside.
Most rooms with loch views.
Open: All Year **Grades:** STB 2 Star
01546 603658 Mr Moore
D: £16.50–£22.00 **S:** £20.00
Beds: 3D 3T **Baths:** 2 En 2 Pr 2 Sh
🐾 (10) 🅿 (16) ⅙ ⊡ ✕ ▥. Ⅴ ≛ cc

The Argyll Hotel, *Lochnell Street,*
Lochgilphead, Argyll, PA31 8JN.
Friendly village centre inn, quality
restaurant, bar and value accommodation.
Open: All Year
01546 602221 Mr Smith **Fax: 01546 603576**
argyll.hotel@btclick.com
D: £19.00–£25.00 **S:** £19.00–£25.00
Beds: 4D 4T 4S **Baths:** 6 En 2 Sh
🐾 🅿 (4) ⊡ � ✕ ▥. Ⅴ ≛ cc

Luss

NS3592   ◀ *Colquhoun Arms*

Shantron Farm, *Shantron Cottage, Luss,*
Alexandria, Dunbartonshire, G83 8RH.
5000-acre farm with spectacular views of
Loch and surrounding area.
Open: Mar to Nov **Grades:** STB 3 Star
01389 850231 (also fax) Mrs Lennox
rjlennox@shantron.u-net.com
D: £22.00–£30.00 **S:** £25.00–£30.00
Beds: 1F 1D 1T **Baths:** 3 En
🐾 🅿 (3) ⊡ Ⅴ ≛ cc

Doune of Glen Douglas Farm, *Luss,*
Loch Lomond, Alexandria, Argyll & Bute,
G83 8PD.
Open: Easter to Oct **Grades:** STB 4 Star
01301 702312 Mrs Robertson
Fax: 01301 702916
pjrobertson@glendouglas.u-net.com
D: £22.00–£30.00 **S:** £25.00–£35.00
Beds: 2D 1T **Baths:** 1 En 2 Sh
🐾 🅿 ⊡ ♲ ▥. Ⅴ cc
Remote working hill sheep farm set in 6000
acres hills above Loch Lomond, where a
warm welcome awaits you. You can enjoy
home cooking and home made preserves
and eggs from our own hens before hill
walking or observing the sheep and
Highland cattle.

RATES
D = Price range per person
sharing in a double room
S = Price range for a
single room

Blairglas, *Luss, Alexandria, Dunbartonshire,*
G83 8RG.
Between Luss and Cameron house 25 mins
from Glasgow airport.
Open: All Year (not Xmas)
Grades: STB 3 Star
01389 850278 (also fax)
Mrs Buchanan
D: £18.00–£23.00
Beds: 1F 1D 1T **Baths:** 3 En
🐾 🅿 ⊡ ♲ ✕ ▥. Ⅴ ≛ ♿

The Corries, *Inverbeg, Luss, Alexandria,*
Dunbartonshire, G83 8PD.
Beautiful easily accessible rural location.
Panoramic views of Loch Lomond.
Open: All Year (not Xmas)
Grades: STB 3 Star
01436 860275 Mrs Carruthers
the_corries@hotmail.com
D: £20.00–£25.00 **S:** £25.00–£35.00
Beds: 1F 1D 1T **Baths:** 3 En
🅿 (4) ⅙ ♲ ▥. Ⅴ ≛ cc

Minard

NR9896   ◀ *Lochgair Hotel*

Minard Castle, *Minard, Inveraray, Argyll,*
PA32 8YB.
Warm welcome in our nineteenth-century
castle beside Loch Fyne.
Open: April to Oct
Grades: STB 4 Star
01546 886272 (also fax)
Mr Gayre
reinoldgayre@bizonline.co.uk
D: £30.00–£40.00 **S:** £30.00–£40.00
Beds: 1F 2T **Baths:** 3 En
🐾 🅿 (6) ⅙ ⊡ ♲ ▥. Ⅴ ≛ cc

Oban

NM8630 🍺 *Oban Inn, Aulays Bar, Kelvin Hotel, Lorne, Soroba House, Barn Bar, Kings Knoll, Donellys, Rowantree Hotel, Step Inn*

Thelwillows, *Glenslellgh Road, Oban, Argyll, PA34 4PP.*
Open: All Year (not Xmas/New Year)
01631 566240 D F Coates
Fax: 01631 566783
enquiries@obanaccommodation.com
D: £20.00–£25.00 **S:** £20.00–£25.00
Beds: 1T 1D **Baths:** 2 En
🅿 (4) ⊬ ⛵ 🖳 Ⅴ ⚓
Also self catering £15-£17.50 per person nightly. Large garden, private road, idyllic wooded country hillside, tree preservation area overlooking pleasant mile walk to town, golf course, hills gateway to the islands. Ferry 1 mile. Bicycles/scooters available.

Harbour View Guest House, *Shore Street, Oban, Argyll, PA34 4LQ.*
Centrally situated town house.
Open: All Year (not Xmas)
Grades: STB 1 Star
01631 563462 Mrs McDougall
D: £15.00–£17.00
Beds: 2F 1D 1T **Baths:** 2 Sh
🛏 ⛵ 🐾 🖳 ⚓

The Torrans, *Drummore Road, Oban, Argyll, PA34 4JL.*
Detached bungalow overlooking Oban in pleasant peaceful residential area. Private parking.
Open: All Year
Grades: STB 3 Star
01631 565342
Mrs Calderwood
D: £16.00 **S:** £20.00
Beds: 1T 2D **Baths:** 2 En 1 Pr
🛏 🅿 (3) ⛵ 🐾 🖳 ⚓

Planning a longer stay?
Always ask for any special rates

Glenara Guest House, *Rockfield Road, Oban, Argyll, PA34 5DQ.*
Open: Feb to Nov
Grades: STB 4 Star
01631 563172 Mrs Bingham
Fax: 01631 571125
glenara_oban@hotmail.com
D: £21.00–£27.00 **S:** £25.00–£35.00
Beds: 1F/T 3D **Baths:** 4 En
🛏 (12) 🅿 (5) ⊬ ⛵ 🖳 Ⅴ ⚓
We offer to our guests a quality of room, breakfast & welcome which will ensure your return. Centrally situated, sea views, off-street parking. Individually furnished rooms with king-sized beds reflecting Dorothy's commitment to quality. Glenara is a no-smoking guest house.

Alltavona, *Corran Esplanade, Oban, Argyll, PA34 5AQ.*
Open: Feb to Nov
01631 565067 (also fax)
Ms Harris
carol@alltavona.co.uk
D: £20.00–£33.00 **S:** £20.00–£55.00
Beds: 1F 5D 2T
🛏 (5) 🅿 ⊬ ⛵ 🖳 Ⅴ ⚓
Alltavona - a Victorian villa lying on Oban's esplanade. Visitors arriving at Alltavona for the first time are immediately aware that it is a house of outstanding quality, where no effort has been spared. Outstanding views of Oban Bay and surrounding islands.

Dana Villa, *Dunollie Road, Oban, Argyll, PA34 5PJ.*
Scottish hospitality, family run. Close to all amenities and waterfront.
Open: All Year
01631 564063 Mrs Payne
ednacp@aol.com
D: £15.00 **S:** £20.00
Beds: 2F 2D 3T 1S **Baths:** 3 En 1 Pr 2 Sh
🛏 ⛵ 🐾 ✗ 🖳 Ⅴ ⚓

Feorlin, *Longsdale Road, Oban, Argyll,*
PA34 5DZ.
Open: Mar to Nov
Grades: STB 3 Star
01631 562930
Mrs Campbell
Fax: 01631 564199
campbellsmith@btinternet.com
D: £17.50–£20.00 **S:** £27.50
Beds: 1F **Baths:** 1 En
⚬ 🅿 (2) ⚊ 📺 ▥ Ⓥ ♨

A warm welcome and traditional Scottish
hospitality awaits you at Feorlin, a charming
bungalow less than 8 mins walk from town
and leisure sports complex. Great breakfasts
with fresh produce, free range eggs, home
made jams and marmalade.

Elmbank Guest House, *Croft Road, Oban,*
Argyll, PA34 5JN.
Situated in quiet residential area. Large
garden, 1 mile to station/ pier.
Open: Easter to Oct
01631 562545
Mrs Douglas
D: £16.00–£20.00 **S:** £16.00–£20.00
Beds: 4D 2T 1S **Baths:** 2 En 2 Sh
🅿 📺 ▥ Ⓥ ♨

Thornlea, *Laurel Road, Oban, Argyll,*
PA34 5EA.
Small private bungalow in quiet residential
area, 10 mins from town centre.
Open: Easter to Sep
01631 562792
Mrs Millar
D: £13.50 **S:** £13.50
Beds: 1D 1S
⚬ 🅿 (2) 📺 ♙ ▥ ♨

Glenview, *Soroba Road, Oban, Argyll,*
PA34 4JF.
Warm friendly welcome, good breakfasts,
close to all travel terminals.
Open: All Year
01631 562267
Mrs Stewart
D: £15.00–£17.50 **S:** £16.00–£17.50
Beds: 2F 2T **Baths:** 1 Sh
⚬ 🅿 (6) 📺 ♙ ✕ ▥ Ⓥ ♨

Ardenlee, *Pulpit Hill, Oban, Argyll, PA34.*
Comfortable bungalow close to viewpoint
over Oban Bay.
Open: Easter to Oct
Grades: STB 2 Star
01631 564255 Mrs Campbell
D: £16.00–£19.50
Beds: 2D 1T **Baths:** 3 En
🅿 (3) ⚊ 📺 ♙ ▥ ♨

Glenvista, *Mossfield Avenue, Oban, Argyll,*
PA34 4EL.
Semi-detached villa, pleasant location, very
comfortable, good Scottish breakfast.
Open: Easter to Sep
Grades: STB 2 Star
01631 563557 Mrs Carter
D: £16.00–£17.50
Beds: 2D **Baths:** 1 Sh
🅿 (1) ⚊ 📺 ▥ Ⓥ ♨

Carradale, *Glenmore Road, Oban, Argyll,*
PA34 4ND.
10 minutes walk from ferries, bus and train
station, town centre.
Open: May to Oct
Grades: STB 3 Star
01631 564827 Mrs Thompson
fkthompson@talk21.com
D: £16.00–£19.00
Beds: 2D **Baths:** 2 En
🅿 (2) ⚊ 📺 ▥ ♨

Lancaster Hotel, *Esplanade, Oban, Argyll,*
PA34 5AD.
Seafront family hotel, fully licensed,
adequate parking with leisure facilities.
Open: All Year
Grades: STB 2 Star, AA 2 Star, RAC 2 Star
01631 562587 (also fax)
Mrs Ramage
john@lancasterhotel.fresserve.co.uk
D: £24.50 **S:** £27.80
Beds: 3F 5D 10T 7S **Baths:** 24 En 4 Sh
⚬ 🅿 (20) 📺 ♙ ✕ ▥ Ⓥ ♨ & cc

Bringing children with you?
Always ask for any special rates

RATES

D = Price range per person sharing in a double room
S = Price range for a single room

Kildonan, *Mossfield Avenue, Oban, Argyll, PA34 4EL.*
Small friendly guest house in quiet area near to golf courses.
Open: All Year (not Xmas)
01631 565872 Ms Barbour
D: £15.00
Beds: 2D

Raschoille, *Glenshellach Road, Oban, Argyll, PA34 4PP.*
In a quiet glen, 15 minutes' walk from town centre.
Open: Easter to Oct
01631 566064 Ms Dougall
D: £15.00–£19.00 **S:** £15.00–£19.00
Beds: 1F 1D **Baths:** 1 En 1 Pr
ॐ ▣ (4) ▥ ⴕ ▦. Ⅴ ≛

Suilven, *58 Nant Drive, Oban, Argyll, PA34 4LA.*
Modern detached family bungalow. Bookings for 1-3 welcome.
Open: All Year (not Xmas)
01631 562711 (also fax)
Mrs Chapman
D: £15.00 **S:** £16.50
Beds: 1F **Baths:** 1 Sh
ॐ ▣ (2) ⅍ ▥ ≛

Rahoy Lodge, *Gallach Road, Oban, Argyll, PA34 4PD.*
Beautiful seafront Victorian lodge. Most rooms overlook garden to seafront.
Open: All Year (not Xmas)
01631 562301 (also fax)
C Howard
christinehoward@tesco.net
D: £20.00–£27.00 **S:** £25.00–£32.00
Beds: 1F 3D 2T **Baths:** 2 En 1 Pr 1 Sh
ॐ ▣ (6) ⅍ ▥ ✕ ▦. Ⅴ ≛ cc

Shandon

NS2586 ◖ *Ardencaple Hotel*

Garemount Lodge, *Shandon, Helensburgh, G84 8NP.*
Delightful lochside home; large garden; convenient Loch Lomond, Glasgow, Highlands.
Open: All Year (not Xmas)
Grades: STB 3 Star
01436 820780 (also fax)
Mrs Cowie
nickcowie@compuserve.com
D: £20.00–£23.00 **S:** £28.00–£36.00
Beds: 1F 1D **Baths:** 1 En 1 Pr
ॐ ▣ (4) ⅍ ▥ ⴕ ▦. Ⅴ ≛

St Catherines

NN1207 ◖ *Creggans Inn*

Arnish Cottage Christian Guest House, *Poll Bay, St Catherines, Cairndow, Argyll, PA25 8BA.*
Idyllically situated on the shores of Loch Fyne.
Open: All Year (not Xmas)
01499 302405 (also fax) Mr Mercer
D: £25.00 **S:** £25.00
Beds: 2D 1T **Baths:** 3 En
ॐ (14) ▣ (3) ⅍ ▥ ▦. ≛

Tarbert (Kintyre)

NR8668 ◖ *Callums Bar, Tarbot Hotel, West Loch*

Kintarbert Lodge, *Kilberry Road, Tarbert, Argyll, PA29 6XX.*
Open: Apr to Oct
Grades: STB 3 Star
01880 820237 Mrs Chainey
Fax: 01880 821149
bdchainey@aol.com
D: £18.00–£20.00 **S:** £18.00–£20.00
Beds: 1F 2T **Baths:** 2 En 1 Pr
ॐ ▣ ▥ ⴕ ▦. Ⅴ ≛ & cc
Former farm house, 200 ft above West Loch Tarbert with panoramic views. Outside play area for children. 3 miles from Tarbert and 7,10 miles from Islay, Arran ferries. A quiet place to relax from the stresses of daily life.

Tarbert Hotel, *Harbour Street, Tarbert, Argyll, PA29 6UB.*
Open: All Year
Grades: STB 2 Star, AA 2 Star
01880 820264
Fax: 01880 820847
ian.robertson@tarberthotel.com
D: £22.50–£25.00 **S:** £27.50–£30.00
Beds: 1F 5D 10T 4S
Baths: 18 En 1 Sh
🛏 🖾 ⊁ ✕ 🕮 Ⓥ ♨ cc
The hub of the local community - a lively meeting place, giving a true reflection of Scottish hospitality. Our food is famous and its value unsurpassed. Ideal base for touring or relaxing overlooking the bustling fishing and sailing harbour of Tarbert.

Tarbet

NN3104 **Corner Stone,** *7 Ballyhennan Cresent, Tarbet, Arrochar, G83 7DB.*
Beautiful stone built house, overlooking Loch Lomond's, breathtaking Mountains.
Open: All Year
Grades: STB 3 Star
01301 702592
Mr & Mrs McKinley
s.mckinley@talk21.com
D: £16.00–£18.00 **S:** £20.00–£25.00
Beds: 1T 1F **Baths:** 1 Sh
🛏 🅿 ⊁ 🖾 🕮 Ⓥ

Lochview, *Tarbet, Arrochar, Dunbartonshire, G83 7DD.*
Clean, comfortable, friendly welcome in 200-year-old Georgian house.
Open: All Year (not Xmas)
Grades: STB 1 Star
01301 702200 Mrs Fairfield
D: £15.00–£17.00 **S:** £20.00
Beds: 1F 1D 1T **Baths:** 1 Sh
🛏 🅿 🖾 ⊁ 🕮 ♨ ❂

Bon-Etive, *Tarbet, Arrochar, Dunbartonshire, G83 7D.*
Private home, quiet location, view of Loch and Ben Lomond. **Open:** Easter to Oct
01301 702219 Mrs Kelly
D: £16.50–£17.00
Beds: 1D 1T **Baths:** 1 Sh
🛏 🖾 ⊁ 🕮 Ⓥ ♨

Tighnabruaich

NR9773 🛥 *Royal Hotel*

Ferguslie, *Seafront, Tighnabruaich, Argyll, PA21 2BE.*
Superior Victorian villa, on sea front, with landscaped garden. Quality throughout.
Open: Easter to Oct **Grades:** STB 3 Star
01700 811414 Mrs McLachlan
D: £17.00 **S:** £18.00
Beds: 2D **Baths:** 1 Sh
🅿 (3) ⊁ 🖾 🕮 Ⓥ ♨

Ayrshire & Arran

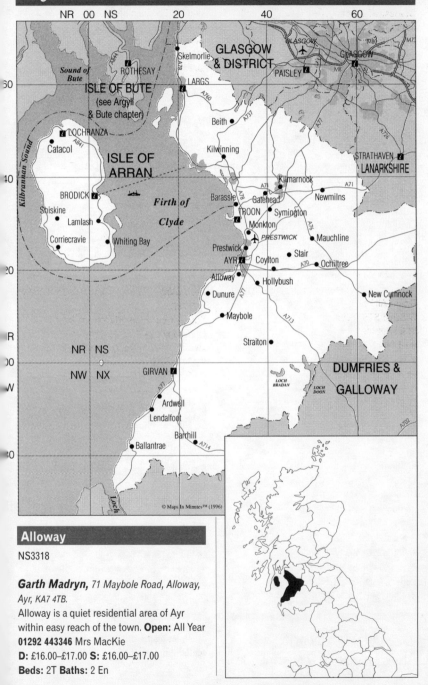

NR 00 NS   20   40   60

GLASGOW
& DISTRICT

Sound of
Bute

ISLE OF BUTE
(see Argyll
& Bute chapter)

ISLE OF
ARRAN

Firth of
Clyde

LANARKSHIRE

DUMFRIES &
GALLOWAY

© Maps In Minutes™ (1996)

Alloway

NS3318

Garth Madryn, *71 Maybole Road, Alloway,*
Ayr, KA7 4TB.
Alloway is a quiet residential area of Ayr
within easy reach of the town. **Open:** All Year
01292 443346 Mrs MacKie
D: £16.00–£17.00 **S:** £16.00–£17.00
Beds: 2T **Baths:** 2 En

AIRPORTS ⊕
Prestwick International,
tel. 01292 479822.

AIR SERVICES & AIRLINES ✈
Ryanair: *Prestwick to Belfast, Dublin, London (Stansted)*, tel. 0870 156 9569.

RAIL ⇌
For rail information, telephone the National Rail Enquiries line on 08457 484950. For the Minicom service for the deaf and hard of hearing, tel. 0845 605 0600.

BUS 🚌
For services from *Ayr*, phone **Scottish Citylink** on 08705 505050.

FERRIES ⛴
Caledonian MacBrayne:
Ardrossan to Brodick (Isle of Arran),
tel. 01475 650100.

TOURIST INFORMATION OFFICES 🛈

339 Sandgate, **Ayr**, KA7 1BG, 01292 288688.

The Pier, **Brodick**, Isle of Arran, KA27 8AU, 01770 302140.

Bridge Street, **Girvan**, Ayrshire, KA26 9HH, 01465 714950 (Easter to Oct).

New Street, **Irvine**, Ayrshire, KA12 8AG, 01294 313886.

62 Bank Street, **Kilmarnock**, Ayrshire, KA1 1ER, 01563 539090.

The Promenade, **Largs**, Ayrshire, KA30 8BG, 01475 673765.

Stuart Street, **Millport**, Isle of Cumbrae, KA28 0AN, 01475 530753 (Easter to Oct).

Municipal Buildings, South Beach, **Troon**, Ayrshire, KA10 6EF, 01292 317696 (Easter to Oct).

Ardwell
NX1693

Ardwell Farm, *Ardwell, Girvan, Ayrshire, KA26 0HP.*
Picturesque farmhouse with rooms overlooking the Firth of Clyde.
Open: All Year
Grades: STB 2 Star
01465 713389 Mrs Melville
D: £14.00–£15.00 **S:** £14.00–£16.00
Beds: 2T 1D **Baths:** 1 Sh
🛇 🅿 (3) ⅌ 📺 🛏 ✕ 🛍 Ⓥ 🛢

Planning a longer stay?
Always ask for any special rates

ARRAN Brodick
NS0136 🍴 *Pirates Cove, Ormidale Bar, Brodick Bar, Duncan's Bar, Arran Hotel, Ingledene Hotel*

Kingsley Hotel, *Brodick, Isle of Arran, KA27 8AJ.*
Open: Easter to Sep
01770 302226 kingsleyhotel@connectfree
D: £29.00–£29.50 **S:** £29.00–£29.50
Beds: 2F 6D 11T 8S **Baths:** 27 En
🛇 🅿 (30) 📺 🛏 ✕ 🛍 Ⓥ 🛢 cc
Situated on Brodick seafront, overlooking the Arran hills, Kingsley is one of Arran's well known hotels with a reputation for warm welcome, good food and relaxing friendly atmosphere. Golf and family packages a speciality, with our small indoor heated swimming pool adding to the experience.

Sunnyside, *Kings Cross, Brodick, Isle of Arran, KA27 8RG.*
Open: All year (not Xmas)
Grades: STB 2 Star
01770 700422
D: £17.50–£20.00 **S:** £18.50–£24.00
Beds: 1D 1T/S **Baths:** 1 En 1 Pr
ॐ ⅍ 📺 🍴 🕮 ♨ **cc**
Private entrance to comfortably furnished double ensuite room with superb view across the Clyde. Also one Twin/single room having private facilities. Deck and secluded sun trap garden. A haven for peace and tranquillity. Private parking. 8.5 miles south Brodick.

Rosaburn Lodge, *Brodick, Isle of Arran, KA27 8DP.*
Open: All Year
01770 302383
D: £24.00–£27.50 **S:** £24.00–£27.50
Beds: 1T 2D **Baths:** 3 En
ॐ 🅿 ⅍ 📺 🍴 🕮 ♨ ✿ ♨ ♿
The lodge stands on the beautiful banks of river Rosa within 2 acres of private landscaped gardens. An ideal location for hill walking golf cycling or relaxing on this wonderful island. A warm welcome awaits you from Paul and Leen.

Tigh Na Mara, *Seafront, Brodick, Isle of Arran, KA27 8AJ.*
Beautifully situated on seafront overlooking the mountains and Brodick Bay.
Open: All Year
Grades: STB 2 Star
01770 302538
Terry & Leslie Dunleavy
Fax: 01770 302546
arran.tighnamara@btinternet.com
D: £20.00–£24.00 **S:** £20.00–£24.00
Beds: 2F 5D 2T **Baths:** 2 En 3 Sh
ॐ (4) 🅿 (2) 📺 🕮 ♨ ✿ ♨ **cc**

BEDROOMS

F - Family   **T** - Twin
D - Double   **S** - Single

ARRAN Catacol
NR9149

Catacol Bay Hotel, *Catacol, Brodick, Isle of Arran, KA27 8HN.*
Open: All Year (not Xmas)
01770 830231
Mr Ashcroft
Fax: 01770 830350
davecatbay@lineone.net
D: £20.00–£25.00 **S:** £20.00–£25.00
Beds: 3F 1D 1T 1S
Baths: 2 Sh
ॐ 🅿 (30) 📺 🍴 ✕ 🕮 ♨ ♨ **cc**
Small friendly fully licensed hotel nestling in hills at the picturesque north end of Arran situated on the seashore overlooking the Kilbrannan Sound & Kintyre. Self-catering bungalow also available - sleeps 7.

ARRAN Corriecravie
NR9223 ⌘ *Lagg inn*

Rosebank, *Corriecravie, Brodick, Isle of Arran, KA27 8PD.*
Locally owned; ideal for walking, golf, birdwatching and relaxing.
Open: All Year (not Xmas)
Grades: STB 2 Star
01770 870228 (also fax)
Mrs Adamson
D: £17.00–£18.00 **S:** £17.00–£18.00
Beds: 1F 1D 1T 1S
Baths: 1 En 1 Sh
ॐ 🅿 📺 🍴 🕮 ♨ ♨

ARRAN Lamlash
NS0230 ⌘ *Drift Inn, Breadalbane*

Westfield Guest House, *Lamlash, Brodick, Isle of Arran, KA27 8NN.*
Typical island house, close to the sea, overlooking Holy Isle.
Open: All Year
01770 600428
Mrs Sloan
D: £16.00–£18.00 **S:** £16.00–£18.00
Beds: 2D 1T 2S **Baths:** 2 Sh
ॐ 🅿 (6) ⅍ 📺 🕮 ♨ ♨

ARRAN   Lochranza

NR9349

Butt Lodge Country House Hotel,
Lochranza, Brodick, Isle of Arran, KA27 8JF.
Open: Feb to Jan
Grades: STB 4 Star
01770 830240 Fax: 01770 830211
butt.lodge@virgin.net
D: £25.00–£40.00 **S:** £25.00–£48.00
Beds: 5F 1D 1T 3S **Baths:** 1 Pr
ॐ 🅿 ⊬ 📺 ✕ 🛏 📖 Ⅴ ✿ 🌡 ♿ cc
Beautiful 4 star family-run hotel, with
residential licence. Standing in 2 acres of
gardens with an abundance of wildlife,
nestling under the hills at the head of the
sea loch. Log fires, all rooms ensuite. Private
off-road parking. We are renowned for our
cuisine and fine dining.

ARRAN   Shiskine

NR9129   ⚓ *Black Waterfoot Hotel*

Croftlea, *Shiskine, Brodick, Isle of Arran,*
KA27 8EN.
Comfortable house with garden. Quiet
location 2 miles beach/golf course.
Open: Easter to Oct
Grades: STB 2 Star
01770 860259
Mrs Henderson
D: £18.00–£20.00 **S:** £25.00
Beds: 2D 3T **Baths:** 3 En 1 Sh
🅿 (5) ⊬ 📺 🛏 📖 Ⅴ

ARRAN   Whiting Bay

NS0425   ⚓ *Burlington Hotel, Trafalgar, Kiscadale Hotel, The Cameronia, The Shurrig*

Argentine House Hotel, *Whiting Bay,*
Brodick, Isle of Arran, KA27 8PZ.
Swiss owners, superb views over Clyde, first
class cooking. Licensed.
Open: Mar to Jan
01770 700662
info@argentinearran.co.uk
D: £20.00–£32.00 **S:** £24.00–£50.00
Beds: 4D 1T **Baths:** 5 En
ॐ 🅿 (6) 📺 🛏 ✕ 📖 Ⅴ ✿ 🌡 cc

Ayr

NS3422   ⚓ *Tam O'Shanter, Kylestrome Hotel, Finlay's Bar, Burroffield's Bar, Carrick Lodge, Durward Hotel, Hollybush Inn, Balgarth, Littlejohns*

Inverlea Guest House, *42 Carrick Road,*
Ayr, KA7 2RB.
Open: All Year
01292 266756 (also fax)
Mr & Mrs Bryson
D: £15.00–£20.00 **S:** £18.00–£25.00
Beds: 3F 2D 2T 1S **Baths:** 3 En 2 Pr 3 Sh
ॐ 🅿 (5) 📺 🛏 📖 Ⅴ 🌡
Family-run Victorian guest house which has
ensured personal attention for 15 years. Few
minutes walk from beach and town centre.
Burns Cottage and 7 golf courses nearby.
Large enclosed car park at rear of house.

Belmont Guest House, *15 Park Circus,*
Ayr, KA7 2DJ.
Open: All Year (not Xmas)
Grades: STB 2 Star, AA 3 Diamond
01292 265588
Mr Hillhouse
Fax: 01292 290303
belmontguesthouse@btinternet.com
D: £20.00–£22.00 **S:** £24.00
Beds: 2F 2D 1T **Baths:** 5 En
ॐ 🅿 (5) 📺 🛏 📖 Ⅴ 🌡 ♿
Try a breath of fresh 'Ayr'. Warm, comfortable
hospitality assured in this Victorian town
house, situated in a quiet residential area
within easy walking distance of the town
centre and beach. Ground floor bedrooms
available. Glasgow (Prestwick) Airport 6
miles. Green Tourism Silver Award.

Kilkerran, *15 Prestwick Road, Ayr, KA8 8LD.*
Friendly family-run guest house on main A74
Ayr-Prestwick route.
Open: All Year
Grades: STB 2 Star
01292 266477
Ms Ferguson
margaret@kilkerran-gh.demon.co.uk
D: £16.00–£20.00 **S:** £16.00–£20.00
Beds: 3F 2D 2T 2S **Baths:** 2 En 1 Pr 3 Sh
ॐ 🅿 (10) 📺 🛏 ✕ 📖 Ⅴ ✿ 🌡 ♿

Finlayson Arms Hotel, *Coylton, Ayr,*
KA6 6JT.
Superbly located for golfing holiday, with
over 30 courses, nearby including Turnberry
and Troon.
Open: All Year (not Xmas/New Year)
01292 570298
D: £22.50–£27.50 **S:** £25.00–£35.00
Beds: 1F 7T **Baths:** 8 En
🛏 🄿 (12) ⌇ 📺 ✕ 🖿 Ⓥ 🔔 ♿ cc

Deanbank, *44 Ashgrove Street, Ayr, KA7 3BG.*
Convenient for town centre, station, golf and
Burns Country.
Open: All Year (not Xmas)
Grades: STB 4 Star
01292 263745 Ms Wilson
D: £18.00–£20.00 **S:** £20.00–£25.00
Beds: 1F 1T **Baths:** 1 Sh
🛏 (1) ⌇ 📺 🐾 🖿 Ⓥ 🔔

Sunnyside, *26 Dunure Road, Doonfoot, Ayr,*
KA7 4HR.
Close to Burns Cottage, Brig O'Doon;
spacious rooms: family welcome.
Open: All Year (not Xmas)
Grades: STB 3 Star
01292 441234 (also fax) Mrs Malcolm
D: £20.00–£22.00 **S:** £26.00–£28.00
Beds: 2F **Baths:** 2 En
🛏 🄿 (4) ⌇ 📺 🖿 Ⓥ 🔔

Ferguslea, *98 New Road, Ayr, KA8 8JG.*
Family run, good food, traditional Scottish
hospitality.
Open: All Year (not Xmas/New Year)
Grades: STB 2 Star
01292 268551 Mrs Campbell
D: £14.00–£16.00 **S:** £14.00–£16.00
Beds: 2T 1S **Baths:** 2 Sh
🛏 🄿 (3) 📺 🐾 🖿 Ⓥ 🔔

Tramore Guest House, *17 Eglinton*
Terrace, Ayr, KA7 1JJ.
In C12th old fort area, 2 mins from town
centre. **Open:** All Year
Grades: STB 3 Star
01292 266019 (also fax) E R Tumilty
D: £17.00–£18.00 **S:** £17.00–£19.00
Beds: 1D 2T **Baths:** 2 Sh
🛏 📺 🐾 ✕ 🖿 Ⓥ 🔔

Langley Bank Guest House, *39 Carrick*
Road, Ayr, KA7 2RD.
A well appointed Victorian house. Centrally
situated, see website.
Open: All Year **Grades:** STB 3 Star
01292 264246 Mr & Mrs Mitchell
Fax: 01292 282628
D: £15.00–£25.00 **S:** £20.00–£45.00
Beds: 1F 3D 2T **Baths:** 4 Pr 1 En
🛏 🄿 (4) 📺 🖿 🔔 cc

Dunedin, *10 Montgomerie Terrace, Ayr,*
KA7 1JL.
Comfortable family home from home.
Open: Easter to Sept **Grades:** STB 2 Star
01292 261224 Mrs Grant
D: £18.00–£19.00 **S:** £36.00–£46.00
Beds: 1F 1D **Baths:** 2 En
🛏 🄿 (2) ⌇ 📺 🖿 🔔

Windsor Hotel, *6 Alloway Place, Ayr,*
KA7 2AA.
Town house hotel within 15 min drive of 14
golf courses.
Open: All Year (not Xmas)
Grades: STB 2 Star, AA 3 Diamond
01292 264689 Mrs Hamilton
D: £22.00–£25.00 **S:** £22.00–£35.00
Beds: 4F 3D 1T 2S **Baths:** 7 En 1 Pr 1 Sh
🛏 ⌇ 📺 🐾 ✕ 🖿 Ⓥ 🔔 ♿ cc

Town Hotel, *9-11 Barns Street, Ayr, KA7 1XB.*
Family run hotel, close to town centre and 10
local golf courses. **Open:** All Year
01292 267595
D: £20.00–£25.00 **S:** £20.00–£25.00
Beds: 3F 1D 14T **Baths:** 18 En
🛏 (1) 🄿 (1) 📺 🐾 ✕ 🖿 Ⓥ ❀ 🔔 ♿

Ballantrae

NX0982 🏨 *Kings Arms, Royal Hotel*

Orchard Lea, *14 Main Street, Ballantrae,*
Girvan, Ayrshire, KA26 0NB.
Comfortable house offers superb breakfast.
Quiet coastal village, ferries nearby.
Open: All Year (not Xmas)
01465 831509 Mr & Mrs Ward
D: £15.00 **S:** £15.00
Beds: 2D 1T **Baths:** 1 Sh
🛏 🄿 (12) ⌇ 📺 🐾 🖿 ❀ 🔔

Ardstinchar Cottage, *81 Main Street, Ballantrae, Girvan, Ayrshire, KA26 0NA.*
Beautiful cottage in magnificent countryside.
Open: All Year (not Xmas/New Year)
01465 831343 Mrs Drummond
D: £16.00–£20.00 **S:** £20.00–£25.00
Beds: 2D 1T **Baths:** 1 Sh
ॐ 🅿 (3) 📺 🛋, 🖪 ❄ 🗷

Laggan Farm, *Ballantrae, Girvan, Ayrshire, KA26 0JZ.*
Comfortable Georgian House on dairy farm close to Ayrshire Coast.
Open: Easter to Oct **Grades:** STB 3 Star
01465 831402 Mrs McKinley
j&r@lagganfm.freeserve.co.uk
D: £16.00–£19.00 **S:** £18.00–£21.00
Beds: 1F 1D 1T **Baths:** 1 En 2 Sh
ॐ 🅿 🍴 📺 🛦 ✕ 🛋, 🖪 🗷

Barassie

NS3232 ◀ *Tower Hotel*

Fordell, *43 Beach Road, Barassie, Troon, KA10 6SU.*
Open: All Year (not Xmas/New Year)
Grades: STB 3 Star
01292 313224 Mrs Mathieson
Fax: 01292 312141
morag@fordell.junglelink.co.uk
D: £18.00–£20.00 **S:** £20.00–£25.00
Beds: 1F 2T **Baths:** 2 Sh
🍴 📺 🛦 🛋, 🖪 🗷
Relax in this Victorian House overlooking the sea or use as a base to visit Ayrshire's famed golf courses or many other attractions. Comfortable rooms, good breakfasts, secure parking for cycles or motor bikes. A warm welcome awaits.

Barrhill

NX2382 ◀ *Galloway Hotel*

14 Main Street, *Barrhill, Girvan, Ayrshire, KA26 0PQ.*
Comfortable, homely, in small village. Central for local beauty spots. **Open:** All Year
01465 821344 Mrs Hegarty
D: £15.00–£18.00 **S:** £18.00
Beds: 1F **Baths:** 1 Pr 1 Sh
ॐ 🍴 📺 🛦 ✕ 🛋, 🗷

Blair Farm, *Barrhill, Girvan, Ayrshire, KA26 0RD.*
Beautiful farmhouse, lovely views. Enjoy peace, comfort & friendly hospitality.
Open: Easter to Nov **Grades:** STB 4 Star
01465 821247 Mrs Hughes
D: £20.00–£22.00 **S:** £25.00
Beds: 1D 1T **Baths:** 1 En 1 Pr
ॐ 🅿 📺 🛦 ✕ 🛋, 🗷

Beith

NS3553 ◀ *Parrafin Lamp*

Townend of Shuterflat Farm, *Beith, Ayrshire, KA15 2LW.*
Comfortable farmhouse, warm welcome, 15 minutes Glasgow Airport and city centre.
Open: All Year
01505 502342 Mrs Lamont
D: £17.50 **S:** £17.50
Beds: 1T 2D **Baths:** 1 Sh
ॐ 🅿 (4) 📺 🛦 🛋, 🗷

Coylton

NS4219 ◀ *The Kyle Hotel, The Finlayson Arms*

The Kyle Hotel, *Main Street, Coylton, Ayr, KA6 6JW.*
Close to many Ayrshire top golf courses and Ayr Racecourse. **Open:** All Year
01292 570312 Mr Finlayson
Fax: 01292 571493
D: £22.50–£25.00 **S:** £22.50–£25.00
Beds: 3F 1T **Baths:** 2 En 1 Sh
ॐ 📺 🛦 ✕ 🛋, 🖪 ❄ 🗷 cc

Dunure

NS2515 ◀ *Anchorage*

Cruachan, *38 Station Road, Dunure, Ayr, KA7 4LL.*
Magnificent views to Arran; close to harbour and castle park.
Open: Apr to Oct **Grades:** STB 4 Star
01292 500494 Mr Evans
Fax: 01292 500266
dnevans@lineone.net
D: £20.00–£25.00 **S:** £20.00–£30.00
Beds: 1D 1T **Baths:** 1 En 1 Pr
🅿 (4) 🍴 📺 🛋, 🗷

Gatehead

NS3936

Muirhouse Farm, *Gatehead, Kilmarnock, Ayrshire, KA2 0BT.*
Comfortable farmhouse. Convenient to town.
Open: All Year (not Xmas)
01563 523975 (also fax)
Mrs Love
D: £16.00–£20.00 **S:** £17.00–£20.00
Beds: 1F 1D 1T **Baths:** 2 En 1 Pr
🛇 🅿 (6) 📺 🏲 🛏 🖵 ᐧ

Girvan

NX1897 🍺 *Southfield Hotel, Aisa Graig Hotel, Roxy Bar*

Hotel Westcliffe, *15-16 Louisa Drive, Girvan, Ayrshire, KA26 9AH.*
Family run hotel on sea front, all rooms ensuite. Spa/steam room.
Open: All Year
Grades: STB 2 Star
01465 712128 (also fax)
Mrs Jardine
D: £23.00–£26.00 **S:** £24.00–£28.00
Beds: 6F 5D 8T 5S **Baths:** 24 En
🛇 🅿 (6) 📺 ✕ 🖵 ❁ ᐧ & cc

Thistleneuk Guest House, *19 Louisa Drive, Girvan, Ayrshire, KA26 9AH.*
Victorian terrace, original features overlooking Ailsa Craig. Local shops nearby.
Open: Easter to Oct **Grades:** STB 2 Star
01465 712137 (also fax) Mr & Mrs Lacey
reservations@thistleneuk.freeserve.co.uk
D: £23.00 **S:** £23.00–£31.00
Beds: 2F 2D 2T 1S **Baths:** 7 En
🛇 (2) 📺 ✕ 🖵 🖵 ᐧ

Hollybush

NS3914 🍺 *Hollybush Inn*

Malcolmston Farm, *Hollybush, Ayr, KA6 6EZ.*
Farmhouse on A713 near Ayr, (near Turnberry and Troon). **Open:** Easter to Nov
01292 560238 Mrs Drummond
D: £16.00–£18.00 **S:** £16.00–£18.00
Beds: 1F 2D **Baths:** 1 En 2 Sh
🛇 🅿 (4) 📺 🏲 🖵 ᐧ &

Kilmarnock

NS4238 🍺 *Cochrane Inn, Wheatsheaf, Kings Arms, The Gathering, Ellerslie Inn*

Hillhouse Farm, *Grassyards Road, Kilmarnock, Ayrshire, KA3 6HG.*
Open: All Year
Grades: STB 4 Star
01563 523370 Mrs Howie
D: £18.00–£21.00 **S:** £18.00–£21.00
Beds: 3F 1T **Baths:** 2 En 2 Sh
🛇 🅿 (8) 📺 🏲 🖵 🖵 ᐧ
The Howie family extend a warm welcome to their working dairy farm. Large bedrooms with superb views over garden and Ayrshire countryside. Central location for coast, golf, fishing, Glasgow and Prestwick Airports. Real farmhouse breakfast, home baking for supper.

Tamarind, *24 Arran Avenue, Kilmarnock, Ayrshire, KA3 1TP.*
Large ranch-style bungalow on one level. Located at end of quiet tree-lined avenue.
Open: All Year
Grades: STB 3 Star
01563 571788 Mrs Turner
james@tamarind25.freeserve.co.uk
D: £17.50–£20.00 **S:** £25.00–£30.00
Beds: 1F 2T 1S **Baths:** 4 En
🛇 🅿 (4) ⅍ 📺 🖵 ᐧ & cc

Kilwinning

NS3043 🍺 *Blair Inn, Claremont Hotel*

Claremont Guest House, *27 Howgate, Kilwinning, Ayrshire, KA13 6EW.*
Friendly family B&B close to town centre and public transport.
Open: All Year (not Xmas)
01294 553905 Mrs Filby
D: £17.00–£20.00 **S:** £17.00–£20.00
Beds: 1F 1S **Baths:** 2 Sh
🛇 🅿 (10) ⅍ 📺 🖵

Planning a longer stay?
Always ask for any special rates

Largs

NS2059 ◀ *George, Morris's, Regattas, Haylie Hotel, Inverkip Hotel, Brisbane House, Flannigans*

South Whittleburn Farm, *Brisbane Glen, Largs, Ayrshire, KA30 8SN.*
Superb farmhouse accommodation, enormous, delicious breakfasts. Warm, friendly hospitality, highly recommended.
Open: All Year (not Xmas)
Grades: STB 4 Star, AA 4 Diamond
01475 675881 Mrs Watson
Fax: 01475 675080
D: £20.00 **S:** £20.00
Beds: 1F 1D 1T **Baths:** 3 En
🛇 🅿 (10) ⌿ 📺 🛏 🎛 �V 🛢

Belmont House, *2 Broomfield Place, Largs, Ayrshire, KA30 8DR.*
Interesting old waterfront house. Spacious rooms. Views of Islands and Highlands.
Open: All Year
01475 676264 Mr & Mrs Clarke
belmont.house@i12.com
D: £20.00–£25.00 **S:** £20.00–£25.00
Beds: 2D 1T **Baths:** 1 En 2 Pr
🛇 (4) 🅿 (2) 🛏 🎛 ☑ 🛢

Stonehaven Guest House, *8 Netherpark Crescent, Largs, KA30 8QB.*
Open: All Year (not Xmas)
Grades: STB 4 Star
01475 673319 Mr Martin
stonehaven.martin@virgin.net
D: £20.00–£25.00 **S:** £18.00–£23.00
Beds: 1D 1T 1S **Baths:** 1 En 1 Sh
⌿ 📺 🎛 ☑ 🛢
Situated in an elevated position with magnificent views over the bay to the Isles of Cumbrae, Arran, Bute and Ailsa Craig with Routenburn Golf Course and The Clyde. Muirsheil regional park at the rear. High standards and personal attention given to all.

Planning a longer stay?
Always ask for any special rates

Rutland Guest House, *22 Charles Street, Largs, Ayrshire, KA30 8HJ.*
Comfortable, family-run guest house. 1 minute walk to view panoramic sites of Arran.
Open: All Year
Grades: STB 2 Star
01475 675642 Mrs Russell
rutland@22largs.freeserve.co.uk
D: £17.00–£18.00 **S:** £18.00–£20.00
Beds: 3F 1D 1T **Baths:** 1 En 1 Pr 2 Sh
🛇 📺 🛏 🎛 🛢

Inverie, *16 Charles Street, Largs, Ayrshire, KA30 8HJ.*
Attractive comfortable home, warm hospitality, Scottish breakfast, central, adjacent to sea.
Open: All Year (not Xmas/New Year)
01475 675903 Mrs MacLeod
D: £17.00–£18.00 **S:** £17.00–£18.00
Beds: 1D 1T 1S **Baths:** 1 Sh
🅿 (3) ⌿ 📺 🎛 🛢

Lendalfoot

NX1389

The Smiddy, *Lendalfoot, Girvan, KA26 0JF.*
Make yourself at home in comfortable home with panoramic views.
Open: May to Sep
01465 891204 Mrs Bell
D: £14.00 **S:** £14.00
Beds: 1D 1T **Baths:** 1 Sh
🛇 🅿 📺 ✕ 🎛 ☑ 🛢

Mauchline

NS4927 ◀ *Maxwood Inn, Stair Inn*

Treborane, *Dykefield Farm, Mauchline, Ayrshire, KA5 6EY.*
This is a new cottage on farm; friendly atmosphere.
Open: All Year
Grades: STB 2 Star
01290 550328 Ms Smith
D: £12.00–£15.00
Beds: 2F **Baths:** 1 En 1 Sh
🛇 🅿 ⌿ 📺 🛏 ✕ ☑

Ardwell, *103 Loudoun Street, Mauchline, KA5 5BH.*
Beautiful rooms, near centre of historic village. Great golf locally.
Open: All Year
01290 552987 Mrs Houston
D: £15.00–£17.00 **S:** £17.00–£19.00
Beds: 2F **Baths:** 2 En
ᗙ 🅿 (2) ⅍ 📺 🛏, 🍵

Dykefield Farm, *Mauchline, KA5 6EY.*
Farmhouse B&B with friendly, family atmosphere. Private lounge for guests.
Open: All Year
Grades: STB 1 Star
01290 553170
Mrs Smith
D: £12.00 **S:** £12.00
Beds: 2F **Baths:** 1 Sh
ᗙ 🅿 (3) 📺 🛏,

NS2909 🍺 *Welltrees Inn*

Homelea, *62 Culzean Road, Maybole, Ayrshire, KA19 8AH.*
Homelea is a spacious red sandstone Victorian family home, retaining many original features.
Open: Easter to Oct
Grades: STB 3 Star
01655 882736
Mrs McKellar
Fax: 01655 883557
gilmour_mck@msn.com
D: £17.50–£18.50 **S:** £20.00–£22.00
Beds: 1F 1T 1S **Baths:** 2 Sh
ᗙ 🅿 (3) ⅍ 📺 🛏, 🍵

Garpin Farm, *Crosshill, Maybole, Ayrshire, KA19 7PX.*
Comfortable family farmhouse in beautiful Ayrshire countryside. Home baking.
Open: All Year
01655 740214
Mrs Young
D: £18.00–£20.00 **S:** £21.00–£20.00
Beds: 1F 1T 1D **Baths:** 1 Sh
ᗙ 🅿 📺 ✕ 🛏, Ⓥ 🍵

Monkton
NS3627 🍺 *Wheatsheaf, North Beach Hotel*

Crookside Farm, *Kerrix Road, Monkton, Prestwick, Ayrshire, KA9 2QU.*
Comfortable farmhouse central heating throughout, ideal for golfing, close to airport.
Open: All Year (not Xmas)
01563 830266 Mrs Gault
D: £12.00 **S:** £12.00
Beds: 1F 1D **Baths:** 1 Sh
ᗙ 🅿 📺 🐾 🛏, Ⓥ 🍵 ♿

New Cumnock
NS6113

Low Polquheys Farm, *New Cumnock, Cumnock, Ayrshire, KA18 4NX.*
Modern farmhouse, very friendly and central.
Open: Easter to Oct
01290 338307
Mrs Caldwell
marjorie@low-polquheys.freeserve.co.uk
D: £13.00–£15.00 **S:** £15.00
Beds: 1F 1T 1S **Baths:** 1 Sh
ᗙ (2) 📺 🛏, 🍵

Newmilns
NS5237 🍺 *Wee Train*

Whatriggs Farm, *Newmilns, Ayrshire, KA16 9LJ.*
Family-run 700-acre farm, with golf and family attractions nearby.
Open: All Year (not Xmas)
Grades: STB 2 Star
01560 700279
Mrs Mitchell
whatriggs@farming.co.uk
D: £15.00–£17.50 **S:** £15.00–£17.50
Beds: 2F **Baths:** 1 Sh
ᗙ 🅿 (6) 📺 🐾 ✕ Ⓥ 🍵

BEDROOMS
F - Family   **T** - Twin
D - Double   **S** - Single

Ochiltree

NS5121 ⚓ *Stair Inn*

Laigh Tareg Farm, *Ochiltree, Cymnock, KA18 2RL.*
Modern working dairy farm traditional farmhouse of great character with a warm family welcome.
Open: Easter to Oct
Grades: STB 2 Star
01290 700242 (also fax)
Mrs Watson
D: £18.00–£20.00 **S:** £18.00–£22.00
Beds: 2F **Baths:** 1 Pr 1 Sh
🛏 (1) 🅿 📺 🐾 🛏️ ♨

Prestwick

NS3425 ⚓ *North Beach Hotel, Golf Inn, Carlton Hotel*

Knox Bed & Breakfast, *105 Ayr Road, Prestwick, Ayrshire, KA9 1TN.*
Superb accommodation, homely welcome, excellent value, close to all amenities, airport and Centrum Arena.
Open: All Year (not Xmas)
01292 478808
Mrs Wardrope
knox-bed-breakfast@talk21.com
D: £15.00–£18.00 **S:** £16.00–£20.00
Beds: 1D 1T 1S
Baths: 1 Sh
🛏 (2) 🅿 (4) ⊬ 📺 🛏️ Ⅴ ♨

Skelmorlie

NS1967

Balvonie Conference & Holiday Centre, *Halketburn Road, Skelmorlie, Ayrshire, PA17 5BP.*
Tudor style manor house, for a perfect conference/retreat or holiday.
Open: All Year (not Xmas)
01475 520122
Fax: 01475 522668
D: £17.00 **S:** £17.00
Beds: 2F 1D 16T 1S
Baths: 17 En 3 Pr
🛏 🅿 (17) ⊬ 📺 ✕ 🛏️ Ⅴ ♨ ♿

Stair

NS4423

Stair Inn, *Stair, Mauchline, KA5 5HW.*
Conservation area. Guest rooms of a very high standard.
Open: All Year
01292 591562 Mr Boyd
Fax: 01292 591650
D: £22.50–£25.00 **S:** £35.00–£39.00
Beds: 2F 3T 1D **Baths:** 6 En
⊬ 📺 ✕ 🛏️ Ⅴ ♨ cc

Straiton

NS3804 ⚓ *Black Bull*

Three Thorns Farm, *Straiton, Maybole, Ayrshire, KA19 7QR.*
Good wholesome food, scenic views, C18th farmhouse, Culzean and Blairguham Castles nearby.
Open: All Year
01655 770221 (also fax)
Mrs Henry
D: £20.00 **S:** £22.00–£25.00
Beds: 1F 2D 1T **Baths:** 2 En 2 Pr
🛏 🅿 (10) 📺 🐾 🛏️ Ⅴ ♨ ♿

Symington

NS3831 ⚓ *Wheatsheaf Inn*

Muirhouse Farm, *Symington, Kilmarnock, Ayrshire, KA1 5PA.*
Traditional comfortable farmhouse, excellent food, near golf, leisure, equestrian centre.
Open: All Year
Grades: STB 2 Star
01563 830218 Mrs Howie
D: £18.00–£20.00 **S:** £20.00
Beds: 1D 1T **Baths:** 1 Sh
🛏 🅿 (20) 📺 🛏️ Ⅴ ♨

BATHROOMS
Pr - Private
Sh - Shared
En - Ensuite

Troon

NS3230 ◁ *Old Loans Inn, Lookout, Wheatsheaf, South Beach Hotel, Anchorage, Towers*

The Cherries, *50 Ottoline Drive, Troon, Ayrshire, KA10 7AW.*
Beautiful quiet home on golf course near beaches and restaurants.
Open: All Year **Grades:** STB 3 Star
01292 313312 Mrs Tweedie
Fax: 01292 319007
thecherries50@hotmail.com
D: £20.00–£24.00 **S:** £20.00–£25.00
Beds: 1F 1T 1S **Baths:** 1 En 1 Pr 1 Sh
🛇 🅿 (5) ⊬ 📺 🐓 🛏 📶 🆅 🍵

Rosedale, *9 Firth Road, Barassie, Troon, KA10 6TF.*
Quiet seafront location - ideal for Sea Cat ferry to Ireland. **Open:** All Year (not Xmas)
Grades: STB 2 Star
01292 314371 Mrs Risk hmrisk@hotmail.com
D: £20.00 **S:** £20.00
Beds: 1D 1T 1S
🛇 (5) ⊬ 📺 📶 🆅 🍵

Mossgiel, *56 Bentinck Drive, Troon, KA10 6HY.*
5 minutes from beach, 10 minutes' walk from golf courses.
Open: All Year
Grades: STB 2 Star
01292 314937 (also fax)
Mrs Rankin
mossgiel@aol.com
D: £19.00–£22.00 **S:** £22.00–£25.00
Beds: 1F 1D 1T **Baths:** 3 En
🛇 🅿 (3) 📺 📶 🆅 ❋ 🍵 ♿

The Beeches, *63 Ottoline Drive, Troon, KA10 7AN.*
Bright spacious house, wooded gardens. Every amenity, beaches, golf, marina.
Open: All Year
Grades: STB 2 Star
01292 314180
Mrs Sinclair
D: £16.00–£18.00
S: £18.00–£20.00
Beds: 1D 1T 1S **Baths:** 2 Pr
🛇 🅿 (4) ⊬ 📺 📶 🆅 🍵

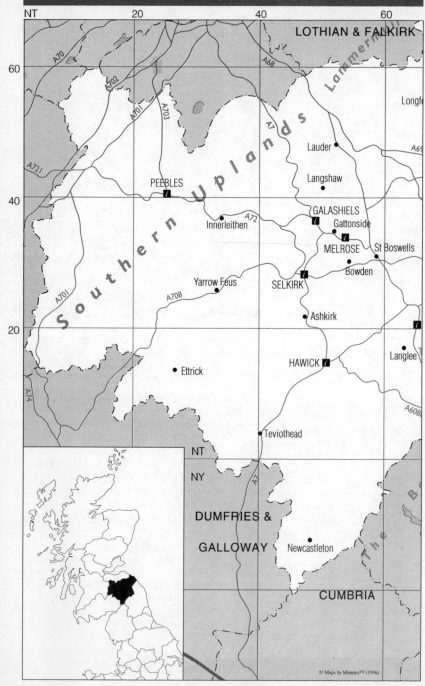

Borders & Berwickshire

LOTHIAN & FALKIRK

Southern Uplands

Lammermuir

Longf

Lauder

Langshaw

PEEBLES *i*

Innerleithen

GALASHIELS *i*

Gattonside *i*

MELROSE

St Boswells

Bowden

Yarrow Feus

SELKIRK *i*

Ashkirk *i*

Ettrick

HAWICK *i*

Langlee

Teviothead

DUMFRIES &

GALLOWAY

Newcastleton

The B

CUMBRIA

© Maps In Minutes™ (1996)

```
40  NT              60              80              00
```

LOTHIAN & FALKIRK

Lammermuir Hills

St Abb's Head

A1107 St Abbs •

Coldingham •

EYEMOUTH

Reston •

60

Longformacus •   Duns •

A6105

Allanton •

BERWICK UPON-TWEED

A697   Greenlaw •   Swinton •

A6112

Lauder •

Langshaw •

A698

40

GALASHIELS

A8089 Ednam • Birgham •

NORTHUMBERLAND

Gattonside

MELROSE   St Boswells   KELSO

Bowden •   Heiton •

Town Yetholm •

SELKIRK   Eckford •

Kirk Yetholm

Ashkirk •   *Cheviot Hills*

20   JEDBURGH

HAWICK

We include Berwick-upon-Tweed since, although part of England continuously for over half a millennium, it was historically Scottish. Having changed hands 14 times between 1174 and 1482 it was finally annexed by the Sassenach and separated from the shire in Scotland that bore its name. The Tweed is in some degree still the psychological border: Berwick Rangers FC is the only English club in the Scottish Football League.

© Maps In Minutes™ (1996)

BUS 🚌
The border towns are well served by **Scottish Citylink**. Tel. 08750 505050.

RAIL ⇌
For rail information, telephone the National Rail Enquiries line on 08457 484950. For the Minicom service for the deaf and hard of hearing, tel. 0845 605 0600.

TOURIST INFORMATION OFFICES ℹ

Castlegate Car Park, **Berwick-upon-Tweed,** Northumberland, TD15 1JS, 01289 330733.

Henderson Park, High Street, **Coldstream**, Berwickshire, TD12 4AG, 01890 882607 (Easter to Oct).

Auld Kirk, Manse Road, **Eyemouth**, Berwickshire, TD14 5JE, 01890 750678 (Easter to Oct).

Bank Street, **Galashiels**, Selkirkshire, TD1 1EL, 01896 755551 (Easter to Oct).

Common Haugh, **Hawick**, Roxburghshire, TD9 7AR, 01450 372547.

Murray's Green, **Jedburgh**, Roxburghshire, TD8 6BE, 01835 863435.

Turret House, Abbey Court, **Kelso**, Roxburghshire, TD5 7JA, 01573 223464 (Easter to Oct).

Priorwood Gardens, **Melrose**, Roxburghshire, TD6 9EQ, 01896 822555 (Easter to Oct).

High Street, **Peebles**, EH45 8HG, 01721 720138.

Halliwell's House, **Selkirk**, TD7 4BL, 01750 20054 (Easter to Oct).

We include Berwick-upon-Tweed since, although part of England continuously for over half a millennium, it was historically Scottish. Having changed hands 14 times between 1174 and 1482 it was finally annexed by the Sassenach and separated from the shire in Scotland that bore its name. The Tweed is in some degree still the psychological border: Berwick Rangers FC is the only English club in the Scottish Football League.

Allanton

NT8654 *Allanton Inn*

Allanton Inn, *Allanton, Chirnside, Duns, Berwickshire, TD11 3JZ.*
Historic coaching inn, set in a Scottish Borders Conservation village.
Open: All Year (not Xmas/New Year)
Grades: STB 3 Star
01890 818260
Mrs Ward
Fax: 01890 817186
allantoninn@supanet.com
D: £40.00 **S:** £46.00
Beds: 1F 1D 2T
🐕 🅿 (8) 📺 🍴 ✕ ▥ 💷 ⚓ cc

Ashkirk

NT4722 *Queens Head*

Ashkirktown Farm, *Ashkirk, Selkirk, TD7 4PB.*
Farmhouse in beautiful countryside. Tastefully furnished. Warm welcome assured.
Open: All Year (not Xmas/New Year)
Grades: STB 3 Star
01750 32315 (also fax)
Mrs Lamont
D: £18.00 **S:** £18.00
Beds: 1F 2D **Baths:** 2 Sh
🐕 🅿 (6) ✂ 📺 ▥ 💷 ⚓

RATES

D = Price range per person sharing in a double room
S = Price range for a single room

Berwick-upon-Tweed

NT9953 *Bluebell, Foxton's, Cobbled Yard, Barrels, Leaping Salmon, Elizabethan, The Plough, Meadow House, Salutation Inn, Rob Roy, White Swan, Magnus*

40 Ravensdowne, *Berwick-upon-Tweed, Northumberland, TD15 1DQ.*
Open: All Year (not Xmas)
Grades: STB 4 Diamond
01289 306992
Mrs Muckle
petedot@dmuckle.freeserve.co.uk
D: £18.00–£25.00
Beds: 1F 2D 1T
Baths: 4 En
🐕 ✂ 📺 ▥ ⚓
A warm welcome awaits you, 3 luxury ensuite rooms furnished to a very high standard. Hearty breakfast including home cured bacon, free range eggs, real coffee. 1 minute to Elizabethan walls. 2 minutes to town centre. Resident parking tickets supplied. No smoking.

The Friendly Hound, *Ford Common, Berwick-upon-Tweed, Northumberland, TD15 2QD.*
Open: All Year
Grades: STB 4 Diamond
01289 388554
Mrs Maycock
friendlyhound.bb@talk21.com
D: £21.50–£23.00 **S:** £21.50–£23.00
Beds: 1F 2D **Baths:** 3 En
The Friendly Hound, recently sympathetically restored to create a welcoming home, offers comfortable accommodation, good food, super views and convenient quiet location for touring North Northumberland and the Scottish borders. Arrive as guests and leave as friends.

Rob Roy Pub & Restaurant, *Dock Road, Tweedmouth, Berwick-upon-Tweed, Northumberland, TD15 2BQ.*
Open: All Year (not Xmas)
Grades: STB 3 Diamond
01289 306428 Mr Wilson
D: £23.00 **S:** £27.00
Beds: 1D 1T **Baths:** 2 En
TV ✕ ▦ V ♿
Stone-built cosy riverside pub with open coal fire. Bar/restaurant menus offer fresh Northumbrian salmon and seafood, lobster, crab, oysters etc. 2 mins Berwick centre or sea front. Excellent situation to explore Northumberland. Twenty years with the Wilsons.

Cobbled Yard Hotel, *40 Walkergate, Berwick-upon-Tweed, Northumberland, TD15 1DJ.*
Open: All Year
Grades: STB 3 Diamond
01289 308407
Ms Miller
Fax: 01289 330623
D: £25.00 **S:** £30.00
Beds: 3F 2D **Baths:** 5 En
♿ P TV ♞ ✕ ▦ V ♿ cc
Surrounded by Berwick's Elizabethan walls we are situated two minutes' walk from town centre, one minute from Barracks Museum, near golf course, beaches, sports complex. Family-run hotel. Food to cater to all tastes, pick up service from railway station.

6 North Road, *Berwick-upon-Tweed, Northumberland, TD15 1PL.*
Open: All Year (not Xmas)
Grades: STB 4 Diamond
01289 308949 (also fax)
Ms Booth
D: £17.00–£19.00
Beds: 1F 1D **Baths:** 1 Sh
♿ P ⚥ TV ▦ V ♿
Beautiful Edwardian house; spacious, comfortable rooms near town centre and railway station. Perfect for exploring the Northumberland coast and the Scottish borders. Private off road parking, non smoking.

Wallace Guest House, *1 Wallace Green, Berwick-upon-Tweed, Northumberland, TD15 1EB.*
Open: Easter to Nov **Grades:** STB 3 Diamond
01289 306539 Mrs Hoggan
Fax: 01289 332617
wallaceguesthouse@yahoo.com
D: £22.00 **S:** £30.00
Beds: 1D 2T **Baths:** 1 Pr 2 En
♿ P (5) ⚥ TV ✕ ▦ V ♿
Berwick-upon-Tweed, the forgotten jewel of the North. This ancient and historic town offers so much you will never get bored. There are many Castles and historic houses to visit in the area and also many Nature Reserves.

Dervaig Guest House, *1 North Road, Berwick-upon-Tweed, TD15 1PW.*
Large Victorian guest house, close railway station/town, ample private parking.
Open: All Year
Grades: STB 4 Diamond, AA 4 Diamond
01289 307378 Mr Doyle
dervaig@btinternet.com
D: £20.00–£27.00 **S:** £25.00–£45.00
Beds: 1F 2D 2T **Baths:** 4 En 1 Pr
♿ P (8) TV ▦ V ♿

The Old Vicarage Guest House, *Church Road, Tweedmouth, Berwick-upon-Tweed, Northumberland, TD15 2AN.*
Attractive C19th detached house, refurbished to highest standards. 10 minutes walk from town centre.
Open: All Year (not Xmas)
Grades: STB 4 Diamond, AA 4 Diamond
01289 306909 Mrs Richardson
D: £17.00–£54.00 **S:** £17.00–£18.00
Beds: 1F 4D 1T 1S **Baths:** 4 En 1 Sh
♿ P (5) TV ♞ ▦ V ♿

Bridge View, *14 Tweed Street, Berwick-upon-Tweed, Northumberland, TD15 1NG.*
200 year old house overlooking Royal Border Bridge with splendid views.
Open: All Year
01289 308098 Mrs Weatherley
D: £20.00–£25.00 **S:** £25.00–£28.00
Beds: 1F **Baths:** 1 En

Queens Head Hotel, *6 Sandgate, Berwick-upon-Tweed, TD15 1EP.*
Family-run hotel situated in town centre near historic town walls.
Open: All Year **Grades:** AA 1 Star, RAC 1 Star
01289 307852 Mr Kerr
Fax: 01289 307858
D: £35.00–£40.00 **S:** £35.00–£40.00
Beds: 2F 1D 2T 1S **Baths:** 6 En
🛇 ⅏ 📺 🐕 ✕ ⬛ 🔽 🛒 **cc**

3 Scotts Place, *Berwick-upon-Tweed, Northd, TD15 1LQ.*
Georgian town house near town centre and station. Residents parking permit available.
Open: All Year
01289 305323 Mrs Blaaser
scottsplace@btinternet.com
D: £18.00–£25.00 **S:** £25.00
Beds: 2D 1T **Baths:** 3 En
🛇 (7) 📺 🐕 ✕ ⬛ 🔽 🛒

Meadow Hill Guest House, *Duns Road, Berwick-upon-Tweed, Northumberland, TD15 1UB.*
Enjoys spectacular views over River Tweed, Cheviots and coast to Holy Island.
Open: All Year
01289 306325 Mr Hall
D: £20.00–£35.00 **S:** £30.00–£50.00
Beds: 3F 1D 2T **Baths:** 6 En
🛇 🅿 (12) 📺 🐕 ✕ ⬛ 🔽 🛒 ♿ **2**

4 North Road, *Berwick-upon-Tweed, TD15 1PL.*
Beautifully furnished and decorated Edwardian house. Comfortable stay assured.
Open: Easter to Oct
01289 306146 (also fax) Mrs Thornton
sandra@thorntonfour.freeserve.co.uk
D: £16.00–£19.00 **S:** £16.00–£19.00
Beds: 1D 1T 1S **Baths:** 1 Sh
🛇 (5) 🅿 (3) ⅏ 📺 ⬛ 🔽 🛒

West Sunnyside House, *Tweedmouth, Berwick-upon-Tweed, Northd, TD15 2QN.*
C19th farmhouse 1.5 miles from town centre on the southern approach road.
Open: All Year
01289 305387 Ms Jamieson
D: £17.00 **S:** £22.50–£25.00
Beds: 1F 1T **Baths:** 1 Sh
🛇 🅿 (3) ⅏ 📺 ⬛ 🛒

Birgham

NT7939 🍺 *Cobbles Inn*

Tweedview, *Birgham, Coldstream, Berwickshire, TD12 4NF.*
Friendly family house in beautiful Scottish Borders. Good touring base.
Open: All Year
018908 30312
Mrs Jarvis
D: £14.00 **S:** £14.00
Beds: 1D 1T
🛇 🅿 (4) 🐕 🐕 ✕ ⬛ 🔽 🛒

Bowden

NT5530

Glenwhit, *Bowden, Melrose, Roxburgh, TD6 0SX.*
Open: All Year
Grades: STB 3 Star
01865 822408 Mrs Pryde
D: £15.00–£23.00 **S:** £20.00–£30.00
Beds: 1T 2D **Baths:** 1 En 1 Sh
🛇 🅿 ⅏ 📺 🐕 ✕ ⬛ 🛒
Small country house with lovely garden, surrounded by panoramic views of countryside and hills. Situated in the centre of the beautiful Scottish borders, within easy reach of all historic buildings and many other attractions.

Coldingham

NT9066 🍺 *Red Lion*

St Abbs Haven Hotel, *Coldingham Sands, Coldingham, Eyemouth, Berwickshire, TD14 5PA.*
Spectacular sea views overlooking bay. Exceptional wildlife and sealife, excellent walks.
Open: All Year
Grades: STB 3 Star
018907 71779
Mrs Ross
Fax: 018907 71847
D: £30.00–£35.00 **S:** £30.00–£35.00
Beds: 2F 6D 4T 3S **Baths:** 12 En
🛇 🅿 📺 🐕 ✕ ⬛ 🔽 🛒

Duns

NT7854 🍺 *Barniken House, Black Ball, Wheatsheaf, Allanton Inn*

St Albans, *Clouds, Duns, Berwickshire, TD11 3BB.*
Georgian manse, with period furnishings, overlooking small town.
Open: All Year (not Xmas/New Year)
Grades: STB 4 Star
01361 883285 Fax: 01361 884534
st_albans@email.msn.com
D: £19.50–£25.00 **S:** £22.00–£30.00
Beds: 2D/T 2S **Baths:** 2 Sh
🛏 (12) ⌇ 📺 🍖 🖳 Ⓥ 🎣 **cc**

Eckford

NT7126

The Old Joiners Cottage, *Eckford, Kelso, Roxburghshire, TD5 8LG.*
Charming Borders style cottage with picturesque views over rolling countryside.
Open: All Year
Grades: STB 3 Star
01835 850323 (also fax)
Mr Butterfield
joiners.cottage@virgin.net
D: £18.00–£21.00 **S:** £21.00–£30.00
Beds: 1F 1D **Baths:** 2 En
🛏 🅿 (3) ⌇ 📺 🍖 ✕ 🖳 Ⓥ 🎣 **cc**

Ettrick

NT2714 🍺 *Cross Keys*

West Deloraine Farm, *Ettrick, Selkirk, TD7 5HR.*
1000 acre farm situated in James Hogg and Sir Walter Scott country.
Open: Easter to Oct
01750 62207 Mrs Bernard
D: £16.00 **S:** £16.00
Beds: 1T 2D **Baths:** 2 Sh
🛏 🅿 📺 🖳

Planning a longer stay?
Always ask for any special rates

Galashiels

NT4936 🍺 *Kings Hotel, Woodlands Hotel, Cobbles Inn, Thistle Inn, Herges Bistro, Abbotsford Arms, Hunters Hall*

Watson Lodge, *15 Bridge Street, Galashiels, Selkirkshire, TD1 1SW.*
Open: All Year **01896 750551** Mrs Reid
D: £16.00–£20.00 **S:** £18.00–£20.00
Beds: 2T 1D **Baths:** 3 En
🛏 🅿 ⌇ 📺 🖳 Ⓥ 🎣
Centrally situated B&B; all guest rooms overlook quiet back garden. Bright comfortable rooms - all ensuite. Shopping, golf, fishing, walks, historic landmarks all at hand. Perfect location for touring all the borders. Good food close by. A friendly welcome awaits.

Island House, *65 Island Street, Galashiels, Selkirkshire, TD1 1PA.*
Comfortable family home. Town centre. Ideally situated for touring the Borders.
Open: All Year **Grades:** AA 3 Diamond
01896 752649 Mr Brown
D: £15.00–£18.00 **S:** £15.00–£20.00
Beds: 1D 2T **Baths:** 2 En 1 Sh
🛏 🅿 (2) ⌇ 📺 🍖 🖳 🎣

Ettrickvale, *33 Abbotsford Road, Galashiels, Selkirkshire, TD1 3HW.*
Warm, comfortable bungalow, ideally situated for touring Borders & Edinburgh.
Open: All Year (not Xmas)
Grades: STB 2 Star
01896 755224 Mrs Field
D: £16.00 **S:** £20.00
Beds: 1D 2T **Baths:** 2 Sh
🛏 🅿 (3) 📺 🍖 ✕ 🖳 Ⓥ 🎣 ♿ 3

Gattonside

NT5435 🍺 *Marmions*

Fauhope House, *Fauhope, Gattonside, Melrose, Roxburghshire, TD6 9LU.*
An Edwardian house looking over the river Tweed to Melrose Abbey.
Open: All Year **Grades:** STB 4 Star
01896 823184 (also fax) Mrs Robson
D: £25.00 **S:** £32.00
Beds: 2T 1D **Baths:** 3 En
🅿 ⌇ 🍖 🖳 🎣 **cc**

Greenlaw

NT7146   🍺 *Blackadder, Cross Keys*

Bridgend House, West High Street,
Greenlaw, Duns, Berwickshire, TD10 6XA.
Built 1816 with trout fishing in pretty
riverside garden.
Open: All Year
Grades: STB 2 Star
01361 810270 (also fax)
Mrs Carruthers
aproposdes@fsbdial.co.uk
D: £18.00–£20.00 **S:** £24.00
Beds: 1F 1D 2T **Baths:** 3 En 1 Pr
🛏 🅿 (4) ⌀ 📺 🛐 ✕ 🏛 🖾 🌡

Hawick

NT5015   🍺 *Cross Keys, Mansfield House,
Buccleuch Hotel, Elm House*

Wiltonburn Farm, Hawick, Roxburghshire,
TD9 7LL.
Delightful setting on hill farm with designer
cashmere knitwear shop.
Open: All Year (not Xmas)
Grades: STB 3 Star
01450 372414
Mrs Shell
Fax: 01450 378098
shell@wiltonburnfarm.u-net.com
D: £20.00 **S:** £20.00
Beds: 1F 1D 1T **Baths:** 1 En 1 Pr 1 Sh
🛏 🅿 (6) ⌀ 📺 🛐 ✕ 🏛 🖾 🌡 cc

Ellistrin, 6 Fenwick Park, Hawick,
Roxburghshire, TD9 9PA.
Welcoming family home in quiet area, close
to all amenities.
Open: Easter to Oct
Grades: STB 3 Star
01450 374216
Mrs Smith
Fax: 01450 373619
ellistrin@compuserve.com
D: £18.00 **S:** £18.00
Beds: 2D 1T **Baths:** 3 En
🛏 🅿 (3) 📺 🛐 🏛 🖾 🌡

Heiton

NT7130   🍺 *Queens Head Hotel*

Goldilands, Roxburgh Road, Heiton, Kelso,
TD5 8TP.
New bungalow, 2 miles from Kelso, adjacent
to golf course.
Open: All Year
01573 450671 (also fax)
Mrs Brotherston
jimbroth@aol.com
D: £20.00 **S:** £25.00
Beds: 2T 1D **Baths:** 3 En
🛏 (2) 🅿 (3) ⌀ 📺 🛐 🏛 ❋ 🌡 ♿

Innerleithen

NT3336   🍺 *St Ronan's Hotel, Traquair Arms*

Caddon View Guest House, 14 Pirn
Road, Innerleithen, Peebles-shire, EH44 6HH.
Open: All Year (not Xmas)
Grades: STB 4 Star
01896 830208 Mr & Mrs Djellil
caddonview@aol.com
D: £24.00–£30.00 **S:** £35.00–£40.00
Beds: 1F 3D 2T **Baths:** 6 En
🛏 🅿 (5) ⌀ 📺 🛐 ✕ 🖾 ❋ 🌡 cc
Charming Victorian family house by the
River Tweed, ideally situated for walking,
fishing, touring or just relaxing. All rooms
individually designed and equipped to make
you feel at home. French restaurant and
sauna available.

Jedburgh

NT6520   🍺 *Royal Hotel, Simply Scottish, Pheasant
Inn, Forresters*

Riverview, Newmill Farm, Jedburgh,
Roxburghshire, TD8 6TH.
Spacious modern villa overlooking River Jed
with country views.
Open: April to Oct
Grades: STB 3 Star
01835 862145
Mrs Kinghorn
D: £18.00–£20.00 **S:** £25.00
Beds: 1T 2D **Baths:** 3 En
🅿 (4) 📺 🏛 🌡

Edgerston Rink Smithy, *Jedburgh,*
Roxburghshire, TD8 6PP.
Open: All Year
Grades: STB 3 Star
01835 840328 Mr & Mrs Smart
royglen.rink@btinternet.com
D: £16.00–£18.00 **S:** £23.00
Beds: 2D **Baths:** 1 Sh
🛏 (12) 🅿 (4) 📺 🐾 ✕ 🎵 🚲
Converted smithy overlooking the Cheviot
Hills backing on to natural woodland. Very
private facilities of a superior standard.
Warm welcome assured. Private visitors
lounge with TV, music centre etc. Rural
location alongside A68, 7 miles south of
Jedburgh.

Hundalee House, *Jedburgh,*
Roxburghshire, TD8 6PA.
Open: Mar to Nov
01835 863011 (also fax)
Mrs Whittaker
sheila.whittaker@btinternet.com
D: £20.00–£23.00 **S:** £25.00–£35.00
Beds: 1F 3D 1T **Baths:** 4 En 1 Pr
🛏 (5) 🅿 (10) ⚡ 📺 🎵 📺 🚲
Large Victorian private house.

Froylehurst, *The Friars, Jedburgh,*
Roxburghshire, TD8 6BN.
Detached Victorian house in large garden.
Spacious guest rooms, 2 mins town centre.
Open: Mar to Nov
Grades: STB 4 Star
01835 862477 (also fax) Mrs Irvine
D: £15.50–£18.00 **S:** £20.00–£25.00
Beds: 2F 1D 1T **Baths:** 2 Sh
🛏 (5) 🅿 (5) 📺 🎵 📺 🚲

Ferniehirst Mill Lodge, *Jedburgh,*
Roxburghshire, TD8 6PQ.
Modern guest house in peaceful setting,
country lovers' paradise.
Open: All Year
Grades: STB 1 Star, AA 3 Diamond,
RAC 3 Diamond
01835 863279 Mr Swanston
ferniemill@aol.com
D: £23.00 **S:** £23.00
Beds: 1F 3D 4T 1S **Baths:** 9 En 1 Sh
🛏 🅿 (10) 📺 🐾 ✕ 🎵 📺 ❄ 🚲 cc

Kelso

NT7234 🍺 *Black Swan, Border Hotel, Cobbles Inn,*
Plough Hotel, Queen's Head, Wagon & Horses

Craignethan House, *Jedburgh Road,*
Kelso, Roxburghshire, TD5 8AZ.
Open: All Year
Grades: STB 3 Star
01573 224818
Mrs McDonald
D: £18.50 **S:** £18.50
Beds: 2D 1T **Baths:** 1 Pr 1 Sh
🛏 🅿 (6) 📺 🐾 🎵 📺 🚲 ⚕ 3
Comfortable welcoming family home with
relaxed informal atmosphere. Breakfast to
suit all tastes and times. Afternoon tea,
tea/coffee in evening, home baking,
attractive garden, breathtaking panoramic
views of Kelso/Tweed Valley to Floors Castle
from all bedrooms. Scottish Border Abbeys,
Floors Castle, Tweed Valley, Walter Scott
country.

Lochside, *Town Yetholm, Kelso,*
Roxburghshire, TD5 8PD.
Victorian country house. Peaceful, spacious,
ensuite bedrooms. Beautiful countryside.
Open: Apr to Oct
Grades: STB 3 Star B&B
01573 420349
Mrs Hurst
D: £20.00–£22.50 **S:** £22.50
Beds: 1D 1T **Baths:** 2 En
🛏 (2) 🅿 (2) ⚡ 📺 🐾 🎵 🚲

Duncan House, *Chalkheugh Terrace,*
Kelso, Roxburghshire, TD5 7DX.
Georgian riverside house, spectacular views
river & castle. 2 mins to centre town.
Open: All Year (not Xmas)
01573 225682
Mrs Robertson
D: £15.00–£17.00 **S:** £20.00–£30.00
Beds: 3F 1D **Baths:** 3 En 3 Pr 1 Sh
🛏 🅿 (6) 📺 🐾 🎵 📺 🚲 ⚕

Planning a longer stay?
Always ask for any special rates

Kirk Yetholm

NT8228 🍴 *Border Hotel, Cobbles Inn, Plough Hotel*

Valleydene, *High Street, Kirk Yetholm, Kelso, Roxburghshire, TD5 8PH.*
Traditional Scottish welcome. Log fire. Comfortable rooms with excellent views.
Open: All Year
01573 420286 Mrs Campbell
D: £22.00 **S:** £25.00–£30.00
Beds: 2T 1D **Baths:** 2 En 1 Pr
🐕 (12) 🅿 (4) 📺 🐾 ✕ 🛏 Ⓥ ♿

Blunty's Mill, *Kirk Yetholm, Kelso, Roxburghshire, TD5 6PG.*
Fabulous rural location set in 6 acres. Friendly welcome guaranteed.
Open: All Year **Grades:** STB 2 Star
01573 420288 Mrs Brooker
gail_rowan@hotmail.com
D: £22.00–£30.00
Beds: 2T **Baths:** 1 Sh
🐕 🅿 (10) 📺 🐾 ✕ Ⓥ ❋ ♿ &

Langlee

NT6417 🍴 *The Pheasant, Simply Scottish*

The Spinney, *Langlee, Jedburgh, Roxburghshire, TD8 6PB.*
Spacious house in main house and in nearby pine cabins. **Open:** Mar to Nov
Grades: STB 4 Star, AA 5 Diamond
01835 863525 Mrs Fry **Fax: 01835 864883**
thespinney@btinternet.com
D: £21.00–£23.00
Beds: 2D 1T 3F **Baths:** 5 En 1 Pr
🐕 🅿 (6) ✕ 📺 🐾 🛏 Ⓥ ♿ cc

Langshaw

NT5139

Over Langshaw Farm, *Langshaw, Galashiels, Selkirkshire, TD1 2PE.*
Welcoming family farm superb location in unspoilt border countryside.
Open: All Year **Grades:** STB 2 Star
01896 860244 Mrs Bergius
D: £20.00–£22.00 **S:** £25.00
Beds: 1F 1D **Baths:** 1 En 1 Pr 1 Sh
🐕 🅿 ✕ 📺 🐾 ✕ 🛏 Ⓥ ♿ &

Lauder

NT5247 🍴 *Lauderdale Hotel, Eagle Hotel, Black Bull Hotel*

The Grange, *6 Edinburgh Road, Lauder, Berwickshire, TD2 6TW.*
Open: All Year (not Xmas)
Grades: STB 3 Star, AA 3 Diamond
01578 722649 (also fax)
Tricia and Peter Gilardi
D: £17.00–£20.00 **S:** £18.00–£20.00
Beds: 1D 2T **Baths:** 1 Sh
🐕 🅿 (3) ✕ 📺 🛏 Ⓥ ♿
A peaceful haven from which to explore the tranquil Scottish and English borders, yet less than an hour's drive from Edinburgh. Overlooking the rolling Lammermuir Hills and on the Southern Upland Way, an ideal base for walking, cycling or relaxing.

Longformacus

NT6957

Eildon Cottage, *Longformacus, Duns, Berwickshire, TD11 3NX.*
Leave crowds behind set in beautiful rolling Lammermuir Hill Village.
Open: All Year (not Xmas/New Year)
01361 890230 Mrs Amos
D: £20.00–£25.00 **S:** £20.00–£25.00
Beds: 1F 1T 1D **Baths:** 2 En 1 Pr
🅿 (3) 📺 🐾 ✕ 🛏 Ⓥ ♿

Kintra Ha, *Gifford Road, Longformacus, Duns, Berwickshire, TD11 3NZ.*
Recently converted, detached property. Edinburgh 50 mins. Access to rural pursuits.
Open: All Year
Grades: STB 3 Star
01361 890660 (also fax)
Mrs Lamb
lamb@kintrastell.co.uk
D: £20.00 **S:** £25.00
Beds: 1D 1T **Baths:** 2 En
✕ 📺 🐾 ✕ 🛏 Ⓥ ♿ &

Bringing children with you?
Always ask for any special rates

Melrose

NT5433 🍺 *Buccleuch Arms, Burts Hotel, Marmions*

Fauhope House, *Fauhope, Gattonside, Melrose, Roxburghshire, TD6 9LU.*
Open: All Year
Grades: STB 4 Star
01896 823184 (also fax)
Mrs Robson
D: £25.00 **S:** £32.00
Beds: 2T 1D **Baths:** 3 En
🅿 ⌀ 🏕 🛏 🎗 CC
An Edwardian house looking over the river Tweed to Melrose Abbey and the Eildon Hills. Fauhope within its spacious grounds offers seclusion with easy access to Melrose, shops and restaurants, golf courses, salmon fishing.

Old Abbey School House, *Waverley Road, Melrose, Roxburghshire, TD6 9SH.*
Charming old school house with character. Large bedrooms, restful atmosphere.
Open: March to November
01896 823432
Mrs O'Neill
D: £17.00–£21.00
S: £20.00–£25.00
Beds: 1T 2D **Baths:** 1 Pr 1 Sh
🍳 🅿 (5) ⌀ 📺 🛏 🎗 🖍

Rivendell, *The Croft, St Boswells, Melrose, TD6 0AE.*
Open: All Year (not Xmas/New Year)
Grades: STB 4 Star
01835 822498
Mrs Mitchell
LizRivBB@cs.com
D: £18.00–£22.50
S: £25.00–£30.00
Beds: 2D 1T **Baths:** 2 En 1 Pr
🅿 (3) ⌀ 📺 🛏 🖍
Relax in our spacious family Victorian home overlooking Scotland's largest village green. Ideal central Scottish Borders location. Only 10 minutes from Kelso, Melrose, Jedburgh - Edinburgh one hour. River Tweed, Dryburgh Abbey & golf club all within easy walking distance.

Newcastleton

NY4887 🍺 *Bailey Mill*

Bailey Mill, *Bailey, Newcastleton, Roxburghshire, TD9 0TR.*
Remote 18th century grain mill by river. Ideal retreat, jacuzzi, pony trekking. **Open:** All Year
016977 48617 Mrs Copeland
Fax: 016977 48074
D: £20.00–£25.00 **S:** £22.00–£28.00
Beds: 4F 6T 3D 4S **Baths:** 6 En 4 Pr 6 Sh
🍳 🅿 📺 🛏 🎗 🖍 ✳ 🖍 🛗 CC

Peebles

NT2540 🍺 *The Crown*

Lyne Farmhouse, *Lyne Farm, Peebles, EH45 8NR.*
Open: All Year (not Xmas)
Grades: STB 2 Star
01721 740255 (also fax) Mrs Waddell
awaddell@farming.co.uk
D: £18.00–£20.00 **S:** £20.00
Beds: 2D 1T **Baths:** 2 Sh
🍳 🅿 📺 🛏 🎗 🖍
Beautiful Georgian farmhouse, with tastefully decorated rooms overlooking scenic Stobo Valley. Walled garden plus hill-walking, picnic areas and major Roman fort all on farm. Ideally placed for Edinburgh and picturesque town of Peebles, plus Border towns and historic houses.

Reston

NT8862

Stoneshiel Hall, *Reston, Eyemouth, Berwickshire, TD14 5LU.*
Open: All Year (not Xmas/New Year)
01890 761267 Mr & Mrs Olley
D: £24.00 **S:** £24.00
Beds: 1T 1D **Baths:** 2 Pr
🍳 🅿 (25) ⌀ 📺 ✕ 🖍 🖍
A warm welcome awaits you at this historic mansion, set in extensive grounds and gardens overlooking beautiful Borders countryside. Traditionally furnished, the accommodation is spacious with an aura of stately splendour, where the emphasis is on flexibility and personal service.

Selkirk

NT4728   🍺 *Queen's Head, Plough Inn, Cross Keys Inn, County Hotel*

Ivy Bank, *Hillside Terrace, Selkirk, TD7 2LT.*
Set back from A7 with fine views over hills beyond.
Open: Easter to Dec
Grades: STB 2 Star
01750 21270 Mrs MacKenzie
nettamackenzie@
ivybankselkirk.freeserve.co.uk
D: £17.50–£18.00 **S:** £18.00
Beds: 1D 1T 1S **Baths:** 2 En 1 Pr 1 Sh
🏇 🅿 (4) 📺 🐾 🛏 📺 ♨ cc

St Abbs

NT9167   🍺 *St Abbs Haven, Anchor*

Castle Rock Guest House, *Murrayfield, St Abbs, Eyemouth, Berwickshire, TD14 5PP.*
Victorian house with superb views over sea and rocks.
Open: Feb to Nov
Grades: STB 3 Star
018907 71715 Mrs Wood
Fax: 018907 71520
boowood@compuserve.com
D: £23.00–£25.00 **S:** £23.00–£25.00
Beds: 1F 1D 1T 1S **Baths:** 4 En
🏇 🅿 (4) ⚡ 📺 🐾 ✕ 🛏 📺 ♨ cc

7 Murrayfield, *St Abbs, Eyemouth, Berwickshire, TD14 5PP.*
Former fisherman's cottage in quiet village, close to beach/harbour.
Open: All Year
Grades: STB 3 Star
018907 71468
Mrs Wilson
D: £16.50–£19.00 **S:** £21.50–£24.00
Beds: 1F 1D **Baths:** 1 En 1 Sh
🏇 ⚡ 📺 🐾 🛏

High season, bank holidays
and special events mean low
availability anywhere

St Boswells

NT5930   🍺 *Buccleuch Arms Hotel*

Rivendell, *The Croft, St Boswells, Melrose, TD6 0AE.*
Relax in our spacious family Victorian home overlooking Scotland's largest village green.
Open: All Year (not Xmas/New Year)
Grades: STB 4 Star
01835 822498 Mrs Mitchell
LizRivBB@cs.com
D: £18.00–£22.50 **S:** £25.00–£30.00
Beds: 2D 1T **Baths:** 2 En 1 Pr
🅿 (3) ⚡ 📺 🛏 ♨

Swinton

NT8347   🍺 *Wheatsheaf Hotel*

Three to Six The Green, *Swinton, Duns, Berwickshire, TD11 3JQ.*
Comfortable ensuite accommodation in quiet village. Guest rooms overlook garden.
Open: All Year
Grades: STB 3 Star
01890 860322 L Robertson
D: £20.00–£22.00 **S:** £26.00–£27.50
Beds: 1T 1D **Baths:** 2 En
🏇 (5) 🅿 (2) ⚡ 📺 🛏 📺 ♨

Teviothead

NT4004

The Quiet Garden, *Hislop, Teviothead, Hawick, Roxburghshire, TD9 0PS.*
Open: Easter to Oct
Grades: STB 3 Star
01450 850310 (also fax)
Mrs Armitage
D: £16.00–£18.00 **S:** £16.00–£18.00
Beds: 1T 1D **Baths:** 1 Sh 1 Pr
🏇 🅿 (2) ⚡ 📺 ✕ 🛏 📺 ♨ ♿
Small privately run, eco-friendly B&B with ground floor accommodation. 1 acre garden with organic vegetables, free range hens and ducks. Superb location for bird watchers, botanists and walkers. Quiet private position on border hill farm. 3 miles from A7. Need own transport.

Town Yetholm

NT8127 ◖ *Border Hotel, Cobbles Inn, Plough Hotel*

Lochside, *Town Yetholm, Kelso, Roxburghshire, TD5 8PD.*
Victorian country house. Peaceful, spacious, ensuite bedrooms. Beautiful countryside.
Open: Apr to Oct
Grades: STB 3 Star B&B
01573 420349 Mrs Hurst
D: £20.00–£22.50 **S:** £22.50
Beds: 1D 1T **Baths:** 2 En
🛏 (2) 🅿 (2) ⅊ 📺 🍴 🛆 ☕

Blunty's Mill, *Kirk Yetholm, Kelso, Roxburghshire, TD5 6PG.*
Fabulous rural location set in 6 acres. Friendly welcome guaranteed.
Open: All Year **Grades:** STB 2 Star
01573 420288 Mrs Brooker
gail_rowan@hotmail.com
D: £22.00–£30.00
Beds: 2T **Baths:** 1 Sh
🛏 🅿 (10) 📺 🍴 ✕ 📺 ❈ ☕ ♿

RATES

D = Price range per person sharing in a double room
S = Price range for a single room

Yarrow Feus

NT3426 ◖ *Cross Keys*

Ladhope Farm, *Yarrow Feus, Yarrow Valley, Selkirk, TD7 5NE.*
Beautiful farmhouse, log fires, very peaceful. Ideal for hunting, touring.
Open: Easter to Oct
01750 82216
Mrs Turnbull
anne@scottish.borders.com
D: £18.00–£20.00 **S:** £20.00–£22.00
Beds: 1F 1D **Baths:** 1 Sh
🛏 🅿 (4) 📺 🍴 ✕ 📺 ☕

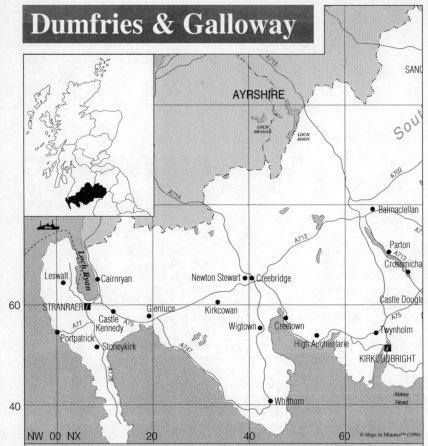

Dumfries & Galloway

AYRSHIRE

SANQ

LOCH BRADAN

LOCH DOON

Sou

A713

A702

A714

A712

Balmaclellan

A7

Parton

A713

Crossmicha

Leswalt

Loch Ryan

Cairnryan

Newton Stewart · Creebridge

Castle Dougla

60 STRANRAER

Glenluce

Kirkcowan

A75

Castle Douglas

Castle Kennedy

A75

A77

Portpatrick

Wigtown · Crestown

Twynholm

Stoneykirk

A747

High Auchenlarie

KIRKCUDBRIGHT

A716

40

Whithorn

Abbey Head

NW 00 NX   20   40   60   © Maps In Minutes™ (1996)

RAIL

For rail information, telephone the National Rail Enquiries line on 08457 484950. For the Minicom service for the deaf and hard of hearing, tel. 0845 605 0600.

FERRIES

Stena Sealink: *Stranraer to Belfast* (3 hrs) tel. 08705 505050.

P&O European Ferries: *Cairnryan*, near *Stranraer*, to *Larne* (2 ¼ hrs) tel. 01581 200276.

SeaCat: *Stranraer* to *Belfast* (1 ½ hrs) tel. 08705 523523.

TOURIST INFORMATION OFFICES

Markethill Car Park, **Castle Douglas**, Kirkudbrightshire, 01556 502611 (Easter to Oct).

Whitesands, **Dumfries**, DG1 2SB, 01387 253862.

Markethill, **Gatehouse of Fleet**, Castle Douglas, Kirkcudbrightshire, DG7 2JQ, 01557 814212 (Easter to Oct).

Old Blacksmith's Shop, **Gretna Green**, Gretna, Dumfriesshire, DG16 5DU, 01461 337834 (Easter to Oct).

Harbour Square, **Kirkcudbright**, DG6 4HY, 01557 330494 (Easter to Oct).

Churchgate, **Moffat**, Dumfriesshire, DG10 9EJ, 01683 220620 (Easter to Oct).

Dashwood Square, **Newton Stewart**, Wigtownshire, DG8 6EQ, 01671 402431.

Port Rodie Car Park, **Stranraer**, Wigtownshire, DG9 7EE, 01776 702595.

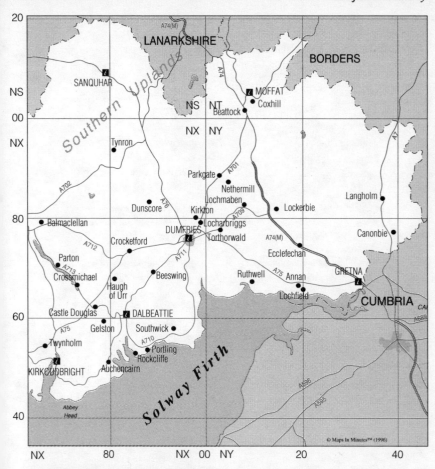

© Maps In Minutes™ (1996)

Annan

NY1966 🍺 *Queensbury Arms*

The Old Rectory Guest House, *12 St Johns Road, Annan, Dumfriesshire, DG12 6AW.*
Open: All Year **01461 202029 (also fax)**
J Buchanan & J Alexander
old-rectory-guest1@supanet.com
D: £22.00–£25.00 **S:** £22.00–£25.00
Beds: 2F 2D 1T 1S **Baths:** 5 En 1 Pr
🛇 (4) 🅿 (6) ⅟ 📺 🐾 ✕ 🎗 📺 ❄ ♨
Charming C19th manse in the centre of
Annan, 7 miles from famous wedding town
Gretna, be assured of warm welcome,
ensuite bedrooms, great Scottish breakfasts,
home cooking, licensed, main Euro & Irish
routes. Walkers, cyclist, small wedding
parties welcome. Smoking lounge available.

Milnfield Farm, *Low Road, Annan, Dumfriesshire, DG12 5QP.*
Working farm, riverside walks, large garden;
ideal for touring base.
Open: All Year (not Xmas)
Grades: STB 2 Star
01461 201811
R Robinson
D: £16.00–£18.00 **S:** £16.00–£18.00
Beds: 1F 1D
🛇 🅿 ⅟ 📺 🐾 🎗 ♨

High season, bank holidays
and special events mean low
availability anywhere

Auchencairn

NX7951 ◁ *Glenisle Inn, Old Smugglers Inn*

Torbay, *Blue Hill, Auchencairn, Castle Douglas, DG7 1QW.*
Open: Easter to Oct
Grades: STB 5 Star
01556 640180
J T Cannon
Fax: 01556 640228
cannontorbay@aol.com
D: £25.00 **S:** £30.00
Beds: 1T 1D **Baths:** 2 En
P ⅍ 📺 🖳 ▲
Enjoy the tranquillity of the unspoilt countryside and relax in the tastefully furnished rooms. Wonderful views across the Solway. Lovely walks. Follow Heritage Trail for castles and abbeys. Coast 1 mile. Excellent pub in village - 0.5 mile.

The Rossan, *Auchencairn, Castle Douglas, Kirkcudbrightshire, DG7 1QR.*
Georgian style house 1869. Large secluded garden - bird watchers paradise. Resident owls.
Open: All Year
Grades: STB 2 Star
01556 640269
Mrs Bardsley
Fax: 01556 640278
bardsley@rossan.freeserve.co.uk
D: £15.00 **S:** £20.00
Beds: 3D **Baths:** 2 Sh
P (4) ⅍ 📺 🐾 ✕ 🖳 📹 ❋ ▲

Gallowa House, *The Square, Auchencairn, Castle Douglas, Kirkcudbrightshire, DG7 1QT.*
Families welcomed. Ideally situated for touring South West Scotland.
Open: All Year (not Xmas/New Year)
Grades: STB 3 Star
01556 640234 (also fax)
J Smith
smith@gallowahouse.freeserve.co.uk
D: £16.00 **S:** £20.00
Beds: 1F 1D **Baths:** 1 Sh
🐉 ⅍ 📺 🖳 📹 ▲

Burnside House, *23 Main Street, Auchencairn, Castle Douglas, Kirkcudbrightshire, DG7 1QU.*
Friendly atmosphere with a good breakfast and comfortable rooms.
Open: All Year (not Xmas)
01556 640283
Mrs Norcross
bev-jade@supanet.com
D: £15.00 **S:** £15.00
Beds: 2F **Baths:** 1 En 1 Pr
🐉 P (1) 📺 🐾 🖳 📹 ▲

Balmaclellan

NX6579 ◁ *Lochinvar Hotel*

High Park, *Balmaclellan, Castle Douglas, Kirkcudbrightshire, DG7 3PT.*
Open: Easter to Oct
Grades: STB 2 Star
01644 420298 (also fax)
Mrs Shaw
high.park@farming.co.uk
D: £16.00–£17.00 **S:** £16.00–£17.00
Beds: 2D 1T **Baths:** 1 Sh
🐉 P (4) ⅍ 📺 🐾 ✕ 🖳 📹 ▲ ♿
A warm welcome awaits you at our comfortable farmhouse by Loch Ken. Double bedroom and bathroom on ground floor, double and twin bedrooms and toilet upstairs. All have tea/coffee facilities, wash basins and TV. Comfortable lounge. Brochure available.

Beattock

NT0802

Middlegill, *Beattock, Moffat, Dumfriesshire, DG10 9SW.*
Manor farmhouse, 4 miles from Moffat. Deer, peacocks, lovely walks.
Open: All year (not Xmas)
01683 300612
Mr Ramsden
D: £15.00–£19.00 **S:** £15.00–£19.00
Beds: 2F 2D 3S **Baths:** 2 Sh
🐉 ⅍ 📺 🐾 ✕ 🖳 📹 ▲

Beeswing

NX8969

Locharthur House, *Beeswing, Dumfries, DG2 8JG.*
Georgian house in beautiful countryside.
Open: All Year
Grades: STB 2 Star
01387 760235 Mrs Schooling
D: £18.00–£20.00 **S:** £20.00–£22.00
Beds: 1F 1D **Baths:** 2 En
🐾 🅿 (6) 📺 🛏 ✕ 🛢 Ⓥ 🛴

Cairnryan

NX0668

Albannach, *Loch Ryan, Cairnryan, Stranraer, Wigtownshire, DG9 8QX.*
Victorian manse on the shores of Loch Ryan, ideally situated for ferries to Ireland.
Open: All Year
01581 200624
Mrs Craig
D: £19.00 **S:** £19.00
Beds: 1F 1D 1T 1S **Baths:** 4 En
🐾 🅿 (10) 📺 🛏 ✕ 🛢 Ⓥ 🛴

Canonbie

NY3876 🍺 *Cross Keys Hotel, Riverside Inn*

Meadow View, *Watch Hill Road, Canonbie, DG14 0TF.*
A warm Scottish welcome assured in this friendly home.
Open: Easter to Oct
Grades: STB 3 Star
013873 71786
Mrs Bell
D: £17.50 **S:** £20.00
Beds: 1F 1D **Baths:** 2 En
🐾 🅿 (3) 💤 📺 🛢 Ⓥ 🛴

BATHROOMS

Pr - Private

Sh - Shared

En - Ensuite

Castle Douglas

NX7662 🍺 *Old Smugglers, King's Arms, Laurie Arms, Douglas Arms, Grapes, Imperial Hotel, Thistle Inn*

Rose Cottage Guest House, *Gelston, Castle Douglas, Kirkcudbrightshire, DG7 1SH.*
Open: All Year (not Xmas)
Grades: STB 3 Star
01556 502513 (also fax)
Mr Steele
D: £18.00–£20.50 **S:** £18.00
Beds: 2D 3T 1S **Baths:** 1 En 2 Sh
🐾 🅿 (10) 📺 🛏 ✕ 🛢 Ⓥ 🛴
Quiet country guest house in small village, 2.5 miles from Castle Douglas.

Smithy House, *The Buchan, Castle Douglas, Kirkcudbrightshire, DG7 1TH.*
Comfortable Galloway cottage overlooking Carlingwark Loch. Central for exploring Galloway.
Open: All Year (not Xmas/New Year)
Grades: STB 4 Star
01556 503841 Mrs Carcas
enquiries@smithyhouse.co.uk
D: £20.00–£27.50 **S:** £30.00–£35.00
Beds: 1T 2D **Baths:** 2 En 1 Pr
🅿 (4) 💤 📺 🛢 Ⓥ 🛴 cc

Airds Farm, *Crossmichael, Castle Douglas, Kirkcudbrightshire, DG7 3BG.*
Scenic views over Loch Ken and the Galloway Hills.
Open: All Year
Grades: STB 3 Star
01556 670418 (also fax)
Mrs Keith
tricia@airds.com
D: £18.00–£23.00 **S:** £23.00–£27.00
Beds: 1F 1T 2D 1S **Baths:** 2 En 1 Sh
🐾 🅿 (6) 💤 📺 🛏 🛢 🛴

Milton Park Farm, *Castle Douglas, DG7 3JJ.*
A warm welcome and good food awaits you in this comfortable farmhouse.
Open: Easter to Oct
01556 660212 Mrs Muir
D: £18.00–£20.00 **S:** £18.00–£20.00
Beds: 2D 1T **Baths:** 2 Sh
🐾 (9) 🅿 (4) 📺 🛢 🛴

Craigadam, *Castle Douglas,*
Kirkcudbrightshire, DG7 3HV.
Elegant country house within working farm.
Antique furnishings, log fires and friendly
atmosphere.
Open: All Year (not Xmas)
01556 650233 (also fax)
Mrs Pickup
inquiry@craigadam.com
D: £23.00 **S:** £28.00
Beds: 1F 2D 4T **Baths:** 3 Pr
ॐ **P** (10) 📺 🍴 ✕ 🏛 Ⓥ ⚓ **cc**

Imperial Hotel, *King Street, Castle*
Douglas, Kircudbrightshire, DG7 1AA.
Former coaching inn and Listed building. All
rooms ensuite. Warm friendly welcome.
Open: All Year (not Xmas)
01556 502086 Fax: 01556 503009
david@thegolfhotel.co.uk
D: £27.00–£29.00 **S:** £35.00–£45.00
Beds: 5D 5T 2S **Baths:** 12 En
ॐ **P** (20) 📺 🍴 ✕ 🏛 Ⓥ ⚓ **cc**

Dalcroy, *24 Abercromby Road, Castle*
Douglas, Kircudbrightshire, DG7 1BA.
A warm Scottish welcome assured in this
long established spacious detached house.
Open: May to Oct
01556 502674 Mrs Coates
ashley@academy67.freeserve.co.uk
D: £16.50–£17.50 **S:** £13.00
Beds: 1D 1T **Baths:** 1 Sh
P (3) ⚡ 📺 🍴 🏛 ⚓

Castle Kennedy

NX1160

Chlenry Farmhouse, *Castle Kennedy,*
Stranraer, Wigtownshire, DG9 8SL.
Situated in a private glen in the heart of
Galloway, comfortable old farmhouse.
Open: All Year (not Xmas)
01776 705316 Mrs Wolseley Brinton
Fax: 01776 889488
brinton@aol.com
D: £26.00 **S:** £30.00
Beds: 1D 1T **Baths:** 1 Pr 1 Sh
ॐ **P** (4) ⚡ 📺 🍴 ✕ 🏛 Ⓥ ⚓

Coxhill

NT0904

Coxhill Farm, *Old Carlisle Road, Coxhill,*
Moffat, Dumfriesshire, DG10 9QN.
Stylish farmhouse set in 70 acres,
outstanding views, private parking.
Open: All Year (not Xmas/New Year)
Grades: STB 4 Star
01683 220471
Mrs Long
Fax: 01683 220871
D: £22.50 **S:** £30.00
Beds: 1D 1T **Baths:** 2 En
ॐ **P** ⚡ 📺 ✕ 🏛 Ⓥ ⚓

Creebridge

NX4165

Villa Cree, *Creebridge, Newton Stewart,*
Wigtownshire, DG8 6NR.
Quiet riverside family house, excellent for
walking, wildlife, touring or business.
Open: All Year (not Xmas)
01671 403914 Mr Rankin
sad_rankin@tinyonline.co.uk
D: £18.00–£20.00 **S:** £18.00–£20.00
Beds: 2D 1T 1S **Baths:** 1 En 1 Pr
ॐ **P** (3) ⚡ 📺 🏛 Ⓥ ⚓

Creetown

NX4758   🍺 *Barholm Arms*

Wal-d-mar, *Mill Street, Creetown, Newton*
Stewart, Wigtownshire, DG8 7JN.
Open: All Year (not Xmas)
01671 820369
M Lockett
Fax: 01671 820266
howie@thebogue.freeserve.co.uk
D: £16.00 **S:** £16.00
Beds: 1D 1S **Baths:** 1 Sh
ॐ **P** (3) 📺 🍴 🏛 Ⓥ ⚓ ♿
Modern bungalow in quiet village location,
ideal base for touring, walking, golf, etc.
Comfortable beds, good breakfasts, private
off-road parking, warm Scottish welcome
assured. Situated between Dumfries and
Stranraer on the Cree estuary.

Crocketford

NX8372

Henderland Farm, *Crocketford Road, Crocketford or Ninemile Bar, Dumfries, DG2 8QD.*
Substantial farmhouse, comfortably furnished with views of lovely open countryside. **Open:** All Year (not Xmas)
Grades: STB 3 Star
01387 730270 Mrs Smyth
D: £17.00–£18.00 **S:** £18.00–£20.00
Beds: 1F 1D 1T **Baths:** 3 En
🛇 🅿 (4) 📺 🐾 ✗ 📖 ♥ ⚓

Crossmichael

NX7366 🍴 *King's Arms, Imperial Hotel, Thistle Inn*

Culgruff House Hotel, *Crossmichael, Castle Douglas, Kirkcudbrightshire, DG7 3BB.*
Victorian baronial mansion, own grounds, overlooking loch, village, Galloway Hills.
Open: All Year
01556 670230 Mr Grayson
D: £17.50–£27.50 **S:** £20.00–£27.50
Beds: 4F 4D 7T 2S **Baths:** 4 En 4 Sh
🛇 🅿 (40) 📺 🐾 ✗ 📖 ♥ ⚓ cc

Airds Farm, *Crossmichael, Castle Douglas, Kirkcudbrightshire, DG7 3BG.*
Scenic views over Loch Ken and the Galloway Hills.
Open: All Year
Grades: STB 3 Star
01556 670418 (also fax) Mrs Keith
tricia@airds.com
D: £18.00–£23.00 **S:** £23.00–£27.00
Beds: 1F 1T 2D 1S **Baths:** 2 En 1 Sh
🛇 🅿 (6) ⚡ 📺 🐾 📖 ⚓

Deeside, *42 Main Street, Crossmichael, Castle Douglas, Kirkcudbrightshire, DG7 3AU.*
Friendly welcome and good breakfast. In Galloway.
Open: All Year (not Xmas/New Year)
Grades: STB 3 Star
01556 670239 Mrs Cowan
D: £17.00 **S:** £20.00
Beds: 1F 1D 1S **Baths:** 1 Sh
🛇 🅿 (2) ⚡ 📺 🐾 ✗ 📖 ♥ ⚓

Dalbeattie

NX8361

Belle Vue, *Port Road, Dalbeattie, Kirkcudbrightshire, DG5 4AZ.*
Beautiful granite house on the edge of Dalbeattie, facing the Galloway Hills.
Open: All Year (not Xmas)
01556 611833 Mrs Lock
Snraajj@bellevuebandb.freeserve.co.uk
D: £18.00–£22.00 **S:** £22.50–£25.00
Beds: 1F 1D 1T **Baths:** 1 En 2 Pr
🛇 🅿 (8) ⚡ 📺 ✗ 📖 ♥ ⚓ &

13 Maxwell Park, *Dalbeattie, Kirkcudbrightshire, DG5 4LR.*
Family run house close to beach, fishing, golf and walks. **Open:** All Year
01556 610830 Mrs Tattersfield
D: £18.00–£21.00 **S:** £20.00–£25.00
Beds: 2D 1T **Baths:** 1 En 1 Sh
🛇 🅿 (3) ⚡ 📺 📖 ♥ ❄

Dumfries

NX9776 🍴 *Hill Hotel, Auldgirth Inn, Station Hotel, Courtyard, Rat & Carrot, Queensbury, Waverley Bar, Aberdour Hotel*

Hazeldean Guest House, *4 Moffat Road, Dumfries, DG1 1NJ.*
4 star Victorian villa. Non-smoking. Parking. Near town centre.
Open: All Year (not Xmas)
Grades: STB 4 Star
01387 266178 (also fax)
Mr & Mrs Harper
D: £20.00 **S:** £25.00–£28.00
Beds: 2F 2D 2T 1S **Baths:** 6 En
🛇 🅿 (8) ⚡ 📺 ✗ 📖 ♥ ⚓ & cc

Fernwood, *4 Casslands, Dumfries, DG2 7NS.*
Victorian sandstone villa, close to golf course and town centre.
Open: All Year (not Xmas)
Grades: STB 3 Star
01387 253701 (also fax) Mrs Vaughan
pamelavaughan@yahoo.com
D: £17.50–£18.50 **S:** £17.50
Beds: 1F 1D 2S **Baths:** 2 Sh
🛇 🅿 (6) ⚡ 📺 📖 ⚓

Wallamhill House, *Kirkton, Dumfries,*
DG1 1SL.
Country house, beautiful views, spacious
rooms, leisure suite, safe parking.
Open: All Year (not Xmas)
Grades: STB 4 Star
01387 248249 (also fax)
Mrs Hood
wallamhill@aol.com
D: £19.00–£22.00 **S:** £22.00–£28.00
Beds: 1F 2D 1T **Baths:** 4 En
🛏 🅿 (8) ⅌ 📺 📖 Ⓥ 🍴 CC

30 Hardthorn Avenue, *Dumfries, DG2 9JA.*
Open: Easter to Oct
Grades: STB 2 Star B&B
01387 253502 (also fax)
Ms Sloan
anniesbandb@aol.com
D: £16.00–£18.00 **S:** £23.00–£25.00
Beds: 1D 1T **Baths:** 1 Sh
🅿 (2) ⅌ 📺 📖 🍴
A warm Scottish welcome awaits you at No
30, a non-smoking private house with car
parking in quiet residential area. Easy
access from Dumfries bypass (A75) and less
than a mile from town centre. Ideal base to
explore SW Scotland.

Henderland Farm, *Crocketford Road,*
Crocketford or Ninemile Bar, Dumfries,
DG2 8QD.
Substantial farmhouse, comfortably
furnished with views of lovely open
countryside.
Open: All Year (not Xmas)
Grades: STB 3 Star
01387 730270 Mrs Smyth
D: £17.00–£18.00 **S:** £18.00–£20.00
Beds: 1F 1D 1T **Baths:** 3 En
🛏 🅿 (4) 📺 🐕 ✗ 📖 Ⓥ 🍴

Lindean, *50 Rae Street, Dumfries, DG1 1JE.*
Town centre house in quiet residential area,
near railway station.
Open: All Year
Grades: STB 3 Star
01387 251888 Mrs Stein
D: £18.00–£20.00 **S:** £25.00
Beds: 2T 1D **Baths:** 2 En 1 Pr
🛏 🅿 ⅌ 📺 📖 Ⓥ 🍴

Brackenbridge, *67 New Abbey Road,*
Dumfries, DG2 7JY.
Brackenridge bed and breakfast, walking
distance into the town centre and all local
attractions.
Open: All Year
Grades: STB 3 Star, AA 3 Diamond
01387 263962
Mr & Mrs Thomson
D: £18.50–£25.00 **S:** £20.00
Beds: 3F 3T 1D 1S **Baths:** 2 En 1 Pr
🛏 🅿 📺 🐕 ✗ 📖 Ⓥ 🍴 ♿

Waverley Guest House, *21 St Mary's*
Street, Dumfries, DG1 1HB.
5 minutes from town centre, across from
Railway station. On main road.
Open: All Year
01387 254080
F Meikle-Latta
Fax: 01387 254848
southwest.lumber@virgin.net
D: £14.50–£20.00 **S:** £14.50–£24.00
Beds: 5F 3T 1D 5S **Baths:** 6 En
🛏 📺 🐕 📖 Ⓥ 🍴 CC

Cairndoon, *14 Newall Terrace, Dumfries,*
DG1 1LW.
Elegant 1880 town house, graciously quiet.
Warm and friendly welcome.
Open: All Year
01387 256991
Mrs Stevenson
stevenson.george@talk21.com
D: £20.00–£24.00 **S:** £21.00–£25.00
Beds: 3F 1S **Baths:** 2 En 1 Pr 1 Sh
🛏 🅿 (1) ⅌ 📺 📖 Ⓥ ❀ 🍴

The Knock Guest House, *1 Lockerbie*
Road, Dumfries, DG1 3AP.
Warm welcome. Convenient for golfing,
fishing, touring. Cyclists welcome.
Open: All Year
Grades: STB 1 Star
01387 253487 Mr Sutherland
D: £16.00–£16.50 **S:** £16.00–£16.50
Beds: 3F 1D 1T 1S
🛏 🅿 (1) 📺 🐕 ✗ 📖 Ⓥ 🍴

Franklea Guest House, *Castle Douglas Road, Dumfries, DG2 8PP.*
Bungalow 1 mile from Dumfries; ideal for golf next door, hill walking, Galloway park.
Open: Easter to Nov
Grades: STB 3 Star
01387 253004 Mrs Wild
Fax: 01387 259301
D: £18.00–£20.00 **S:** £20.00–£22.00
Beds: 1F 1D **Baths:** 2 En
🛇 (5) 🅿 (5) 📺 🛏 ✕ 📖 Ⓥ ⚓ ♿

Fulwood Hotel, *Lovers Walk, Dumfries, DG1 1LX.*
Beautiful Victorian house opposite railway station in the heart of Burns country.
Open: All Year (not Xmas)
01387 252262 / 0411 260246
Fax: 01387 252262
D: £17.00–£21.00 **S:** £20.00–£30.00
Beds: 1F 2D 2T 1S **Baths:** 3 En 1 Pr 1 Sh
✁ 📺 📖 Ⓥ ⚓

Dunscore

NX8684 🍺 *Craigdarroch Arms, George Hotel*

Boreland Farm, *Dunscore, Dumfries, DG2 0XA.*
Organic farm in beautiful countryside by the River Cairn.
Open: All Year
01387 820287 Mr & Mrs Barnes
barnes@borelandfarm.co.uk
D: £16.00 **S:** £17.00–£18.00
Beds: 1F 1D **Baths:** 2 En
🛇 🅿 (10) ✁ 📺 🛏 📖 Ⓥ ⚓

Low Kirkbride Farmhouse, *Dunscore, Dumfries, DG2 0SP.*
Warm, comfortable farmhouse set amid beautiful countryside, lovely views from every room.
Open: All Year (not Xmas)
01387 820258 (also fax)
Mrs Kirk
D: £16.00–£18.00 **S:** £16.00–£18.00
Beds: 1D 1T **Baths:** 2 En
🛇 (8) 🅿 (4) 📺 ✕ 📖 Ⓥ ⚓

Ecclefechan

NY1974 🍺 *Cressfield Hotel*

Carlyle House, *Ecclefechan, Lockerbie, Dumfriesshire, DG11 3DG.*
C18th house in small village.
Open: All Year (not Xmas/New Year)
Grades: STB 1 Star
01576 300322 (also fax) Mrs Martin
D: £14.00 **S:** £14.00
Beds: 1F 1T 1S **Baths:** 2 Sh
🛇 🅿 (6) 📺 🛏 📖 ⚓

2 Garthwaite Place, *High Street, Ecclefechan, Lockerbie, Dumfriesshire, DG11 3DF.*
Above average accommodation, just off A74/M6. Home from home.
Open: All Year
01576 300846 Mrs Arbuckle
D: £15.00–£17.50 **S:** £20.00–£22.50
Beds: 2T **Baths:** 1 Sh
🛇 📺 🛏 ✕ 📖 ⚓

Gelston

NX7658 🍺 *Old Smugglers, Kings Arms*

Rose Cottage Guest House, *Gelston, Castle Douglas, Kirkcudbrightshire, DG7 1SH.*
Quiet country guest house in small village, 2.5 miles from Castle Douglas.
Open: All Year (not Xmas)
Grades: STB 3 Star
01556 502513 (also fax) Mr Steele
D: £18.00–£20.50 **S:** £18.00
Beds: 2D 3T 1S **Baths:** 1 En 2 Sh
🛇 🅿 (10) 📺 🛏 ✕ 📖 Ⓥ ⚓

Glenluce

NX1957 🍺 *Kelvin House, Crown Hotel, Inglenook Rest*

Bankfield Farm, *Glenluce, Newton Stewart, Wigtownshire, DG8 0JF.*
Large spacious farmhouse on the outskirts of quiet country village.
Open: All Year **Grades:** STB 2 Star
01581 300281 (also fax) Mrs Stewart
D: £17.00 **S:** £20.00
Beds: 1F 1D 1T **Baths:** 2 En 1 Pr
🅿 📺 📖 ⚓

Rowantree Guest House, *38 Main Street, Glenluce, Newton Stewart, Wigtownshire, DG8 0PS.*
Clean and tidy family run, central to all amenities.
Open: All Year
Grades: STB 2 Star
01581 300244 Mr Thomas
Fax: 01581 300366
D: £15.50–£18.00 **S:** £17.00–£24.00
Beds: 2F 2D 1T **Baths:** 2 En 1 Pr
🛏 🅿 (8) 📺 🛏 ✕ 🖳 📺 ❋ 🛁 ♿

Gretna

NY3167 🍺 *Solway Lodge*

The Braids, *Annan Road, Gretna, Dumfriesshire, DG16 5DQ.*
Open: All Year
01461 337409 (also fax)
Mrs Copeland
D: £16.00–£18.00 **S:** £25.00–£28.00
Beds: 2T **Baths:** 1 Sh
🛏 🅿 (2) 📺 🖳 📺 🛁
Small friendly family B&B in bungalow inside the entrance to our (BGHP Grade 4) caravan park. Open all year. Gretna marriage centre, golf, Sunday market. Good area for birdwatching in winter months. Advice on fishing in the area.

Haugh of Urr

NX8066 🍺 *The Grapes, Laurie Arms*

Corbieton Cottage, *Haugh of Urr, Castle Douglas, Kirkcudbrightshire, DG7 3JJ.*
Charming country cottage, lovely views, good food and a warm welcome.
Open: Feb to Dec
01556 660413 Mr Jones
ann&don@corbieton.demon.uk
D: £16.00–£18.00 **S:** £17.00–£18.00
Beds: 1D 1T **Baths:** 1 Sh
🅿 (2) 📺 ✕ 🖳 🛁

Planning a longer stay?
Always ask for any special rates

High Auchenlarie

NX5353

High Auchenlarie Farmhouse, *High Auchenlarie, Gatehouse of Fleet, Castle Douglas, Kirkcudbrightshire, DG7 2HB.*
Traditional farmhouse overlooking fleet, Wigtown Bay, Isle of Man. Superb location.
Open: Feb to Dec
Grades: STB 3 Star
01557 840231 (also fax)
Mrs Johnstone
D: £22.00–£26.00 **S:** £30.00–£36.00
Beds: 1F 1T 1D **Baths:** 3 En
🛏 🅿 (4) 📺 ✕ 🖳 🛁

Kirkcowan

NX3261 🍺 *Bladnoch Inn*

Tarff House, *Kirkcowan, Newton Stewart, Wigtownshire, DG8 0HW.*
Victorian house set in 1 acre of garden, within 5 miles good eating places.
Open: All Year
01671 830312 Mrs McGeoch
sandra@tarffhouse.ndo.co.uk
D: £15.00 **S:** £15.00
Beds: 1D 1T **Baths:** 2 Pr
🛏 🅿 (4) 📺 🛏 🖳 🛁 cc

Kirkcudbright

NX6850 🍺 *Selkirk Arms*

Number 3 B&B, *3 High Street, Kirkcudbright, DG6 4JZ.*
Open: All Year
Grades: STB 3 Star
01557 330881 Miriam Baker
ham_wwk@hotmail.com
D: £22.50–£25.00 **S:** £25.00–£30.00
Beds: 2T 1D **Baths:** 2 En 1 Pr
🛏 📺 🛏 🖳 ❋ 🛁

A 'B' Listed Georgian townhouse with a C17th dining area and elegant guest drawing room. No 3 is opposite the National Trust for Scotland's Broughton House and behind MacLellans Castle at the end of Kirkcudbright's historic old High Street.

Benutium, *2 Rossway Road, Kirkcudbright, DG6 4BS.*
Excellent quality. Ensuite bedroom and private lounge/dining room. Magnificent views. **Open:** All Year
Grades: STB 4 Star
01557 330788 Mr & Mrs Garroch-Mackay
eileen.malcolm@benutium.freeserve.co.uk
D: £18.00–£24.00 **S:** £25.00
Beds: 1D 1T **Baths:** 1Pr 1Sh
P (2) ⌇ 🖵 🕮 ⓥ ⛴

Baytree House, *110 High Street, Kirkcudbright, DG6 4JQ.*
Georgian town house in artist colony near harbour, private parking. **Open:** All Year
Grades: STB 4 Star, AA 5 Diamond
01557 330824 (also fax)
baytree@currantbun.com
D: £27.00 **S:** £27.00
Beds: 1D 2T **Baths:** 3 En

Kirkton

NX9782 ◀ *Auldgirth Inn*

Wallamhill House, *Kirkton, Dumfries, DG1 1SL.*
Country house, beautiful views, spacious rooms, leisure suite, safe parking.
Open: All Year (not Xmas)
Grades: STB 4 Star
01387 248249 (also fax) Mrs Hood
wallamhill@aol.com
D: £19.00–£22.00 **S:** £22.00–£28.00
Beds: 1F 2D 1T **Baths:** 4 En
🛏 P (8) ⌇ 🖵 🕮 ⓥ ⛴ cc

Langholm

NY3684 ◀ *Reivers Rest, Cross Keys*

Burnfoot House, *Westerkirk, Langholm, Dumfriesshire, DG13 0NG.*
Spacious country home set in quiet and beautiful Eskdale Valley.
Open: March to Jan **Grades:** STB 3 Star
01387 370611 Mr & Mrs Laverack
Fax: 01387 370616
sg.laverack@burnft.co.uk
D: £24.00 **S:** £27.00
Beds: 1T 3D **Baths:** 3 En 1 Pr
🛏 ⌇ 🖵 🕮 ⓥ ⛴ cc

Esk Brae, *Langholm, Dumfriesshire, DG13 0DP.*
Quiet bungalow, near town and river. Comfortable with good food.
Open: Mar to Oct
013873 80377 Mrs Geddes
D: £17.00 **S:** £17.00
Beds: 1D 1T **Baths:** 1 Sh
P (2) ⌇ 🖵 🕅 🕮 ⓥ ⛴ &

Leswalt

NX0163 ◀ *The Crown, Dunskey Golf Hotel*

Windyridge, *Auchnotteroch, Leswalt, Stranraer, Wigtownshire, DG9 0XL.*
Set in rolling countryside between Stranraer and Portpatrick 10 mins all ferries.
Open: All Year (not Xmas)
Grades: STB 1 Star
01776 870280 (also fax) Mrs Rushworth
rushworth@windyridge96.fsnet.co.uk
D: £15.00 **S:** £15.00
Beds: 1D 1T **Baths:** 1 Sh
🛏 P (3) 🖵 🕅 🕮 ⛴

Locharbriggs

NX9980 ◀ *Hill Hotel, Auldgirth Inn, Station Hotel, The Courtyard*

Southpark Guest House, *Quarry Road, Locharbriggs, Dumfries, DG1 1QG.*
Peaceful edge of town location. Easy access from all major routes. **Open:** All Year
01387 711188 (also fax) Mr Maxwell
ewan@emaxwell.freeserve.co.uk
D: £17.00–£18.00 **S:** £17.00–£23.00
Beds: 1F 1D 1T 1S **Baths:** 2 En 2 Pr
🛏 P (15) ⌇ 🖵 🕮 ⛴ cc

Lochfield

NY2066 ◀ *Rat & Carrot*

20 Hardthorn Road, *Lochfield, Dumfries, DG2 9JQ.*
Comfortable accommodation in family home. Full Scottish breakfast. Warm welcome. **Open:** Mar to Oct
01387 264415 Mrs Cherrington
pcherrington@hotmail.com
D: £15.00 **S:** £20.00
Beds: 1D **Baths:** 1 Pr
🛏 P (1) ⌇ 🖵 🕮 ⛴

Lochmaben

NY0882 ◖ *Crown*

Smallrigg, *Lochmaben, Lockerbie, DG11 1JH.*
Open: All Year (not Xmas/New Year)
Grades: STB 3 Star
01387 810462
Janet Newbould
jnewbould@ukgateway.net
D: £15.00 **S:** £18.00
Beds: 1T 1D
Baths: 1 En 1 Pr
ॐ ⯿ (4) ⊬ 🇹🇻 ✕ 🎍 Ⓥ ₤
Smallrigg, only ten minutes drive from
motorway network, is a small working dairy
farm. Smallrigg's situation enjoys extensive
views of surrounding countryside in an area
suited to cycling, walking, fishing, and is
approximately half mile from Lochmaben
Golf Course.

Ardbeg Cottage, *19 Castle Street,*
Lochmaben, Lockerbie, Dumfriesshire,
DG11 1NY.
Open: Feb to Dec
Grades: STB 3 Star
01387 811855 (also fax)
Mr & Mrs Neilson
bill@neilson.net
D: £18.00 **S:** £18.00
Beds: 1D 1T **Baths:** 2 En
⊬ 🇹🇻 ✕ 🎍 ₤ ⅋ 3
Quiet, comfortable, friendly ground floor
B&B in centre of village just 4 miles from
A74 at Lockerbie. Ideal centre for exploring
beautiful south-west Scotland.

Magdalene House, *Bruce Street,*
Lochmaben, Lockerbie, DG11 1PD.
An elegant and comfortable home in historic
village built around lochs.
Open: All Year
01387 810439 (also fax)
Lady Hillhouse
D: £20.00–£28.00
S: £25.00–£33.00
Beds: 1F 1T 1D
ॐ ⯿ (4) ⊬ 🇹🇻 🐾 ✕ 🎍 Ⓥ ✳ ₤ cc

Lockerbie

NY1381 ◖ *Kings Arms, Somerton Hotel*

Rosehill Guest House, *9 Carlisle Road,*
Lockerbie, Dumfriesshire, DG11 2DR.
Victorian sandstone house (1871). Half-acre
garden. Easy access M74.
Open: All Year (not Xmas)
Grades: BF 3 Star, AA 4 Diamond
01576 202378 Mr & Mrs Callander
D: £20.00 **S:** £20.00–£25.00
Beds: 1F 1D 2T 1S **Baths:** 3 En 2 Pr
ॐ ⯿ (5) 🇹🇻 🐾 🎍 Ⓥ ₤

Ravenshill House Hotel, *Dumfries Road,*
Lockerbie, Dumfriesshire, DG11 2EF.
Large Victorian house, good food, quiet
location, gardens, private car park.
Open: All Year
Grades: STB 2 Star, AA 1 Star
01576 202882 (also fax) Ms Tindal
ravenshillhouse.hotel@virgin.net
D: £22.00–£25.00 **S:** £35.00
Beds: 2F 3D 3T **Baths:** 7 En 1 Pr
ॐ ⯿ (30) 🇹🇻 🐾 ✕ 🎍 Ⓥ ₤ cc

Kings Arms Hotel, *29 High Street,*
Lockerbie, DG11 2JL.
C16th former coaching inn; cosy barn log
fires.
Open: All Year
Grades: STB 2 Star, AA 2 Star
01576 202410 (also fax)
Mr Spence
D: £30.00 **S:** £35.00–£40.00
Beds: 3F 4D 2T 5S
ॐ ⯿ (10) ⊬ 🇹🇻 🐾 ✕ 🎍 Ⓥ ₤ cc

The Elms, *Dumfries Road, Lockerbie,*
Dumfriesshire, DG11 2EF.
Comfortable detached house. Friendly
personal welcome. Private parking.
Open: Mar to Nov
Grades: STB 4 Star
01576 203898 (also fax)
Mrs Rae
theelms@gofornet.co.uk
D: £19.00–£22.00 **S:** £22.00–£25.00
Beds: 1D 1T **Baths:** 2 En
ॐ (12) ⯿ (2) ⊬ 🇹🇻 🎍 Ⓥ ₤

Corrie Lodge Country House, *Lockerbie, Dumfriesshire, DG11 2NG.*
B&B in lovely country house. Hunting, shooting, fishing. Golf course nearby.
Open: All Year
Grades: STB 3 Star
01576 710237 Mr & Mrs Spence
D: £20.00 **S:** £20.00
Beds: 2D 1T 1S **Baths:** 2 Pr
🄿 (6) ⅍ 📺 ⅋ ✕ Ⓥ ♨

Moffat

NT0805 ◖ *Black Bull, Allanton House, Star Hotel*

Woodhead Farm, *Moffat, Dumfriesshire, DG10 9LU.*
Open: All Year **Grades:** STB 4 Star
01683 220225 Mrs Jackson
D: £24.00–£26.00 **S:** £26.00–£30.00
Beds: 1D 2T **Baths:** 3 En
🐫 🄿 (3) ⅍ 📺 ✕ ▥ Ⓥ ♨
Luxuriously appointed farmhouse breakfast served in large conservatory, overlooking mature garden and surrounding hills. Working sheep farm. Ample safe parking. 2 miles from spa town of Moffat. All bedrooms have panoramic views.

Morlich House, *Ballplay Road, Moffat, Dumfriesshire, DG10 9JU.*
Open: Feb to Nov
01683 220589 Mrs Wells
Fax: 01683 221032
morlich.house@ndirect.co.uk
D: £20.00–£23.00 **S:** £20.00–£33.00
Beds: 2F 1D 1T 1S **Baths:** 4 En 1 Pr
🐫 🄿 (6) ⅍ 📺 ⅋ ✕ ▥ Ⓥ ♨ cc
A superb Victorian country house set in quiet elevated grounds overlooking town.

Kirkland House, *Well Road, Moffat, Dumfriesshire, DG10 9AR.*
Listed former manse with many interesting features, set in peaceful gardens.
Open: All Year
Grades: STB 3 Star
01683 221133 (also fax) Mr Watkins
Derekwatkins@Kirklandhouse.freeserve.co.uk
D: £18.00–£20.00 **S:** £18.00
Beds: 1F 1T 1D **Baths:** 2 En 1 Pr
🄿 (6) ⅍ 📺 ▥ Ⓥ ♨

Waterside, *Moffat, Dumfriesshire, DG10 9LF.*
Open: Easter to Oct
01683 220092 Mrs Edwards
D: £19.00–£21.00 **S:** £21.00
Beds: 2D 2T **Baths:** 1 Pr 1 Sh
🐫 🄿 (4) ⅍ 📺 ▥ ♨
Large country house set in 12 acres of woodland garden with private stretch of river. The house is tastefully decorated throughout. We have a dog and cat, donkeys, peafowl, ducks, geese and hens. Ideal for walking, fishing, golf and bird watching.

Hartfell House, *Hartfell Crescent, Moffat, Dumfriesshire, DG10 9AL.*
Splendid Victorian manor house in peaceful location.
Open: All Year (not Xmas/New Year)
Grades: STB 4 Star, AA 4 Diamond
01683 220153 Mrs White
robert.white@virgin.net
D: £23.00 **S:** £25.00
Beds: 2F 4D 1T 1S **Baths:** 7 En 1 Sh
🐫 🄿 (8) 📺 ⅋ ✕ ▥ Ⓥ ♨

Morag, *19 Old Carlisle Road, Moffat, Dumfriesshire, DG10 9QJ.*
Beautiful quiet location in charming town near Southern Upland Way.
Open: All Year
Grades: STB 3 Star
01683 220690 Mr & Mrs Taylor
D: £16.00–£18.00 **S:** £18.00–£19.00
Beds: 1D 1T 1S **Baths:** 1 Sh
🐫 (10) 🄿 (5) ⅍ 📺 ⅋ ✕ ▥ Ⓥ ♨

Ericstane, *Moffat, Dumfriesshire, DG10 9LT.*
Working hill farm in a peaceful valley. Moffat 4 miles.
Open: All Year
Grades: STB 3 Star
01683 220127 Mr Jackson
D: £20.00 **S:** £25.00
Beds: 1D 1S **Baths:** 2 En
🐫 (8) 🄿 📺 ▥ Ⓥ ♨

Bringing children with you?
Always ask for any special rates

Allanton Hotel, *21-22 High Street, Moffat,*
Dumfriesshire, DG10 9HL.
Small inn in the scenic town of Moffat.
Home cooking. **Open:** All Year
01683 220343 Mr Kennedy
Fax: 01683 220914
D: £22.00–£30.00 **S:** £24.00–£32.00
Beds: 1F 2T 3D 1 S **Baths:** 2 En 6 Pr 1 Sh
🛏 🧺 📺 🐾 ✕ ▥ Ⓥ 🛢 cc

Wellview Hotel, *Ballplay Road, Moffat,*
Dumfriesshire, DG10 9JU.
Excellent centre to explore Borders.
Open: All Year **Grades:** STB 4 Star
01683 220184 (also fax) Mr Schuckardt
info@wellview.co.uk
D: £36.00–£50.00 **S:** £53.00–£63.00
Beds: 4D 2T **Baths:** 6 En
🛏 🅿 (8) 🧺 📺 🐾 ✕ ▥ Ⓥ ❋ 🛢 cc

Coxhill Farm, *Old Carlisle Road, Coxhill,*
Moffat, Dumfriesshire, DG10 9QN.
Stylish farmhouse set in 70 acres,
outstanding views, private parking.
Open: All Year (not Xmas/New Year)
Grades: STB 4 Star
01683 220471 Mrs Long
Fax: 01683 220871
D: £22.50 **S:** £30.00
Beds: 1D 1T **Baths:** 2 En
🛏 🅿 🧺 📺 ✕ ▥ Ⓥ 🛢

Stratford House, *Academy Road, Moffat,*
Dumfriesshire, DG10 9HR.
Family-run B&B, 2 minutes from town centre.
Off-road parking.
Open: All Year (not Xmas)
01683 220297 Mrs Forrester
D: £18.00–£20.00 **S:** £20.00–£25.00
Beds: 1F 2T **Baths:** 2 En 1 Pr
🛏 (10) 🅿 (2) 📺 🐾 ▥ Ⓥ 🛢

Hazel Bank, *Academy Road, Moffat,*
Dumfriesshire, DG10 9HP.
Welcome to Hazel Bank. A warm and
personal welcome awaits all our guests.
Open: All Year
01683 220294 Mrs Watson
D: £17.00–£20.00 **S:** £23.00–£25.00
Beds: 1F 1D **Baths:** 1 En 1 Sh
🛏 📺 🐾 ▥ Ⓥ 🛢 ♿

Merkland House, *Buccleuch Place, Moffat,*
Dumfriesshire, DG10 9AN.
Spacious early Victorian house set in
tranquil woodland gardens.
Open: All Year (not Xmas)
01683 220957 Mr & Mrs Tavener
D: £17.50–£22.00 **S:** £17.50–£22.00
Beds: 2F 2D 1T 1S **Baths:** 5 En 1 Pr
🛏 🅿 (8) 📺 🐾 ✕ ▥ Ⓥ 🛢 ♿

Nineoaks, *Reid Street, Moffat, DG10 9JE.*
Large spacious family bungalow situated in
3 acres with paddocks and horse.
Open: Easter to Nov
01683 220658 Mrs Jones
D: £17.00 **S:** £18.00
Beds: 1F 1D 1S **Baths:** 1 En 1 Pr
🅿 (3) 🧺 📺 ▥ 🛢

Marvig Guest House, *Academy Road,*
Moffat, Dumfriesshire, DG10 9HW.
Hello! Welcome to Marvig, a renovated
Victorian guest house offering personal
attention.
Open: All Year (not Xmas)
01683 220628 (also fax)
Mr Muirhead
marvig.moffat@tesco.net
D: £18.00–£20.00 **S:** £20.00–£25.00
Beds: 1F 2D 2T 1S **Baths:** 2 En 2 Sh
🛏 🅿 (4) 🧺 📺 ▥ Ⓥ 🛢

Nethermill

NY0487 🏰 *Balcastle*

Lochrigghead Farmhouse, *Nethermill,*
Parkgate, Dumfries, DG1 3NG.
Farmhouse, picturesque surroundings. Good
food, hospitality. Ideal for touring Scotland.
Open: All Year
01387 860381 Mrs Burgoyne
D: £17.00 **S:** £17.00
Beds: 3F 1D 1T 1S **Baths:** 2 En 1 Pr 1 Sh
🛏 🅿 (10) 📺 🐾 ✕ ▥ Ⓥ ❋ 🛢

All details shown are as
supplied by B&B owners in
Autumn 2000

Newton Stewart

NX4065

Rowallan House, *Corsbie Road, Newton Stewart, DG8 6JB.*
Visit our website - www.rowallan.co.uk - see what our guests say about Rowallan.
Open: All Year
Grades: STB 4 Star
01671 402520 Mrs Henderson
rowallan@sol.co.uk
D: £27.00–£30.00 **S:** £27.00–£40.00
Beds: 2D 2T **Baths:** 4 En
☻ (10) ᛈ (6) ⌿ 🖵 ▥ Ⅴ ᵹ

Kilwarlin, *Corvisel Road, Newton Stewart, Wigtownshire, DG8 6LN.*
Victorian house, beautiful garden, central location, home-baking, golf, fishing.
Open: Easter to Oct
01671 403047
Mrs Dickson
D: £16.50 **S:** £16.50
Beds: 1F 1D 1S **Baths:** 1 Sh
☻ (3) ᛈ (3) 🖵 ▥ Ⅴ ᵹ

Eskdale, *Princess Avenue, Newton Stewart, DG8 6ES.*
Attractive detached house, very quiet residential area, 5 mins' walk town centre.
Open: All Year
01671 404195 Mrs Smith
D: £16.00–£18.00 **S:** £16.00–£20.00
Beds: 1D 1T 1S **Baths:** 1 Pr 1 Sh
ᛈ (4) ⌿ 🖵 ▥ Ⅴ ᵹ

Parkgate

NY0288 ᛃ *Balcastle*

Lochrigghead Farmhouse, *Nethermill, Parkgate, Dumfries, DG1 3NG.*
Farmhouse, picturesque surroundings. Good food, hospitality. Ideal for touring Scotland.
Open: All Year
01387 860381
Mrs Burgoyne
D: £17.00 **S:** £17.00
Beds: 3F 1D 1T 1S **Baths:** 2 En 1 Pr 1 Sh
☻ ᛈ (10) 🖵 ʄ ✕ ▥ Ⅴ ✳ ᵹ

High season, bank holidays and special events mean low availability anywhere

Parton

NX6970 ᛃ *Welcome Tavern*

Drumrash Farm, *Parton, Castle Douglas, Kirkcudbrightshire, DG7 3NF.*
Traditional farmhouse, 300 yards from working farm. Superb views over Loch Ken.
Open: All Year
Grades: STB 2 Star
01644 470274 Mrs Cruikshank
D: £14.00–£16.00 **S:** £15.00–£18.00
Beds: 2F 1D **Baths:** 1 En 2 Sh
☻ ᛈ (6) ⌿ 🖵 ʄ ✕ ▥ Ⅴ ᵹ

Portling

NX8854 ᛃ *The Anchor*

Braemar, *Portling, Dalbeattie, Kirkcudbrightshire, DG5 4PZ.*
Welcome to Braemar, a charming friendly Victorian villa in picturesque Portling.
Open: May to Oct
01556 630414 (also fax)
Mrs Dennis
D: £19.00–£21.00 **S:** £25.00
Beds: 2D 1T **Baths:** 1 En 1 Sh
ᛈ (3) ⌿ 🖵 ʄ ▥ Ⅴ ᵹ

Portpatrick

NW9954 ᛃ *Campbells, Mount Stewart, Downshire, Crown*

Melvin Lodge Guest House, *South Crescent, Portpatrick, Stranraer, Wigtownshire, DG9 8LE.*
Very comfortable, friendly house starting southern upland way.
Open: All Year
Grades: STB 2 Star GH
01776 810238 Mr & Mrs Pinder
D: £20.00–£23.00 **S:** £20.00–£23.00
Beds: 4F 3D 1T 2S **Baths:** 5 En 1 Sh
☻ ᛈ (8) ⌿ 🖵 ʄ ▥ Ⅴ ᵹ cc

Torrs Warren Hotel, *Stoneykirk,*
Portpatrick, Stranraer, Wigtownshire, DG9 9DH.
Delightful former manse set in peaceful
countryside location. Warm welcome.
Open: All Year
Grades: STB 2 Star
01776 830298 Mrs Camlin
Fax: 01776 830204
torrswarren@btinternet.com
D: £24.00 **S:** £28.00
Beds: 2F 2T 2D 2S **Baths:** 8 En
🛏 🅿 (30) 📺 ✕ 🛏 📺 ❋ ♨ cc

Rickwood Private Hotel, *Portpatrick,*
Stranraer, Wigtownshire, DG9 8TD.
Large Victorian house in acre of garden
south facing overlooking village and sea.
Open: Mar to Oct
01776 810270 D: £21.50–£22.50 **S:**
£21.50–£22.50
Beds: 1F 2D 2T **Baths:** 4 En 1 Pr
🅿 (5) 📺 ★ ✕ 🛏 📺 ♨ cc

Mansewood, *Dean Place, Portpatrick,*
Stranraer, Wigtownshire, DG9 8TX.
Quiet central location. Lovely views over
putting green towards harbour.
Open: All Year (not Xmas)
01776 810256
Mrs Anderson
D: £18.00–£20.00 **S:** £20.00
Beds: 1D 2T **Baths:** 2 En 1 Sh
🛏 🅿 (5) 📺 🛏 ♨ ⅙

NX8453   🚢 *Anchor Hotel*

The Cottage, *1 Barcloy Mill, Rockcliffe,*
Dalbeattie, Kirkcudbrightshire, DG5 4QL.
Quiet cottage in central village guest rooms
overlooking garden and coast.
Open: All Year (not Xmas/New Year)
Grades: STB 3 Star
01556 630460
Mrs Bailey
elizabeth-bailey@rockcliffe-
bandb.freeserve.co.uk
D: £17.50–£18.50 **S:** £23.00–£25.00
Beds: 1T 1D **Baths:** 1 En 1 Sh
🛏 🅿 ⅙ 📺 ✕ 🛏 📺 ♨

Ruthwell
NY0967

Kirkland Country House Hotel,
Ruthwell, Dumfries, DG1 4NP.
Small country house hotel offering good
food and friendly service.
Open: All Year
Grades: STB 3 Star
01387 870284 Mrs Coatsworth
kirklands@hotel72.freeserve.co.uk
D: £25.00–£27.00 **S:** £35.00–£45.00
Beds: 1F 2T 3D **Baths:** 6 En
🛏 🅿 (12) 📺 ✕ 🛏 📺 ♨ ⅙ **3** cc

Sanquhar
NS7809   🚢 *Blackaddie Hotel*

4 Barons Court, *Sanquhar, Dumfriesshire,*
DG4 6EB.
Comfortable self-contained flat. Ideal fishing,
walking, golf and touring.
Open: All Year (not Xmas)
01659 50361 Mrs Clark
D: £17.00 **S:** £17.00
Beds: 1F 1D **Baths:** 2 En
★ ✕ 🛏 📺 ⅙ cc

Penhurst, *Townhead Street, Sanquhar,*
Dumfriesshire, DG4 6DA.
Family run bed and breakfast. Excellent
home cooking. **Open:** All Year
01659 50751 (also fax) Mrs McDowall
D: £15.00 **S:** £15.00
Beds: 1F 1D 1T **Baths:** 1 Sh
🛏 📺 ★ ✕ 🛏 📺 ♨

Southwick
NX9357

Boreland of Southwick, *Southwick,*
Dumfries, DG2 8AN.
Warm and friendly welcome awaits you on
the beautiful Solway Coast.
Open: All Year **Grades:** STB 4 Star
01387 780225 Mrs Dodd
boreland.southwic@virgin.net
D: £20.00–£25.00 **S:** £20.00–£25.00
Beds: 1T 2D **Baths:** 3 En
🛏 🅿 ⅙ 📺 ✕ 🛏 📺 ❋ ♨ cc

Stoneykirk

NX0853

Torrs Warren Hotel, *Stoneykirk, Portpatrick, Stranraer, Wigtownshire, DG9 9DH.*
Delightful former manse set in peaceful countryside location. Warm welcome.
Open: All Year
Grades: STB 2 Star
01776 830298
Mrs Camlin
Fax: 01776 830204
torrswarren@btinternet.com
D: £24.00 **S:** £28.00
Beds: 2F 2T 2D 2S **Baths:** 8 En
🛏 🅿 (30) 📺 ✕ 🛏 Ⅴ ❋ ⚓ cc

Stranraer

NX0560 🍴 *Crown Inn, Harbour House, Swan Inn, Marine House, L'Aperitif, Dunskey Golf Hotel*

Windyridge, *Auchnotteroch, Leswalt, Stranraer, Wigtownshire, DG9 0XL.*
Set in rolling countryside between Stranraer and Portpatrick 10 mins all ferries.
Open: All Year (not Xmas)
Grades: STB 1 Star
01776 870280 (also fax)
Mrs Rushworth
rushworth@windyridge96.fsnet.co.uk
D: £15.00 **S:** £15.00
Beds: 1D 1T **Baths:** 1 Sh
🛏 🅿 (3) 📺 🛏 🛏 ⚓

Neptune's Rest, *25 Agnew Crescent, Stranraer, Wigtownshire, DG9 7JZ.*
Open: All Year
Grades: STB 2 Star
01776 704729
Mr McClymont
D: £15.00–£20.00 **S:** £16.00–£22.00
Beds: 2F 2D 1T 1S **Baths:** 3 En 2 Sh
🛏 📺 ✕ Ⅴ ❋ ⚓ cc
Neptune's Rest overlooks Agnew Park with its boating lake and miniature railway, situated on the shores of Loch Ryan with its busy ferry routes. All bedrooms are pleasantly decorated & co-ordinated. You are assured of a warm welcome in this family-run guest house.

Windyridge Villa, *5 Royal Crescent, Stranraer, DG9 8HB.*
Overlooking Loch Ryan. Convenient for ferry terminal and railway station.
Open: All Year (not Xmas/New Year)
Grades: STB 4 Star, AA 4 Diamond
01776 889900 (also fax) Mrs Kelly
windyridge_villa@hotmail.com
D: £20.00–£22.00 **S:** £25.00–£28.00
Beds: 1T 1D **Baths:** 2 En
🛏 🅿 (3) ⚓ 📺 🛏 🛏 Ⅴ ⚓

Ivy House, *London Road, Stranraer, DG9 8ER.*
Lovely old town house, situated at the foot of Loch Ryan.
Open: All Year
Grades: STB 2 Star
01776 704176 Mr & Mrs Mcmillan
gregormcmillan@hotmail.com
D: £16.00–£19.00 **S:** £18.00–£25.00
Beds: 1F 1D 1T **Baths:** 2 En 1 Pr
🛏 🅿 (10) 📺 🛏 🛏 Ⅴ ⚓

Lorenza, *2 Birnam Place, Station Street, Stranraer, Wigtownshire, DG9 7HN.*
Terraced house, central located, close to ferries, trains & buses. **Open:** Jan to Dec
01776 703935 Mrs Jameson
D: £17.00 **S:** £15.00
Beds: 2D 1T **Baths:** 2 En 1 Sh
🅿 (4) 📺 🛏 ⚓

Fernlea Guest House, *Lewis Street, Stranraer, Wigtownshire, DG9 7AQ.*
Friendly guest house, close to town centre and all ferries. **Open:** All Year (not Xmas)
01776 703037 Mrs Drysdale
fernlea@tinyworld.co.uk
D: £16.00–£20.00 **S:** £23.00–£28.00
Beds: 2D 1T **Baths:** 3 En
🛏 🅿 (5) ⚓ 📺 🛏 ⚓

Jan Da Mar, *1 Ivy Place, London Road, Stranraer, Wigtownshire, DG9 8ER.*
Updated Georgian town house with many original features. **Open:** All Year
01776 706194 Mrs Bewley
bewley@tinyonline.co.uk
D: £16.00–£20.00 **S:** £18.00
Beds: 3F 3T 2S **Baths:** 2 En 2 Sh
🛏 🅿 📺 🛏 🛏 Ⅴ ⚓

Abonny House, *10 Academy Street, Stranraer, Wigtownshire, DG9 7DR.*
Warm friendly welcome awaits you at this family run B&B, day or night.
Open: All Year (not Xmas)
01776 706313 Mrs Harvey
D: £22.00–£24.00 **S:** £18.00–£30.00
Beds: 1F 1D 1T 1S **Baths:** 2 En 1 Sh
ﾟﾐ⌇⛰💤🛏✕▥⚘

Rawer Cottage, *South Glenstockadale, Stranraer, DG9 8TS.*
Former farm cottage, remote, peaceful yet only 10 mins from ferries to Northern Ireland.
Open: All Year
01776 810328 (also fax)
Mrs Ross
rawer@freenet.co.uk
D: £15.00–£18.00 **S:** £15.00–£18.00
Beds: 1F 1D 1T **Baths:** 1 Sh
ﾟﾐ🅿 (4) ▥🛏✕⚘

Torthorwald

NY0378 🍺 *Four Crowns, The Manor Country House*

Branetrigg Farm, *Torthorwald, Dumfries, DG1 3QB.*
Farmhouse with panoramic views; ideal for touring, cycling, fishing and golfing.
Open: Easter to Nov
Grades: STB 3 Star
01387 750650 Mrs Huston
D: £16.00–£18.00 **S:** £18.00
Beds: 1F 1D **Baths:** 1 Sh
▥▦

Twynholm

NX6654 🍺 *Murray Arms*

Barbey Farm, *Twynholm, Kirkcudbright, Kirkcudbrightshire, DG6 4PN.*
Farmhouse accommodation with beautiful gardens in quiet rural area.
Open: Easter to Sep
01557 860229 Miss Service
D: £14.00 **S:** £14.00
Beds: 1F 1T
ﾟﾐ🅿 (2) ▥🛏⚘

Tynron

NX8193 🍺 *Craigdarroch Arms*

Dalmakerran, *Tynron, Thornhill, Dumfriesshire, DG3 4LA.*
Country house in 36 acres of pasture and woodland. Warm, friendly atmosphere.
Open: All Year (not Xmas)
01848 200379 (also fax)
M Newbould
maryn@dalmakerran.freeserve.co.uk
D: £18.00–£20.00 **S:** £20.00
Beds: 1F 1D 1T 1S **Baths:** 1 En 1 Sh
ﾟﾐ🅿▥🛏▦⚘

Whithorn

NX4440 🍺 *Queen's Arms*

Slan A Stigh, *34 George Street, Whithorn, Dumfries & Galloway, DG8 8NZ.*
Open: All Year
01988 500699 Mr Burford
alexburford@supanet.com
D: £20.00 **S:** £20.00
Beds: 1F 2D **Baths:** 1 Sh
ﾟﾐ🅿 (2) ⌇▥✕▥⚘
Slan A Stigh is a 1700 Georgian townhouse in historic Whithorn, site of the Whithorn Dig, the earliest Christian community in Scotland. We are close to sea with good fishing in sea, loch, rivers. Ideal walking and cycling country.

Belmont, *St John Street, Whithorn, Newton Stewart, Wigtownshire, DG8 8PG.*
Visit nearby gardens, Whithorn, St Ninian's cave, many beautiful walks.
Open: All Year
01988 500890 (also fax)
Mrs Fleming
D: £18.00–£21.00 **S:** £18.00–£21.00
Beds: 1D 1T 1S **Baths:** 1 Pr 1 Sh
ﾟﾐ (12) 🅿 (8) ⌇▥🛏✕▥⚘

High season, bank holidays
and special events mean low
availability anywhere

Wigtown

NX4355 🍺 *Bladnoch Inn, Fordbank Hotel*

Glaisnock House, *20 South Main Street,*
Wigtown, Wigtownshire, DG8 9EH.
Set in the heart of Scotland's book town with
licensed restaurant.
Open: All Year (not Xmas)
Grades: STB 2 Star
01988 402249 (also fax)
Mr & Mrs Cairns
cairns@glaisnock1.freeserve.co.uk
D: £17.50–£18.50 **S:** £18.50–£19.50
Beds: 2F 1T 1S **Baths:** 2 En 1 Pr 1 Sh
🛏 📺 🍴 ✕ 🏛 Ⅴ 🛢 cc

Craigmount Guest House, *High Street,*
Wigtown, Wigtownshire, DG8 9EQ.
Welcoming licensed family run home with
space to relax. Safe, off-road parking.
Open: All Year
01988 402291 / 0800 980 4510 Mrs Taylor
D: £17.00–£20.00 **S:** £17.00–£20.00
Beds: 2F 1D 1T 1S **Baths:** 2 En 1 Sh
🛏 📅 (10) 📺 🍴 ✕ 🏛 Ⅴ 🛢

The Old Coach House, *34 Bladnoch,*
Wigtown, Newton Stewart, DG8 9AB.
Grade C listed. Overlooking river. 35 minutes
Stranraer ferry. Home baking. Brochure.
Open: All Year
01988 402316 Mrs Key
D: £18.50–£20.00 **S:** £21.00
Beds: 1F 1T **Baths:** 2 En
🛏 📅 (5) 📺 🍴 ✕ 🏛 Ⅴ ❀ 🛢

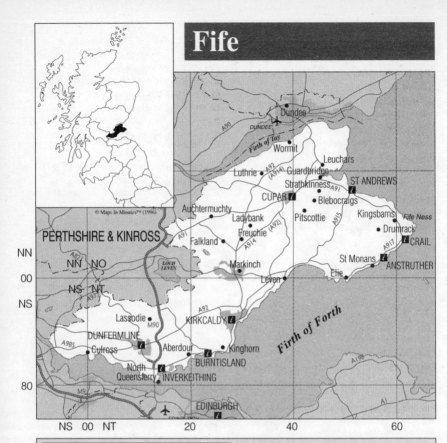

Fife

PERTHSHIRE & KINROSS

NN
00
NS
80

NS 00 NT   20   40   60

AIRPORTS ⊕

The nearest well served airport is
Edinburgh (see Lothian chapter).

BUS 🚌

Scottish Citylink, tel. 08705 505050.

RAIL ⇥

For rail information, telephone the National
Rail Enquiries line on 08457 484950. For
the Minicom service for the deaf and hard
of hearing, tel. 0845 605 0600.

TOURIST INFORMATION OFFICES *i*

Scottish Fisheries Museum, **Anstruther**,
Fife, KY10 3DQ, 01333 311073
(Easter to Oct).

Marketgate Museum & Heritage Centre,
Crail, Anstruther, Fife, KY10 3TL,
01333 450869 (Easter to Oct).

Abbot House, Maygate, **Dunfermline**, Fife,
KY12 7NH, 01383 720999 (Easter to Oct).

19 Whyte's Causeway, **Kirkcaldy**, Fife,
KY1 1XF, 01592 267775.

South Street, **Leven**, Fife, KY8 4NU,
01592 267775.

Queensferry Lodge Hotel, **North
Queensferry**, Inverkeithing, Fife,
KY11 1JH, 01383 417759.

78 South Street, **St Andrews**, Fife,
KY16 9JT, 01334 472021.

Aberdour

NT1985 🍴 *Aberdour Hotel*

Aberdour Hotel, *38 High Street, Aberdour, Burntisland, Fife, KY3 0SW.*
Friendly village inn, traditional cooking, real ales, Edinburgh half hour car/rail.
Open: All Year
Grades: STB 3 Star, AA 2 Star
01383 860325 Mr Thomson
Fax: 01383 860808
reception@aberdourhotel.co.uk
D: £25.00–£30.00 **S:** £35.00–£45.00
Beds: 4F 7D 5T **Baths:** 16 En
🛏 🅿 (8) 📺 🐴 ✕ 🖿 📋 ♨ ♿ 1 cc

Anstruther

NO5603 🍴 *Crow's Nest, Salutation, Haven Restaurant, Dreel Tavern, Cellar*

Harefield Cottage, *Carvenom, Anstruther, Fife, KY10 3JU.*
Open: Easter to Oct
Grades: STB 3 Star
01333 310346 Mrs Robinson
D: £20.00–£21.50 **S:** £24.00
Beds: 1T 1D **Baths:** 1 Pr 1 Sh
🅿 (4) 📺 🐴 🖿 📋
Large, stone built, single storey cottage, large garden. All rooms have extensive view over fields and woods to firth of forth with May Island and Bass Rock. Private parking. Very Peaceful. Quiet location, one and half miles from town centre.

Royal Hotel, *20 Rodger Street, Anstruther, Fife, KY10 3HU.*
Family-run hotel, 100 yards seashore. Small harbour, sea trips to May Island Bird Sanctuary.
Open: All Year
01333 310581 Mr Cook
D: £18.00–£22.00 **S:** £18.00
Beds: 1F 4T 4D 2S **Baths:** 1 En
🛏 📺 🐴 ✕ 🖿 📋 ♨

Bringing children with you?
Always ask for any special rates

The Sheiling, *32 Glenogil Gardens, Anstruther, Fife, KY10 3ET.*
Pretty white bungalow, ground floor bedrooms overlook garden. Harbour 200m.
Open: Easter to Sept **Grades:** STB 3 Star
01333 310697 Mrs Ritchie
D: £16.00–£22.00 **S:** £22.00
Beds: 2D **Baths:** 1 Sh 1 Pr
🅿 (2) ⅍ 📺 ✕ 🖿 📋 ♨ ♿

The Hermitage, *Ladywalk, Anstruther, Fife, KY10 3EX.*
Home from home, quiet situation near harbour, superb walled garden.
Open: All Year
Grades: STB 4 Star, AA 4 Diamond
01333 310909 Mrs McDonald
Fax: 01333 311505
b&b@thehermitage.co.uk
D: £20.00–£30.00 **S:** £25.00–£30.00
Beds: 3D 1T **Baths:** 2 Sh
🛏 🅿 (4) ⅍ 📺 ✕ 🖿 📋 ♨ cc

Auchtermuchty

NO2311

Forest Hills Hotel, *High Street, Auchtermuchty, Cupar, Fife, KY14 7DP.*
Old inn situated in village square, surrounded by rolling countryside.
Open: All Year
01337 828318 (also fax) Mr Van Beuskom
lomond.foresthotels@dtn.ntl.com
D: £25.00–£42.00 **S:** £37.00–£42.00
Beds: 2F 4D 2T 2S **Baths:** 8 Pr 1 Sh
🛏 📺 🐴 ✕ 🖿 📋 ♨

Blebocraigs

NO4215 🍴 *Pitscottie Inn*

Torridon, *16 Main Street, Blebocraigs, Cupar, Fife, KY15 5UF.*
In quiet country village by St Andrews. Lovely views. Friendly.
Open: All Year **Grades:** STB 3 Star
01334 850766 (also fax) Mrs Grice
tonyw@gricet.freeserve.co.uk
D: £18.00–£21.00 **S:** £23.00–£26.00
Beds: 1T 1D **Baths:** 1 En 1 Pr
🛏 (10) 🅿 (6) ⅍ 📺 🐴 🖿 ♨

Burntisland

NT2386   *Kingswood Hotel, Inchview Hotel*

148a Kinghorn Road, *Burntisland, Fife, KY3 9JU.*
Panoramic views over River Forth, golf courses and water sports nearby.
Open: All Year
01592 872266 (also fax)
Mrs Redford
c148m@aol.com
D: £20.00–£25.00 **S:** £25.00–£30.00
Beds: 1F 1D **Baths:** 2 En
🛏 🅿 (2) 📺 🐾 🛢 Ⓥ 🛢

Crail

NO6107   *Marine Hotel, East Neuk Hotel, Balcomie Hotel*

Woodlands Guest House, *Balcomie Road, Crail, Anstruther, Fife, KY10 3TN.*
Detached villa, superb views, beach half a minute, St Andrews 10 mins, golf courses.
Open: Feb to Dec
01333 450147 Mrs Wood
rachelwoodlandsbb@easicom.com
D: £18.00–£19.00 **S:** £20.00–£21.00
Beds: 1F 2D **Baths:** 2 Sh
🛏 (2) 🅿 (10) ✠ 📺 🐾 🛢 🛢 ♿

Caiplie House, *53 High Street, Crail, Anstruther, KY10 3RA.*
Friendly, informal guest house. Taste of Scotland member.
Open: Feb to Nov
01333 450564 (also fax)
Mr & Mrs Strachan
caipliehouse@talk21.com
D: £17.00–£24.00 **S:** £18.00–£22.00
Beds: 1F 4D 1T 1S **Baths:** 3 En 1 Pr 2 Sh
🛏 🅿 (3) 📺 🐾 ✗ 🛢 Ⓥ 🛢

RATES

D = Price range per person sharing in a double room
S = Price range for a single room

Culross

NS9886

Dundonald Arms Hotel, *Mid Causeway, Culross, Dunfermline, Fife, KY12 8HS.*
C16th time warp riverside village; white cottages, cobbled causeways.
Open: All Year
01383 882443
Mrs Finlayson
Fax: 01383 881137
D: £20.00–£30.00 **S:** £30.00–£40.00
Beds: 7F 3D 2T **Baths:** 7 En 7 Pr
🛏 🅿 (30) 📺 ✗ 🛢 Ⓥ 🛢 cc

Cupar

NO3714   *Springfield Tavern, Ceres Inn, Eden House Hotel, St Michaels Inn, Guardbridge Hotel, Dairsie Inn, Dolls House*

Todhall House, *off A91, Cupar, Fife, KY15 4RQ.*
Welcoming country house near St Andrews - come explore the Kingdom of Fife.
Open: Mar to Oct
01334 656344
Mrs Donald
Fax: 01334 650791
todhallhouse@ukgateway.net
D: £25.00–£32.00 **S:** £30.00–£38.00
Beds: 2D 1T **Baths:** 3 En
🛏 (10) 🅿 (5) ✠ 📺 ✗ 🛢 Ⓥ 🛢

Drumrack

NO5408   *Cambo Arms, Kings Barns*

Drumrack Farm, *Drumrack, St Andrews, Fife, KY16 8QQ.*
Open: All Year (not Xmas)
01333 310520 Mrs Watson
D: £16.00 **S:** £16.00
Beds: 1D 1T 1S **Baths:** 1 Sh
🛏 🅿 (5) ✠ 📺 ✗ Ⓥ 🛢
Situated 6 miles south of St Andrews on the B9131, a family-run farm of 350 acres with sheep and cattle. House and garden have fine views over River Forth. Ideally placed for golf, beaches and many places of interest.

Dunfermline

NT1087 🍴 *Roadhouse, Saline Hotel, St Margaret's Hotel*

Broomfield Guest House, *1 Bloomfield Drive, Dunfermline, Fife, KY12 7DZ.*
Large Victorian house, near golf course, swimming pool and town centre.
Open: All Year (not Xmas/New Year)
01383 732498 Mrs Taylor
D: £19.00–£25.00 **S:** £16.00–£20.00
Beds: 1F 2D 1T 2S **Baths:** 5 En 1 Pr
🛏 🅿 (7) 📺 🛋 ⊻ ♨ ♿

Bowleys Farm, *Roscobie, Dunfermline, Fife, KY12 0SG.*
Sample Scottish hospitality at its best! (30 minutes from Edinburgh).
Open: Feb to Dec **Grades:** STB 3 Star
01383 721056 Mrs Fotheringham
bowleysfarm@hotmail.com
D: £18.00–£22.00 **S:** £25.00
Beds: 2F **Baths:** 1 En 1 Sh
🛏 🅿 (6) ⊁ 📺 🐴 ✗ 🛋 ⊻ ♨

Pitreavie Guest House, *3 Aberdour Road, Dunfermline, Fife, KY12 4PB.*
Family-run guest house on bus route to Edinburgh, well-appointed rooms.
Open: All Year
01383 724244 (also fax) Mr & Mrs Walker
pitreavieg@aol.com
D: £19.00–£21.00 **S:** £21.00–£25.00
Beds: 1F 1D 2T 2S **Baths:** 3 Sh
🛏 🅿 (6) ⊁ 📺 🐴 ✗ 🛋 ⊻ ❀ ♨ cc

Elie

NO4900 🍴 *Ship Inn, The Toft*

Millford House, *19 High Street, Elie, Leven, Fife, KY9 1BY.*
Large Georgian house in peaceful seaside village. Golf, tennis, sailing.
Open: All Year
Grades: STB 2 Star
01333 330567 Mr Cowan
millfordhouse@netscapeonline.co.uk
D: £17.50–£20.00 **S:** £20.00–£25.00
Beds: 2D 1T
🛏 📺 🛋 ⊻ ♨ ♿

Falkland

NO2507 🍴 *Warbecks*

Templelands Farm, *Falkland, Cupar, Fife, KY15 7DE.*
Panoramic views, National Trust properties nearby - Abundance of golf courses.
Open: Easter to Oct
Grades: STB 2 Star
01337 857383 Ms McGregor
D: £15.00 **S:** £15.00–£18.00
Beds: 1F 1D 1S **Baths:** 2 Sh
🛏 🅿 (3) ⊁ 📺 🛋 ♨

Freuchie

NO2806

Lomond Hills Hotel, *Parliament Square, Freuchie, Cupar, Fife, KY7 7EY.*
Comfortable coaching inn, candle-lit restaurant and leisure centre.
Open: All Year
01337 857329 (also fax)
lomond.foresthotels@dtn.ntl.com
D: £27.50–£39.00 **S:** £40.00–£54.00
Beds: 4F 11D 7T 2S **Baths:** 24 En
🛏 🅿 ⊁ 📺 🐴 ✗ 🛋 ⊻ ♨

Guardbridge

NO4519 🍴 *Guardbridge Hotel*

The Larches, *7 River Terrace, Guardbridge, St Andrews, Fife, KY16 0XA.*
Large, comfortable memorial hall. Wonderful food. Fully ensuite/private rooms.
Open: All Year
01334 838008 (also fax)
Mrs Mayner
thelarches@aol.com
D: £18.00–£28.00 **S:** £22.00–£32.00
Beds: 2D 1T **Baths:** 2 En 1 Pr
🛏 🅿 (4) ⊁ 📺 🐴 🛋 ⊻

High season, bank holidays
and special events mean low
availability anywhere

Bringing children with you?
Always ask for any special rates

Inverkeithing
NT1382

The Roods, *16 Bannerman Avenue,*
Inverkeithing, Fife, KY11 1NG.
Award winning B&B set in quiet gardens
close to costal path.
Open: All Year
Grades: STB 3 Star, AA 4 Diamond
01383 415049 (also fax)
Mrs Marley
bookings@theroods.com
D: £20.00–£25.00 **S:** £20.00–£25.00
Beds: 1D 1T 1F **Baths:** 3 En
⌂ 🅿 ⅍ 📺 ✕ ▥ Ⓥ 🎿 cc

Kinghorn
NT2687 🚢 *The Bay*

Craigo-Er, *45 Pettycur Road, Kinghorn, Fife,*
KY3 9RN.
Victorian house, panoramic sea views, direct
regular Edinburgh rail links.
Open: All Year
01592 890527 Mrs Thomson
D: £19.00 **S:** £19.00
Beds: 1D 2T **Baths:** 2 Sh
⌂ 🅿 (1) 📺 ✿ ▥ 🎿

Kingsbarns
NO5912 🚢 *Cambo Arms Hotel*

Kingsbarns Bed & Breakfast, *3 Main*
Street, Kingsbarns, St Andrews, Fife, KY16 8SL.
Warm, friendly, comfortable B&B in
picturesque coastal village. Golf courses
nearby.
Open: Apr to Oct
Grades: STB 4 Star
01334 880234 Mrs Hay
hay@itek-uk.com
D: £22.00–£25.00 **S:** £22.00
Beds: 2D 1T **Baths:** 3 En
⌂ 🅿 (2) 📺 ▥ Ⓥ 🎿

Kirkcaldy
NT2791 🚢 *Kingswood, Victoria, Wheatsheaf,*
Mullins

Crawford Hall, *2 Kinghorn Road, Kirkcaldy,*
Fife, KY1 1SU.
Open: All Year (not Xmas)
01592 262658 Mrs Crawford
D: £17.00–£19.00 **S:** £17.00–£19.00
Beds: 1F 1T **Baths:** 1 Sh
⌂ 🅿 (4) 📺 ✿ ✕ ▥ 🎿 ♿
Large, rambling old C19th house, once local
manse, set in lovely gardens. 2 minutes from
beach, 10 minute walk to town centre,
bus/railway stations. Comfortable rooms,
hearty breakfast, handy for golfers, near St
Andrews.

Cameron House, *44 Glebe Park, Kirkcaldy,*
Fife, KY1 1BL.
Quiet, friendly, good food central for
Edinburgh, Perth, St Andrews.
Open: All Year (not Xmas)
Grades: STB 2 Star B&B
01592 264531 Mrs Nicol
D: £15.00 **S:** £15.00–£17.00
Beds: 1F 1D **Baths:** 1 Sh
⌂ (1) ⅍ 📺 ✿ ✕ ▥ Ⓥ 🎿

Castleview, *17 Dysart Road, Kirkcaldy, Fife,*
KY1 2AY.
Situated on Fife coast near M90, within
reach Edinburgh, Perth, Dundee.
Open: All Year (not Xmas)
Grades: STB 1 Star B&B
01592 269275 Mrs Dick
D: £16.00–£17.00 **S:** £16.00–£17.00
Beds: 1F 2T **Baths:** 1 Sh
⌂ 🅿 📺 ✿ ✕ ▥ Ⓥ 🎿

Invertiel Guest House, *21 Pratt Street,*
Kirkcaldy, Fife, KY1 1RZ.
Quality accommodation where you can
come & go as you please.
Open: All Year
01592 264849 Mrs Duffy
Fax: 01592 592440
invertiel@fife.ac.uk
D: £20.00–£25.00 **S:** £25.00–£50.00
Beds: 2F 1D 1T 1S **Baths:** 1 En 1 Sh
⌂ 🅿 (7) 📺 ✕ ▥ Ⓥ 🎿

Cherrydene, *44 Bennochy Road, Kirkcaldy, Fife, KY2 5RB.*
Victorian house retaining many original features. Situated 5 minutes from bus and rail stations.
Open: All Year
01592 202147 Mrs Nicol
Fax: 01592 644618
D: £16.00–£25.00 **S:** £22.00–£35.00
Beds: 1F 1D 1S **Baths:** 2 En 1 Sh
🛏 🅿 (3) 📺 🐾 ✕ 🏠 📶 🖶

Arboretum, *20 Southerton Road, Kirkcaldy, Fife, KY2 5NB.*
Extended bungalow - quiet area courtyard for private parking, overlooking park.
Open: All Year
01592 643673 Mrs Duncan
D: £17.00–£20.00 **S:** £18.00–£22.00
Beds: 2D 1T **Baths:** 2 En 1 Pr
🛏 (8) 🅿 (6) 📺 🐾 🏠 📶 🖶

Dunedin House, *25 Townsend Place, Kirkcaldy, Fife, KY1 1HB.*
Excellent accommodation, central location. Superb breakfast, private parking, 35 mins Edinburgh & St Andrews.
Open: All Year
01592 203874 Mr & Mrs Duffy
Fax: 01592 265274
info@dunedin-house.co.uk
D: £20.00–£22.00 **S:** £25.00–£28.00
Beds: 1F 1D 1S **Baths:** 1 Sh
🛏 🅿 (5) 🍽 📺 ✕ 🏠 📶 🖶

Ladybank

NO3009

Redlands Country Lodge, *Pitlessie Road, Ladybank, Cupar, Fife, KY15 7SH.*
An attractive country cottage and pine lodge, surrounded by trees and fields.
Open: Feb to Nov
01337 831091 (also fax)
Jim & Dorothy McGregor
D: £24.00 **S:** £24.00–£30.00
Beds: 2D 2T **Baths:** 4 En
🛏 🅿 (6) 🍽 📺 🐾 ✕ 🏠 📶 🖶 cc

Lassodie

NT1292 🍺 *Halfway House*

Loch Fitty Cottage, *Lassodie, Dunfermline, Fife, KY12 0SP.*
Enjoy the comfort of a family home, in rural setting.
Open: All Year
Grades: STB 2 Star
01383 831081
Mr Woolley
n.woolley@btinternet.com
D: £18.00–£20.00 **S:** £18.00–£20.00
Beds: 1F 1D **Baths:** 1 En 1 Pr
🛏 🅿 (4) 📺 🐾 🏠 📶 🖶

Leuchars

NO4521 🍺 *St Michaels Inn*

Pinewood Country House, *Tayport Road, St Michaels, Leuchars, St Andrews, Fife, KY16 0DU.*
A quiet wooded area setting ideal for short breaks or golfing holidays.
Open: All Year (not Xmas/New Year)
Grades: STB 3 Star
01334 839860 Mr Bedwell
Fax: 01334 839868
accommodation@pinewoodhouse.com
D: £22.00–£25.00 **S:** £32.00–£44.00
Beds: 2T 3D **Baths:** 4 En 1 Pr
📺 🐾 ✕ 🏠 📶 🖶 cc

Pitlethie Farm, *Leuchars, St Andrews, Fife, KY16 0DP.*
Attractive comfortable farmhouse set in open farmland.
Open: All Year (not Xmas)
01334 838649
Mrs Black
Fax: 01334 839281
D: £25.00 **S:** £26.50
Beds: 2T, 1S
🛏 🍽 📺

High season, bank holidays and special events mean low availability anywhere

Leven

NO3800 ⌑ *Burns Tavern, Fettykil Fox*

Duniface Farm, *Windygates, Leven, Fife, KY8 5RH.*
Charming C19th farmhouse - comfortable & welcoming, hearty breakfasts, ideal touring base.
Open: All Year
01333 350272 (also fax)
Mrs Hamilton
auderymhamilton@tinyworld.co.uk
D: £15.00–£17.00 **S:** £15.00–£20.00
Beds: 1D 1F **Baths:** 1 Sh
🛏 🅿 ⌧ 📺 🏠 Ⓥ ♨

Luthrie

NO3319 ⌑ *Fernie Castle*

Easter Kinsleith, *Luthrie, Cupar, Fife, KY15 4NR.*
Gaplair is ideally situated for touring East and Central Scotland.
Open: Feb to Nov
Grades: STB 3 Star
01337 870363 Mr Rieu-Clarke
gapplair@compuserve.com
D: £18.00–£20.00 **S:** £18.00–£20.00
Beds: 1F 1D **Baths:** 2 En
🛏 (6) 🅿 (2) ⌧ 📺 🐕 🏠 ♨ cc

Markinch

NO2901 ⌑ *Town House, Laurel Bank Hotel*

Wester Markinch Cottage, *Balbirnie Estate, Markinch, Glenrothes, Fife, KY7 6JN.*
Extended Victorian cottage, convenient for Edinburgh, Glasgow and St Andrews.
Open: All Year (not Xmas/New Year)
01592 756719 (also fax) Ms Tjeransen
D: £18.00–£25.00 **S:** £16.00
Beds: 1D 2S 1T **Baths:** 1 En 1 Sh
🛏 🅿 (4) 📺 🐕 🏠 Ⓥ ♨

High season, bank holidays and special events mean low availability anywhere

Planning a longer stay?
Always ask for any special rates

Shythrum Farm, *Markinch, Glenrothes, Fife, KY7 6HB.*
Peaceful farmhouse. Markinch 1 mile golfers haven, excellent touring base.
Open: Mar to Oct
Grades: STB 2 Star
01592 758372 Mrs Craig
D: £19.00 **S:** £19.00
Beds: 1F 1T **Baths:** 1 En 1 Pr
🛏 🅿 (3) 📺 🏠 Ⓥ ♨

North Queensferry

NT1380 ⌑ *Ferry Bridge Hotel, Albert Hotel*

Fourteen Falls, *Chapel Place, North Queensferry, Inverkeithing, Fife, KY11 1JT.*
C18th cottage under Forth Bridge, enclosed garden, emphasis on hospitality.
Open: All Year
01383 412749 (also fax)
Mrs Evans
b&b@fourteen-falls.in2home.co.uk
D: £22.00 **S:** £22.00
Beds: 1T **Baths:** 1 Sh
🅿 (3) ⌧ 📺 🐕 ✕ 🏠 Ⓥ ♨

Pitscottie

NO4113 ⌑ *Pitscottie Inn*

Rockmount Cottage, *Dura Den Road, Pitscottie, Cupar, Fife, KY15 5TG.*
Open: All Year (not Xmas/New Year)
Grades: STB 3 Star
01334 828164 Mrs Reid
annmreid@rockmount1.freeserve.co.uk
D: £18.00–£25.00 **S:** £18.00–£25.00
Beds: 1F 1D 1S **Baths:** 1 Pr 2 Sh
🛏 🅿 (3) ⌧ 📺 🏠 Ⓥ ♨ ♿ 3
Lovely nineteenth century cottage tastefully modernised to a high standard just 7 miles from St. Andrews. Beautiful bedrooms with colour TV, tea, coffee and home baking. Good breakfasts and private parking. Children welcome and non smoking throughout.

St Andrews

NO5116 ◀ *Tavern, Pitscottie Inn, Guardbridge Hotel, Dolls House, Strathkinness Tavern, Cambo, Playfairs, Russell Hotel*

The Paddock, *Sunnyside, Strathkinness, St Andrews, KY16 9XP.*
Open: All Year (not Xmas/New Year)
Grades: STB 4 Star
01334 850888
Mrs Taylor
Fax: 01334 850870
thepaddock@btinternet.com
D: £20.00–£26.00 **S:** £25.00–£40.00
Beds: 1T 2D
P (8) **TV** **IIII.** **♨**
Quality ensuite accommodation in a modern residence with outstanding country views. Positioned in a secluded spot. Ample private parking. Guests may use the conservatory overlooking the gardens. St Andrews 2 miles.

Edenside House, *Edenside, St Andrews, Fife, KY16 9SQ.*
Pre 1775 farmhouse, 2.5 miles from St Andrews. Parking guaranteed.
Open: All Year (not Xmas)
Grades: STB 3 Star, AA 4 Diamond
01334 838108
Douglas & Yvonne Reid
Fax: 01334 838493
yreid19154@aol.com
D: £20.00–£27.00 **S:** £32.00–£38.00
Beds: 1F 2D 5T **Baths:** 8 En
ॐ **P** (10) **⚥** **TV** **ħ** **IIII.** **V** **♨** **Ġ** cc

Cairnsden B&B, *2 King Street, St Andrews, Fife, KY16 8JQ.*
Comfortable family house, 7 mins town centre, early breakfasts for golfers.
Open: All Year (not Xmas)
Grades: STB 2 Star
01334 476326
Mrs Allan
Fax: 01334 840355
D: £16.00–£20.00 **S:** £18.00–£22.00
Beds: 1D 1T **Baths:** 1 Sh
P (1) **⚥** **TV** **ħ** **IIII.** **V** **♨**

Coppercantie, *8 Lawhead Road West, St Andrews, Fife, KY16 9NE.*
A warm welcome awaits in the home of Scottish historian.
Open: All Year (not Xmas)
Grades: STB 4 Star
01334 476544 Mrs Dobson
Fax: 01334 470322
f.dobson@zetnet.co.uk
D: £18.00–£24.00 **S:** £34.00–£40.00
Beds: 1F 1D 1T **Baths:** 1 En 2 Sh
ॐ (9) **⚥** **TV** **IIII.** **V** **♨** cc

23 Kilrymont Road, *St Andrews, Fife, KY16 8DE.*
Detached home, harbour area, East Sands, 10 mins famous golf course.
Open: April-Dec
01334 477946 Mrs Kier
mkier@talk21.com
D: £17.00–£19.00 **S:** £17.00–£20.00
Beds: 1D 1S
ॐ (7) **P** (1) **⚥** **TV** **IIII.** **♨** **Ġ**

12 Newmill Gardens, *St Andrews, Fife, KY16 8RY.*
Spacious, bright room. Tranquil area. Conveniently situated.
Open: All Year (not Xmas/New Year)
Grades: STB 3 Star
01334 474552 (also fax)
Mrs Irvine
D: £18.00–£20.00 **S:** £20.00–£22.00
Beds: 1D **Baths:** 1 Pr
P (1) **⚥** **TV** **IIII.** **V** **♨**

Amberside Guest House, *4 Murray Park, St Andrews, Fife, KY16 9AW.*
Amberside has become well known for its wonderful breakfast and lovely warm welcome.
Open: All Year
Grades: STB 3 Star, AA 3 Diamond
01334 474644 (also fax)
Mr Carney
amberside@talk21.com
D: £18.00–£28.00 **S:** £35.00–£45.00
Beds: 1F 2D 2T 1S **Baths:** 1 Pr
ॐ **P** **TV** **ħ** **IIII.** **V** **❄** **♨** cc

Spinkstown Farmhouse, *St Andrews,*
Fife, KY16 8PN.
Two miles from St Andrews on A917.
Open: All Year (not Xmas)
01334 473475 (also fax) Mrs Duncan
D: £20.00 **S:** £25.00
Beds: 2D 1T **Baths:** 3 Pr
🅿 (4) ✤ 📺 ▥ ⃝ 🖾

Ardmore, *1 Drumcarrow Road, St Andrews,*
Fife, KY16 8SE.
Comfortable, non-smoking, family bungalow
in quiet residential area opposite Botanical
Gardens. **Open:** Jan to Nov
01334 474574 Mrs Methven
D: £16.00–£18.00
Beds: 2D
🅿 (2) ✤ 📺 ▥ ⃝

Whitecroft Guest Lodges, *33*
Strathkinness High Road, St Andrews, Fife,
KY16 9UA.
Whitecroft has modern ensuite rooms with
parking, private entrances.
Open: All Year
01334 474448 (also fax) Mr & Mrs Horn
whitecroft@tesco.net
D: £22.00–£27.00 **S:** £30.00–£35.00
Beds: 3F 2D 1T **Baths:** 5 En
🐾 🅿 (5) ✤ 📺 🐾 ▥ 🖾 cc

NO5201   🍴 *Mayview Hotel, Cabin Bar*

Inverforth, *20 Braehead, St Monans, Fife,*
KY10 2AN.
Comfortable homely accommodation, home
baking. Seaview, near St Andrews golf.
Open: Jun to Oct **Grades:** STB 2 Star B&B
01333 730205 Miss Aitken
D: £17.50–£18.00 **S:** £17.50–£18.00
Beds: 1D 2T **Baths:** 1 Sh
🐾 (8) ✤ 📺 ▥

Strathkinness

NO4616

Brig-A-Doon, *6 High Road, Strathkinness,*
St Andrews, Fife, KY16 9XY.
Open: Easter to October
01334 850268
Mrs Watson
D: £20.00–£25.00 **S:** £25.00
Beds: 1T 1D **Baths:** 1 En 1 Pr
🐾 (5) 🅿 (2) ✤ 📺 ▥
Brig-A-Doon was one time a Toll House.
Panoramic views over St Andrews Bay and
Tay Estuary. Very handy for local golf
courses. Dundee, Perth within easy distance.
Hospitality tray in bedrooms with extras.
Wake up to a good Scottish breakfast.

Wormit

NO3925   🍴 *Sandford Country House Hotel*

Newton Farm, *Wormit, Newport-on-Tay,*
Fife, DD6 8RL.
Traditional farmhouse overlooking our own
trout loch, fly fishing, quad biking.
Open: Easter to Oct
Grades: STB 2 Star
01382 540125
K Crawford
Fax: 01382 542513
ghcrawford@ukonline.co.uk
D: £17.00
Beds: 1F 2T **Baths:** 1 Sh
🐾 🅿 (8) ✤ 📺 🐾 🖾

Stilwell's Britain Cycleway Companion

23 Long Distance Cycleways – Where to Stay * Where to Eat

County Cycleways – Sustrans Routes

The first guide of its kind, **Stilwell's Britain Cycleway Companion** makes planning accommodation for your cycling trip easy. It lists B&Bs, hostels, campsites and pubs– in the order they appear along the selected cycleways – allowing the cyclist to book ahead. No more hunting for a room, a hot meal or a cold drink after a long day in the saddle. Stilwell's gives descriptions of the featured routes and includes such relevant information as maps, grid references and distance from route; Tourist Board ratings; and the availability of drying facilities and packed lunches. No matter which route – or part of a route – you decide to ride, let the **Cycleway Companion** show you where to sleep and eat.

As essential as your tyre pump – the perfect cycling companion: **Stilwell's Britain Cycleway Companion**.

Cycleways

Sustrans

Carlisle to Inverness – Clyde to Forth - Devon Coast to Coast - Hull to Harwich – Kingfisher Cycle Trail - Lon Las Cymru – Sea to Sea (C2C) – Severn and Thames – West Country Way – White Rose Cycle Route

County

Round Berkshire Cycle Route – Cheshire Cycleway – Cumbria Cycleway – Essex Cycle Route – Icknield Way - Lancashire Cycleway – Leicestershire County Cycleway – Oxfordshire Cycleway – Reivers Cycle Route – South Downs Way - Surrey Cycleway – Wiltshire Cycleway – Yorkshire Dales Cycleway

£9.95 from all good bookstores (ISBN 1-900861-26-7) or £10.95 (inc p&p) from Stilwell Publishing Ltd, 59 Charlotte Road, London EC2A 3QW (020 7739 7179)

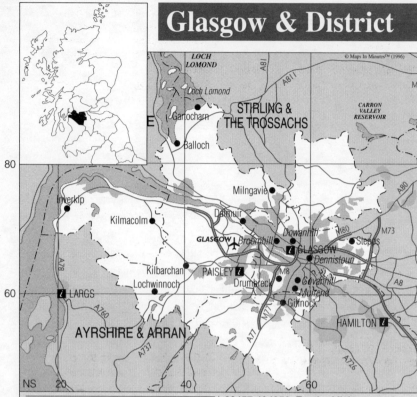

Glasgow & District

© Maps In Minutes™ (1996)

AIRPORTS ⊕

Glasgow Airport (Paisley), tel. 0141 887 1111.

AIR SERVICES & AIRLINES ✈

British Airways (into Scotland): *Glasgow to Belfast, Birmingham, Bristol, Derry, London (Heathrow), Manchester.* Tel. (local rate) 0345 222111.

British Airways (within Scotland): *Glasgow to Aberdeen, Barra (Western Isles), Benbecula (Western Isles), Campbeltown (Argyll), Inverness, Isle of Islay, Kirkwall (Orkney), Stornoway (Western Isles), Sumburgh (Shetland), Isle of Tiree, Wick.* Tel. (local rate) 0345 222111.

KLM UK: *Glasgow to London (Gatwick & Stansted).* Tel. (local rate) 08705 074074.

RAIL ⇌

For rail information, telephone the National Rail Enquiries line on 08457 484950. For the Minicom service for the deaf and hard of hearing, tel. 0845 605 0600.

BUS 🚌

Scottish Citylink, tel. 08705 505050; **National Express**, 0141 226 4826.

TOURIST INFORMATION OFFICES 𝑖

Balloch Road, **Balloch**, Alexandria, Dunbartonshire, G83 8LQ, 01389 753533 (Easter to Oct).

35 St Vincent Place, **Glasgow**, G1 2ER, 0141 204 4400.

Pierhead, **Gourock**, Renfrewshire, PA19 1QS, 01475 722007 (Easter to Oct).

A82 Northbound, **Milton**, Dumbarton, G82 2TD, 01389 742306 (Easter to Oct).

Town Hall, Abbey Close, **Paisley**, Renfrewshire, PA1 1JF, 0141 889 0711.

Glasgow Airport, **Paisley**, Renfrewshire, 0141 848 4440.

Balloch

NS3982 🍺 *Roundabout Inn, Balloch Hotel, Corries, Stables, Clachan Inn*

Glyndale, *6 McKenzie Drive, Lomond Road Estate, Balloch, Alexandria, Dunbartonshire, G83 8HL.*
Easy access to Loch Lomond, Glasgow Airport, public transport.
Open: All Year (not Xmas)
Grades: STB 3 Star B&B
01389 758238 Mrs Ross
glyndale_b_and_b@tinyworld.co.uk
D: £16.50–£17.50 **S:** £20.00
Beds: 1D 1T **Baths:** 1 Sh
🛏 🅿 (2) ⅍ 📺 🐾 🛏 Ⓥ ♨

Anchorage Guest House, *Balloch Road, Balloch, Alexandria, Dunbartonshire, G83 8SS.*
Situated on the banks of Loch Lomond. Ideal base for touring, fishing, sailing & walking.
Open: All Year **Grades:** STB 1 Star
01389 753336 Mr Bowman
D: £18.00–£25.00
Beds: 1F 2D 4T **Baths:** 5 En 2 Sh
🛏 (1) 🅿 (6) 📺 🐾 ✕ 🛏 Ⓥ ✴ ♨ ⚓ 3

Dumbain Farm, *Balloch, Alexandria, Dunbartonshire, G83 8DS.*
Newly converted byre on working farm. Aga cooked breakfast. Homemade raspberry jam.
Open: All Year
Grades: STB 3 Star
01389 752263 Mrs Watson
D: £20.00–£22.00 **S:** £18.00–£25.00
Beds: 1F 1T 1D **Baths:** 3 En
🛏 🅿 (5) ⅍ 📺 🛏 Ⓥ ♨

Gowanlea Guest House, *Drymen Road, Balloch, Alexandria, Dunbartonshire, G83 8HS.*
Open: All Year (not Xmas/New Year)
Grades: STB 4 Star
01389 752456 Mrs Campbell
Fax: 01389 710543 gowanlea@aol.com
D: £19.00–£23.00 **S:** £22.00–£30.00
Beds: 1T 3D **Baths:** 4 En
🛏 🅿 (4) ⅍ 📺 🛏 Ⓥ ♨ cc
Warm welcome awaits you at Campbell's award winning family run guest house B&B. Superior accommodation, excellent hospitality. Ideal touring base.

Heathpete, *24 Balloch Road, Balloch, Alexandria, Dunbartonshire, G83 8LE.*
Superb hospitality offered in luxurious accommodation central to all amenities.
Open: All Year
Grades: STB 3 Star
01389 752195 Mrs Hamill
sheathpete@aol.com
D: £12.00–£25.00 **S:** £18.00–£25.00
Beds: 2F 2D **Baths:** 4 En
🛏 🅿 (5) 📺 🐾 🛏 Ⓥ ♨ ♿

Auchry, *24 Boturich Drive, Balloch, Alexandria, Dunbartonshire, G83 8JP.*
Set in quiet cul de sac; walking distance to Loch Lomond.
Open: All Year (not Xmas/New Year)
Grades: STB 3 Star
01389 753208 Mrs McIntosh
auchry@ic24.net
D: £17.00–£19.00 **S:** £18.00–£20.00
Beds: 1D 1S **Baths:** 1 En 1 Sh
🅿 (4) ⅍ 📺 🛏 ♨ cc

7 Carrochan Crescent, *Balloch, Alexandria, Dunbartonshire, G83 8PX.*
A warm welcome awaits you; ideally situated for touring etc.
Open: Easter to Oct
Grades: STB 3 Star
01389 750078 Mrs Campbell
D: £16.00 **S:** £18
Beds: 2D **Baths:** 1 Sh
🛏 🅿 (2) 📺 🛏 Ⓥ ♨

Gartocharn

NS4286 🍺 *Hungry Monk, Clachan Inn*

Mardella Farm, *Old School Road, Gartocharn, Loch Lomond, Alexandria, Dunbartonshire, G83 8SD.*
Friendly, welcoming, homely atmosphere. Come and meet the quackers (ducks)!
Open: All Year
Grades: AA 4 Diamond
01389 830428 Mrs MacDonell
D: £18.50–£22.00 **S:** £31.00–£37.00
Beds: 1F 1D 1T **Baths:** 1 En 1 Sh
🛏 🅿 (4) ⅍ 📺 🐾 🛏 Ⓥ ✴ ♨

Giffnock

NS5658 🍴 *Orchard Park*

Forres Guest House, *10 Forres Avenue,*
Giffnock, Glasgow, G46 6LJ.
Located in quiet south side suburbs. 5
minutes from city centre.
Open: All Year (not Xmas)
Grades: STB 3 Star
0141 638 5554 Mrs Davies
Fax: 0141 571 9301
june@10forres.freeserve.co.uk
D: £18.00–£20.00 **S:** £18.00–£20.00
Beds: 2D
🅿 (4) 📺 ▥ 🛁

GLASGOW Broomhill

NS5467 🍴 *Air Organic, Bellahoustow Hotel,*
Dino's, Dorsey's, Garfield House, Highlanders Park,
Mitchell's, Orchard Park, Pablo's, Park Bar,
Stravaigan's, Snaffil Bit

Lochgilvie House, *117 Randolph Road,*
Broomhill, Glasgow, G11 7DS.
Open: All Year
Grades: STB 3 Star
0141 357 1593 Mrs Ogilvie
Fax: 0141 334 5828
reservations@lochgilvie.demon.co.uk
D: £25.00–£30.00 **S:** £25.00–£35.00
Beds: 1F 2D 3T **Baths:** 4 En
🐾 (10) 🅿 ⅟ 📺 ▥ Ⅴ 🛁
Luxurious Victorian town house situated in
Glasgow's prestigious West End, adjacent to
rail station, beside the art galleries,
university, SECC, convenient for
International Airport.

Park House, *13 Victoria Park Gardens*
South, Glasgow, G11 7BX.
Magnificent Victorian residence overlooking
private parkland in quiet residential area.
Open: All Year
Grades: STB 4 Star
0141 339 1559 Mrs Hallam
Fax: 0141 576 0915
richardanddi.parkhouse.glasgow@
dial.pipex.com
D: £25.00–£27.50 **S:** £32.00–£37.50
Beds: 2D 1T **Baths:** 2 En 1 Pr
🐾 🅿 (3) 📺 ✕ ▥ Ⅴ 🛁 cc

GLASGOW Central

NS5865 🍴 *Dorsey's, Park Bar, Mitchell's,*
Stravaigan's, Orchard Park, Bellahoustow Hotel,
Garfield House, Highlanders Park, Snaffil Bit

Kirkland House, *42 St Vincent Crescent,*
Glasgow, G3 8NG.
Open: All Year
Grades: STB 3 Star
0141 248 3458 Mrs Divers
Fax: 0141 221 5174
admin@kirkland.gispnet.com
D: £27.00–£30.00 **S:** £27.00–£30.00
Beds: 3D 2T 2S **Baths:** 6 En 2 Sh
🐾 (1) ⅟ 📺 ▥ 🛁
City centre guest house with excellent rooms
on beautiful Victorian Crescent in Finnieston
(Glasgow's 'little Chelsea'). Short walk to
Scottish Exhibition Centre, Museum/Art
Gallery, Kelvingrove Park and all West End
facilities. Glasgow airport 10 minutes,
member of the Harry James society.

Kelvingrove Hotel, *944 Sauchiehall Street,*
Glasgow, G3 7TH.
Open: All Year (not Xmas)
Grades: STB 2 Star
0141 339 5011 Mr Wills
Fax: 0141 339 6566
kelvingrove.hotel@business.ntl.com
D: £24.00–£29.00 **S:** £33.00–£38.00
Beds: 8D 4T 4F **Baths:** 10 En
🐾 🅿 (20) ⅟ 📺 🛏 ✕ ▥ Ⅴ 🛁 cc
Centrally located family-run hotel, set in
Glasgow's fashionable West End. Close to
pubs, clubs, art galleries, museums,
University, shops, rail and bus links - all
within walking distance.

Adelaide's, *209 Bath Street, Glasgow,*
G2 4HZ.
Central location, close to all major
attractions of revitalised city.
Open: All Year (not Xmas/New Year)
Grades: STB 2 Star
0141 248 4970 A R Meiklejohn
Fax: 0141 226 4247
info@adelaides.freeserve.co.uk
D: £25.00–£28.00 **S:** £35.00–£45.00
Beds: 2F 2T 2D 2S **Baths:** 6 En 2 Sh
🐾 ⅟ 📺 🛁 cc

Number Thirty Six, *36 St Vincent Crescent, Glasgow, G3 8NG.*
Situated in a Georgian terrace on the edge of Glasgow city centre.
Open: All Year (not Xmas)
0141 248 2086 Mrs MacKay
Fax: 0141 221 1477
admin@no36.gisp.net
D: £25.00–£30.00 **S:** £30.00–£35.00
Beds: 4D 2T **Baths:** 4 En 2 Pr
⌦ ⊡ ⠇ ♨

GLASGOW   Dalmuir
NS4970 ◀ *Radnor Park Hotel, Whiskey Joes*

13 Southview, *Dalmuir, Clydebank, Dunbartonshire, G81 3LA.*
Semi-villa: near Station/Glasgow Airport. Tourist board highly commended.
Open: All Year
0141 952 7007 Mrs McCay
D: £15.00–£18.00 **S:** £18.00–£20.00
Beds: 1T 1D 1S **Baths:** 1 En 1 Sh
⊡ (1) ⌦ ⊡ ⠇

GLASGOW   Dennistoun
NS6065 ◀ *Fire Station Resturant, Dorsey's, Park Bar, Mitchell's, Stravaigan's, Orchard Park, Bellahoustow Hotel, Garfield House, Highlanders Park, Snaffil Bit*

Seton Guest House, *6 Seton Terrace, Glasgow, G31 2HU.*
Warm and friendly welcome assured. Five minutes from city centre.
Open: All Year (not Xmas)
Grades: STB 2 Star
0141 556 7654 Mr Passway
Fax: 0141 402 3655
passway@seton.prestel.co.uk
D: £16.00–£17.00 **S:** £17.00–£18.00
Beds: 4F 2D 2T 1S **Baths:** 3 Sh
⌂ ⊡ ⠇ ⠇ ⊡ ♨

All details shown are as supplied by B&B owners in Autumn 2000

Rosewood Guest House, *4 Seton Terrace, Glasgow, G31 2HU.*
Victorian House near City Centre, close to many city attractions.
Open: All Year
Grades: STB 2 Star
0141 550 1500
Ms Turner
Fax: 01555 393876
rosewoodguesthouse@hotmail.com
D: £17.00–£20.00 **S:** £19.00–£22.00
Beds: 3F 2T 1D 2S **Baths:** 3 Sh
⌂ ⊡ ⊡ ⠇ ⠇ ⊡ ♨ cc

GLASGOW   Dowanhill
NS5667 ◀ *Orchard Park Hotel, Bellahoustow Hotel*

The Terrace House Hotel, *14 Belhaven Terrace, Glasgow, G12 0TG.*
Open: All Year
Grades: STB 2 Star
0141 337 3377 (also fax)
Mrs Black
admin@the-terrace.fsnet.co.uk
D: £29.00–£39.00 **S:** £49.00–£65.00
Beds: 4F 3D 5T 1S **Baths:** 12 En 1 Pr
⌂ ⌦ ⊡ ⠇ ✕ ⠇ ⊡ ♨ cc
'B' Listed terraced townhouse, built circa 1860, boasting fine period features, such as ornate cornices, wall friezes and columned entrance. Well connected to transport links to city centre, Glasgow Airport and Loch Lomond. A friendly welcome awaits you.

GLASGOW   Drumbreck
NS5663 ◀ *Sherbrock Castle*

Glasgow Guest House, *56 Dumbreck Road, Glasgow, G41 5NP.*
Turn of the century, red sandstone house, antique decoration, friendly welcome.
Open: All Year
Grades: STB 3 Star
0141 427 0129
Mr Bristow
brian.muir@ukonline.co.uk
D: £20.00 **S:** £25.00
Beds: 3D 3T 1S 1F **Baths:** 8 En
⌂ ⊡ (2) ⊡ ⠇ ⠇ ♨ ⌖ cc

GLASGOW   Govanhill

NS5862

Dunkeld Hotel, *10-12 Queens Drive,*
Glasgow, G42 8BS.
Open: All Year
Grades: STB 2 Star, RAC 1 Star
0141 424 0160 P Martin
Fax: 0141 423 4437
dunkeldhot@aol.com
D: £22.00–£29.95 **S:** £30.00–£44.95
Beds: 4F 8T 11D 4S **Baths:** 21 En 6 Sh
🛏 🅿 (10) ⅙ 📺 🐾 ✕ 🏛 Ⓥ ⓛ cc
Set in one of Glasgow's premier conservation
streets overlooking Queen's Park. Elegant
Victorian villa has bar, restaurant, comfortable
rooms with satellite TV/tea/coffee
facilities/hairdryers/ironing boards & mostly
ensuite. Private parking. Near Hampden
National Stadium/Burrell Collection.

GLASGOW   Muirend

NS5760

16 Bogton Avenue, *Muirend, Glasgow,*
G44 3JJ.
Quiet red sandstone terraced private house
adjacent station, 12 mins city centre.
Open: All Year (not Xmas)
0141 637 4402 (also fax)
Mrs Paterson
apaterson@gofornet.co.uk
D: £20.00 **S:** £22.00
Beds: 1D 2S **Baths:** 2 Sh
🅿 (2) ⅙ 📺 ✕ 🏛 Ⓥ ⓛ

Inverkip

NS2072

The Foresters, *Station Road, Inverkip,*
Greenock, Renfrewshire, PA16 0AY.
Charming Victorian villa in conservation
village. Five minutes walk to Scotland's
premier marina. **Open:** All Year (not Xmas)
01475 521433 (also fax) Mrs Wallace
forestershouse@msn.com
D: £22.00–£26.00 **S:** £20.00–£31.00
Beds: 1D 2T **Baths:** 3 En
🅿 (2) ⅙ 📺 🐾 🏛 Ⓥ ⓛ cc

Kilbarchan

NS4063 🍺 *Trust Inn*

Gladstone Farmhouse, *Burntshields*
Road, Kilbarchan, Johnstone, Renfrewshire,
PA10 2PB.
Quiet countryside, 10 minutes Glasgow
airport on direct route.
Open: All Year
01505 702579 (also fax)
Mrs Douglas
D: £18.00 **S:** £20.00
Beds: 1F 1D 1T **Baths:** 1 Sh
🛏 🅿 (6) 📺 🐾 ✕ 🏛 Ⓥ ⓛ ♿

Kilmacolm

NS3669 🍺 *Pullman*

Margaret's Mill Farm, *High Greenock*
Road, Kilmacolm, Renfrewshire, PA13 4TG.
200-year-old farmhouse set in beautiful
valley. Comfortable spacious bedrooms with
colour TV.
Open: All Year
01505 873716 Mrs Henderson
D: £15.00–£18.00 **S:** £15.00–£18.00
Beds: 1F 1D 1T
🛏 🅿 (8) ⅙ 📺 ✺ ⓛ

Lochwinnoch

NS3559 🍺 *Mossend Hotel, Gateside Inn, Brown*
Bull

Garnock Lodge, *Lochwinnoch,*
Renfrewshire, PA12 4JT.
Open: All Year
Grades: STB 4 Star, AA 4 Diamond
01505 503680 (also fax)
Mr & Mrs McMeechan
garnocklodge@cwcom.net
D: £18.00–£21.00 **S:** £25.00–£30.00
Beds: 1D 2T 1S **Baths:** 2 En 1 Sh
🛏 🅿 (4) 📺 🐾 ✕ 🏛 Ⓥ ⓛ cc
A warm welcome awaits you at detached
house in rural situation easy access to
Glasgow Airport via main route also Loch
Lomond and Ayrshire coast, walking, fishing,
golf, cycling and bird watching, home
baking, log fires, ensuite, off road parking.

East Lochhead, Largs Road, Lochwinnoch, Renfrewshire, PA12 4DX.
Beautifully restored farmhouse. Loch views, gardens. Taste of Scotland. **Open:** All Year
Grades: STB 4 Star,
AA 5 Diamond, Premier Select
01505 842610 (also fax) Mrs Anderson
winnoch@aol.com
D: £30.00–£32.50 **S:** £30.00–£35.00
Beds: 1T 2D **Baths:** 3 En
ॐ ▣ (6) ⊬ ⊡ ♉ ✕ ▥ Ⅴ ⚐ ⅍ cc

Milngavie

NS5574 ⬛ *Allander Bar, Cross Keys*

13 Craigdhu Avenue, Milngavie, Glasgow, G62 6DX.
Very comfortable family house where a warm welcome is assured.
Open: Mar to Oct **Grades:** STB 3 Star
0141 956 3439 Mrs Ogilvie
D: £18.00 **S:** £20.00–£25.00
Beds: 1F 1T
ॐ ▣ (4) ⊬ ⊡ ♉ ▥ Ⅴ ⚐

Westview, 1 Dougalston Gardens South, Milngavie, Glasgow, G62 6HS.
Modern detached, unique, comfortable, convenient to West Highland Way.
Open: All Year
0141 956 5973 Mr & Mrs McColl
D: £20.00 **S:** £24.00
Beds: 1F 1D 1T **Baths:** 3 En
ॐ ▣ (6) ⊬ Ⅴ ⚐

Paisley

NS4863 ⬛ *Lord Lounsdale, Paraffin Lamp*

Accara Guest House, 75 Maxwellton Road, Paisley, Renfrewshire, PA1 2RB.
Grade II Listed building close to airport, museum, university, hospital.
Open: All Year **Grades:** STB 2 Star
0141 887 7604 Mrs Stevens
Fax: 0141 887 1589
D: £20.00 **S:** £25.00
Beds: 1F 1T 1S **Baths:** 2 Sh
ॐ (4) ⊬ ⊡ ▥ Ⅴ ⚐ cc

Myfarrclan Guest House, 146 Corsebar Road, Paisley, Renfrewshire, PA2 9NA.
Nestling in leafy suburb of Paisley, lovingly restored bungalow offering many thoughtful extras.
Open: All Year
0141 884 8285
Mr & Mrs Farr
Fax: 0141 581 1566
myfarrclan_qwest@compuserve.com
D: £32.50–£35.00 **S:** £40.00–£60.00
Beds: 2D 1T **Baths:** 2 En 1 Pr
ॐ ▣ (2) ⊬ ⊡ ✕ ▥ Ⅴ ❀ ⚐

Stepps

NS6668 ⬛ *Dorsey's, Park Bar, Mitchell's, Stravaigan's, Orchard Park, Bellahoustow Hotel, Garfield House, Highlanders Park, Snaffil Bit*

Avenue End B&B, 21 West Avenue, Stepps, Glasgow, G33 6ES.
Open: All Year
Grades: STB 3 Star B&B
0141 779 1990
Mrs Wells
Fax: 0141 779 1990
avenueend@aol.com
D: £20.00–£25.00 **S:** £25.00–£27.50
Beds: 1F 1D 1S **Baths:** 2 En 1 Pr
ॐ ▣ (2) ⊬ ⊡ ▥ Ⅴ ⚐
Self built family home situated down quiet tree-lined lane. Glasgow east off A80, main route to Stirling (Braveheart Country) and the North. Easy commuting by public or own transport. M8 Exit 12. Home from home - warm welcome assured.

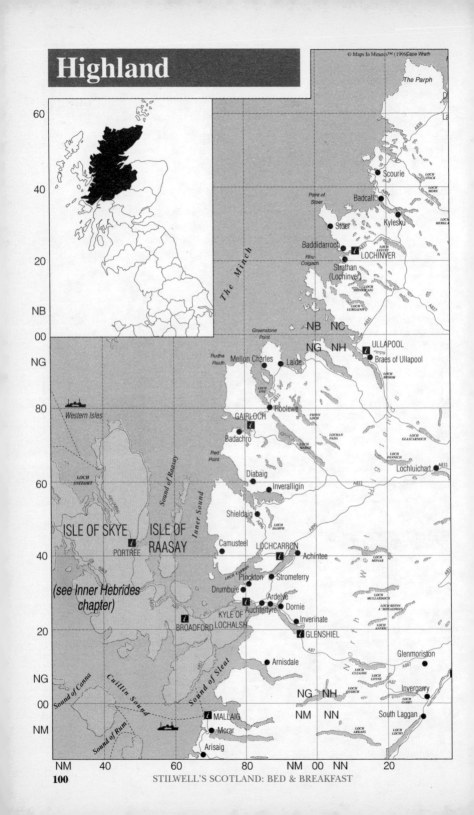

© Maps In Minutes™ (1996)

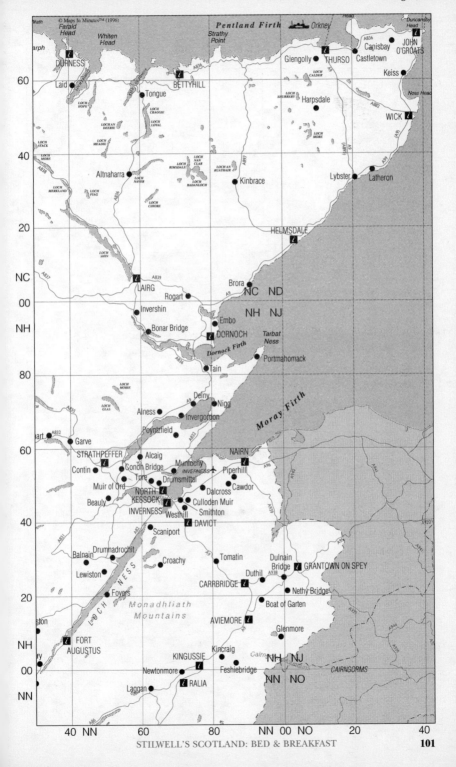

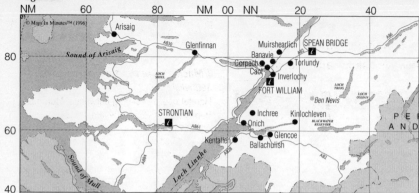

AIRPORTS ⊕

Inverness Airport (tel. 01463 232471).
Wick Airport (tel. 01856 872421).

AIR SERVICES & AIRLINES ✈

British Airways: *Inverness to Glasgow, Kirkwall (Orkney), London (Heathrow), Stornoway (Western Isles), Sumburgh (Shetland). Wick to Edinburgh, Glasgow, Kirkwall (Orkney), Sumburgh (Shetland).* Tel. (local rate): 0345 222111.

BUS 🚌

Scottish Citylink, tel. 08705 505050, **National Express**, tel. 0141 226 4826.

RAIL ⇌

For rail information, telephone the National Rail Enquiries line, on 08457 484950. For the Minicom service for the deaf and hard of hearing, tel. 0845 605 0600. There are local lines serving *Dingwall, Fort William, Inverness, Kyle of Lochalsh, Mallaig and Wick.* There are sleeper services between *London (Euston)/Inverness* and *London (Euston)/ Fort William.*

FERRIES 🛥

Caledonian MacBrayne: *Mallaig to Armadale (Skye)* 30 mins; *to Isle of Eigg* (1½ hrs); *to Isle of Rhum* (3½ hrs); *to Isle of Muck* (2¼ hrs). *Uig (Skye) to Tarbert or Lochmaddy (Western Isles)* 45 mins. Tel. 01475 650100. **P&O Scottish Ferries:** *Scrabster (near Thurso) to Stromness (Orkney)* 50 mins. Tel. 01224 572615.
Thomas & Bews: *John O'Groats to Burwick (Orkney)* 45 mins. Tel. 01955 611353.

TOURIST INFORMATION OFFICES 🛈

Grampian Road, **Aviemore**, Inverness-shire, PH22 1RH, 01479 810363.

Clachan, **Bettyhill**, Thurso, Caithness, KW14 7SZ, 01641 521342 (Easter to Oct).

Daviot Wood, A9, **Daviot**, Inverness-shire, IV1 2ER, 01463 772203 (Easter to Oct).

The Square, **Dornoch**, Sutherland, IV25 3SD, 01862 810400.

Sango, **Durness**, Lairg, Sutherland, V27 4PZ, 01971 511259 (Easter to Oct).

Car Park, **Fort Augustus**, Inverness-shire, PH32 4DG, 01320 366367 (Easter to Oct).

Cameron Centre, Cameron Square, **Fort William**, Inverness-shire, PH33 6AJ, 01397 703781.

Auchtercairn, **Gairloch**, Ross-shire, IV21 2BP, 01445 712130.

Glenshiel, Kyle of Lochalsh, Ross-shire, IV40 8HN, 01599 511264 (Easter to Oct).

High Street, **Grantown-on-Spey**, Moray, PH26 3EG, 01479 872773 (Easter to Oct).

Coupar Park, **Helmsdale**, Sutherland, KW8 6JX, 01431 821640 (Easter to Oct).

23 Church St, **Inverness**, IV1 1DY, 01463 234353.

County Road, **John o' Groats**, Wick, Caithness, KW1 4YR, 01955 611373 (Easter to Oct).

King Street, **Kingussie**, Inverness-shire, PH21 1HW, 01540 661297 (Easter to Oct).

Car Park, **Kyle of Lochalsh**, Ross-shire, IV40 8DA, 01599 534276 (Easter to Oct).

Lairg, Sutherland, 01549 402160 (Easter to Oct).

Main Street, **Lochcarron**, Strathcarron, Ross-shire, IV54 8YB, 01520 722357 (Easter to Oct).

Main Street, **Lochinver**, Lairg, Sutherland, IV27 4AR, 01571 844330 (Easter to Oct).

Mallaig, Inverness-shire, PH41 4QS, 01687 462170 (Easter to Oct).

62 King Street, **Nairn**, IV12 4DN, 01667 452753 (Easter to Oct).

North Kessock, Inverness, IV1 1XD, 01463 731505.

A9 North, **Ralia**, Newtonmore, Inverness-shire, PH20 1BD, 01540 673253 (Easter to Oct).

Spean Bridge, Inverness-shire, PH34 4EU, 01397 712576 (Easter to Oct).

The Square, **Strathpeffer**, Ross-shire, IV14 9DW, 01997 421415 (Easter to Oct).

Strontian, Acharacle, Argyll, PH36 4JA, 01967 402131 (Easter to Oct).

Riverside, **Thurso**, Caithness, KW14 8BU, 01847 892371 (Easter to Oct).

West Shore Street, **Ullapool**, Ross-shire, IV26 2UR, 01854 612135 (Easter to Oct).

Whitechapel Road, **Wick**, Caithness, KW1 4EA, 01955 602596.

Bringing children with you? Always ask for any special rates

Achintee

NG9441 ◀ *Carron Restaurant, Strathcarron Hotel*

The Shieling, *Achintee, Strathcarron, Ross-shire, IV54 8YX.*
Open: All Year
01520 722364 Mrs Levy
jlevyshieling@talk21.com
D: £18.00–£20.00 **S:** £17.00
Beds: 2T 1S **Baths:** 1 En 1 Sh
🛏 🅿 (3) ⊬ 📺 🛏, 🅅 ♨
Comfortable, homely, croft cottage, tastefully extended and modernised, only minutes from Strathcarron Railway station, surrounded by spectacular scenery; a central base for many leisure activities, particularly hill waking and climbing, and for day trips to such places as Skye and Inverewe Gardens.

Alcaig

NH5657 ◀ *Mallard, Cottage Bar*

Dun Eistein, *Alcaig, Conon Bridge, Dingwall, Ross-shire, IV7 8HS.*
Highland country cottage.
Open: May to Oct
Grades: STB 4 Star
01349 862210 Mrs Morrison
D: £18.50–£19.50 **S:** £24.00
Beds: 1F 1D **Baths:** 1 En 1 Pr
🛏 🅿 (3) ⊬ 📺 🛏, ♨

Alness

NH6569

An Laimhrig, *82 Obsdale Park, Alness, IV17 0TR.*
Modern detached house ideal touring centre, cyclists stopover for John o' Groats.
Open: All Year
Grades: STB 3 Star
01349 882016 Ms MacDonald
D: £17.00–£22.00 **S:** £18.00–£25.00
Beds: 1F 2T 1D **Baths:** 2 En 1 Sh
⊬ 📺 ✕ 🛏, ♨

Altnaharra

NC5635

1 Macleod Crescent, *Altnaharra, Lairg, Sutherland, IV27 4UG.*
Hamlet pop. 31 nestling between 2 Munros, Ben Klebrig & Ben Hope, ideal base hillwalking.
Open: Easter to
Grades: STB 3 Star
01549 411258 Mrs Barrie
D: £18.00 **S:** £23.00
Beds: 1F 2T **Baths:** 3 En
🛏 🅿 (3) ⊬ 📺 ✕ 🛏, ♨

Ardelve

NG8727 ◀ *Loch Duich Hotel*

Caberfeidh House, *Ardelve, Kyle of Lochalsh, IV40 8DY.*
Beautiful lochside house with superb views of Eilean Donan Castle.
Open: All Year (not Xmas/New Year)
Grades: STB 2 Star
01599 555293 Mr Newton
D: £18.00–£22.00 **S:** £25.00–£30.00
Beds: 2T 3D 1S **Baths:** 2 En 1 Sh
🅿 (6) ⊬ 📺 🛏, ♨ cc

Arisaig

NM6586 ◀ *Old Library*

Cnoc Na Faire Hotel, *Back of Keppoch, Arisaig, Inverness-shire, PH39 4NS.*
Family hotel overlooking Skye, sandy beaches. 9-hole golf course nearby.
Open: Mar to Oct
01687 450249 Miss MacDonald
D: £20.00–£25.00 **S:** £20.00–£35.00
Beds: 3D 2T 2S **Baths:** 2 En 1 Sh
🛏 🅿 (16) 🍴 ✕ 🅅 cc

BATHROOMS
Pr - Private
Sh - Shared
En - Ensuite

Arnisdale

NG8410   ◀ *Glenelg Inn*

Corran, *Arnisdale, Kyle of Lochalsh, Ross-shire, IV40 8JJ.*
House is situated in small village surrounded by massive mountains overlooking Loch Horn.
Open: All Year
01599 522336 Mrs Nash
D: £13.00–£16.00 **S:** £13.00–£16.00
Beds: 1F 1S **Baths:** 1 Sh
🖵 🛏 ✕ 🎖 ⬤

Auchtertyre

NG8328

Caladh Solas, *Auchtertyre, Kyle of Lochalsh, Ross-shire, IV40 8EG.*
Open: All Year (not Xmas)
Grades: STB 3 Star
01599 566317 Mrs Knowles
knowles@caladhsolas.freeserve.co.uk
D: £16.00–£22.00 **S:** £16.00–£30.00
Beds: 1D 1T 1S **Baths:** 1 En 1 Sh
🐾 🅿 (2) ✄ 🖵 ✕ 🎖 ⬤
Quality bed and breakfast with a warm welcome guaranteed. Set amid spectacular scenery, an ideal location for exploring Skye and the highlands. An experience you will want to repeat.

Aviemore

NH8912   ◀ *Glenmore Lodge, Cairngorm Hotel, Old Bridge Inn, Mackenzie's, Winking Owl*

Cairngorm Guest House, *Grampian Road, Aviemore, Inverness-shire, PH22 1RP.*
Open: Easter to Easter
01479 810630 (also fax) Mrs Conn
conns@lineone.net
D: £18.00–£25.00 **S:** £20.00–£28.00
Beds: 1F 5D 3T **Baths:** 9 En
🐾 (2) 🅿 (10) ✄ 🖵 🎖 ⬤ cc
Experience a real Scottish welcome. Have coffee with us on arrival. Relax in our guest lounge in front of a real fire with views of the Cairngorm mountains. Handy for train/bus. Two minutes walk to the centre. 24 hour access to rooms.

Cairn Eilrig, *Glenmore, Aviemore, Inverness-shire, PH22 1QU.*
Highland welcome. Secluded bungalow in Glenmore forest park panoramic views.
Open: All Year
Grades: STB 3 Star
01479 861223
Mrs Ferguson
D: £17.00–£18.00 **S:** £17.00–£20.00
Beds: 1F 1T **Baths:** 1 Sh
🐾 🅿 (2) 🖵 🛏 🎖 ⬤

Ravenscraig Guest House, *Aviemore, Inverness-shire, PH22 1RP.*
Central village location. Ideal for exploring highlands or just relaxing.
Open: All Year
Grades: STB 2 Star GH, AA 3 Diamond, RAC 3 Diamond
01479 810278
Mr & Mrs Gatenby
Fax: 01479 812742
ravenscrg@aol.com
D: £18.00–£24.00 **S:** £18.00–£24.00
Beds: 2F 5D 4T 1S **Baths:** 12 En
🐾 🅿 (16) 🖵 🛏 🎖 ⬤ cc

Rowan Tree Country Hotel, *Loch Alvie, Aviemore, Inverness-shire, PH22 1QB.*
C17th Coaching Inn. Characterful bedrooms. Comfortable lounges. A warm welcome.
Open: All Year
Grades: STB 3 Star
01479 810207 (also fax)
enquires@rowantreehotel.com
D: £26.50–£31.50 **S:** £36.50–£41.50
Beds: 2F 3T 4D 1S **Baths:** 10 En 1 Sh
🐾 (12) 🅿 🖵 🛏 ✕ 🎖 ⬤ ❋ cc

Eriskay, *Craig-na-gower, Aviemore, Inverness-shire, PH22 1RW.*
Quietly situated warm and comfortable house good base for touring.
Open: All Year
Grades: STB 4 Star
01479 810717 Fax: 01479 812312
eriskay@cali.co.uk
D: £17.00–£20.00 **S:** £22.00–£26.00
Beds: 2D 1T **Baths:** 3 En
🅿 (4) 🖵 🎖 ⬤

Dunroamin, *Craig Gower Avenue, Aviemore, Inverness-shire, PH22 1RN.*
Comfortable, friendly, family-run home. Rooms tasteful and spacious.
Open: All Year
Grades: STB 2 Star
01479 810698 (also fax)
Mrs Sheffield
D: £16.00–£25.00
S: £20.00–£40.00
Beds: 2F 2D **Baths:** 3 En 1 Pr
🛏 🅿 (4) ⅍ 📺 📖 Ⅴ ✤ 🕏

Waverley, *35 Strathspey Avenue, Aviemore, Inverness-shire, PH22 1SN.*
Modern comfortable bungalow in quiet area.
Open: All Year (not Xmas)
01479 811226 Mrs Fraser
maggie.fraser@talk21.com
D: £17.00–£20.00 **S:** £20.00–£25.00
Beds: 1D 1T **Baths:** 1 En 1 Pr
🛏 (8) ⅍ 📺 📖 Ⅴ 🕏 &

Ardlogie Guest House, *Dalfaber Road, Aviemore, Inverness-shire, PH22 1PU.*
Centre of Aviemore views over River Spey to Cairngorm Mountains.
Open: All Year
Grades: STB 2 Star
01479 810747 D: £17.00 **S:** £17.00
Beds: 4D 1T **Baths:** 5 En
🛏 🅿 (3) 📺 🐕 📖 🕏 cc

Ryvoan, *Grampian Road, Aviemore, Inverness-shire, PH22 1RY.*
Beautiful modern bungalow with patio overlooking the Cairngorms situated at north end of village.
Open: Dec to Oct
01479 810805
Mrs Cristall
D: £16.00 **S:** £18.00
Beds: 1T 1D **Baths:** 2 En
🅿 (3) 📺 🐕 📖 🕏

High season, bank holidays and special events mean low availability anywhere

---

Badachro

NG7773 🍺 *Badachro Inn*

Lochside, *Aird Road, Badachro, Gairloch, Wester Ross, IV21 2AB.*
Open: All Year
Grades: STB 3 Star
01445 741295 Mrs Foster
D: £21.00–£22.00
Beds: 1F 1D **Baths:** 2 En
🛏 🅿 ⅍ 📺 📖 🕏

All rooms face south across beautiful sheltered Badachro Bay with its many boats to the Torridon Mountains and the village with its unique Inn serving excellent food. Large sized bedrooms with large superior bathrooms. Exclusive situation with immediate shoreline access.

Badcall (Scourie)

NC1542 🍺 *Scourie Hotel, Anchorage Rest*

Mountain View, *Upper Badcall, Scourie, Lairg, Sutherland, IV27 4TH.*
All rooms overlooking beautiful Badcall Bay. Near village, bird sanctuary.
Open: All Year
01971 502343
Mrs Macleod
olivmcl@aol.com
D: £15.50 **S:** £25.00
Beds: 1F 1T 1D **Baths:** 2 Sh
🛏 🅿 (3) 📺 ✕ 📖 🕏

Baddidarroch

NC0822

Veyatie, *66 Baddidarroch, Lochinver, Lairg, Sutherland, IV27 4LP.*
Veyatie is a modern bungalow situated in a beautiful, peaceful setting.
Open: All Year (not Xmas)
Grades: STB 4 Star
01571 844424
Mrs Chapman
veyatie@baddid.freeserve.co.uk
D: £20.00–£25.00 **S:** £30.00–£50.00
Beds: 2D 1T **Baths:** 2 En 1 Pr
🅿 (3) ⅍ 📺 🐕 📖 🕏

Ballachulish

NN0858   🍷 *Glencoe Hotel, Laroch Bar*

Fern Villa Guest House, *Loanfern, Ballachulish, Argyll, PH49 4JE.*
Open: All Year
Grades: STB 3 Star, AA 4 Diamond
01855 811393 Mr Chandler
Fax: 01855 811727
fernvilla@aol.com
D: £20.00–£22.00 **S:** £25.00–£27.00
Beds: 3D 2T **Baths:** 5 En
🛇 🅿 (5) ⅙ 📺 ✕ 🛏. Ⅵ ♨
A warm welcome awaits you in this beautifully upgraded Victorian house. The village is surrounded by the spectacular lochs & mountains of Glencoe. Natural cooking of Scotland forms the basis of our home made dinner menus. Non-smoking.

Lyn Leven Guest House, *West Laroch, Ballachulish, Argyll, PA39 4JP.*
Very warm Highland welcome in modern comfortable family-run award-winning guest house. **Open:** All Year
Grades: STB 4 Star, AA 4 Diamond, RAC 4 Diamond
01855 811392 Mrs Macleod
Fax: 01855 811600
D: £20.00–£25.00 **S:** £25.00–£30.00
Beds: 4F 4D 4T **Baths:** 12 En
🛇 🅿 (10) 📺 🐕 ✕ 🛏. Ⅵ ♨ cc

Riverside House, *Ballachulish, Argyll, PH49 4JE.*
Spacious rooms in modern house overlooking river mountains and loch.
Open: Easter to Oct
Grades: STB 3 Star
01855 811473 Mrs Watt
D: £16.00–£20.00 **S:** £18.00–£22.00
Beds: 2D 1T **Baths:** 1 En 1 Sh
🛇 (2) 🅿 (4) ⅙ 📺 🛏. ♨

High season, bank holidays and special events mean low availability anywhere

---

Inverlaroch, *Albert Road, Ballachulish, Argyll, PH49 4JR.*
Modern, comfortable, spacious, homely bungalow. Excellent for walking and climbing.
Open: All Year (not Xmas)
01855 811726 Mrs Castles
inverlaroch@talk21.com
D: £17.00–£21.00 **S:** £34.00–£42.00
Beds: 1F 1D 1T **Baths:** 3 En
🛇 (3) 🅿 (5) ⅙ 📺 🛏. ♨

Tigh Ard, *Brecklet, Ballachulish, Argyll, PA39 4JG.*
Lovely family bungalow panoramic view, private parking.
Open: Easter to Sep
01855 811328 Mrs Dow
D: £16.00
Beds: 1D 1T **Baths:** 2 Sh
🅿 (2) ⅙ 📺 🛏.

Balnain

NH4430

Glenurquhart House Hotel, *Balnain, Drumnadrochit, Inverness, IV63 6TJ.*
In a scenic location between Loch Ness and Glen Affric.
Open: Mar to Dec
Grades: STB 3 Star
01456 476234 C Hughes
D: £25.00–£35.00 **S:** £25.00–£40.00
Beds: 2F 2D 2T 2S **Baths:** 6 En 1 Sh
🛇 🅿 (8) 📺 ✕ 🛏. Ⅵ ♨ cc

Banavie

NN1177   🍷 *Moorings Hotel, Lochy Bar*

Rushfield House, *Tomonie, Banavie, Fort William, Inverness-shire, PH33 7LX.*
Modern house with excellent views of Ben Nevis situated 3 miles from Fort William.
Open: Mar to Oct
Grades: STB 3 Star
01397 772063 Ms Corbett
rushbb0063@aol.com
D: £18.00–£25.00
Beds: 2F 1D **Baths:** 3 En
🛇 🅿 (3) ⅙ 📺 🛏. Ⅵ ♨

New House, *Shenghan Bridge, Banavie,*
Fort William, Inverness-shire, PH33 7PB.
Open: March to Nov
01397 772228 Miss Ross
shenghan-chalets@
fortwilliam59.freeserve.co.uk
D: £18.00–£20.00 **S:** £18.00
Beds: 1T 1D **Baths:** 2 En
☒ ⅀ ⅏ ♉ ✕ ▥ Ⅴ ♨ cc
Stunning views to Ben Nevis and Anoch
Moe. Friendly family atmosphere. Situated
on the banks of the Caledonian Canal.
Converted barn restaurant adjacent to the
Bed & Breakfast.

Grianan, *4 Lochiel Crescent, Banavie, Fort*
William, Inverness-shire, PH33 7LZ.
Situated by Caledonian Canal. Fine views
towards Ben Nevis.
Open: May to Sept
Grades: STB 3 Star
01397 772659 Mrs Maclean
imacleangrianan@hotmail.com
D: £15.00–£17.00 **S:** £18.00–£23.50
Beds: 1D 1F
☒ (5) ᴘ (3) ⅏ ♉ ▥ ♨ ♿

Quaich Cottage, *Upper Banavie, Banavie,*
Fort William, Inverness-shire, PH33 7LX.
Modern home on an elevated rural site.
Spacious accommodation and a warm
welcome. **Open:** All Year (not Xmas)
01397 772799 (also fax)
D: £17.00–£20.00 **S:** £25.00–£35.00
Beds: 1F 1D 1T **Baths:** 3 En
☒ (8) ᴘ (3) ⅏ ▥ Ⅴ ♨

Beauly

NH5246 ⬤ *Old Arms Hotel, North Kessock*
Hotel, Moorings Hotel, Achilty Hotel

Hillview Park, *Muir of Ord, Ross-shire,*
IV6 7XS.
Rural situation, adjacent to golf course.
Ground floor bungalow.
Open: Easter to Oct
Grades: STB 3 Star
01463 870787 Mrs Peterkin
D: £17.00–£19.00 **S:** £18.00–£20.00
Beds: 1F 1D 1T **Baths:** 3 En
ᴘ (3) ⅀ ⅏ ▥ ♨

Planning a longer stay?
Always ask for any special rates

Bettyhill

NC7061

Shenley, *Bettyhill, Thurso, Caithness,*
KW14 7SS.
Ideal centre for touring North Highlands,
river and sandy beaches.
Open: Easter to Oct
01641 521421 Mrs Allan
D: £12.50–£18.00 **S:** £12.50–£18.00
Beds: 2T 1S **Baths:** 2 Sh
☒ (5) ᴘ ⅏ ♉ ✕ ▥ ♨

Boat of Garten

NH9418 ⬤ *Boat, Craigard Hotel, Heatherbank,*
Lisi's

The Old Ferrymans House, *Boat of*
Garten, Inverness-shire, PH24 3BY.
Open: All Year
01479 831370 (also fax)
Ms Matthews
D: £19.50 **S:** £19.50
Beds: 1T 1D 2S **Baths:** 2 Sh
☒ ᴘ (4) ⅀ ♉ ✕ ▥ Ⅴ ♨
Which? Recommended former ferryman's
house, just across River Spey from village,
welcoming, homely, comfortable. Sitting
room with wood stove, many books, no TV.
No set breakfast times, home-cooked meals
with Highland specialities. Numerous walks,
beautiful Strathspey countryside and
Cairngorm mountains, castles, distilleries.

Avingormack Guest House, *Boat of*
Garten, Inverness-shire, PH24 3BT.
Breathtaking views of the mountains, award
winning food - just perfect.
Open: All Year
Grades: STB 3 Star
01479 831614 Mrs Ferguson
avin.gormack@ukgateway.net
D: £19.00–£22.00 **S:** £19.50
Beds: 1F 2D 1T **Baths:** 2 En 1 Sh
☒ ᴘ (6) ⅀ ⅏ ✕ ▥ Ⅴ ♨ cc

Chapelton Steading, *Boat Of Garten, Inverness-shire, PH24 3BU.*
Spacious rural retreat. Charming garden with views of Cairngorm Mountains.
Open: March to Nov **Grades:** STB 4 Star
01479 831327 Mrs Smyth
chapelton@btinternet.com
D: £21.00–£22.00 **S:** £23.00–£25.00
Beds: 2T 1D **Baths:** 3 En
🛏 (10) 🅿 (4) ✕ 📺 ♨

Heathbank - The Victorian House,
Drumuillie Road, Boat of Garten, Inverness-shire, PH24 3BD.
Beautiful of character, house full of curiosities; each bedroom different in style and atmosphere. **Open:** All Year
01479 831234 Mr Burge
quirky@heathbank32.freeserve.co.uk
D: £25.00–£35.00 **S:** £30.00–£50.00
Beds: 5D 2T **Baths:** 7 En
🛏 (8) 🅿 (8) ✕ 📺 ✕ 🖿 📺 ♨

Bonar Bridge
NH6191 ⬤ *Dornoch Bridge Inn, Lady Ross, The Dunroamin*

Kyle House, *Dornoch Road, Bonar Bridge, Ardgay, Sutherland, IV24 3EB.*
Superb old Scottish house offering excellent accommodation. Ideal touring base.
Open: Feb to Nov
Grades: AA 3 Diamond, RAC 3 Diamond
01863 766360 (also fax) Mrs Thomson
kyle.hse@talk21.com
D: £19.00–£22.00 **S:** £24.00
Beds: 2F 1D 2T 1S **Baths:** 3 En 1 Sh
🛏 (4) 🅿 (6) ✕ 📺 🖿 ♨

Braes of Ullapool
NH1493 ⬤ *Argyll Hotel*

Blawearie, *16 Corry Heights, Braes of Ullapool, Ullapool, Ross-shire, IV26 2SZ.*
Modern detached house with spectacular lochside views and warm hospitality.
Open: May to Sep
01854 612790 Mrs Clark
D: £16.00–£18.00 **S:** £16.00–£18.00
Beds: 1D 1T 1S **Baths:** 2 Sh
🛏 🅿 (3) ✕ 📺 ✕ 🖿 📺 ♨

Brora
NC9004 ⬤ *Royal Marine Hotel, Links Hotel, Sutherland Arms*

Non Smokers Haven, *Tigh Fada, 18 Golf Road, Brora, Sutherland, KW9 6QS.*
Top quality welcoming home. Also self-catering, prime seaside location.
Open: All Year (not Xmas/New Year)
Grades: STB 4 Star
01408 621332 (also fax)
Mr & Mrs Clarkson
D: £18.00 **S:** £20.00
Beds: 1D 2T **Baths:** 1 En 2 Pr
🛏 (5) 🅿 (6) ✕ 📺 🖿 ♨

Glenaveron, *Golf Road, Brora, Sutherland, KW9 6QS.*
Open: All Year
Grades: STB 4 Star, AA 4 Diamond
01408 621601 (also fax)
Mr Fortune
glenaveron@hotmail.com
D: £24.00–£28.00 **S:** £28.00–£34.00
Beds: 1F 1D 1T **Baths:** 3 En
🛏 🅿 (3) ✕ 📺 🖿 ♨ 🐾 2 cc
A luxurious Edwardian house in mature gardens close to Brora golf club and beaches. Only a 25 minute drive to the famous Royal Dornoch golf club. Ideal base for touring the Highlands and Orkney. Non smoking. Friendly family home.

Ar Dachaidh, *Badnellan, Brora, Sutherland, KW9 6NQ.*
Traditional croft house, quiet crofting area, ideal golf, fishing, touring.
Open: Mar to Nov
Grades: STB 2 Star
01408 621658 (also fax)
Ms MacDonald
badnellan@madasafish.com
D: £17.00 **S:** £17.00
Beds: 1D 1T 1S **Baths:** 1 Sh
🛏 (12) 🅿 (3) 📺 🐾 ✕ 🖿 📺

Bringing children with you?
Always ask for any special rates

Carrbridge

NH9022 ◖ *Cairn Hotel, Rowanlea, Struan Hotel*

Cairn Hotel, *Main Road, Carrbridge, Inverness-shire, PH23 3AS.*
Open: All Year (not Xmas)
Grades: STB 3 Star
01479 841212 Mr Kirk
Fax: 01479 841362
cairn.carrbridge@talk21.com
D: £19.00–£22.00 **S:** £19.00–£26.00
Beds: 2F 2D 1T 2S **Baths:** 4 En 1 Sh
ॐ ℗ (15) ⊡ ≟ cc
Enjoy the country pub atmosphere; log fire, malt whiskies, real ales and affordable food in this family-owned village centre hotel close to the historic bridge. A perfect base for touring Cairngorms, Loch Ness, Whisky Trail and beyond.

Carrmoor Guest House, *Carr Road, Carrbridge, Inverness-shire, PH23 3AD.*
Licensed, family-run, warm welcome. Popular restaurant, chef proprietor.
Open: All Year
Grades: STB 3 Star, AA 4 Diamond
01479 841244 (also fax)
Mrs Stitt
christine@carrmoorguesthouse.co.uk
D: £19.50–£21.50 **S:** £22.00
Beds: 1F 3D 2T **Baths:** 6 En
ॐ ℗ (6) ⊡ ┮ ✗ ▥ Ⓥ ✻ ≟ cc

Craigellachie House, *Main Street, Carrbridge, Inverness-shire, PH23 3AS.*
Traditional house in centre of small Highland village on main tourist routes.
Open: All Year
Grades: STB 3 Star GH
01479 841641 Mrs Pedersen
e.pedersen@talk21.com
D: £16.00–£19.00 **S:** £16.00–£25.00
Beds: 2F 2D 2T 1S **Baths:** 3 En 2 Sh
ॐ ℗ (8) ⅟ ⊡ ✗ ▥ Ⓥ ≟ cc

High season, bank holidays and special events mean low availability anywhere

Camusteel

NG7042 ◖ *Applecross Inn, Flower Tunnel*

Raon Mor, *Camusteel, Applecross, Strathcarron, Ross-shire, IV54 8LT.*
Modern croft house wonderful views. Ideal for hill walking and wildlife.
Open: May to Oct
01520 744260 Mrs Thompson
D: £14.50–£15.00
Beds: 2D 1T **Baths:** 1 Sh
ॐ ℗ (3) ⊡ ▥ Ⓥ

Canisbay

ND3472

Bencorragh House, *Upper Gills, Canisbay, John o' Groats, Wick, Caithness, KW1 4YB.*
Working croft. Panoramic views across Pentland Firth near seasonal Orkney ferry.
Open: Mar to Oct
Grades: STB 3 Star, AA 3 Diamond
01955 611449 (also fax)
Mrs Barton
D: £20.00–£21.00 **S:** £23.00–£25.00
Beds: 1F 2D 1T **Baths:** 4 En
ॐ (5) ℗ (6) ⅟ ⊡ ┮ ✗ ▥ Ⓥ ≟ cc

Caol

NN1076 ◖ *Lochy Bar*

Connamara, *27 Camaghael Road, Caol, Fort William, PH33 7HU.*
The front of the house faces Ben Nevis, back looks onto Caledonian Canal.
Open: All Year
Grades: STB 2 Star
01397 702901 Mrs Mcginlay
Fax: 01397 700566
e.mcginlay@amserve.net
D: £17.00–£18.00 **S:** £20.00–£25.00
Beds: 2F
ॐ ℗ ⅟ ⊡ ≟

Planning a longer stay?
Always ask for any special rates

Pine Ridge, Carrbridge, Inverness-shire,
PH23 3AA.
Pine Ridge is a beautiful 100 year old home.
Open: All Year
01479 841646 Mrs Weston
jane.weston@tesco.net
D: £16.00–£20.00 **S:** £20.00–£25.00
Beds: 1F 1D 1T **Baths:** 1 En 1 Sh
ॐ 🅿 (6) ⅍ 🖵 🛏 🚪, ♨

Castletown (Thurso)

ND1967 ⚓ *Northern Sands Hotel*

Greenland House, Main Street,
Castletown, Thurso, Caithness, *KW14 8TU.*
Greenland Guest House is a Victorian period
house, restored retaining many original
features.
Open: All Year (not Xmas)
01847 821694 (also fax) Y Pollard
dgpolla@aol.com
D: £16.00–£20.00 **S:** £20.00–£25.00
Beds: 3D 2T **Baths:** 3 En 2 Sh
ॐ 🅿 ⅍ 🖵 🛏 🚪, Ⅴ ♨

Cawdor

NH8449 ⚓ *Cawdor Tavern*

Dallaschyle, Cawdor, Nairn, *IV12 5XS.*
A gardener's delight. Only birds and wildlife
disturb the peace. **Open:** All Year
01667 493422 Mrs MacLeod
Fax: 01667 493638
bookings@dallaschyle.fsnet.co.uk
D: £17.00 **S:** £25.00–£20.00
Beds: 1F 1D 1S **Baths:** 2 Sh
ॐ (2) 🅿 (4) ⅍ 🖵 🚪, ♨ ♿ cc

Conon Bridge

NH5455 ⚓ *Conon Bridge Hotel*

Conon Bridge Hotel, Conon Bridge,
Dingwall, Ross-shire, *IV7 8HD.*
Charming Scottish Highland inn offering
excellent comfort & fresh traditional food.
Open: All Year
01349 861500 Mr Jack
D: £17.50–£20.00 **S:** £21.00–£23.00
Beds: 1F 5D 2T 5S
ॐ 🅿 (20) 🖵 🛏 ✕ 🚪, Ⅴ ♨ cc

Contin

NH4555 ⚓ *Achilty Hotel*

Millbrae, Contin, Strathpeffer, Ross-shire,
IV14 9EB.
Traditional highland house, 100 years old,
relax in peace, watch wildlife, feel welcome.
Open: All Year
01997 421368 Mrs Redfern
D: £13.50–£15.00 **S:** £20.00
Beds: 1F 1D **Baths:** 1 Sh
ॐ 🅿 (4) 🖵 🛏 🚪, Ⅴ ♨

Corpach

NN0976 ⚓ *Lochy Bar, Mooring Hotel*

Ben Nevis View, Corpach, Fort William,
Inverness-shire, PH33 7JH.
Modern, comfortable house, 5 minutes by
car from Fort William.
Open: Mar to Oct
Grades: STB 3 Star
01397 772131 Mrs Mooney
D: £18.00–£20.00 **S:** £20.00–£25.00
Beds: 1F 1D **Baths:** 2 En
🅿 (4) ⅍ 🖵 🚪, ♨

The Neuk, Corpach, Fort William, Inverness-
shire, *PH33 7LR.*
Modern, privately run, home cooking. Views
over Ben Nevis. Private garden.
Open: All Year (not Xmas)
Grades: STB 2 Star
01397 772244 Mrs McCallum
D: £18.00–£24.00 **S:** £27.00–£36.00
Beds: 2F 1D 1T **Baths:** 4 En
ॐ 🅿 (6) ⅍ 🖵 🛏 ✕ 🚪, Ⅴ ♨

Heston, Corpach, Fort William, Inverness-
shire, *PH33 7LT.*
Comfortable house with excellent views on
road to the Isles.
Open: March - November
Grades: STB 2 Star
01397 772425 Mrs Wynne
D: £18.00–£20.00 **S:** £22.00
Beds: 1F 1D 1T **Baths:** 2 En
ॐ (3) 🅿 (3) ⅍ 🖵 🛏 🚪, ♨

Croachy

NH6427 ◀ *Dores Inn*

The Old Parsonage, *Croachy, Inverness,*
IV2 6UE.
Our family-run guest house offers superior
accommodation. Ensuite rooms, lounge and
large garden room.
Open: All Year
01808 521441 (also fax)
Isabell Steel
D: £17.50–£25.00 **S:** £20.00–£27.00
Beds: 3D **Baths:** 2 En 1 Pr
🛏 🅿 (6) 📺 🐕 🛋 🍽 cc

Culloden Moor

NH7345 ◀ *Cawdor Tavern, Culloden Moor Inn*

Westhill House, *Westhill, Inverness, IV1 5BP.*
Open: Easter to Oct
Grades: STB 2 Star
01463 793225 Mrs Honnor
Fax: 01463 792503
janethon@piccolopress.demon.co.uk
D: £18.00–£20.00 **S:** £16.00–£18.00
Beds: 1F 1T 1S **Baths:** 2 En 1 Sh
🛏 🅿 (4) ⚡ 📺 🐕 🛋 🍽
Spacious, comfortable family home in lovely
garden amidst trees, wildlife and glorious
views. One mile Culloden Battlefield, three
miles Inverness. Perfect for touring
Highlands.

Culdoich Farm, *Culloden Muir, Inverness,*
IV2 5EL.
Old farmhouse in peaceful surroundings.
Good farmhouse cooking.
Open: May to Oct
Grades: STB 3 Star
01463 790268 Mrs Alexander
D: £17.00 **S:** £34.00
Beds: 1F 1T/D **Baths:** 1 Sh
🛏 🅿 📺 🍽

All details shown are as
supplied by B&B owners in
Autumn 2000

Dalcross

NH7748 ◀ *Gun Lodge*

Easter Dalziel Farm, *Dalcross, Inverness,*
IV2 7JL.
Lovely Victorian farmhouse home on a
working stock/arable farm.
Open: All Year (not Xmas/New Year)
01667 462213 (also fax)
Mrs Pottie
D: £17.00–£20.00 **S:** £20.00–£28.00
Beds: 2D 1T **Baths:** 2 Sh
🛏 🅿 (6) 📺 🐕 🍽 🛋 📺 🍽 cc

Daviot

NH7239 ◀ *Deerstalker, Tomatin Inn*

Torguish House, *Daviot, Inverness, IV2 5XQ.*
Former manse set in quiet rural area,
childhood home of late author Alistair
McLean.
Open: All Year
01463 772208
Mr & Mrs Allan
Fax: 01463 772308
amallan@torguish.com
D: £16.00–£22.00 **S:** £20.00–£25.00
Beds: 3F 3D 1T **Baths:** 5 En 2 Pr
🛏 🅿 (20) 📺 🐕 🛋 📺 🍽

Delny

NH7372 ◀ *Johnnny Foxes*

Under Beechwood, *Delny, Kilmvir Easter,*
Ross-shire, IV18 0NW.
Open: Feb to Nov
01862 842685
Mrs Horn
D: £16.00–£17.00 **S:** £16.00–£17.00
Beds: 1F 1T 1D 1S **Baths:** 1 Sh
🛏 🅿 (6) ⚡ 📺 🐕 🍽 🛋 📺 🍽
Overlooking Cromarty Firth offering
Traditional and friendly accommodation with
good cooking and baking. Babies free.
Children from 3 yrs sharing half price. Ideal
for touring north and west coasts. Excellent
golf, fishing, hill walking, dolphin sea trips.
Beautiful beaches.

Diabaig

NG7960

Ben Bhraggie, *Diabaig, Torridon,*
Achnasheen, Ross-shire, IV22 2HE.
Comfortable homely cottage - fishing and
hill walkers paradise.
Open: Easter to Nov
01445 790268 Mrs Ross
D: £14.00 **S:** £14.00
Beds: 1D 1T
🛏 (3) 🅿 (4) ⅍ 📺 ✕ ▦ 📺 ₠

Dornie

NG8826

Castle View, *Upper Ardelve, Dornie, Kyle of*
Lochalsh, Ross-shire, IV40 8EY.
Outstanding views across Loch Alsh to
Eilean Donan, Loch Duich, Five Sisters of
Kintail. **Open:** Easter to Oct
01599 555453 (also fax) Ms McClelland
castleview@j-c-m.freeserve.co.uk
D: £20.00
Beds: 2D 1T **Baths:** 3 En
🅿 (3) ⅍ 📺 ✕ ▦ ₠

Dornoch

NH8089 ◀ *Ragle Hotel, Castle Hotel, Sutherland*
House, Mallin House, Eagle Hotel, Grannie's
Heiland Hame

Achandean Bungalow, *The Meadows,*
Dornoch, Sutherland, IV25 3SF.
Open: Easter to Oct
Grades: AA 3 Diamond
01862 810413 (also fax)
Mrs Hellier
bhellier@lineone.net
D: £18.00–£22.00
Beds: 2D 1T **Baths:** 2 En 1 Pr
🅿 (3) 📺 🐾 ✕ ▦ ₠ 🚹
Audrey & Basil Hellier welcome you to our
lovely home. Secluded, central position.
Tastefully decorated ensuite bedrooms with
every comfort. Ideal disabled and OAPs.
Weekly rates. Reductions OAPs. Superb
touring, walks, beach, golf, birdwatching,
countryside, relaxation. Private parking. EM
available.

Amalfi, *River Street, Dornoch, Sutherland,*
IV25 3LY.
Modern comfortable house alongside golf
course. Award winning beach 300m. Friendly
highland hospitality.
Open: All Year (not Xmas/New Year)
Grades: STB 3 Star
01862 810015 Mrs MacKay
mackay.amalfi@talk21.com
D: £18.00–£21.00 **S:** £20.00–£33.00
Beds: 1F 1T **Baths:** 2 En
🛏 (2) 🅿 (2) 📺 🐾 ▦ ₠

Corven, *Station Road, Embo, Dornoch,*
Sutherland, IV25 3PR.
Detached bungalow with panoramic views.
Ideal base for touring North Scotland.
Open: Feb to Nov
Grades: STB 2 Star
01862 810128 Mrs Fraser
D: £16.00 **S:** £18.00
Beds: 2D 1T **Baths:** 1 En 1 Sh
🛏 (10) 🅿 (4) ⅍ 📺 🐾 ▦ 📺 ₠ 🚹

Tordarroch, *Castle Street, Dornoch,*
Sutherland, IV25 3SN.
Traditional stone built house set within
walled gardens, ensuring peace & quiet.
Open: Easter to Oct
Grades: STB 3 Star
01862 810855 Mrs Matherson
D: £19.00–£21.00 **S:** £19.00–£21.00
Beds: 1D 1T 1S **Baths:** 1 En 1 Pr 1 Sh
🅿 (3) ⅍ 📺 🐾 ▦ ₠ 🚹

Rosslyn Villa, *Castle Street, Dornoch,*
Sutherland, IV25 3SR.
Comfortable ensuite rooms (non-smoking).
Beautiful scenery, beach, golf and wildlife.
Open: All Year
01862 810237 Mr Miles
D: £15.00–£19.00 **S:** £15.00–£19.00
Beds: 1D 1T 1S **Baths:** 2 En 1 Pr
🛏 (1) ⅍ 📺 ₠

Planning a longer stay?
Always ask for any special rates

Drumbuie

NG7731 ◀ *Plockton Inn, Plockton Hotel, Off The Rails, Old School House, Tingle Creek Hotel*

Glenmarvin, *Drumbuie, Kyle of Lochalsh, Ross-shire, IV40 8BD.*
Modern crofthouse in picturesque village between Plockton and Kyle of Lochalsh.
Open: All Year
01599 544380 (also fax) Mrs Finlayson
D: £18.00
Beds: 1F 1T **Baths:** 2 En
🛏 🅿 (3) ⅍ 📺 🛁 Ⓥ ♨

Drumnadrochit

NH5030 ◀ *Fiddlers, Hunters Bar, Drumnadrochit Hotel*

Ferness Cottage, *Lewiston, Drumnadrochit, Inverness, IV3 6UW.*
200 year old cottage within walking distance of Loch Ness.
Open: Easter to Oct **Grades:** STB 3 Star
01456 450564 Mrs Campbell
ferness@freezone.co.uk
D: £18.00–£25.00 **S:** £20.00–£30.00
Beds: 1F 1T 2D **Baths:** 4 En

Westwood, *Lower Balmacaan, Drumnadrochit, Inverness, IV63 6WU.*
Comfortable bungalow near Loch Ness. Ideal walking and touring base. **Open:** All Year
Grades: STB 3 Star B&B
01456 450826 (also fax) S Silke
sandra@westwoodbb.freeserve.co.uk
D: £17.00–£21.00 **S:** £20.00
Beds: 1D 1T 1S **Baths:** 2 En 1 Sh
🛏 (8) 🅿 (4) 📺 ♞ ✕ 🛁 Ⓥ ♨ cc

Glen Rowan House, *West Lewiston, Drumnadrochit, Inverness, IV63 6UW.*
Very comfortable riverside village house near Urquhart Castle, Monster Exhibition.
Open: All Year (not Xmas)
01456 450235 Mrs Harrod
Fax: 01456 450817
glenrowan@loch-ness.demon.co.uk
D: £16.00–£25.00 **S:** £25.00–£42.00
Beds: 1D 2T **Baths:** 3 Pr
🛏 🅿 ⅍ 📺 ✕ 🛁 Ⓥ ♨ ♿

Twin Birches, *Milton, Drumnadrochit, IV63 6UA.*
Homely, good breakfast, comfortable rooms. Loch Ness, Urquhart Castle nearby.
Open: All Year (not Xmas/New Year)
01456 450359 Mrs Seeburg
D: £15.00–£16.00 **S:** £17.50–£18.00
Beds: 1T 1D
🅿 (3) ⅍ 📺 🛁

Bridgend House, *The Green, Drumnadrochit, Inverness, IV63 6TX.*
Highland home overlooking village green. Comfortable rooms. Imaginative evening meals. **Open:** Feb to Dec
Grades: STB 3 Star
01456 450865 (also fax) Mrs Luffman
D: £18.00–£22.00 **S:** £18.00–£20.00
Beds: 1F/T 1D 1S **Baths:** 1 En 1 Sh
🛏 (10) 🅿 (5) ⅍ 📺 ♞ ✕ Ⓥ ♨

Gillyflowers, *Drumnadrochit, Inverness, IV63 6UJ.*
Renovated C18th farmhouse in beautiful rural setting.
Open: All Year **Grades:** STB 3 Star
01456 450641 (also fax) J Benzie
gillyflowers@cali.co.uk
D: £14.00–£18.00 **S:** £20.00–£28.00
Beds: 2D 1T **Baths:** 1 En 1 Sh
🛏 (7) 🅿 (3) ⅍ 📺 🛁 Ⓥ ♨

Drumsmittal

NH6449 ◀ *North Kessock Hotel*

Culbin Drumsmittal Croft, *Drumsmittal, North Kessock, Inverness, IV1 3XF.*
Open: All Year (not Xmas)
Grades: STB 2 Star
01463 731455 (also fax) Mrs Ross
ian-eliz@rossculbin.freeserve.co.uk
D: £15.00–£18.00
Beds: 1F 1T 1D **Baths:** 1 Pr 1 Sh
🛏 🅿 (4) ⅍ 📺 🛁 ♨
Situated on a Highland working croft. Set in beautiful countryside and making the Ideal touring base for seeing what the Scottish Highlands and Islands offer - Moray Firth, Dolphins, Red Kites, wildlife park, riding centre etc. Good pubs + restaurants + night clubs + theatres.

Dulnain Bridge

NH9924   ◀ *Skye of Curr Hotel, Strathspey Hotel*

Broomlands, *Dulnain Bridge, Grantown-on-Spey, Moray, PH26 3LT.*
Open: Easter to Sept
01479 851255
Mrs Noble
ernest@noble56.fsnet.co.uk
D: £16.00–£17.00 **S:** £16.00–£20.00
Beds: 1F 1D 1S **Baths:** 1 Sh
♿ P (4) 📺 ⽝ ✕ 🛏.
A Traditional Scottish house in a quiet village. Ideal centre for touring the highlands. Close to Cairngorm Mountains, walks, distilleries. Several good golf courses. Fishing and bird watching.

Auchendean Lodge, *Dulnain Bridge, Grantown-on-Spey, Moray, PH26 3LU.*
A popular and friendly country house hotel in a sensational setting.
Open: All Year
Grades: STB 4 Star
01479 851347 (also fax)
Mr Kirk
hotel@auchendean.com
D: £35.00–£47.00 **S:** £37.00–£58.00
Beds: 1F 1T 2D 1S **Baths:** 5 En
♿ P (8) 📺 ⽝ ✕ 🛏. 🅅 ❋ 🏌 ⅙ cc

Durness

NC4067   ◀ *Parkill Hotel, Smoo Cave Hotel, Sango Sands*

Glengolly House, *Durine, Durness, Lairg, Sutherland, IV27 4PN.*
Open: All Year
01971 511255 (also fax)
Mr Mackay
D: £16.00–£18.00 **S:** £18.00–£20.00
Beds: 1F 1T 1D
Baths: 1 En 1 Pr 1 Sh
♿ P (4) ✂ 📺 🛏. 🅅 🏌
Prepare to be enchanted by spectacular sunsets and breathtaking scenery. Come and stay at a traditional croft where you can watch Border Collies at work or listen to the corncrake. Enjoy outdoor pursuits in an area steeped in history.

Port Na Con House, *Loch Eriboll, Lairg, Sutherland, IV27 4UN.*
Open: All Year
Grades: AA 4 Diamond
01971 511367 (also fax)
Mrs Black
portnacon70@hotmail.com
D: £19.00–£20.00 **S:** £27.00–£28.00
Beds: 1F 2D 1T **Baths:** 1 En 1 Pr 1 Sh
♿ P (4) ✂ ⽝ ✕ 🛏. 🅅 🏌 cc
Former customs house, sited on the shore of Loch Eriboll. All rooms overlook the sea and our raised conservatory offers magnificent views to Ben Hope (the most far Northerly Munro) and Ben Loyal. We have a restricted Licence.

Puffin Cottage, *Durness, Lairg, Sutherland, IV27 4PN.*
Close to the village with spectacular sea and country views.
Open: Easter to Oct
Grades: STB 3 Star
01971 511208 (also fax)
Mrs Frazer
puffincottage@aol.com
D: £17.00–£21.00 **S:** £25.00–£30.00
Beds: 2D **Baths:** 1 En 1 Sh
P (2) ✂ 📺 🛏. 🏌

Duthil

NH9324

The Pines Country House, *Duthil, Carrbridge, Inverness-shire, PH23 3ND.*
Relax and enjoy our Highland hospitality. Set in mature woodlands where nature comes alive.
Open: All Year
01479 841220 Mrs Benge
thepines@dbenge.freeserve.co.uk
D: £19.00–£20.00 **S:** £21.50–£22.50
Beds: 1F 2D 1T **Baths:** 4 En
♿ P ✂ 📺 ⽝ ✕ 🛏. 🅅 ❋ 🏌

All details shown are as
supplied by B&B owners in
Autumn 2000

Planning a longer stay?
Always ask for any special rates

Embo

NH8193 🍷 *Grannie's Heiland Hame*

Corven, *Station Road, Embo, Dornoch,*
Sutherland, IV25 3PR.
Detached bungalow with panoramic views.
Ideal base for touring North Scotland.
Open: Feb to Nov
Grades: STB 2 Star
01862 810128 Mrs Fraser
D: £16.00 **S:** £18.00
Beds: 2D 1T **Baths:** 1 En 1 Sh
🛏 (10) 🅿 (4) ⌇ 📺 🐾 ▥ Ⅴ ☕ ᎑

Feshiebridge

NH8504

Balcraggan House, *Feshiebridge, Kincraig,*
Kingussie, Inverness-shire, PH21 1NG.
Wonderful setting where wildlife, walks and
cycle routes abound.
Open: All Year
01540 651488 Mrs Gillies
D: £25.00 **S:** £30.00–£35.00
Beds: 1D 1T **Baths:** 2 En
🛏 (10) 🅿 (3) ⌇ 📺 ✕ ▥ Ⅴ ☕

Fort Augustus

NH3709 🍷 *Lock Inn, Lovat Arms, Bothy*

Lorien House, *Station Road, Fort*
Augustus, Inverness-shire, PH32 4AY.
Open: All Year
Grades: STB 2 Star
01320 366736 E Dickie
Fax: 01320 366263
lorienhouse@aol.com
D: £20.00–£25.00 **S:** £25.00–£30.00
Beds: 3D 2T **Baths:** 2 En
🅿 (2) ⌇ 📺 🐾 ▥ Ⅴ ☕
Excellent full Scottish, Continental or fresh
fruits breakfasts. Central for sightseeing
Inverness, Ben Nevis, Isle of Skye, Aonach
Mor skiing. Great pubs and restaurants
nearby.

Caledonian Hotel, *Fort Augustus,*
Inverness-shire, PH32 4BQ.
Typical small highland hotel centrally
positioned for exploring Scotland.
Open: Easter to Oct.
Grades: STB 2 Star
01320 366256 J M MacLellan
Fax: 0870 284 1287
hotel-scotland.co.uk
D: £20.00–£30.00 **S:** £25.00–£35.00
Beds: 3F 3T 5D **Baths:** 7 En 2 Sh
🛏 (10) 🅿 (20) ⌇ 📺 ✕ ▥ Ⅴ ☕ cc

Tigh Na Mairi, *Canalside, Fort Augustus,*
Inverness-shire, PH32 4BA.
Stunning views all rooms ideal for Nessie
hunting very welcoming.
Open: Easter to Oct
Grades: STB 2 Star
01320 366766 (also fax)
S V Callcutt
D: £11.00–£22.00 **S:** £14.00–£30.00
Beds: 2D 1T **Baths:** 1 Sh
🛏 (8) 🅿 (2) ⌇ 📺 ▥ Ⅴ ☕

Fort William

NN1073 🍷 *Moorings Hotel, Lochy Bar, Nevis*
Bank Hotel, Glen Nevis Rest, Cafe Beag, Pat's Bar,
Grogg & Gruel, Ben Nevis Rest, West End

Glenlochy Guest House, *Nevis Bridge,*
Fort William, Inverness-shire, PH33 6PF.
Open: All Year
Grades: STB 3 Star, AA 3 Diamond
01397 702909 Mrs MacBeth
D: £17.00
Beds: 1F 4D 5T **Baths:** 8 En 1 Sh
🛏 🅿 (14) 📺 ▥ ❀ ☕
Situated 0.5 mile north of Fort William town
centre, close to Ben Nevis. The famous West
Highland walk ends at our guest house
grounds. 8 of 10 bedrooms are ensuite. Large
private car park.

BATHROOMS
Pr - Private
Sh - Shared
En - Ensuite

Alltonside, *Achintore Road, Fort William, Inverness-shire, PH33 6RW.*
Open: All Year **Grades:** STB 3 Star
01397 703542 (also fax) Mrs Allton
altonside@aol.com
D: £16.00 **S:** £20.00
Beds: 1F 3D 2T **Baths:** 6 Pr
🛏 🅿 (8) 📺 🐾 🛋 Ⓥ ❋ 🔔
Alltonside guest house commands magnificent views over Loch Linnhe to the hills beyond. Being close to the town of Fort William and Ben Nevis makes it an ideal base for sightseeing and visiting the many beautiful places in the Highlands.

Rushfield House, *Tomonie, Banavie, Fort William, Inverness-shire, PH33 7LX.*
Modern house with excellent views of Ben Nevis situated 3 miles from Fort William.
Open: Mar to Oct
Grades: STB 3 Star
01397 772063 Ms Corbett
rushbb0063@aol.com
D: £18.00–£25.00
Beds: 2F 1D **Baths:** 3 En
🛏 🅿 (3) ✄ 📺 🛋 Ⓥ 🔔

Ben Nevis View, *Corpach, Fort William, Inverness-shire, PH33 7JH.*
Open: Mar to Oct
Grades: STB 3 Star
01397 772131 Mrs Mooney
D: £18.00–£20.00 **S:** £20.00–£25.00
Beds: 1F 1D **Baths:** 2 En
🅿 (4) ✄ 📺 🛋 🔔
Modern, comfortable house, 5 minutes by car from Fort William.

Ossian's Hotel, *High Street, Fort William, Inverness-shire, PH33 6DH.*
Open: All Year
01397 700857 J Wallace
Fax: 01397 701030
ossiansfw@aol.com
D: £16.00–£25.00 **S:** £18.00–£32.00
Beds: 10F 10D 10T 5S **Baths:** 32 En 3 Sh
🛏 🅿 📺 🐾 ✕ 🛋 Ⓥ 🔔
Accommodation, food and drink for the budget traveller. Ideal town centre location. Couple of minutes wall from railway or bus. Warm, friendly and relaxed atmosphere.

11 Castle Drive, *Lochyside, Fort William, PH33 7NR.*
Open: All Year
Grades: STB 3 Star
01397 702659 Mrs Grant
D: £16.00–£18.00 **S:** £20.00–£24.00
Beds: 1T 1D **Baths:** 1 Sh
🛏 🅿 (2) ✄ 📺 🐾 ✕ 🛋 Ⓥ ❋ 🔔
Quiet residential area near castle. Views to Ben Nevis. Ideal base for walking, climbing, skiing. Intimate family home with cosy log fire in lounge where you can be assured of a warm and friendly welcome. Breakfast is the best in the west.

Ferndale, *Tomacharrich, Torlundy, Fort William, PH33 6SP.*
Open: All Year **Grades:** STB 3 Star
01397 703593 Mrs Riley
D: £15.00–£20.00
Beds: 1F 2D **Baths:** 2 En 1 Pr
🛏 🅿 (6) ✄ 📺 🐾 🛋 Ⓥ 🔔
Large bungalow in beautiful country setting, with wonderful views of Ben Nevis and Nevis Range Ski Slope. Ideal base for walking, cycling, skiing and touring. Pony trekking, trout fishing and golfing all nearby. Breakfast served in conservatory. Nearest B&B to skiing.

Melantee, *Achintore Road, Fort William, Inverness-shire, PH33 6RW.*
Comfortable bungalow overlooking Loch Linnhe and the Ardgour hills.
Open: All Year (not Xmas)
Grades: STB 2 Star
01397 705329 Mrs Cook
Fax: 01397 700453
D: £15.50–£16.00 **S:** £15.50–£16.00
Beds: 1F 1D 1T 1S **Baths:** 2 Sh
🛏 (5) 🅿 (6) 📺 🛋 Ⓥ 🔔

Glen Shiel Guest House, *Achintore Road, Fort William, Inverness-shire, PH33 6RW.*
Lochside location, panoramic views. Large car park. Tea makers, colour TV in all rooms.
Open: Easter to Oct
Grades: STB 2 Star
01397 702271 D: £17.00–£20.00
Beds: 1F 3D 1T **Baths:** 3 En 1 Pr 1 Sh
🛏 (8) 🅿 (7) ✄ 📺 🛋 Ⓥ 🔔

Stronchreggan View Guest House,
Achintore Road, Fort William, Inverness-shire, PH33 6RW.
Our house overlooks Loch Linnhe with views to Ardgour Hills.
Open: Easter to Oct
Grades: STB 3 Star GH
01397 704644 (also fax)
patricia@apmac.freeserve.co.uk
D: £19.00–£24.00
Beds: 5D 2T **Baths:** 5 En 2 Pr
🛏 (8) 🅿 (7) ⅍ 📺 ✕ 🛏 Ⓥ 🛎

Abrach, *4 Caithness Place, Fort William, Inverness-shire, PH33 6JP.*
Modern house in elevated position overlooking Loch Linnhe.
Open: All Year (not Xmas)
Grades: STB 3 Star
01397 702535 Mr & Mrs Moore
Fax: 01397 705629
cmoore3050@aol.com
D: £17.50–£23.00 **S:** £20.00–£30.00
Beds: 1F 1D 1T 1S **Baths:** 2 En 1 Pr 1 Sh
🛏 🅿 (6) ⅍ 📺 🐾 🛏 Ⓥ 🛎 cc

Distillery House, *Nevis Bridge, North Road, Fort William, Inverness-shire, PH33 6LR.*
Well-run guest house, ideally situated at end of Glen Nevis and West Highland Way.
Open: All Year
Grades: STB 4 Star, AA 4 Diamond, RAC 4 Diamond, Sparkling
01397 700103 Mr MacPherson
Fax: 01397 702980
disthouse@aol.com
D: £20.00–£36.00 **S:** £22.00–£38.00
Beds: 1F 3D 2T 1S **Baths:** 7 En
🛏 🅿 (12) ⅍ 📺 🐾 🛏 🛎 cc

Rhu Mhor Guest House, *Alma Road, Fort William, Inverness-shire, PH33 6BP.*
Old fashioned in acre of wild and enchanting garden.
Open: Easter to Oct
Grades: STB 2 Star
01397 702213 Mr MacPherson
ian@rhumhor.co.uk
D: £16.00–£24.00 **S:** £17.00–£44.00
Beds: 1F 3D 1T 2S **Baths:** 2 Sh 4 En
🛏 (1) 🅿 (7) 📺 🐾 ✕ 🛏 Ⓥ 🛎 cc

Innseagan House Hotel, *Highland Holidays Scotland Ltd, Achintore Road, Fort William, Inverness-shire, PH33 6RW.*
In its own grounds overlooking Loch Linnhe only 1.5 miles from Fort William.
Open: Easter to Oct
Grades: STB 3 Star Hotel
01397 702452
Mr Maclean
Fax: 01397 702606
frontdesk@innseagan-holidays.com
D: £22.50 **S:** £30.00
Beds: 14D 8T 2S **Baths:** 23 En 1 Pr
🅿 📺 ✕ 🛏 🛎 cc

Stobahn, *Fassifern Road, Fort William, Inverness-shire, PH33 6BD.*
Guest rooms overlooking Loch Linnhe. Just off High Street.
Open: All Year
Grades: STB 2 Star
01397 702790 (also fax)
boggi@supanet.com
D: £15.00–£20.00 **S:** £18.00–£23.00
Beds: 1F 1T 2D **Baths:** 2 En 2 Sh
🛏 🅿 📺 🐾 ✕ 🛏 Ⓥ 🛎 ♿ cc

Voringfoss, *5 Stirling Place, Fort William, Inverness-shire, PH33 6UW.*
Experience the best of the highland hospitality in a quiet situation.
Open: All Year
Grades: STB 4 Star
01397 704062 Mr & Mrs Fraser
D: £20.00–£26.00 **S:** £20.00–£26.00
Beds: 2D 1T **Baths:** 3 En
🅿 (4) 📺 🛏 Ⓥ 🛎 cc

19 Lundy Road, *Inverlochy, Fort William, Inverness-shire, PH33 6NY.*
Family-run B&B. Views of Ben Nevis, passing steam trains.
Open: All Year
Grades: STB 2 Star
01397 704918
Mrs Campbell
acampbell@talk21.com
D: £13.00–£17.00 **S:** £15.00–£20.00
Beds: 2F **Baths:** 1 Sh
🛏 🅿 (2) 📺 🐾 ✕ 🛏 Ⓥ 🛎

Foyers

NH4920   ⚓ *Foyers Hotel*

Intake House, *Foyers, Inverness, IV2 6YA.*
Overlooking the River Foyers near the famous Falls of Foyers.
Open: Easter to Nov
Grades: STB 4 Star
01456 486258 (also fax)
Mrs Grant
D: £15.00–£18.00 **S:** £20.00–£25.00
Beds: 1T 2D **Baths:** 1 En 1 Sh
🛏 (14) 🅿 (5) ⅏ 📺 🛏, 🛢

Gairloch

NG8076   ⚓ *Myrtle Bank Hotel, Gairloch Sands Hotel, Old Inn, Millcroft Hotel*

Croit Mo Sheanair, *29 Strath, Gairloch, Ross-shire, IV21 2DA.*
Relax in our cosy family home; hand decorated throughout with stencilling & original artworks.
Open: Easter to Oct
Grades: STB 3 Star
01445 712389 L Bennett-Mackenzie
D: £15.00–£22.00
Beds: 1D 1T **Baths:** 1 En 1 Sh
🛏 🅿 (3) ⅏ 📺 🛢, 🛢

The Mountain Restaurant & Lodge,
Strath Square, Gairloch, Ross-shire, IV21 2BX.
Unique informal coffee shop/restaurant. Lochside sun terrace, views across water to Torridon Mountains.
Open: Apr to Oct, Dec to Jan
01445 712316 (also fax)
Mr Rudge
D: £18.00–£29.95 **S:** £29.00–£59.90
Beds: 2D 1T **Baths:** 3 En
🛏 🅿 (3) 📺 🛏 ✕ 🛢, 🛢 ❄ 🛢 cc

BATHROOMS
Pr - Private
Sh - Shared
En - Ensuite

Garve

NH3961   ⚓ *Garve Hotel, Inchbae Lodge Hotel, Achilty Hotel*

The Old Manse, *Garve, Ross-shire, IV23 2PX.*
Former manse c1860 set in quiet location amidst beautiful scenery.
Open: All Year (not Xmas)
Grades: AA 3 Diamond
01997 414201 (also fax)
Mr & Mrs Hollingdale
D: £16.00–£17.00 **S:** £16.00–£17.00
Beds: 2D 1T **Baths:** 1 En 1 Sh
🛏 (10) 🅿 (6) ⅏ 🛢, 🛢

Birch Cottage, *Station Road, Garve, Ross-shire, IV23 2PS.*
Traditional Highland cottage, modernised to a very high standard.
Open: Feb to Nov
Grades: STB 4 Star
01997 414237 (also fax) Mrs Hayton
D: £15.00–£18.00 **S:** £17.00–£18.00
Beds: 2D 1T **Baths:** 3 En
🛏 (3) 🅿 (4) ⅏ 📺 🛏 🛢, 🛢 🛢

Glencoe

NN1058   ⚓ *Glencoe Hotel, Clachaid Inn*

Scorrybreac Guest House, *Glencoe, Ballachulish, Argyll, PH49 4HT.*
Comfortable, secluded, overlooking Loch Leven. All rooms on ground floor.
Open: 26 Dec to Oct
Grades: STB 3 Star, AA 3 Diamond
01855 811354 (also fax) Mr Mortimer
john@scorrybreac.freeserve.co.uk
D: £16.00 **S:** £17.00
Beds: 3D 3T **Baths:** 5 En 1 Pr
🛏 🅿 (8) ⅏ 📺 🛏 ✕ 🛢, 🛢 🛢 ♿ cc

Dunire Guest House, *Glencoe, Ballachulish, Argyll, PA39 4HS.*
Family run set in large garden.
Open: All Year (not Xmas)
01855 811305 Mrs Cameron
D: £16.00–£22.00
Beds: 33D 2T **Baths:** 5 En
🛏 🅿 (8) 📺 🛏 🛢, ❄ 🛢

Glenfinnan

NM8980

Craigag Lodge Guest House,
Glenfinnan, Inverness-shire, PH37 4LT.
Victorian shooting lodge among superb
mountain scenery. Ideal walking/wildlife.
Open: Easter to Oct
01397 722240
Mr & Mrs Scott
D: £15.00–£20.00 **S:** £18.00
Beds: 1F 1D 1T **Baths:** 1 Sh
🛏 (9) 🅿 (4) ⊬ 📺 🐾 ✕ 🏠 Ⅴ 🛢 ᴊ

Glengolly

ND1066 🍴 *Pentland Hotel*

Shinval, *Glengolly, Thurso, Caithness,*
KW14 7XN.
Modern house with large garden. Four miles
from Orkney ferry.
Open: Jan to Dec
01847 894306 Mrs Sinclair
Fax: 01847 890711
mary@shinval.swinternet.co.uk
D: £15.00 **S:** £15.00
Beds: 1F 1D 1T **Baths:** 1 En 2 Sh
🛏 🅿 (4) 📺 🐾 🏠 Ⅴ 🛢 ᴊ

Glenmore

NH9809 🍴 *Glenmore Lodge, Cairngorm Hotel*

Cairn Eilrig, *Glenmore, Aviemore,*
Inverness-shire, PH22 1QU.
Highland welcome. Secluded bungalow in
Glenmore forest park panoramic views.
Open: All Year
Grades: STB 3 Star
01479 861223
Mrs Ferguson
D: £17.00–£18.00 **S:** £17.00–£20.00
Beds: 1F 1T **Baths:** 1 Sh
🛏 🅿 (2) 📺 🐾 🏠 Ⅴ 🛢

BEDROOMS

F - Family   **T** - Twin

D - Double   **S** - Single

Glenmoriston

NH2912 🍴 *Glenmoriston Arms Hotel*

Burnside Guest House, *Bhlaraidh,*
Glenmoriston, Inverness, IV63 7YH.
Open: Mar to Nov **Grades:** STB 2 Star
01320 351269 (also fax) Mr & Mrs Lowe
D: £16.00–£17.50 **S:** £16.00–£17.50
Beds: 2D 1T 1S **Baths:** 2 Sh
🛏 🅿 (5) ⊬ 📺 🐾 ✕ 🏠 🛢
A comfortable family home situated in a
forested mountain area of Glenmoriston.
Burnside is on the A887 road to the Isles,
just 3 miles from Invermoriston and Loch
Ness. Comfortable beds, good breakfast,
excellent hospitality, private off road parking.

Glenshiel

NG9318

10 MacInnes Place, *Glenshiel, Kyle of*
Lochalsh, Ross-shire, IV40 8HX.
Beautiful view overlooking Loch Duich and
mountains. Ideal for hillwalkers.
Open: All Year (not Xmas)
01599 511384 (also fax) L Macrae
D: £16.00–£20.00 **S:** £18.00–£20.00
Beds: 1F 1D 1T **Baths:** 1 En 1 Pr 1 Sh
🛏 📺 🐾 ✕ 🏠 Ⅴ 🛢

Grantown-on-Spey

NJ0327 🍴 *Tyree House, Ben Mhorh, Garth Hotel,*
Strathspey Hotel, Craggan Mill

Strathallan House, *Grant Road,*
Grantown-on-Spey, Moray, PH26 3LD.
Open: Easter to Oct
Grades: STB 3 Star GH
01479 872165 (also fax)
Mr Pearson
D: £18.00–£24.00 **S:** £18.00–£24.00
Beds: 3D 2T 1F **Baths:** 5 En 1 Pr
🛏 (7) 🅿 (6) ⊬ 📺 ✕ 🏠 Ⅴ ❄ 🛢 cc
Charming Victorian home, many original
features, offers first class accommodation in
spacious ensuite bedrooms, comfortable 4
poster and king-size beds available. Freshly
cooked breakfasts with wide choice. A warm
welcome to all guests. No single
supplement.

Garden Park Guest House, *Woodside Avenue, Grantown-on-Spey, Moray, PH26 3JN.*
Charming Victorian guest house set in lovely gardens in malt whisky country.
Open: Mar to Oct
Grades: STB 4 Star, AA 4 Diamond, RAC 4 Diamond
01479 873235 Mr Pattinson
D: £21.00–£24.00
Beds: 3D 2T **Baths:** 5 En
🛇 (12) 🅿 (8) 📺 ✗ ▥ ♨

Gaich Farm, *Grantown-on-Spey, Moray, PH26 3NT.*
Beautiful working farmhouse overlooking Cairngorms, comfortable beds, good breakfast.
Open: May to Sept
01479 851381 Mrs Laing
Fax: 01479 851 381
gaich@tinyworld.co.uk
D: £16.00–£17.00 **S:** £16.00–£17.00
Beds: 1T 1D **Baths:** 1S
🛇 🅿 📺 🐦 ✗ ▥ ♨

Firhall Guest House, *Grant Road, Grantown-on-Spey, Moray, PH26 3LD.*
Beautiful Victorian house set in the heart of Scottish Highlands.
Open: All Year (not Xmas)
Grades: STB 3 Star GH
01479 873097 (also fax)
Mr Salmon
firhall@cs.com
D: £17.00–£24.00 **S:** £17.00–£30.00
Beds: 3F 1D 1T 1S **Baths:** 3 En 1 Pr 1 Sh
🛇 🅿 (8) ⌇ 📺 ✗ ▥ Ⓥ ♨

Ravenscourt House Hotel, *Seafield Avenue, Grantown-on-Spey, Moray, PH26 3JG.*
Victorian manse set in beautiful gardens within walking distance of River Spey.
Open: All Year
Grades: RAC 5 Diamond
01479 872286
Mr & Mrs Lockey
Fax: 01479 873260
D: £30.00–£35.00 **S:** £35.00–£40.00
Beds: 2F 3D 2T 1S **Baths:** 9 En 2 Sh
🛇 🅿 (8) ⌇ 📺 🐦 ✗ ▥ Ⓥ ♨ ⅙

Harpsdale

ND1356   🍴 *Ulbster Arms*

The Bungalow, *Bachmore Farm, Harpsdale, Halkirk, Caithness, KW12 6UN.*
Modern comfortable friendly farmhouse.
Open: Easter to Oct
01847 841216 Mr & Mrs Waters
D: £18.00 **S:** £20.00
Beds: 1F 1D 1T **Baths:** 3 En
🛇 🅿 ⌇ 📺 ✗ ▥ Ⓥ ♨

Helmsdale

ND0215   🍴 *Bannock Burn, Belgrave Arms*

The Old Manse, *Stittenham Road, Helmsdale, Sutherland, KW8 6JG.*
Beautiful village settings, garden, access to salmon river, fishing arranged.
Open: All Year
01431 821597 Mrs Goodridge
D: £18.00–£20.00 **S:** £18.00–£20.00
Beds: 1F 2T **Baths:** 1 En 1 Pr 1 Sh
🛇 🅿 (4) ⌇ 📺 ✗ ▥ Ⓥ ♨

Broomhill House, *Helmsdale, Sutherland, KW8 6JS.*
Comfortable crofthouse, panoramic seaview.
Open: Apr to Oct
01431 821259 (also fax)
Mrs Blance
D: £18.00–£21.00 **S:** £25.00–£28.00
Beds: 1D 1T **Baths:** 2 En
🅿 (3) 📺 🐦 ✗ ▥ Ⓥ ♨

Kerloch, *67 Dunrobin Street, Helmsdale, Sutherland, KW8 6JX.*
Superb view of the Harbour and Moray Firth.
Open: All Year
01431 821396 Mrs Smith
D: £14.00 **S:** £14.00
Beds: 1F 1T 1S **Baths:** 2 Sh
🛇 📺 🐦 ▥ Ⓥ ♨

BEDROOMS

F - Family   **T** - Twin

D - Double   **S** - Single

Inchree

NN0263   *Four Seasons*

Foresters Bungalow, *Inchree, Onich, Fort William, Inverness-shire, PH33 6SE.*
Swedish-type bungalow in rural setting by Glenrigh Forest.
Open: Easter to Oct
01855 821285
Mrs Maclean
D: £14.00–£16.00
S: £15.00–£20.00
Beds: 1F 2T **Baths:** 1 Sh
ゐ (2) 🅿 (4) 📺 ✝ ✕ ▥ ♨

Inveralligin

NG8457   *Ben Damph, Tigh-an-eilean*

Heather Cliff, *Inveralligin, Torridon, Achnasheen, Ross-shire, IV22 2HB.*
Enjoy magnificent North West Highlands scenery. Walk, climb or just relax.
Open: Easter to Oct
01445 791256
Mrs Rose
D: £15.00 **S:** £15.00
Beds: 1F 1D 1S **Baths:** 1 Sh
🅿 (4) ▥ ♨

Invergarry

NH3001   *Invergarry Hotel, Glengarry Castle Hotel, Lock Inn*

Lundie View Guest House, *Invergarry, Inverness-shire, PH35 4HN.*
Open: All Year
Grades: STB 4 Star
01809 501291 (also fax)
Mr & Mrs Girdwood
lundieview@talk21.com
D: £18.00–£24.00 **S:** £20.00–£28.00
Beds: 2F 2D 1T
Baths: 4 En 1 Pr
ゐ 🅿 (10) ⚲ 📺 ✝ ✕ ▥ ♨ ✿ ♨ ⅋ cc
Set in heart of Great Glen near to Loch Ness Ben Nevis and much more. Ideal base for touring the Highlands. Excellent hospitality. Home cooked meals. We are licensed, so relax with a drink and enjoy the peace and tranquillity.

Lilac Cottage, *South Laggan, Invergarry, Inverness-shire, PH34 4EA.*
Comfortable accommodation,warm welcome in the heart of the Great Glen.
Open: All Year **Grades:** STB 3 Star
01809 501410 Mrs Jamieson
lilac.cottage@virgin.net
D: £13.00–£16.00 **S:** £13.00–£20.00
Beds: 2D 1T **Baths:** 1 Sh
ゐ 🅿 (4) 📺 ✕ ▥ ♨

Ardgarry Farm, *Faichem, Invergarry, Inverness-shire, PH35 4HG.*
Comfortable Accommodation, warm welcome, ideal for touring, beautiful forest walks.
Open: Easter to October
01809 501226
Mr Wilson
Fax: 01809 501307
ardgarry.farm@lineone.net
D: £14.00–£15.00
Beds: 1F 2T 1D **Baths:** 2 Sh
ゐ (5) 🅿 (5) 📺 ✝ ✕ ▥ 📺 ♨

Invergordon

NH7168   *Foxes Hotel, Marine Hotel*

Craigaron, *17 Saltburn, Invergordon, Ross-shire, IV18 0JX.*
Ground floor bedrooms (some seafront), good breakfast, friendly, value for money.
Open: All Year (not Xmas/New Year)
Grades: STB 3 Star
01349 853640 Mrs Brown
Fax: 01349 853619
jobrown@craigaron.freeserve.co.uk
D: £18.00–£22.00 **S:** £20.00–£22.00
Beds: 4T 1S **Baths:** 2 En 1 Sh
🅿 (6) 📺 ✝ ▥ ♨

RATES

D = Price range per person sharing in a double room
S = Price range for a single room

Inverinate

NG9221   ◀ *Dornie Hotel, Clachan, Loch Duich Hotel, Kintail Lodge Hotel*

Foresters Bungalow, *Inverinate, Kyle of Lochalsh, Ross-shire, IV40 8HE.*
Shores of Loch Duich on main A87, with superb views of the Kintail Mountains.
Open: Easter to Oct
01599 511329 Mrs MacIntosh
Fax: 01599 511407
Donald.MacIntosh@tesco.net
D: £17.50–£20.00
Beds: 1D 1T **Baths:** 1 En 1 Pr
⛺ 🅿 (2) 📺 🛏 🚿 cc

Cruechan, *5 Glebe Road, Inverinate, Glenshiel, Kyle of Lochalsh, Ross-shire, IV40 8HD.*
Seafront location, looking towards Mam Ratagan and Five Sisters of Kintail.
Open: All Year
01599 511328 (also fax) Mrs Fraser
D: £16.00–£18.00 **S:** £18.00–£20.00
Beds: 2F **Baths:** 1 Sh
⛺ 📺 🛏 🚿 🛏

Mo Dhachaidh, *Inverinate, Kyle of Lochalsh, Ross-shire, IV40 8HB.*
Modern house with magnificent views overlooking Loch Duich and Kintail mountains. **Open:** All Year (not Xmas)
01599 511351 (also fax) Mrs Croy
croy-irenwick@currantbun.com
D: £16.00–£20.00 **S:** £16.00–£20.00
Beds: 1F 1D 1T 1S **Baths:** 1 En 1 Sh
⛺ 🅿 (4) 📺 🛏 🚿 🛏

Inverlochy

NN1174

19 Lundy Road, *Inverlochy, Fort William, Inverness-shire, PH33 6NY.*
Family-run B&B. Views of Ben Nevis, passing steam trains. **Open:** All Year
Grades: STB 2 Star
01397 704918 Mrs Campbell
acampbell@talk21.com
D: £13.00–£17.00 **S:** £15.00–£20.00
Beds: 2F **Baths:** 1 Sh
⛺ 🅿 (2) 📺 🛏 ✗ 🚿 🛏

Inverness

NH6645   ◀ *Beaufort Hotel, Castle, Cawdor Tavern, Craigmonie Hotel, Finlay's, Girvans, Harlequin, Heathmount Hotel, Johnny Fox's, Kilcoy Arms, Loch Ness House, Mairten Lodge, No 27 Pub, Redcliffe, Waterfront*

Eskdale Guest House, *41 Greig Street, Inverness, IV3 5PX.*
Open: All Year (not Xmas) **Grades:** STB 3 Star
01463 240933 (also fax) Mrs Mazurek
eskdale.guesthouse@lineone.net
D: £16.00–£25.00 **S:** £22.00–£25.00
Beds: 2F 2D 1T 1S **Baths:** 3 En 1 Sh
⛺ 🅿 (5) 🚭 📺 🛏 🛏
Situated in the heart of Inverness only 5 minutes from bus/rail stations, this impeccably run guest house offers all the comforts of home and a warm Highland welcome. Private parking, discounts for stays over 3 days. Please phone Vera & Alex.

Pitfaranne, *57 Crown Street, Inverness, IV2 3AY.*
Open: All Year
Grades: STB 3 Star
01463 239338 Gwen & Jim Morrison
D: £16.00–£20.00 **S:** £18.00–£26.00
Beds: 1F 2D 4T **Baths:** 1 En 1 Pr 2 Sh
⛺ 🅿 (5) 📺 🛏 🚿 📺 🛏
5 minutes from town centre/rail/bus stations. Find true Highland hospitality in friendly relaxed atmosphere of 100-year-old town house in quiet location. Private showers in all cosy guest rooms. Daily room service. Extensive varied menu. Full Highland breakfast our speciality.

Strathmhor Guest House, *99 Kenneth Street, Inverness, IV3 5QQ.*
Open: All Year **Grades:** STB 2 Star
01463 235397 Mr & Mrs Reid
D: £20.00–£25.00 **S:** £18.00–£25.00
Beds: 2D 2T 1S **Baths:** 2 En 1 Pr 1 Sh
⛺ 🅿 (5) 📺 🚿 📺 🛏
Warm welcome awaits at refurbished Victorian home. Comfortable bedrooms and good food. 10 minutes walk into town centre, theatres, restaurants, leisure centre; golf course and fishing nearby. Easy access for all traffic off A9.

Torridon Guest House, *59 Kenneth Street, Inverness, IV3 5PZ.*
Open: All Year **Grades:** STB 3 Star B&B
01463 236449 (also fax) Mrs Stenhouse
louise@torridon59.freeserve.co.uk
D: £17.00
Beds: 3F **Baths:** 2 En 1 Pr
🛏 (5) 🅿 (4) 📺 ⅢⅢ ⓥ ♨
Comfortable, family-run house, 5 minutes from town centre, good food, good beds, and a warm welcome assured.

30 Culduthel Road, *Inverness, IV2 4AP.*
Open: All Year
01463 717181 Mrs Dunnett
Fax: 01463 717188
puffinexpress@cs.com
D: £12.50–£15.00 **S:** £18.00–£22.00
Beds: 1D 1T **Baths:** 1 En 1 Pr
🛏 (5) 🅿 (4) 📺 ♩ ✕ ⅢⅢ ⓥ ♨ ☕
1930's bungalow set in large garden, pleasant to relax in on summer evenings. Central heating. Lounge with open fire which you may have to share with a cat. Your hosts are both qualified local guides.

Fiveways Bed & Breakfast, *Tore, Muir of Ord, Ross-shire, IV6 7RY.*
TV all rooms, guest lounge, spacious parking, welcome always assured.
Open: Jun to Oct
Grades: STB 2 Star B&B
01463 811408 Mrs MacKenzie
D: £15.00 **S:** £17.00
Beds: 1F 1D 1T **Baths:** 1 En 2 Sh
🛏 🅿 📺 ♩ ⅢⅢ ⓥ ♨

Roseneath Guest House, *39 Greig Street, Inverness, IV3 5PX.*
Open: All Year
Grades: STB 3 Star
01463 220201 (also fax) Mr Morrison
roseneath@lineone.net
D: £15.00–£25.00
Beds: 3F 1T 2D **Baths:** 5 En 1 Pr
🛏 (7) 🅿 (3) 📺 ⅢⅢ ♨ **cc**
Over 100 year old building in centre location 200 yards from River Ness and Grieg Street Bridge. Only 5 minutes to town centre and all tourist excursions. Recently refurbished to very high standards.

Loanfern Guest House, *4 Glenurquhart Road, Inverness, IV3 5NU.*
Victorian house with character. 10 minutes walk from town centre.
Open: All Year (not Xmas/New Year)
Grades: STB 3 Star
01463 221660 (also fax)
Mrs Campbell
D: £16.00–£22.00 **S:** £18.00–£23.00
Beds: 1F 2T 2D **Baths:** 1 En 2 Sh
🛏 🅿 (4) ✄ 📺 ⓥ ♨

Melness Guest House, *8 Old Edinburgh Road, Inverness, IV2 3HF.*
Charming, award-winning guest house close to town centre.
Open: All Year
Grades: STB 3 Star
01463 220963
Fax: 01463 717037
melness@joyce86.freeserve.co.uk
D: £20.00–£26.00 **S:** £25.00–£40.00
Beds: 1F 1T 1D **Baths:** 1 En 1 Sh
🅿 (3) ✄ 📺 ⅢⅢ ⓥ ♨ **cc**

Edenview, *26 Ness Bank, Inverness, IV2 4SF.*
Comfortable friendly Victorian home on River Ness within 5 minutes town, 7 miles airport.
Open: Mar to Oct
Grades: STB 3 Star
01463 234397
Mrs Fraser
Fax: 01463 222742
D: £20.00–£24.00 **S:** £22.00–£28.00
Beds: 1F 1D 1T **Baths:** 2 En 1 Pr
🛏 🅿 (4) 📺 ⅢⅢ ⓥ ♨

The Tilt, *26 Old Perth Road, Inverness, IV2 3UT.*
Family home convenient for A9. Ideal touring base.
Open: All Year (not Xmas)
Grades: STB 3 Star B&B
01463 225352 (also fax)
Mrs Fiddes
D: £15.00 **S:** £17.00
Beds: 1F 1D 1T 1S **Baths:** 1 Sh
🛏 🅿 (4) ✄ 📺 ⅢⅢ ⓥ

Abb Cottage, 11 Douglas Row, Inverness,
IV1 1RE.
Central, quiet, riverside Listed terraced
cottage. Easy access public transport.
Open: Feb to Dec
01463 233486 Miss Storrar
D: £16.00–£18.00 **S:** £18.00–£25.00
Beds: 3T **Baths:** 1 Sh
🐕 (12) 🅿 (2) ⊬ 📺 ✕ 🏛, 🔽 ᷤ ♿

Winmar House Hotel, Kenneth Street,
Inverness, IV3 5QG.
Full Scottish breakfast and friendly welcome.
Ample parking. **Open:** All Year (not Xmas)
01463 239328 (also fax) Mrs Maclellan
winmarguesthouse@
invernessll.freeserve.co.uk
D: £16.00–£22.00 **S:** £16.00–£22.00
Beds: 1D 6T 3S **Baths:** 1 En 4 Pr 2 Sh
🐕 🅿 (10) ⊬ 📺 🐾 🏛, ᷤ ♿ cc

MacGregor's, 36 Ardconnel Street,
Inverness, IV2 3EX.
We are situated minutes from River Ness,
shops and castle.
Open: All Year (not Xmas/New Year)
01463 238357 Mrs MacGregor
james@seafieldorms.orknet.co.uk
D: £14.00–£18.00 **S:** £15.00–£20.00
Beds: 1F 3D 1T 3S **Baths:** 2 En 3 Sh
📺 🐾 🏛, ᷤ

Hazeldean House, 125 Lochalsh Road,
Inverness, IV3 5QS.
Friendly Highland welcome. Only 10 mins'
walk to town centre. **Open:** All Year
Grades: STB 3 Star
01463 241338 Mr Stuart
Fax: 01463 236387
D: £14.00–£20.00 **S:** £16.00–£22.00
Beds: 2F 4D 3T 2S **Baths:** 3 En 2 Sh
🐕 🅿 (6) ⊬ 📺 🐾 🏛, ᷤ

101 Kenneth Street, Inverness, IV3 5QQ.
Ideal base for day trips to North Highland
and Islands.
Open: All Year **Grades:** STB 2 Star
01463 237224 Mrs Reid **Fax: 01463 712249**
D: £16.00–£25.00 **S:** £20.00–£25.00
Beds: 2F 2D 1T 1S **Baths:** 1 En 1 Pr 2 Sh
🐕 🅿 (6) ⊬ 📺 🏛, 🔽 ᷤ ♿ cc

Bringing children with you?
Always ask for any special rates

Strathisla, 42 Charles Street, Inverness,
IV2 3AH.
2 minutes' walk to high street. 5 mins to rail
and bus stations.
Open: All Year (not Xmas)
Grades: STB 3 Star
01463 235657 (also fax)
Mr & Mrs Lewthwaite
strathislabb@talk21.com
D: £15.00–£18.00 **S:** £16.00–£20.00
Beds: 1D 1T 2S **Baths:** 1 Sh
🐕 (8) 🅿 (2) ⊬ 📺 ✕ 🏛, 🔽 ᷤ

Ivybank Guest House, 28 Old Edinburgh
Road, Inverness, IV2 3HJ.
Georgian home, near town centre and with
parking.
Open: All Year
Grades: STB 4 Star
01463 232796 (also fax)
Mrs Cameron
ivybank@talk21.com
D: £20.00–£27.50 **S:** £20.00–£55.00
Beds: 1F 4D 2T 5S **Baths:** 3 En 1 Pr 2 Sh
🐕 🅿 ⊬ 📺 🐾 🏛, 🔽 ❄ ᷤ cc

5 Muirfield Gardens, Inverness, IV2 4HF.
Quiet residential area 15 mins walk to town
centre. All rooms on ground floor.
Open: Easter to Dec
Grades: STB 3 Star
01463 238114 Mrs MacDonald
D: £17.00–£20.00 **S:** £18.00–£20.00
Beds: 2D 1T **Baths:** 2 Sh
🅿 (3) 📺 🏛, ᷤ

6 Broadstone Park, Inverness, IV2 3LA.
Family-run B&B. Victorian house 10 mins
town centre, bus and railway station.
Open: All Year (not Xmas)
Grades: STB 2 Star
01463 221506 Mrs Mackinnon
D: £20.00–£25.00 **S:** £21.00–£25.00
Beds: 1F 1D 1T 1S **Baths:** 2 En 1 Pr
🐕 (5) 🅿 (3) ⊬ 📺 🏛, 🔽 ᷤ

Lyndon, *50 Telford Street, Inverness, IV3 5LE.*
A warm and friendly welcome awaits you at
the Lyndon. **Open:** All Year (not Xmas)
Grades: STB 3 Star
01463 232551 D Smith
donnas@tesco.net
D: £15.00–£22.00 **S:** £30.00–£40.00
Beds: 4F 1D 1T **Baths:** 6 En
❄ 🅿 (6) 📺 🐕 ⛌ 🔥 ♿ cc

Taigh Na Teile, *6 Island Bank Road,
Inverness, IV2 4SY.*
Overlooking the River Ness, this beautifully
appointed Victorian-style house.
Open: All Year (not Xmas)
Grades: STB 4 Star
01463 222842 Mr & Mrs Menzies
Fax: 01463 226844
jenny@omn.co.uk
D: £20.00 **S:** £25.00–£30.00
Beds: 1D 2T **Baths:** All En
🅿 (4) ⅍ 📺 ⛌ 🔥

Invershin

NH5796 ⬛ *Invershin Hotel*

Birkenshaw, *Invershin, Lairg, Sutherland,
IV27 4ET.*
Modern house in woodland setting. Peaceful
surroundings, self-contained entrance.
Open: May to Oct
01549 421226 Mrs Alford
D: £15.00–£16.00 **S:** £15.00–£16.00
Beds: 2T **Baths:** 1 En 1 Pr
❄ (10) 🅿 (4) ⅍ 📺 🐕 ⛌ 🔥

John O' Groats

ND3773 ⬛ *John O' Groats House, Castle Arms*

Seaview Hotel, *John o' Groats, Wick,
Caithness, KW1 4YR.*
Scenic seaside location. Family owned, five
minutes from Orkney ferry.
Open: All Year
Grades: STB 1 Star
01955 611220 (also fax)
Mr Mowat
D: £14.50–£25.00 **S:** £20.00–£35.00
Beds: 3F 3D 2T 1S **Baths:** 5 En 2 Sh
❄ 🅿 (20) 📺 🐕 ✕ ⛌ 🔥

Bencorragh House, *Upper Gills, Canisbay,
John o' Groats, Wick, Caithness, KW1 4YB.*
Working croft. Panoramic views across
Pentland Firth near seasonal Orkney ferry.
Open: Mar to Oct
Grades: STB 3 Star, AA 3 Diamond
01955 611449 (also fax)
Mrs Barton
D: £20.00–£21.00 **S:** £23.00–£25.00
Beds: 1F 2D 1T **Baths:** 4 En
❄ (5) 🅿 (6) ⅍ 📺 🐕 ✕ ⛌ 🔥 cc

Keiss

ND3461 **Links View,** *Keiss, Wick,
Caithness, KW1 4XG.*
Attractive B&B overlooking Sinclair bay. 10
minutes from Orkney ferry.
Open: All Year
01955 631376 Mrs Brooks
D: £14.00–£15.00 **S:** £12.50
Beds: 1F 1D 1T **Baths:** 1 En 1 Sh
❄ 🅿 (8) ⅍ 📺 ✕

Kentallen

NN0157

Ardsheal House, *Kentallen, Appin, Argyll,
PA38 4BX.*
Open: All Year
Grades: STB 4 Star, AA 5 Diamond
01631 740227 N V C Sutherland
Fax: 01631 740342
info@ardsheal.co.uk
D: £45.00 **S:** £45.00
Beds: 1F 2T 4D 1S **Baths:** 8 En
❄ 🅿 🐕 ✕ ⛌ 🔥 cc
Spectacularly situated on the shores of Loch
Linnhe, standing in some 800 acres of
woodlands, fields and gardens, this historic
mansion is furnished with family antiques
and pictures. Ideal for climbing, walking and
touring or for the use of the full size billiards
table.

All details shown are as
supplied by B&B owners in
Autumn 2000

Kinbrace

NC8632

Tigh achen Echan, *Kinbrace, Sutherland, KW11 6UB.*
Natural stone-built house. View of river and distant hills.
Open: All Year
01431 831207 Mrs MacKenzie
D: £15.00 **S:** £15.00
Beds: 2F **Baths:** 1 Sh
ॐ 🅿 📺 ✕ 🎞 Ⅴ ☕ ♨

Kincraig

NH8305   🍴 *Kith & Kin Inn, Ossian Hotel*

Ossian Hotel, *Kincraig, Kingussie, Inverness-shire, PH21 1QD.*
Built in 1880s lochside village. Magnificent mountain views.
Open: Feb to Dec
Grades: STB 2 Star
01540 651242
Mrs Rainbow
Fax: 01540 651633
ossian@kincraig.com
D: £20.00–£31.00 **S:** £20.00–£31.00
Beds: 2F 3D 2T 2S **Baths:** 8 En 1 Pr
ॐ 🅿 (20) ✂ 📺 🐾 ✕ 🎞 Ⅴ ♨ cc

Balcraggan House, *Feshiebridge, Kincraig, Kingussie, Inverness-shire, PH21 1NG.*
Wonderful setting where wildlife, walks and cycle routes abound.
Open: All Year
01540 651488 Mrs Gillies
D: £25.00 **S:** £30.00–£35.00
Beds: 1D 1T **Baths:** 2 En
ॐ (10) 🅿 (3) ✂ 📺 ✕ 🎞 Ⅴ ♨

Braeriach Guest House, *Kincraig, Kingussie, Inverness-shire, PH21 1QA.*
Beautiful riverside country house. Spacious comfortable rooms with incredible views.
Open: All Year
01540 651369
Mrs Johnson
D: £20.00–£25.00 **S:** £20.00–£25.00
Beds: 2D 2T **Baths:** 3 En 1 Pr
ॐ 🅿 (4) 📺 🐾 ✕ 🎞 Ⅴ ❄ ♨

Kirkbeag, *Milehead, Kincraig, Kingussie, Inverness-shire, PH21 1ND.*
Freindly family B&B in converted C19th church. Quiet country location.
Open: All Year
01540 651298 (also fax) Mrs Paisley
D: £16.50–£17.50 **S:** £20.00–£23.00
Beds: 1D 1T **Baths:** 2 Sh
ॐ 🅿 (6) 📺 ✕ 🎞 Ⅴ ♨

Insh House, *Kincraig, Kingussie, Inverness-shire, PH21 1NU.*
Friendly family guest house in splendid rural location near loch & mountains.
Open: All Year (not Xmas)
01540 651377 Nick & Patsy Thompson
inshhouse@btinternet.com
D: £17.00–£20.00 **S:** £17.00–£20.00
Beds: 1F 1D 1T 2S **Baths:** 2 En 1 Sh
ॐ 🅿 ✂ 📺 🐾 ✕ 🎞 Ⅴ ♨

Kingussie

NH7500   🍴 *Scot House Hotel, Tipsy Laird, Osprey Hotel*

The Osprey Hotel, *Kingussie, Inverness-shire, PH21 1EN.*
Open: All Year
Grades: STB 3 Star Hotel, AA 2 Star
01540 661510 (also fax) Mr & Mrs Burrow
aileen@ospreyhotel.co.uk
D: £24.00–£30.00 **S:** £24.00–£30.00
Beds: 3D 3T 2S **Baths:** 8 En
ॐ 🅿 📺 🐾 ✕ 🎞 Ⅴ ♨ & cc
Small hotel in area of outstanding beauty, offering a warm welcome, ensuite accommodation and award-winning food. Aileen & Robert hold AA food rosettes and are members of the 'taste of Scotland'. Ideal base for touring, walking, golf, fishing, etc.

Arden House, *Newtonmore Road, Kingussie, Inverness-shire, PH21 1HE.*
Excellent food and accommodation, delightful centrally situated Victorian villa.
Open: All Year **Grades:** STB 3 Star GH
01540 661369 (also fax) Mrs Spry
ardenhouse@compuserve.com
D: £18.00–£22.00 **S:** £18.00–£22.00
Beds: 2F 2D 1T 1S **Baths:** 3 En 3 Sh
ॐ (1) 🅿 (7) ✂ 📺 🐾 ✕ 🎞 Ⅴ ♨ & 2 cc

The Hermitage, *Spey Street, Kingussie, Inverness-shire, PH21 1HN.*
Warm Highland welcome in heart of Badenoch & Strathspey. Excellent touring base.
Open: All Year (not Xmas)
Grades: STB 4 Star
01540 662137
Mr Taylor
Fax: 01540 662177
thehermitage@clara.net
D: £21.00–£23.00 **S:** £26.00–£28.00
Beds: 1F 1T 3D **Baths:** 5 En
🛏 🅿 📺 🕏 ✕ ▥ Ⓥ 🍴 cc

St Helens, *Ardbroilach Road, Kingussie, Inverness-shire, PH21 1JX.*
Built 100 years ago, St Helens is an elegant Victorian villa.
Open: All Year
Grades: STB 4 Star
01540 661430 Mrs Jarratt
sthelens@talk21.com
D: £20.00 **S:** £38.00
Beds: 1D 1T **Baths:** 1 En 1 Pr
🛏 (12) 🅿 (3) ⚼ 📺 ▥ Ⓥ 🍴

Ruthven Farmhouse, *Kingussie, Inverness-shire, PH21 1NR.*
Spacious farmhouse set amidst an acre of landscaped grounds.
Open: All Year
Grades: STB 3 Star
01540 661226
Mr Morris
D: £18.00–£20.00 **S:** £18.00–£20.00
Beds: 2D 1T **Baths:** 1 En 2 Pr
🛏 (10) 🅿 (3) ⚼ 📺 ▥ Ⓥ ✿ 🍴

Dunmhor House, *67 High Street, Kingussie, Inverness-shire, PH21 1HX.*
Centrally situated for numerous attractions in beautiful scenic Highland village.
Open: All Year
01540 661809 (also fax)
D: £16.00–£18.00 **S:** £16.00–£20.00
Beds: 2F 2D 1S
Baths: 2 Sh
🛏 🅿 (5) 📺 🕏 ✕ ▥ Ⓥ 🍴

Kinlochleven

NN1861 ◀ *Tailrace Inn, Macdonald Hotel, Osprey Hotel*

Macdonald Hotel and Camp Site, *Fort William Road, Kinlochleven, Argyll, PH50 4QL.*
Open: Mar to Dec
Grades: STB 3 Star
01855 831539 Mr & Mrs Reece
Fax: 01855 831416
martin@macdonaldhotel.demon.co.uk
D: £24.00–£32.00 **S:** £24.00–£44.00
Beds: 1F 4D 5T **Baths:** 10 En
🛏 🅿 (20) 📺 🕏 ✕ ▥ Ⓥ ✿ 🍴 cc
A modern hotel in Highland-style on the shore of Loch Leven. Superb views of the loch and surrounding mountains. Only 25 metres from West Highland Way. The walkers' bar provides an informal atmosphere and a wide selection of bar meals.

Edencoille, *Garbhien Road, Kinlochleven, Argyll, PA40 4SE.*
Friendly, comfortable B&B. Home cooking our speciality. Family run.
Open: All Year
Grades: STB 3 Star
01855 831358 (also fax) Mrs Robertson
D: £18.00–£22.00 **S:** £26.00–£34.00
Beds: 2F 1D 2T **Baths:** 2 Sh 2 En
🛏 🅿 (5) 📺 ✕ ▥ Ⓥ ✿ 🍴

Hermon, *Kinlochleven, Argyll, PH50 4RA.*
Spacious bungalow in village surrounded by hills on West Highland Way.
Open: Easter to Sep
01855 831383 Miss MacAngus
D: £16.00–£18.00 **S:** £18.00–£25.00
Beds: 1D 2T **Baths:** 1 En 1 Sh
🛏 🅿 (6) 📺 🕏 ▥ 🍴

Kyle of Lochalsh

NG7627   🍺 *Glenelg Inn, Off The Rails Restaurant*

Kyle Hotel, *Main Street, Kyle of Lochalsh, Ross-shire, IV40 6AB.*
Open: All Year
Grades: STB 3 Star
01599 534204 Fax: 01599 534932
thekylehotel@btinternet.com
D: £25.00–£47.00 **S:** £25.00–£47.00
Beds: 14T 8D 9S **Baths:** 31 En
🛇 🅿 ⅍ 📺 ⛺ ✕ 🛏 �🗂 ❄ 🚻 cc
By the main crossing to the Isle of Skye via
bridge and 200 metres from railway station.
Kyle hotel offers a warm welcome.
Experience superb local cuisine in our
charming restaurant or enjoy a great value
for money bar meal.

Tigh-a-Cladach, *Badicaul, Kyle of Lochalsh, Ross-shire, IV40 8BB.*
Open: Mar to Nov
01599 534891 (also fax)
Mrs Matheson
D: £16.00–£17.50 **S:** £16.00–£17.50
Beds: 1T 2D 1S **Baths:** 2 Sh
🛇 🅿 (5) 📺 🛏 🗂 🚻 ♿
Situated between Kyle of Lochalsh and
Plockton with superb views overlooking the
Isle of Skye, all rooms with sea view. Guests
can relax in the large garden or in the lounge
and watch the seals play. Hotels and
restaurants nearby for meals.

Marabhaig, *7 Coullindune, Glenelg, Kyle of Lochalsh, Ross-shire, IV40 8JU.*
Marabhaig - Situated on the shore of Glenelg
Bay. Fantastic views.
Open: All Year
Grades: STB 3 Diamond
01599 522327 Mrs Cameron
D: £19.00–£21.00 **S:** £21.00–£23.00
Beds: 2T 3D **Baths:** 3 En 2 Sh
🅿 (6) ⅍ 📺 ✕ 🗂 🚻 ♿ 1

BEDROOMS

F - Family   **T** - Twin
D - Double   **S** - Single

Ashgrove, *Balmacara Square, Kyle of Lochalsh, Ross-shire, IV40 8DJ.*
Very central West Highland location for
touring and walking, including hill climbing.
Open: All Year
01599 566259 Mrs Gordon
D: £16.50–£20.00
Beds: 2D 1T **Baths:** 2 En 1 Pr
🛇 🅿 (3) 📺 🛏 🗂 🚻 ♿

Achomraich, *Main Street, Kyle of Lochalsh, Ross-shire, IV40 8DA.*
Friendly family comfortable home. Parking,
guest sitting room, Scottish breakfast.
Open: Easter to Oct
01599 534210 Mrs Murchison
D: £15.00–£17.00 **S:** £15.00–£17.00
Beds: 2D 1T **Baths:** 2 Sh
🛇 (3) 🅿 (4) 📺 🛏 🚻 ♿

Kylesku

NC2233

Newton Lodge, *Kylesku, Lairg, Sutherland, IV27 4HW.*
Lovely new small hotel overlooking seal
colony - spectacular scenery.
Open: Easter to Oct
01971 502070 (also fax)
Mr & Mrs Brauer
newtonlge@aol.com
D: £28.00–£30.00
Beds: 4D 3T **Baths:** 7 En
🅿 (10) ⅍ 📺 🛏 ✕ 🗂 🚻 ♿ cc

Laggan (Newtonmore)

NN6194

Gaskmore House Hotel, *Laggan, Newtonmore, Inverness-shire, PH20 1BS.*
Set in heart of the Highlands a wonderful
place just to be.
Open: Easter to Oct
Grades: STB 3 Star
01528 544250 (also fax)
gaskmorehouse@aol.com
D: £25.00–£45.00 **S:** £30.00–£50.00
Beds: 12T 12D 1S **Baths:** 25 En
🛇 🅿 ⅍ 📺 ✕ 🗂 🚻 ♿ cc

Laid

NC4159

Rowan House, *90 Laid, Laid, Altnaharra, Lairg, Sutherland, IV27 4UN.*
Open: All Year **Grades:** STB 1 Star
01971 511347 (also fax) Mr MacLellan
shm@capetech.co.uk
D: £14.00–£19.00 **S:** £15.00–£20.00
Beds: 1F 2D 1T 1S **Baths:** 1 En 2 Sh
⌚ 🅿 (6) 📺 🕯 ✕ 🛏 Ⓥ ❀ ⚓ ♿
Set in a spectacular setting with uninterrupted views across Loch Eriboll to Ben Hope, Rowan House is in a private position on a 20 acre croft within 400m of the shore line. Launching facilities for diver, compressor nearby.

Laide

NG8992 ◀ *Aultbea Hotel, Ocean View Hotel*

Cul Na Mara Guest House, *Catalina Slipway, Sand passage, Laide, Achnasheen, Ross-shire, IV22 2ND.*
Open: All Year (not Xmas/New Year)
Grades: STB 3 Star
01445 731295 Mr Hart
Fax: 01445 731570
billhart@dircon.co.uk
D: £21.00 **S:** £31.00
Beds: 1F 1D **Baths:** 2 En
⌚ (5) 🅿 (4) 📺 🕯 ✕ 🛏 Ⓥ ♿
A stay at 'Cul Na Mara' (Gaelic - Song of the Sea) is an enjoyable experience with superior Bed & Breakfast accommodation. Guest rooms fully ensuite complete with colour television - private dining room.

Lairg

NC5806 ◀ *Pitentrail Inn*

Muirness, *97 Lower Toroboll, Lairg, Sutherland, IV27 4DH.*
Comfortable croft house, superb open views. Central for day trips, close to railway.
Open: All Year
01549 402489 Mrs Grey
D: £16.00–£18.00 **S:** £18.00
Beds: 2D 1T **Baths:** 1 Pr 1 Sh
⌚ (2) 🅿 ✕ 📺 ✕ 🛏 ⚓

Latheron

ND1933 ◀ *Latheroncoheel Hotel*

Tacher, *Latheron, Caithness, KW5 6DX.*
On A895 (Thurso). Modern, comfortable farmhouse.
Open: May to Oct
Grades: STB 3 Star
01593 741313 Mrs Falconer
D: £16.00–£18.00 **S:** £16.00–£20.00
Beds: 1F 1D 1T **Baths:** 1 En 1 Sh 1 Pr
⌚ 🅿 (8) ✕ 📺 🕯 ✕ 🛏 Ⓥ ⚓ ♿

Lewiston

NH5029 ◀ *Hunters Restaurant*

Woodlands, *East Lewiston, Drumnadrochit, Inverness, IV63 6UL.*
Family home, warm Scottish welcome awaits you. Central for touring.
Open: All Year (not Xmas)
Grades: STB 4 Star, AA 4 Diamond
01456 450356 Mr & Mrs Drysdale
Fax: 01456 450199
drysdale@woodlandsbandb.fsnet.co.uk
D: £18.00–£20.00
Beds: 2D 1T **Baths:** 3 En
⌚ 🅿 (3) 📺 ✕ 🛏 Ⓥ ⚓ cc

Lochcarron

NG8939 ◀ *Locharron Hotel, Rockvilla Hotel*

Aultsigh, *Croft Road, Lochcarron, Strathcarron, Ross-shire, IV54 8YA.*
Spectacular views over Loch Carron. Ideal base for climbing or touring.
Open: All Year
01520 722558 Ms Innes
moyra.innes@talk21.com
D: £16.00–£18.00 **S:** £18.00
Beds: 1F 1D 1T **Baths:** 2 Sh
⌚ 🅿 (6) ✕ 📺 🕯 🛏 ⚓ ♿

All details shown are as supplied by B&B owners in Autumn 2000

Lochinver

NC0922

Veyatie, *66 Baddidarroch, Lochinver, Lairg, Sutherland, IV27 4LP.*
Open: All Year (not Xmas)
Grades: STB 4 Star
01571 844424 Mrs Chapman
veyatie@baddid.freeserve.co.uk
D: £20.00–£25.00 **S:** £30.00–£50.00
Beds: 2D 1T **Baths:** 2 En 1 Pr
🅿 (3) ⅙ 📺 🛏 ▥ ♨
Veyatie is a modern bungalow situated in a beautiful, peaceful setting where our conservatory offers spectacular views over Lochinver bay to mountains beyond. Our bedrooms have many extra refinements for your comfort and the guests' lounge has fascinating character.

Suilven, *Badnaban, Lochinver, Lairg, Sutherland, IV27 4LR.*
3 miles from Lochinver, off Achiltibuie Road. Sea angling available.
Open: All Year (not Xmas/New Year)
01571 844358 Mrs Brown
D: £17.00 **S:** £22.00
Beds: 1T 1D **Baths:** 1 Sh
🅿 (2) 📺 🛏 ✕ ▥ ♨

Lochluichart

NH3263

4 Mossford Cottages, *Lochluichart, Garve, IV232QA.*
Spectacular view across loch. Friendly informal atmosphere. Central touring position.
Open: All Year (not Xmas/New Year)
Grades: STB 3 Star
01997 414334 Mr & Mrs Doyle
D: £15.00–£18.00 **S:** £15.00–£18.00
Beds: 1F 1T 1D 1S **Baths:** 2 En 1 Pr 1 Sh
🐂 ⅙ 🛏 ✕ ▥ ♨

Planning a longer stay?
Always ask for any special rates

Bringing children with you?
Always ask for any special rates

Lybster (Wick)

ND2435

Reisgill House, *Lybster, Caithness, KW3 6BT.*
Country house in quiet location. Traditional Scottish cooking our speciality.
Open: All Year (not Xmas/New Year)
Grades: STB 3 Star
01593 721212 (also fax)
Ms Harper
helen@reisgill-house.com
D: £18.00 **S:** £18.00
Beds: 1F 2T 2D 1S **Baths:** 5 En 1 Pr
🐂 🅿 (6) ⅙ 📺 🛏 ✕ ▥ �V ♨ cc

Mallaig

NM6796 🍴 *Arisaig Hotel, Chlachain Bar, Cabin, Marine Hotel, Cornerstone Rest*

Spring Bank Guest House, *East Bay, Mallaig, Inverness-shire, PH41 4QF.*
Open: All Year (not Xmas/New Year)
01687 462459 (also fax)
Mr Smith
j.t.smith0@talk21.com
D: £16.00–£17.00 **S:** £16.00–£17.00
Beds: 1F 2D 3T 2S **Baths:** 3 Sh
🐂 📺 🛏 ✕ ▥ �V ♨ cc
Spring Bank is a traditional Highland house, situated overlooking the harbour and ferry terminals to Skye, the small Isles and Knoydart. Mallaig is at the end of the world famous West Highland Line and is ideal for walking and touring.

Rockcliffe, *East Bay, Mallaig, Inverness-shire, PH41 4QF.*
Quality accommodation overlooking bay. Trains, ferries and restaurants very close.
Open: Easter to Oct
01687 462484 Mrs Henderson
D: £16.00–£17.00 **S:** £17.00–£18.00
Beds: 2D 1S **Baths:** 2 Sh
🅿 (2) ⅙ 📺 ▥ �V ♨

The Anchorage, *Gillies Park, Mallaig,*
Inverness-shire, PH41 4QS.
Yards from station and ferry terminal.
Open: All Year (not Xmas/New Year)
Grades: STB 2 Star
01687 462454 (also fax) Mrs Summers
anchoragemallaig@talk21.com
D: £18.00–£20.00 **S:** £18.00–£20.00
Beds: 1F 1D 1T 1S **Baths:** 4 En
ॐ ⅏ 📺 🏇 ⏸ Ⅴ 🍵

Mellon Charles

NG8491

Tranquillity, *21 Mellon Charles, Aultbea,*
Achnasheen, Ross-shire, IV22 2JN.
Comfortable house in quiet lochside location
with wonderful mountain views.
Open: All Year (not Xmas)
Grades: STB 3 Star
01445 731241 (also fax) Mr & Mrs Bond
D: £20.00 **S:** £20.00–£30.00
Beds: 1F 1D 1S **Baths:** 2 En 1 Pr
ॐ 🅿 ⅏ 📺 ✕ Ⅴ 🍵

Morar

NM6793 ⊲ *Morar Hotel, Marine Hotel, Cabin*
Hotel

Sunset, *Morar, Mallaig, Inverness-shire,*
PH40 4PA.
Family-run guest house, sea views, Thai food
our speciality.
Open: All Year (not Xmas)
01687 462259 Mrs Clulow **Fax: 01687 460085**
sunsetgh@aol.com
D: £12.50–£18.00 **S:** £12.50–£18.00
Beds: 1F 1D 1T **Baths:** 1 En 1 Sh
ॐ (2) 🅿 (6) ⅏ 📺 ✕ ⏸ Ⅴ 🍵

Glengorm, *Morar, Mallaig, Inverness-shire,*
PH40 4PA.
In Morar Village. Silversand beaches nearby.
Ferry to Skye 2 miles.
Open: All Year **Grades:** STB 2 Star
01687 462165 Mrs Stewart
glengormmorar@talk21.com
D: £15.00–£16.00
Beds: 1D 1T **Baths:** 1 Sh
🅿 (4) 📺 🏇 ⏸ Ⅴ 🍵

Muir of Ord

NH5250 ⊲ *Old Arms Hotel, North Kessock*
Hotel, Moorings Hotel, Achilty Hotel

Birchgrove, *Arcan, Muir of Ord, Ross-shire,*
IV6 7UL.
Comfortable country house in quiet area.
Guest rooms overlooking garden.
Open: All Year (not Xmas)
01997 433245 Mrs Bell
Fax: 01997 433304
D: £15.00–£16.50 **S:** £16.00–£17.00
Beds: 1F 1D 1T **Baths:** 1 En 1 Sh
ॐ 🅿 (3) 📺 🏇 ⏸ 🍵

Hillview Park, *Muir of Ord, Ross-shire,*
IV6 7XS.
Rural situation, adjacent to golf course.
Ground floor bungalow.
Open: Easter to Oct
Grades: STB 3 Star
01463 870787 Mrs Peterkin
D: £17.00–£19.00 **S:** £18.00–£20.00
Beds: 1F 1D 1T **Baths:** 3 En
🅿 (3) ⅏ 📺 ⏸ 🍵

Muirshearlich

NN1380 ⊲ *Moorings Hotel*

Strone Farm, *Muirshearlich, Banavie, Fort*
William, Inverness-shire, PH33 7PB.
Rural setting, panoramic views Ben Nevis,
Caledonian Canal. Traditional food.
Open: Feb to Nov **Grades:** STB 3 Star
01397 712773 (also fax) Mrs Cameron
D: £18.00–£20.00 **S:** £23.00–£25.00
Beds: 2D 1T
ॐ 🅿 (3) 📺 ✕ ⏸ 🍵

Munlochy

NH6453

Craigiehowe, *3 Forestry House, Munlochy,*
Ross-shire, IV8 8NH.
Quiet cul de sac near to all services.
Open: All Year (not Xmas)
01463 811402 Mrs Munro
D: £14.00–£16.00 **S:** £14.00–£16.00
Beds: 1F 1D
ॐ 🅿 ⅏ 📺 ⏸ 🍵

Nairn

NH8856   ◧ *Havelock Hotel, Longhouse, Claymore Hotel, Links Hotel, Lothian Hotel, Newton Hotel, Argdour Hotel, Marine Hotel*

Fonthill, *King Street, Nairn, IV12 4NP.*
Beautiful detached villa, central location, views on website.
Open: All Year
01667 455996 Mrs O'Grady
fonthill@classicfm.net
D: £18.00–£22.00 **S:** £18.00–£22.00
Beds: 1T 2D **Baths:** 1 En, 1 Pr, 1 Sh
♿ ⓟ (6) ⤧ 📺 🐾 ✕ ▥ Ⓥ ❄ ⚓

Redburn, *Queen Street, Nairn, IV12 4AA.*
Extremely attractive Victorian Villa, quiet location, close to all amenities.
Open: Easter to Oct
Grades: STB 3 Star
01667 452238 Mr & Mrs Clucas
clucas@redburnvilla.fsnet.co.uk
D: £17.00–£20.00 **S:** £17.00–£20.00
Beds: 1D 1T 1S **Baths:** 2 Sh
♿ ⓟ (4) ⤧ 📺 ▥ Ⓥ ⚓

Durham House, *4 Academy Street, Nairn, IV12 4RJ.*
Elegant Victorian villa near beaches, golf, castles and historic sites.
Open: All Year (not Xmas)
Grades: STB 3 Star
01667 452345 (also fax)
P J Hudson
durhamhouse@nairn34.freeserve.co.uk
D: £18.00–£22.00 **S:** £16.00–£18.00
Beds: 1F 1D 1T 1S **Baths:** 2 En 1 Pr 1 Sh
♿ ⓟ (4) ⤧ 📺 🐾 ✕ ▥ Ⓥ ⚓ cc

Glenshiel, *Pier Road, Sandbank, Argyll, PA23 8QH.*
Elegant Victorian villa in secluded beautiful garden. Loch and mountain views.
Open: Easter to Oct
01369 701202 Mrs Galliard
ann@galliard.freeserve.co.uk
D: £20.00–£25.00 **S:** £25.00–£30.00
Beds: 1D 1T **Baths:** 2 Pr
♿ ⓟ (20) ⤧ 📺 🐾 ▥ Ⓥ ⚓ ♿

RATES
D = Price range per person sharing in a double room
S = Price range for a single room

Bracadale House, *Albert Street, Nairn, Inverness-shire, IV12 4HF.*
A Victorian villa situated in the championship golfing, seaside town.
Open: Mar to Oct
Grades: STB 4 Star
01667 452547 H M MacLeod
bracadale_house@hotmail.com
D: £20.00–£22.00 **S:** £20.00–£25.00
Beds: 1T 2D **Baths:** 2 En 1 Pr
♿ (13) ⓟ (3) ⤧ 📺 🐾 ✕ ▥ Ⓥ ⚓

Coel Mara, *Links Place, Nairn, IV12 4NH.*
Panoramic view of the Moray Firth, 200 yards from beach.
Open: All Year (not Xmas/New Year)
Grades: STB 4 Star
01667 452495 Mrs Mackintosh
Fax: 01667 451531
ceolmara15@aol.com
D: £20.00–£25.00 **S:** £20.00–£25.00
Beds: 1F 1D 1S **Baths:** 3 En
♿ ⓟ ⤧ 📺 🐾 ▥ Ⓥ ⚓ cc

Nethy Bridge

NJ0020   ◧ *Strathspey Hotel, The Mountview, Heatherbridge Hotel*

Aspen Lodge, *Nethy Bridge, Inverness-shire, PH25 3DA.*
Warm welcome and memorable breakfast in heart of picturesque village.
Open: All Year (not Xmas)
Grades: STB 3 Star B&B
01479 821042 Mrs Renton
linda@aspenlodge.fsnet.co.uk
D: £19.00 **S:** £25.00
Beds: 1D 1T **Baths:** 1 En 1 Pr
♿ (1) ⤧ 📺 ▥ Ⓥ ⚓

Newtonmore

NN7199 🍴 *Braeriach Hotel, Glen Hotel, Ballavile Sport Hotel*

The Pines, *Station Road, Newtonmore, Inverness-shire, PH20 1AR.*
Open: Jan to Oct
01540 673271 Mr Walker
Fax: 01540 673882
D: £20.00–£25.00 **S:** £20.00–£25.00
Beds: 2D 2T 2S **Baths:** 6 En
🛏 (12) 🅿 (5) ⅄ 📺 🛏 ✗ 🛏 Ⅴ 🌢 **cc**
Comfortable Edwardian house with river valley and mountain views. Peaceful wooded gardens rich in bird and wildlife. Conveniently located for public transport, touring, walking, cycling, golf, Cairngorm Mountains and RSPB reserves. Please phone for colour brochure.

Alder Lodge Guest House, *Glen Road, Newtonmore, Inverness-shire, PH20 1EA.*
Beautiful house, quiet situation, 0.25 mile from the shops and hotels.
Open: All Year
01540 673376 Mr Stewart
D: £15.00 **S:** £15.00
Beds: 2 T 2D **Baths:** 1 Sh
🛏 🅿 (6) 🛏 ✗ 🛏 Ⅴ 🌢

Nigg

NH8071 🍴 *Nigg Ferry Hotel*

Carse of Bayfield, *Nigg, Tain, Ross-shire, IV19 1QW.*
Overlooking Cromarty Firth on Pictish Trail. Walking, sandy beaches, golf courses & birdwatching nearby.
Open: All Year (not Xmas)
Grades: STB 3 Star
01862 863230 (also fax)
Mrs Campbell
D: £16.00–£18.00 **S:** £16.00–£18.00
Beds: 1D 1T **Baths:** 1 Sh
🛏 🅿 (6) ⅄ 📺 🛏 ✗ 🛏 Ⅴ 🌢

North Kessock

NH6548 🍴 *North Kessock Hotel, Munlochy Hotel*

The Rowans, *Bogallan, North Kessock, Inverness, Highland, IV1 3XE.*
Open: All Year (not Xmas/New Year)
01463 731428 Mrs Davidson
ruth.davidson@ntlworld.com
D: £15.00–£17.50 **S:** £18.00–£20.00
Beds: 3D **Baths:** 2 En 1 Pr
⅄ 📺 🛏 🌢
The Rowans is a modern family run bungalow on the outskirts of Inverness in area of scenic beauty known as the Black Isle. Ideal base for touring highlands - Loch Ness, Cairngorm Mountains, dolphin watch, golf courses, beaches, Culloden Battlefield close by.

37 Drumsmittal Road, *North Kessock, Inverness, IV1 3JU.*
Warm welcome awaits in comfortable bungalow. Ideal for touring Highlands.
Open: All Year
Grades: STB 3 Star
01463 731777 Mrs Bonthrone
norah@kessock.fsnet.co.uk
D: £16.00–£18.00 **S:** £16.00–£18.00
Beds: 1D 1S **Baths:** 1 Sh
🅿 (2) ⅄ 📺 🛏 Ⅴ

Helen's B&B, *8 Bellfield Drive, North Kessock, Inverness, IV1 3XT.*
Modern house overlooking Beauly Firth where dolphins can be viewed.
Open: Easter to Oct
Grades: STB 2 Star
01463 731317 H C Robertson
D: £16.00–£18.00 **S:** £17.00–£20.00
Beds: 1D 2T **Baths:** 1 Pr 1 Sh
🅿 (4) ⅄ 📺 🛏

Onich

NN0261

Camus House, *Lochside Lodge, Onich, Fort William, Inverness-shire, PH33 6RY.*
Beautiful Victorian country house in outstanding location between Fort William - Glencoe.
Open: Feb to Nov
Grades: STB 3 Star
01855 821200 Fax: 01855 821 200
young@camushouse.freeserve.co.uk
D: £23.50–£30.00 **S:** £27.50–£35.00
Beds: 2F 2T 3D **Baths:** 6 En 1 Sh
ॐ ▣ ⌇ ⊡ ✕ ▥ Ⅴ ♨ cc

Piperhill

NH8651 ◀ *Cawdor Tavern*

Colonsay, *Piperhill Cawdor, Cawdor, Nairn, IV12 5SD.*
Open: All Year (not Xmas/New Year)
01667 404305 Mrs Murray
dmmm16592@aol.com
D: £15.00 **S:** £18.00
Beds: 1F 1D **Baths:** 2 Sh
ॐ ▣ (3) ⌇ ⊡ ▥ Ⅴ
Beautiful new traditionally built detached house set in rural area close to Inverness, Nairn, Cawdor castle and Culloden battlefield, Golf and Fishing close by. Comfortable beds, tastefully decorated rooms and good Scottish breakfasts and evening tea, private off road parking.

Plockton

NG8033 ◀ *Plockton Inn, Plockton Hotel, Off The Rails, Old School House, Tingle Creek Hotel*

Plockton Hotel, *Harbour Street, Plockton, Ross-shire, IV52 8TN.*
Waterfront inn in traditional row of stone houses, picturesque NT village of Plockton.
Open: All Year
01599 544274
Mrs Pearson
Fax: 01599 544475
D: £27.50–£35.00 **S:** £32.50–£40.00
Beds: 9D 4T 1S **Baths:** 13 En 1 Pr
ॐ ⌇ ⊡ ✝ ✕ ▥ Ⅴ ♨ � & 3 cc

Poolewe

NG8580 ◀ *Poolewe Hotel*

Creagan, *Poolewe, Ross-shire, IV22 2LD.*
Quiet country house in highland village. Private off-road parking, good breakfasts with home-baking.
Open: Mar to Oct
01445 781424 (also fax)
Mrs MacKenzie
D: £18.00 **S:** £25.00
Beds: 2D 1T **Baths:** 2 En 1 Pr
ॐ ▣ (4) ⌇ ⊡ ✝ ▥ ♨ cc

Corriness Guest House, *Poolewe, Achnasheen, Ross-shire, IV22 2JU.*
Cherished Edwardian villa by Inverewe Gardens and Loch Ewe.
Open: Easter to Oct
01445 781262 Mrs Rowley
Fax: 01445 781263
D: £23.00–£25.00
Beds: 3T 2D **Baths:** 5 En
ॐ (10) ▣ (10) ⌇ ⊡ ✕ ▥ Ⅴ ♨ & cc

Portmahomack

NH9184 ◀ *Oyster Catcher Restaurant*

Wentworth House , *Tarbatness Road, Portmahomack, Tain, Ross-shire, IV20 1YB.*
Open: All Year
01862 871897 Mrs Elliott
monicaelliott@wentworth39.demon.co.uk
D: £20.00–£22.50 **S:** £25.00
Beds: 3T **Baths:** 1 En 2 Sh
ॐ ▣ (6) ⌇ ⊡ ✝ ✕ Ⅴ ♨
Historic former manse beside golf course, overlooking the Dornoch Firth, home of the bottle-nosed dolphins. Portmahomack is the only West-facing village on East coast, next to Pictish archaeological site (largest in Europe) currently under excavation by York University.

All details shown are as supplied by B&B owners in Autumn 2000

High season, bank holidays
and special events mean low
availability anywhere

Poyntzfield

NH7064 🍴 *Royal Hotel*

Newfield, *Newhall Bridge, Poyntzfield,
Dingwall, Ross-shire, IV7 8LQ.*
Open: All Year **Grades:** STB 4 Star
01381 610333 Mrs Munro
Fax: 01381 610325
jean.munro@tesco.net
D: £18.00–£25.00 **S:** £18.00–£24.00
Beds: 1F 1D 1S **Baths:** 1 En 2 Sh
🛏 (1) 🅿 (6) ✠ 📺 ⅲ 🕯
Newfield is a modernised traditional
Scottish house set in 2 acres of mature
gardens, situated 0.25 mile from Udale Bay
Bird Sanctuary, 6 miles from Cromarty and
17 miles from Inverness. Ideal for touring the
Highlands of Scotland.

Rogart

NC7303 🍴 *Pittentrail Inn*

Benview, *Lower Morness, Rogart,
Sutherland, IV28 3XG.*
Traditional country farmhouse offering peace
and quiet, comfort, good food.
Open: Easter to Oct
01408 641222 Mrs Corbett
D: £15.00–£15.50 **S:** £16.00
Beds: 1T 1S 2D **Baths:** 2 Sh
🛏 (12) 🅿 ✠ 📺 🐾 ✗ ⅲ 🍴 🕯

Tigh Na Fuaran, *Pitfure, Rogart,
Sutherland, IV28 3UA.*
Modern bungalow large garden golfing
fishing walking ideal touring base.
Open: Easter to Oct
Grades: STB 3 Star
01408 641224 (also fax)
Mrs Colquhoun
D: £16.00–£18.00 **S:** £16.00–£18.00
Beds: 1D 1T **Baths:** 1 Sh
🛏 (5) 🅿 (3) 📺 🐾 ⅲ 🕯

Scaniport

NH6239 🍴 *Dores Inn*

Ballindarroch, *Aldourie, Inverness, IV2 6EL.*
Open: All Year
01463 751348 Mrs Parsons
Fax: 01463 751372
ali.phil@cwcom.net
D: £20.00–£30.00 **S:** £20.00–£30.00
Beds: 1F 1D 1T 1S **Baths:** 1 Pr 2 Sh
🛏 🅿 (8) 📺 🐾 ⅲ 🍴 🕯
Situated ten minutes south of Inverness
(B862), Ballindarroch is a unique Victorian
country house in ten acres of woodland
gardens, furnished with period pieces, hand
painted Chinese wallpaper in drawing room.
A warm and friendly house run on very
informal lines.

Scourie

NC1544 🍴 *Scourie Hotel*

Minch View, *Scouriemore, Scourie, Lairg,
Sutherland, IV27 4TG.*
Modern comfortable croft house. Home
cooking. Outstanding views and hospitality.
Open: Easter to Oct
01971 502010 Mrs MacDonald
D: £16.00 **S:** £16.00
Beds: 2D 1T **Baths:** 2 Sh
🛏 🅿 ✠ 📺 🐾 ✗ ⅲ 🍴

Fasgadh, *Scourie, Lairg, Sutherland, IV27 4TG.*
Beautiful views of Scourie, near to
restaurant and Scourie Hotel.
Open: Easter to Oct
Grades: STB 3 Star
01971 502402 Mrs Mackay
sandra@scouriemore.co.uk
D: £17.00–£18.00 **S:** £18.00–£20.00
Beds: 1D 1T **Baths:** 2 En
🛏 🅿 (3) 📺 🐾 ✗ ⅲ 🍴 🕯

BATHROOMS
Pr - Private
Sh - Shared
En - Ensuite

Shieldaig (Loch Shieldaig)

NG8153   ⬛ *Tigh An Cilan Hotel*

Tigh Fada, *117 Doireaonar, Shieldaig, Strathcarron, Ross-shire, IV54 8XH.*
Family home on working croft, magnificent scenery. **Open:** Feb to Nov
Grades: STB 2 Star
01520 755248 (also fax) Mrs Calcott
D: £14.50–£15.50 **S:** £16.00–£18.00
Beds: 1F 1D 1T **Baths:** 2 Sh
⛫ 🄿 (3) 📺 ✕ 🗄 Ⓥ cc

Smithton

NH7145

3a Resaurie, *Smithton, Inverness, IV2 7NH.*
Open: All Year
01463 791714 Mrs Mansfield
mbmansfield@uk2net
D: £17.00–£21.00 **S:** £17.00–£21.00
Beds: 2D 1T **Baths:** 1 En 1 Sh
⛫ 🄿 (3) ✠ 📺 ⊁ ✕ 🗄 Ⓥ 🍴 cc
Quiet residential area 3 miles east of Inverness. Public transport nearby. GB National Cycle Route 7 passes door. Adjacent to Farmland. Views to Moray Firth, Ben Wyvis and Ross-shire Hills. Home baking, high tea, Evening meals. A CHRISTIAN HOME.

South Laggan

NN2996

Forest Lodge, *South Laggan, Invergarry, Inverness-shire, PH34 4EA.*
Open: All Year (not Xmas/New Year)
Grades: STB 3 Star, AA 3 Diamond
01809 501219 Mr & Mrs Shearer
Fax: 01809 501476
info@flgh.co.uk
D: £17.00–£22.00 **S:** £24.00–£29.00
Beds: 2F 2T 3D **Baths:** 6 En 1 Pr
⛫ 🄿 (10) ✠ 📺 ✕ 🗄 Ⓥ 🍴 cc
Ian and Janet Shearer offer friendly hospitality, pleasant en-suite accommodation, and home cooking in their rurally set home close to the Great Glen Way. Walking or touring, Forest Lodge is the perfect stopover.

Bringing children with you?
Always ask for any special rates

Spean Bridge

NN2281   ⬛ *Smiddy House, Spean Bridge Hotel, Aonach Mor Hotel*

Dreamweavers, *Earendil, Spean Bridge, PH34 4EQ.*
Traditional Scottish hospitality and cuisine amidst stunning Highland scenery.
Open: All Year
Grades: STB 2 Star
01397 712548 H Maclean
helen@dreamweavers.co.uk
D: £15.00–£20.00 **S:** £15.00–£20.00
Beds: 1F 1T 1D **Baths:** 1 En 2 Pr
⛫ 🄿 (5) ✠ 📺 ⊁ ✕ 🗄 Ⓥ 🍴 ♿ 3

Coire Glas Guest House, *Spean Bridge, Inverness-shire, PH34 4EU.*
Spectacular views of Grey Corries. Ideal base for climbing / touring.
Open: All Year (not Xmas)
Grades: STB 2 Star, AA 3 Diamond
01397 712272 (also fax)
Mrs MacFarlane
enquiry@coireglas.co.uk
D: £14.50–£19.50 **S:** £14.50–£25.00
Beds: 2F 4D 4T 1S **Baths:** 8 En 3 Sh
⛫ 🄿 (11) 📺 ✕ Ⓥ 🍴 cc

Coinachan Guest House, *Gairlochy Road, Spean Bridge, Inverness-shire, PH34 4EG.*
Open: All Year (not Xmas)
Grades: STB 4 Star
01397 712417 (also fax)
H C Hoare
D: £20.00–£25.00 **S:** £20.00–£35.00
Beds: 2D 1T **Baths:** 3 En
🄿 📺 ✕ 🗄 Ⓥ 🍴
Enjoy a relaxing informal stay in a tastefully modernised C17th highland home offering a high standard of comfort and attention to detail. Privately situated overlooking mountains and moorland, carefully prepared 4 course dinner. Perfect touring base, special 7 day rates.

Corriechoille Lodge, *Spean Bridge, Inverness-shire, PH34 4EY.*
C18th lodge; stunning highland location, home cooked food, drinks licence.
Open: Mar to Oct
Grades: STB 4 Star GH, AA 4 Diamond
01397 712002 Mr & Mrs Swabey
enquiry@corriechoille.com
D: £20.00–£27.00
Beds: 2F 2D 1T **Baths:** 5 En
⌂ (7) ▣ (6) ⅍ ▣ ✕ ▥ � ᕦ cc

Stoer

NC0328   ◀ *Riverside*

Stoer Villa, *Stoer, Lairg, Sutherland, IV27 4JE.*
Victorian villa near Atlantic, sandy beaches, hill walkers and anglers paradise.
Open: All Year (not Xmas/New Year)
01571 855305
Mrs Spykers
D: £15.00–£17.00 **S:** £15.00–£17.00
Beds: 1D 1T **Baths:** 1 Sh
⌂ ▣ (5) ▣ ✕ ▥

Cruachan Guest House, *Stoer, Lochinver, Lairg, Sutherland, IV27 4JE.*
Friendly licensed accommodation. Beautiful beaches and mountains nearby.
Open: Apr to Oct
01571 855303 Miss Gould
D: £17.50–£20.00 **S:** £17.50–£20.00
Beds: 1D 2T 1S **Baths:** 1 Pr 1 Sh
⌂ ▣ (4) ▣ ➤ ✕ ▥ ▣ static

Strathan (Lochinver)

NC0821

Glenview , *Strathan, Lochinver, Lairg, Sutherland, IV27 4LR.*
Peaceful location, 100 yards off minor road, easy parking. 'Home from home'.
Open: March to Oct
01571 844324
Mrs Palmer
jand1@nascr.net
D: £17.00–£18.00 **S:** £16.00–£20.00
Beds: 1T 2D 2S **Baths:** 2 Sh
⌂ (14) ▣ (6) ⅍ ▣ ✕ ▥ ▣ ᕦ

Strathpeffer

NH4858   ◀ *Richmond Hotel, Brunstane Hotel, Holly Lodge Hotel*

Scoraig, *8 Kinnettas Square, Strathpeffer, Ross-shire, IV14 9BD.*
Quiet location in Victorian village ideal base for touring Highlands.
Open: All Year (not Xmas)
Grades: STB 3 Star
01997 421847 Mrs MacDonald
macdonald@kinnettas.freeserve.co.uk
D: £15.00–£17.00 **S:** £15.00–£20.00
Beds: 1F 1D 1T 1S **Baths:** 1 En 1 Sh
⌂ ▣ (6) ▣ ➤ ✕ ▥ ▣ static

Burnhill, *Strathpeffer, Ross-shire, IV14 9DH.*
Victorian house situated at entrance to a former spa village.
Open: Easter to Oct
01997 421292 Mrs Watt
D: £14.00–£18.00 **S:** £18.00
Beds: 1F 1T 1D **Baths:** 1 En 1 Sh
⌂ ▣ ⅍ ▣ ▥ static

Inver Lodge, *Strathpeffer, Ross-shire, IV14 9DH.*
Late Victorian house, large garden, home baking/cooking. Highland hospitality, warm welcome.
Open: March to Dec
Grades: STB 3 Star, AA 3 Diamond
01997 421392 Mrs Derbyshire
debyshire@inverlg.fsnet.co.uk
D: £16.00–£17.00 **S:** £22.00–£25.00
Beds: 1F 1T
⌂ ▣ ⅍ ▣ ➤ ✕ ▥ ▣ static cc

Craigvar, *The Square, Strathpeffer, Ross-shire, IV14 9DL.*
Beautifully situated luxury accommodation in unique Highland Victorian spa village.
Open: All Year (not Xmas/New Year)
Grades: STB 4 Star, AA 5 Diamond
01997 421622 (also fax)
Mrs Scott
craigvar@talk21.com
D: £20.00–£27.00 **S:** £24.00–£31.00
Beds: 1T 1D 1S **Baths:** 3 En
▣ (4) ⅍ ▣ ▥ ▣ static cc

Stromeferry

NG8634

Maple Lodge, *Stromeferry, Ross-shire,*
IV53 8UP.
Detached house in secluded Glen. Mountain
views all rooms.
Open: All Year
Grades: STB 2 Star
01599 577276
Mrs McDermott
jim@maple-lodge.co.uk
D: £16.00–£20.00 **S:** £16.00–£20.00
Beds: 1F 1T **Baths:** 1 En 1 Pr
🐾 🅿 (2) 📺 🐕 ✕ 🛏, Ⓥ ♨

Strontian

NM8161 🍴 *Strothian Hotel, Benview Hotel*

Carm Cottage, *Monument Park, Strontian,*
Acharacle, Argyll, PH36 4HZ.
Ideal stop for visiting Mull and smaller Isles,
plus touring around Ardnamurchan.
Open: April to Oct
01967 402268
Mrs Macnaughton
Fax: 01967 402095
D: £16.00–£19.00
Beds: 3F 1T 2D **Baths:** 1 En 1 Sh
🐾 🅿 (3) 📺 🐕 ✕ 🛏, ♨

Tain (Dornoch Firth)

NH7881 🍴 *Morangie House Hotel, Royal Hotel,*
Carnegie Lodge Hotel

Carringtons, *Morangie Road, Tain, Ross-*
shire, IV19 1PY.
Large Victorian house facing sea. Suitable
stopover for Orkney Isles.
Open: All Year (not Xmas)
Grades: STB 3 Star
01862 892635 (also fax)
Mrs Roberts
mollie1@btinternet,com
D: £16.00–£18.00 **S:** £20.00–£25.00
Beds: 2F 1D **Baths:** 2 En
🐾 🅿 (6) 📺 🐕 🛏, Ⓥ ♨

Golf View Guest House, *13 Knockbreck*
Road, Tain, Ross-shire, IV19 1BN.
Secluded Victorian House, overlooking Tain
Golf Course and Dornoch Firth.
Open: Feb to Nov
Grades: STB 4 Star, AA 4 Diamond
01862 892856 Mrs Ross
Fax: 01862 892172
golfview@btinternet.com
D: £20.00–£25.00 **S:** £25.00–£40.00
Beds: 1F 1D 3T **Baths:** 3 En 1 Sh
🐾 (5) 🅿 (7) ✄ 📺 🛏, Ⓥ ♨ cc

Northfield, *23 Moss Road, Tain, Ross-shire,*
IV19 1HH.
One mile from Glenmorangie Distillery, Tain
golf course and museum.
Open: Jan to Nov
Grades: STB 3 Star
01862 894087 Mrs McLean
may-mclean@northfield23.fsnet.co.uk
D: £16.00–£19.00 **S:** £16.00–£25.00
Beds: 1D 1T 1S **Baths:** 2 En 1 Pr
🐾 (3) 🅿 (3) ✄ 📺 🛏, Ⓥ ♨

Heatherdale, *2 Well Street, Tain, Ross-shire,*
IV19 1HJ.
Centrally situated for travelling north and
west. Golf, fishing, shooting.
Open: All Year (not Xmas/New Year)
01862 894340 Mrs Fraser
D: £18.00–£20.00 **S:** £25.00–£30.00
Beds: 1D 1T 1F **Baths:** 2 En 1 Pr
🐾 🅿 (3) ✄ 📺 🛏, Ⓥ ♨

Thurso

ND1168 🍴 *Halladale Inn, Melvich Hotel,*
Pentland Hotel, Northern Sands Hotel, Viking Bowl,
Upper Deck

Tigh na Clash, *Melvich, Thurso, Caithness,*
KW14 7YJ.
Modern building. Country views. Ideally
situated for touring north coast.
Open: Easter to October
Grades: STB 3 Star, AA 4 Diamond
01641 531262 (also fax) Mrs Ritchie
tignaclash@mywebpage.net
D: £21.50–£23.00 **S:** £21.50–£23.00
Beds: 1F 2T 3D 2S **Baths:** 7 En 1 Pr
🅿 (8) 📺 🛏, ♨ cc

3 Ravenshill Road, *Thurso, Caithness,*
KW14 7PX.
Open: May to Sep
Grades: STB 2 Star
01847 894801 Mrs Milne
D: £16.00 **S:** £17.00
Beds: 1D 1T **Baths:** 1 Sh
Situated in mainland Britain's most northerly town. Comfortable family home, comfortable beds, substantial Scots breakfast, wonderful views of Orkney Islands. Spectacular sea and hill scenery. Access by road and rail.

9 Couper Street, *Thurso, Caithness,*
KW14 8AR.
Friendly welcome, close to ferry to Orkney, beach and Train station.
Open: Jan to Dec
Grades: STB 2 Star
01847 894529 Mrs Oag
D: £15.00 **S:** £15.00
Beds: 1D 1T 2S **Baths:** 1 Sh

Shinval, *Glengolly, Thurso, Caithness,*
KW14 7XN.
Modern house with large garden. Four miles from Orkney ferry.
Open: Jan to Dec
01847 894306 Mrs Sinclair
Fax: 01847 890711
mary@shinval.swinternet.co.uk
D: £15.00 **S:** £15.00
Beds: 1F 1D 1T **Baths:** 1 En 2 Sh

Garth House, *Castletown, Thurso,*
Caithness, KW14 8SL.
Garth house is 280 years old, overlooking Britain's most Northerly point.
Open: All Year
Grades: STB 4 Star
01847 821429 Mr & Mrs Garfield
paul.garfield@tesco.net
D: £20.00–£25.00 **S:** £20.00–£25.00
Beds: 1D 1T **Baths:** 1 En 1 Pr

Tomatin

NH8029 ◀ *Tomatin Inn*

Millcroft, *Old Mill Road, Tomatin, Inverness,*
IV13 7YN.
1850 modernised crofthouse in quiet village. Ideal base for touring.
Open: All Year
Grades: AA 4 Diamond
01808 511405 Mrs Leitch
margaret_tomatin@hotmail.com
D: £18.00 **S:** £20.00–£25.00
Beds: 1D 1F **Baths:** 1 En 1 Pr

Tongue

NC5956 ◀ *Craggan Hotel*

77 Dalcharn, *Tongue, Lairg, Sutherland,*
IV27 4XU.
Croft cottage set in quiet valley. Families welcome. Phone for brochure.
Open: All Year
Grades: STB 2 Star
01847 611251 Mrs MacIntosh
D: £13.00–£15.00 **S:** £15.00
Beds: 1F 1D 1T 1S **Baths:** 1 En 1 Sh

Strathtongue Old Manse, *Tongue, Lairg,*
Sutherland, IV27 4XR.
Attractive Victorian Highland manse. Woodland setting. Beautiful beach, spectacular views.
Open: All Year (not Xmas/New Year)
01847 611252 (also fax)
Mrs MacKay
D: £18.00–£20.00 **S:** £20.00–£25.00
Beds: 2D 1T **Baths:** 1 En 2 Pr

BATHROOMS
Pr - Private
Sh - Shared
En - Ensuite

Tore

NH6052　◀ *Kilcoy Arms*

Fiveways Bed & Breakfast, *Tore, Muir of Ord, Ross-shire, IV6 7RY.*
TV all rooms, guest lounge, spacious parking, welcome always assured.
Open: Jun to Oct
Grades: STB 2 Star B&B
01463 811408 Mrs MacKenzie
D: £15.00 **S:** £17.00
Beds: 1F 1D 1T **Baths:** 1 En 2 Sh
🛏 🅿 📺 🐾 🎵 Ⓥ ☕

Torlundy

NN1476　◀ *Ben Nevis Restaurant*

Ferndale, *Tomacharrich, Torlundy, Fort William, PH33 6SP.*
Large bungalow in beautiful country setting, with wonderful views of Ben Nevis.
Open: All Year
Grades: STB 3 Star
01397 703593 Mrs Riley
D: £15.00–£20.00
Beds: 1F 2D **Baths:** 2 En 1 Pr
🛏 🅿 (6) ✔ 📺 🐾 🎵 Ⓥ ☕

Ullapool

NH1294　◀ *Argyll Hotel, Morefield Hotel, Arch Inn, Ferryboat Inn*

Broombank Bungalow, *Castle Terrace, Ullapool, IV26 2XD.*
A warm welcome awaits. Panoramic views over Loch Broom and Summer Isles.
Open: All Year
Grades: STB 3 Star
01854 612247 Mrs Couper
shirley.couper@tesco.net
D: £17.50–£20.00
Beds: 1T 2D **Baths:** All En
🅿 (3) ✔ 📺 🐾 🎵 ☕

All details shown are as
supplied by B&B owners in
Autumn 2000

Thornlea, *2 Morefield Crescent, Ullapool, IV26 2XN.*
Comfortable accommodation in pleasant surroundings on outskirts of Ullapool.
Open: Easter to Sept
Grades: STB 2 Star
01854 612944 Mrs Harvey
gjharvey@supanet.com
D: £14.00–£18.00 **S:** £15.00–£20.00
Beds: 1T 2D **Baths:** 1 En 1 Pr 1 Sh
🛏 (5) 🅿 (3) ✔ 📺 🐾 ✕ 🎵 Ⓥ ☕

3 Castle Terrace, *Ullapool, Ross-shire, IV26 2XD.*
Overlooking Summer Isles. Pretty rooms, home-made jams, vegetarian speciality. Some French/German spoken.
Open: Easter to Oct
Grades: STB 3 Star
01854 612409
Mrs Browne
D: £16.00–£19.00 **S:** £17.00–£18.00
Beds: 1D 1T 1S **Baths:** 1 En 1 Sh
🅿 (2) ✔ 📺 🐾 🎵 Ⓥ

Oakworth, *Riverside Terrace, Ullapool, Ross-shire, IV26 2TE.*
Modern detached bungalow in the centre of Ullapool.
Open: All Year
Grades: STB 3 Star
01854 612290
Mrs Downey
oakworth@ecosse.net
D: £15.00–£19.00
Beds: 3D **Baths:** 3 En
🛏 (12) 🅿 (3) ✔ 📺 🐾 🎵 ☕

The Sheiling Guest House, *Garve Road, Ullapool, Ross-shire, IV26 2SX.*
Purpose built guest house in one acre private grounds. Trout fishing free.
Open: All Year (not Xmas)
Grades: STB 4 Star, AA 4 Star
01854 612947
Mr MacKenzie
Fax: 01854 612 947
D: £23.00–£26.00 **S:** £23.00–£50.00
Beds: 4D 2T **Baths:** 6 En
🅿 (6) ✔ 📺 🎵 Ⓥ ☕

Westhill

NH7144 🍺 *Snow Goose, Cawdor Tavern*

Easter Muckovie Farm House, *Westhill, Inverness, IV2 5BN.*
Open: All Year
Grades: STB 3 Star
01463 791556 J H MacLellan
dot.westhill@virgin.co.uk
D: £18.00–£20.00 **S:** £25.00
Beds: 2F **Baths:** 1 En 1 Pr
🐾 🅿 (5) ⊬ 📺 🏇 ✗ 🏨 Ⅴ ♨
Original farmhouse modernised set in a rural location overlooking Inverness town, Moray & Beauly Firth with Sutherland & Ross-shire Hills in background. Culloden Battlefield, Cawdor Castle & Clava Cairns nearby. Excellent Scottish breakfast provided in comfortable dining room.

Bayview, *Westhill, Culloden Moor, Inverness, IV2 5BP.*
Open: Easter to Oct **Grades:** STB 3 Star
01463 790386 (also fax) Mrs Campbell
bayviewguesthouse@btinternet.com
D: £18.00–£22.00 **S:** £20.00–£25.00
Beds: 1T 2D **Baths:** 2 En 1 Pr
🅿 (3) ⊬ 📺 🏇 ✗ 🏨 ♨
Modern two storey house situated in 1/2 acre landscaped garden. Beautiful views to Ross-shire hills, Moray Firth and Inverness. 20 mins from Dalcross Airport. 1/2 mile from the famous Culloden Battlefield, 3 miles from Clava Cairns. Choice of breakfast, fresh produce used.

Wick

ND3650 🍺 *Carter's, Mackay's, Silver Darlings*

The Clachan, *South Rd, Wick, Caithness, KW1 5NJ.*
Family-run perfect for exploring the North and Orkney Islands.
Open: All Year (not Xmas)
Grades: STB 4 Star, AA 4 Diamond
01955 605384
Mrs Bremner
enquiry@theclachan.co.uk
D: £20.00–£25.00
S: £25.00–£30.00
Beds: 2D 1T **Baths:** 3 En
🐾 (12) 🅿 (4) ⊬ 📺 🏨 ♨

Quayside, *25 Harbour Quay, Wick, Caithness, KW1 5EP.*
Open: All Year
Grades: STB 2 Star
01955 603229 (also fax)
Mr Turner
quaysidewick@compuserve.com
D: £14.50–£19.50 **S:** £18.00–£28.00
Beds: 2F 2D 1T 2S
Baths: 2 En 2 Sh
🅿 (4) ⊬ 📺 🏨 Ⅴ ♨
We provide comfortable accommodation within a relaxed atmosphere, overlooking a traditional harbour front. For motoring and motorcycle enthusiasts, we provide a warm welcome, secure parking and simple but adequate repair facilities. Advice on daily sightseeing runs is available for all guests.

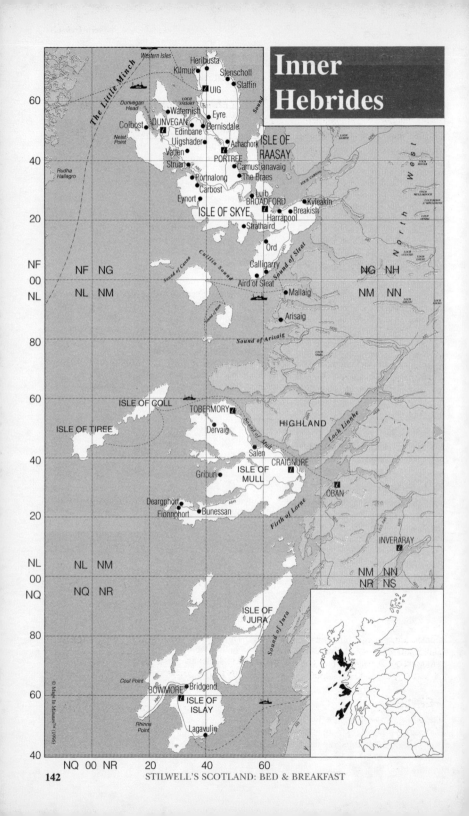

Inner Hebrides

COLL Isle of Coll
NM1955

Garden House, *Isle of Coll, PA78 6TB.*
Isolated comfortable farmhouse in middle of
bird reserve. Unwind on holiday.
Open: Oct
01879 230374 (also fax)
Mrs Graham
D: £18.00–£20.00
S: £24.00–£26.00
Beds: 1D 1T **Baths:** 1 Sh
P (10) ⚹ TV ✗ ▥ ♨

ISLAY Bowmore
NR3159

Lochside Hotel, *Shore Street, Bowmore,
Isle of Islay, PA43 7LB.*
Excellent value accommodation, food and
whisky!.
Open: All Year
01496 810244
Mrs Birse
birse@lochsidehotel.co.uk
D: £20.00 **S:** £20.00
Beds: 1F 1D 1T 5S **Baths:** 8 En
ъ TV ★ ✗ ▥ Ⅴ ♨

ISLAY Bridgend
NR3361

2 Mulindry Cottages, *Bridgend, Isle Of
Islay, PA44 7PZ.*
Open: All Year **Grades:** STB 3 Star B&B
01496 810397 Mrs Macfarlane
Fax: 01469 810397
D: £18.00 **S:** £20.00
Beds: 1T **Baths:** 1 Sh
ъ ⚹ TV ▥ Ⅴ ♨ ♿ 3
Comfortable accommodation in family home.
All on ground floor. Good breakfast provided,
quiet scenic area with views to surrounding
hills and iron age fort. Ideal location for
walking, bird watching and fishing.

ISLAY Lagavulin
NR4045 🕬 *Machrie Hotel*

Tigh Na Suil, *Lagavulin, Port Ellen, Isle of
Islay, PA42 7DX.*
Peaceful village location. Close to
distilleries. A warm welcome always.
Open: Jan to Dec
01496 302483 (also fax) Mrs Bowness
D: £20.00–£22.00 **S:** £22.00–£30.00
Beds: 1T 2D **Baths:** 3 En
P (5) ⚹ TV ▥ Ⅴ ♨

AIRPORTS ⊕
Islay, tel. 01496 302361.
Air Services & Airlines: *Isle of Islay to
Glasgow* and *Campbeltown*.
Tel. (local rate) 0345 222111.

BUS 🚌
Scottish Citylink, tel. 08705 505050,
National Express, tel. 0141 226 4826.

RAIL 🚆
For rail information, telephone the National
Rail Enquiries line, on 08457 484950. For
the Minicom service for the deaf and hard
of hearing, tel. 0845 605 0600.

FERRIES ⛴
Caledonian MacBrayne: *Mallaig to
Armadale (Skye)* 30 mins; *Oban to Mull,
Coll, Colonsay, Tiree, Western Isles;*

Tarbert to Islay.
Tel. 0990 650000 or 01475 650100.

TOURIST INFORMATION OFFICES ℹ

The Square, **Bowmore**, Isle of Islay,
PA43 7JH, 01496 810254.

Car Park, **Broadford**, Isle of Skye,
IV49 9AB, 01471 822361 (Easter to Oct).

The Pierhead, **Craignure**, Isle of Mull,
PA65 6AY, 01680 812377.

Dunvegan, Isle of Skye, 01470 521581.

Meall House, **Portree**, Isle of Skye,
IV51 9BZ, 01478 612137.

Main Street, **Tobermory**, Isle of Mull,
PA75 6NU, 01688 302182 (Easter to Oct).

Ferry Terminal, **Uig**, Isle of Skye,
01470 542404 (Easter to Oct).

MULL Bunessan

NM3821

Ardness House, *Tiraghoil, Bunessan, Isle of Mull, PA67 6DU.*
Family-run B&B near Iona, Staffa, beaches, outstanding sea views.
Open: Easter to Oct
Grades: STB 3 Star
01681 700260 (also fax)
Messrs MacNeill
ardness@supanet.com
D: £18.00–£22.00
Beds: 2D 1T **Baths:** 3 En
🛇 🅿 (3) 🍴 ✕ ▥ Ⓥ ❀

MULL Craignure

NM7136 🍲 *Craignure Inn, Ceilidh Place*

Linnhe View, *Craignure, Isle of Mull, PA65 6AY.*
Comfortable ex-manse built 1850 overlooking Loch Linnhe with view of Ben Nevis.
Open: All Year
01680 812427 (also fax)
Mr & Mrs Roberts
D: £20.00–£25.00 **S:** £20.00–£25.00
Beds: 2D 1T **Baths:** 2 Sh
🛇 🅿 (4) Ⓣ 🐾 ▥ Ⓥ ♨

MULL Deargphort

NM3025 🍲 *Red Bay Cottage*

Red Bay Cottage, *Deargphort, Fionnphort, Isle of Mull, PA66 6BP.*
Isolated, modernised home with restaurant. Ideal for Mull, Iona, Staffa.
Open: All Year (not Jan 1)
01681 700396 Mr Wagstaff
D: £16.50 **S:** £16.50
Beds: 1D 2T **Baths:** 3 Sh
🛇 🅿 (10) 🐾 ✕ ▥ Ⓥ ♨

All details shown are as
supplied by B&B owners in
Autumn 2000

MULL Dervaig

NM4352 🍲 *Ardbeg House, Bellachroy Hotel*

Kengharair Farm, *Dervaig, Isle of Mull, PA75 6QR.*
Victorian farmhouse on hillside overlooking glen and river beautiful scenery.
Open: Easter to
01688 400251 (also fax) Mrs Caskie
D: £16.00–£17.00 **S:** £16.00–£18.00
Beds: 1F 2T **Baths:** 1 Sh
🛇 🅿 (4) Ⓣ ✕ ♨

Antium Farm, *Dervaig, Tobermory, Isle of Mull, PA75 6QW.*
Traditional working farm. Many attractions including sightings of sea eagles.
Open: Easter to Oct
01688 400230 Mrs Boa
D: £18.00–£19.00
Beds: 2F **Baths:** 1 Sh
🛇 (1) 🅿 (2) Ⓣ ▥ Ⓥ ♨

Ardbeg House Hotel, *Dervaig, Tobermory, Isle of Mull, PA75 6QJ.*
Large Victorian picturesque village restaurant, licensed.
Open: All Year
01688 400254 (also fax) Mr Shilling
D: £22.00 **S:** £22.00
Beds: 2F 2D 2T 1S **Baths:** 5 Pr 2 Sh
🛇 🅿 (10) 🐾 ✕ ▥ Ⓥ ❀ ♨ ♿

MULL Fionnphort

NM3023 🍲 *Keel Row*

Caol-Ithe, *Fionnphort, Isle of Mull, PA66 6BL.*
Open: All Year (not Xmas/New Year)
01681 700375 (also fax)
Mrs Dickson
mary@caol-ithe.demon.co.uk
D: £20.00–£22.00 **S:** £20.00–£22.00
Beds: 1T 2D **Baths:** 2 En 1 Sh
🛇 🅿 🍴 Ⓣ 🐾 ▥ ♨
Warm, spacious bungalow. A highland hospitality awaits you. Private car parking. 5 minutes walk to ferry for Iona and Staffa. Ideal location for bird watching, hill walking and relaxation. White, sandy beaches within walking distance.

Staffa House, *Fionnphort, Isle of Mull,*
PA66 6BL.
Open: Marc to Oct
Grades: STB 3 Star
01681 700677 (also fax)
D: £20.00–£25.00 **S:** £25.00–£44.00
Beds: 2T 1D **Baths:** 3 En
☆ ▣ (5) ⚊ �📺 🛏 ✕ ▦ Ⅴ ⚓ cc
Full of antiques and individual touches
which set Staffa House apart from similar
establishments. 2 minutes walk Iona/Staffa
(Fingals Cave) ferries. Conservatory dining
room full of floral extravaganza. Ideal for
dinner watching Hebridean sunset and
views of Iona and Abbey.

Bruach Mhor, *Fionnphort, Isle of Mull,*
PA66 6BL.
Near Iona/Staffa ferries. Beautiful coastline,
walking, wildlife. Vegetarian cooking.
Open: All Year (not Xmas)
01681 700276 (also fax)
Mrs Heald
heather@bruachmhor.ndo.co.uk
D: £16.00–£18.00 **S:** £16.00
Beds: 1F 1D 1T 1S **Baths:** 1 En 1 Sh
☆ ▣ (4) 📺 ✕ ▦ Ⅴ ⚓

MULL Gribun
NM4534 *Salen Hotel*

Derryguaig, *Gribun, Isle of Mull, PA68 6EJ.*
Situated bottom Ben More overlooking Loch
na Keal. Ideal walking, cycling, wildlife.
Open: All Year
01680 300363 R & A MacKenzie
D: £18.00–£20.00 **S:** £18.00–£20.00
Beds: 1T 2D **Baths:** 2 Sh
☆ ▣ (4) ⚊ 📺 ▦ ⚓

RATES
D = Price range per person
sharing in a double room
S = Price range for a
single room

BATHROOMS
Pr - Private
Sh - Shared
En - Ensuite

MULL Salen
NM5743 *Oban Inn, Aulays Bar, Kelvin Hotel,
Soroba House, Barn Bar, Kings Knoll, Studio
Restaurant*

Corriemar House, *Esplanade, Oban,
Argyll, PA34 5AQ.*
Open: All Year
Grades: STB 3 Star, AA 3 Diamond,
RAC 3 Diamond
01631 562476
A Russell
Fax: 01631 564339
corriemar@tinyworld.co.uk
D: £18.00–£38.00 **S:** £20.00–£35.00
Beds: 2F 6D 4T 2S **Baths:** 12 En 2 Pr
☆ ▣ (10) ⚊ 📺 ✕ ▦ Ⅴ ✲ ⚓ cc
Large Victorian house in prime location on
Oban's seafront. Ideal for use as a base for
touring local islands and loch or just relax
and watch the sun setting over Oban Bay.

MULL Tobermory
NM5055 *Western Isles Hotel, Macdonald
Arms, Highland Cottage*

Harbour Heights, *Western Road,
Tobermory, Isle of Mull, PA75 6PR.*
Open: Easter to Oct
Grades: STB 3 Star
01688 302430 (also fax) Mr Stojak
D: £22.50–£25.00 **S:** £25.00–£30.00
Beds: 2T 4D **Baths:** 6 En
☆ (12) ▣ (20) ⚊ 📺 🛏 ▦ Ⅴ ⚓ ♿
Recently refurbished with attention to
comfort and style. Lounge themed in
burgundy with Persian rugs, deep soft sofas
and log fire. Bedrooms in heavy pine
furniture and green tartan furnishings. Guest
rooms overlook garden with views of sea and
gardens.

Tobermory Hotel, *53 Main Street, Tobermory, Isle of Mull, PA75 6NT.*
Open: All Year (not Xmas)
Grades: STB 3 Star
01688 302091 Mr Stevens
Fax: 01688 302254
tobhotel@tinyworld.co.uk
D: £35.00–£45.00 **S:** £39.00–£90.00
Beds: 2F 8D 4T 2S **Baths:** 15 En 1 Pr
🐾 📺 🐕 ✕ 🛏, Ⅴ 🛆 🍴 cc
Set on the waterfront of picturesque Tobermory's Bay, a beautiful sixteen room hotel, all private facilities with two ground floor rooms. A great variety of delicious meals and drinks from our cosy Water's Edge restaurant. A warm welcome guaranteed.

The Cedars, *Dervaig Road, Tobermory, Isle of Mull, PA75 6PY.*
Detached bungalow, separate B&B facilities, set in wooded garden.
Open: All Year (not Xmas)
Grades: STB 2 Star
01688 302096 Mr Bettley
D: £15.00–£16.00 **S:** £16.00–£20.00
Beds: 1D 1T **Baths:** 1 Sh
🐾 📄 (4) 🛏, Ⅴ 🍴

Harbour House, *Main Street, Tobermory, Isle of Mull, PA75 6NU.*
Family-run guest house overlooking Tobermory Bay.
Open: All Year (not Xmas)
01688 302209 Mrs MacLean
Fax: 01688 302750
harbourhou@aol.com
D: £19.50–£22.00 **S:** £19.50–£44.00
Beds: 2F 3D 2T 2S **Baths:** 5 En 2 Sh
🐾 📄 (10) 📺 🐕 🛏, 🍴 🛆 cc

2 Victoria Street, *Tobermory, Isle of Mull, PA75 6PH.*
On-street parking, 5 minutes from shops and harbour.
Open: All Year (not Xmas)
01688 302263 (also fax)
Mrs Harper
D: £14.00–£16.00 **S:** £15.00–£18.00
Beds: 1D 1T **Baths:** 1 Sh
🐾 📺 Ⅴ 🍴

Derwent House, *Raeric Road, Tobermory, Isle of Mull, PA75 6PU.*
Detached house overlooking Tobermory Bay and the Sound of Mull.
Open: Feb to Nov
01688 302420 (also fax)
D: £19.00–£20.00 **S:** £25.00
Beds: 4D **Baths:** 1 En 1 Pr 1 Sh
🐾 📄 (4) ✕ 📺 🐕 🛏, Ⅴ 🍴

SKYE Achachork

NG4745   ◀ *Cuillin Hills Hotel*

Creag An Fhithich, *10 Achachork, Achachork, Portree, Isle of Skye, IV51 9HT.*
Modern farmhouse with panoramic views, situated 2 miles north of Portree.
Open: Easter to Nov
01478 612213 (also fax)
Mrs MacDonald
D: £16.50 **S:** £16.50
Beds: 1F 1D 1T 1S **Baths:** 1 En 2 Sh
🐾 📄 (6) 📺 🛏, Ⅴ 🍴

Myrtlebank, *Achachork, Portree, Isle of Skye, IV51 9HT.*
Modern croft house overlooking Portree. Panoramic view towards Cuillin Mountains.
Open: May-Aug
01478 612597 (also fax)
Mrs Gilmour
skye.gilmour@lineone.net
D: £16.00 **S:** £16.00
Beds: 2F 1D 1S **Baths:** 2 En 1 Sh
🐾 📄 (5) 📺 🐕 Ⅴ 🍴

Jacamar, *5 Achachork Road, Achachork, Portree, Isle of Skye, IV51 9HT.*
Country Bungalow overlooks Portree and Cuillins. Excellent cooking Scottish breakfast.
Open: All Year
01478 612274
Mrs Thorpe
Fax: 01478 611191
normal.pat@jacamar.idps.co.uk
D: £14.00–£19.00 **S:** £15.00–£19.00
Beds: 3F 1D 1S
🐾 📄 ✕ 📺 ✕ 🛏, Ⅴ 🍴

SKYE   Aird of Sleat

NG5900   ◖ *Ardvasar Hotel*

The Old School House, *Aird of Sleat, Ardvasar, Isle of Skye, IV45 8RN.*
Open: Mar to Oct
Grades: STB 2 Star
01471 844218
Mrs Newman
D: £19.50–£24.00 **S:** £19.50–£24.00
Beds: 1D 1T 1S **Baths:** 1 Sh
⌂ (12) 🅿 (6) ⊁ 🎞 ♨
Old school house idyllically situated 30 yards from shore. Panoramic views of mainland mountains across the sea. Otters, dolphins, seals and whales seen from windows. Buzzards, eagles, other birds of prey and wild orchids in the area. Armadale Ferry 4 miles.

SKYE   Bernisdale

NG4050

Rubislaw, *34 Bernisdale, Bernisdale, Skeabost Bridge, Portree, Isle of Skye, IV51 9NS.*
Crofthouse with all rooms on ground level in a quiet lochside village.
Open: Easter to Oct
01470 532212 (also fax)
E M Macdonald
ettamacdonald@hotmail.com
D: £16.00–£22.00
Beds: 2D 1T **Baths:** 2 En 1 Sh
🅿 (4) 🎞 ⊁ ✕ 🎞 🆅 ♨

SKYE   Breakish

NG6623   ◖ *Crofters Kitchen, Claymore, Rendezvous*

Ashfield , *Breakish, Isle of Skye, IV42 9PY.*
Comfortable accommodation, overlooking sea and mountains. Short walk to beach.
Open: Easter to Oct
Grades: STB 3 Star
01471 822301
Mrs Clarke
D: £16.00–£20.00 **S:** £18.00–£20.00
Beds: 2D **Baths:** 1 En 1 Sh
⊁ 🎞 🎞 🆅

Fernlea, *Breakish, Isle of Skye, IV42 8PY.*
Large modern house with excellent sea and mountain views.
Open: Easter to Oct
Grades: STB 3 Star
01471 822107 Mrs Harrison
D: £19.00–£24.00 **S:** £20.00–£26.00
Beds: 2D 1T **Baths:** 3 En
⌂ 🅿 (4) ⊁ 🎞 🎞 ♨

Strathgorm, *15 Upper Breakish, Breakish, Isle of Skye, IV42 8PY.*
Spacious modern house overlooking sea.
Open: Feb to Dec
Grades: STB 4 Star
01471 822508 (also fax)
Mrs Graham
strathgorm@yahoo.com
D: £18.00–£22.00 **S:** £22.00–£25.00
Beds: 1F 1D 1T **Baths:** 2 En 1 Pr
⌂ 🅿 (6) ⊁ 🎞 🎞 🆅 ♨

Shiloh, *Breakish, Isle of Skye, IV42 8PY.*
Modern style bungalow set in own mature garden screened from main road by trees.
Open: Easter to Sep
Grades: STB 3 Star
01471 822346
Mrs MacInnes
D: £18.00–£20.00
Beds: 1F 1D 1T **Baths:** 3 En
⌂ 🅿 (10) 🎞 ♔ 🎞 🆅 ♨

Skye   Broadford

NG6423   ◖ *Claymore, Dunollie Hotel*

Millbrae House, *Broadford, Isle of Skye, IV49 9AE.*
Open: Feb to Nov
01471 822310 (also fax)
P & V Tordoff
D: £16.00–£22.00 **S:** £16.00–£23.00
Beds: 2D 1T 1S **Baths:** 3 Pr 1 Sh
⊁ 🎞 🎞 🆅 ♨
A refurbished croft house looking to the sea and hills. Bedrooms have private facilities with tea/coffee trays. Non-smoking. Antiques. Many foreign languages spoken. Packed lunches. Help with walking/driving tours gladly given. Very friendly.

Tigh Na Mara, *Lower Harrapool, Broadford, Isle of Skye, IV49 9AQ.*
Open: May to Oct **Grades:** STB 2 Star
01471 822475 Mrs Scott
D: £16.00–£18.00
Beds: 1F **Baths:** 1 Pr
🛏 (1) 🅿 ⅍ 📺 ⚲
150 year old traditional croft house in quiet position a few yards from the sea. Varied wildlife. Family room comprising double and single bed plus good sized bunks. Private sitting and bathrooms. French and Italian spoken. TV and toys. Restaurants nearby.

Ashgrove, *11 Black Park, Broadford, Isle of Skye, IV49 9DE.*
Open: All Year
Grades: STB 3 Star
01471 822327 (also fax)
Mrs Fletcher
D: £18.00–£20.00
Beds: 2D 1T **Baths:** 2 En 1 Pr
🛏 (2) 🅿 (4) 📺 ✝ 🎏 ⚲
Comfortable accommodation in bungalow situated within walking distance of hotels and restaurant and other amenities. A warm welcome and a full Scottish breakfast.

Caberfeidh, *1 Lower Harrapool, Broadford, Isle of Skye, IV49 9AQ.*
Modern bungalow with spectacular views. Sea shore location. Warm welcome assured.
Open: All Year (not Xmas/New Year)
Grades: STB 3 Star
01471 822664 Mrs MacKenzie
D: £20.00–£23.00
Beds: 3D **Baths:** 3 En
🅿 (4) ⅍ 📺 ✝ 🎏 ⚲

The Skye Picture House, *Ard Dorch, Broadford, Isle of Skye, IV49 9AJ.*
Comfortable lochside accommodation with panoramic views. Wildlife abounds. Home cooking.
Open: All Year
Grades: STB 3 Star
01471 822531 (also fax) Mrs Terry
holidays@skyepicturehouse.co.uk
D: £20.00–£25.00 **S:** £20.00–£25.00
Beds: 1F 2D 1T 2S **Baths:** 2 En 2 Sh
🛏 🅿 ⅍ 📺 ✝ ✕ 🎏 ⚲ cc

Swordale House, *Swordale, Broadford, Isle of Skye, IV49 9AS.*
Hebridean island hospitality at its best, comfort in a friendly and relaxing atmosphere.
Open: Mar to Nov
01471 822272 (also fax)
Mrs Christie
D: £18.00–£24.00 **S:** £25.00–£35.00
Beds: 3D **Baths:** 2 En 1 Pr
🛏 🅿 (3) ⅍ ✝ 🎏 ⚲ cc

SKYE Calligarry

NG6203

1/2 10 Calligarry, *Calligarry, Ardvasar, Isle of Skye, IV45 8RY.*
Overlooking the Sound of Sleat to the mountains of Knoydart.
Open: Easter to Oct
01471 844312 Mr & Mrs Fraser
D: £15.00 **S:** £12.00
Beds: 1D 1T 1S **Baths:** 1 Sh
🅿 (5) ⅍ 📺 🎏 ⚲ ♿

SKYE Camustianavaig

NG5139 🍴 *Isles Hotel*

An Airigh Shamradh, *1/2 of 8 Camustianavaig, Camustianavaig, Portree, Isle of Skye, IV51 9LQ.*
Outstanding sea views over Camustianavaig Bay to the Cuillin Hills. **Open:** All Year
Grades: STB 4 Star
01478 650224 (also fax) Mrs Smith
D: £20.00
Beds: 1T 1D **Baths:** 2 En
🅿 (4) 📺 🎏 ⚲

SKYE Carbost (Drynoch)

NG3731 🍴 *Old Inn*

The Old Inn, *Carbost, Isle of Skye, IV47 8SR.*
On the shores of Loch Harport, the inn provides an ideal setting for hillwalking.
Open: All Year
01478 640205 Mrs Morrison
D: £22.00–£24.50 **S:** £22.00–£24.50
Beds: 1F 2D 2T 1S **Baths:** 6 En
🛏 🅿 (25) ⅍ 📺 ✝ ✕ 🎏 ⚲ ♿ cc

SKYE Colbost

NG2148 ◀ *Old School House*

An Cala, *1 Colbost, Colbost, Isle of Skye, IV55 8ZT.*
Open: All Year (not Xmas)
01470 511393 Mrs Bohndorf
B&B@ancala.co.uk
D: £18.00 **S:** £21.50
Beds: 1T **Baths:** 1 Pr
🛇 🅿 📺 🐾 🕮 ᣥ
Modern bungalow overlooking Loch Dunvegan, 'The Three Chimneys' award-winning restaurant and a folk museum only 300 metres away. Dunvegan Castle and many other man-made and natural attractions within 10 mile radius and the beauty of the island everywhere.

SKYE Dunvegan

NG2547 ◀ *Dunvegan Hotel, Macleod Tables, Three Chimneys, Chimes*

6 Altavaid, *Harlosh, Dunvegan, Isle of Skye, IV55 8WA.*
Modern house, small garden, open countryside. Loch Bracadale, MacLeods Tables, Dunvegan Castle.
Open: Easter to Oct
Grades: STB 2 Star
01470 521704 Mrs Ewbank
D: £18.00–£20.00 **S:** £18.00–£20.00
Beds: 1F 1T **Baths:** 2 En
🅿 (2) 📺 🕮 ᣥ ᣥ

Sea View, *3 Herebost, Vatten, Dunvegan, Isle of Skye, Isle Of Skye, IV55 8GZ.*
Modern bungalow with sea views, near the famous Dunvegan castle.
Open: Easter to Oct
Grades: STB 3 Star
01470 521705 Mrs Campbell
D: £16.00–£17.50
Beds: 1D 1T **Baths:** 1 En 1 Pr
🅿 (2) ⅍ 📺 🕮 ᣥ

Planning a longer stay?
Always ask for any special rates

Bringing children with you?
Always ask for any special rates

6 Castle Crescent, *Dunvegan, Isle of Skye, IV55 8WE.*
Highland hospitality close to castle shops and restaurants.
Open: All Year
Grades: STB 3 Star
01470 521407
Mrs Stirling
D: £16.00–£17.00 **S:** £18.00–£20.00
Beds: 1F 1T **Baths:** 1 Sh
🛇 (1) 🅿 (2) ⅍ 📺 🐾 🕮 ᣥ ᣥ

Tigh-na-Mara, *2-3 Caroy, Dunvegan, Isle of Skye, IV56 8FQ.*
HIghland welcome. View hills and Loch Caroy. Dunvegan Castle nearby.
Open: All Year
01470 572338 (also fax)
Mrs Cleghorn-Redhead
nanted@tesco.net
D: £15.00 **S:** £15.00
Beds: 1D 2T **Baths:** 1 Sh
🛇 🅿 (5) 📺 🐾 🕮 ᣥ ✳ ᣥ

Herebost, *Dunvegan, Isle of Skye, IV55 8SZ.*
Views of sea & mountain 2 miles from Dunvegan Castle.
Open: Easter to Oct
01470 521255 Mrs MacDonald
D: £17.00–£19.00 **S:** £22.00–£24.00
Beds: 2D **Baths:** 1 En 1 Pr
🛇 🅿 (6) ⅍ 📺 🐾 🕮 ᣥ ᣥ

An Airidh, *6 Roag, Dunvegan, Isle of Skye, IV55 8ZA.*
Very comfortable and welcoming modern house, 4 miles Dunvegan, home of famous castle.
Open: All Year
01470 521738 Mrs Montgomery
Fax: 01470 521600
chrissiemontgomery@dial.pipex.com
D: £18.00–£22.00
Beds: 1F 1D **Baths:** 2 En
🛇 (2) 🅿 (4) 📺 🕮 ᣥ ᣥ

SKYE Edinbane

NG3451 🔲 *Edinbane Hotel, Lodge Hotel*

Eileen Dubh, *Edinbane, Portree, Isle of Skye, IV51 9PW.*
Modern bungalow B&B establishment, situated in North West Skye.
Open: Easter to Oct
01470 582218
Mrs Cumming
D: £16.00–£18.00 **S:** £16.00–£18.00
Beds: 1F 1D **Baths:** 1 Sh
🕏 (8) 🅿 (3) ⚒ 📺 🏃 ✕ ▦ Ⓥ ❋ ♨ & cc

SKYE Eynort

NG3826 🔲 *Old Inn*

The Blue Lobster, *Glen Eynort, Isle of Skye, IV47 8SG.*
Walkers haven: secluded, relaxed, in forest, by sea-loch and eagles!
Open: All Year
01478 640320
Mr Van der Vliet
bluelobster_grula@yahoo.com
D: £18.00 **S:** £23.00
Beds: 1D 2T
🕏 🅿 (4) 📺 🏃 ✕ ▦ Ⓥ

SKYE Eyre

NG4153 🔲 *Skeabost House Hotel*

Cruinn Bheinn, *4 Eyre, Snizort, Portree, Isle of Skye, IV51 9XB.*
Open: Easter to Oct
Grades: STB 4 Star B&B
01470 532459
Mrs Gordon
D: £17.00–£22.00
Beds: 2D 1T **Baths:** 3 En
🕏 🅿 (3) ⚒ 📺 ▦ ♨
Large modern crofthouse situated ten minutes' drive from Portree. We offer true highland hospitality with luxury accommodation and a friendly attentive service. Set in a beautiful tranquil location overlooking Loch Snizort and outer Hebrides and ideal base for exploring Skye.

SKYE Harrapool

NG6522 🔲 *The Claymore*

The Sheiling, *2 Lower Harrapool, Broadford, Isle of Skye, IV49 9AQ.*
Open: All Year (not Xmas)
01471 822533 Mr & Mrs Shearer
D: £14.00–£20.00 **S:** £14.00–£20.00
Beds: 1F 1T 1D 1S **Baths:** 1 En 1 Sh
🕏 ⚒ 📺 🏃 ▦ Ⓥ ♨
A lovely old traditional Skye house where a friendly Scottish welcome and a good breakfast is always assured. An ideal base for touring Skye, close to Broadford village. The area has beautiful views over Broadford bay to the mountains beyond.

SKYE Heribusta

NG4070 🔲 *Flodigarry*

1 Heribusta, *Kilmuir, Portree, Isle of Skye, IV51 9YX.*
Open: Easter to Sep
01470 552341 Mrs Beaton
alanbeaton@yahoo.com
D: £13.00–£15.00 **S:** £14.00–£15.00
Beds: 2D 2S **Baths:** 2 Sh
🕏 🅿 📺 🏃 ▦ ♨
Panoramic sea views towards Outer Hebrides. Set in a peaceful rural community with unrestricted views over unspoilt countryside. Superb base for quiet outdoor holiday with good walks in the vicinity. Excellent fishing, bird watching, sea life, archaeology and historic interest.

SKYE Kilmuir (Uig)

NG3870

Whitewave Activities, *19 Lincro, Kilmuir, Portree, Isle of Skye, IV51 9YN.*
Imagine a cross between an outdoor centre, an inn, & a ceilidh place.
Open: All Year
01470 542414 (also fax)
J White
info@white-wave.co.uk
D: £16.00–£18.00 **S:** £16.00–£18.00
Beds: 4F **Baths:** 1 En 2 Sh
🕏 🅿 (8) ⚒ 🏃 ✕ ▦ Ⓥ & 1 cc

SKYE Kyleakin

NG7526 🔔 *Crofters Kitchen*

Blairdhu House, *Kyle Farm Rd, Kyleakin,*
Isle of Skye, IV41 8PR.
Open: All Year
Grades: STB 4 Star
01599 534760
Ms Scott
Fax: 01599 534623
blairdhuskye@compuserve.com
D: £20.00
Beds: 1F 1D 1T **Baths:** 3 En
🛏 🅿 (6) ✄ 📺 🏲 🟦 🔲 🛎 ♿ cc
Beautifully situated house with panoramic
views. All rooms are ensuite with TV, radio,
hairdryers, tea/coffee making facilities.
Guests also have their own lounge, excellent
breakfast with a choice menu, private
parking, 2 minutes walk from Skye Bridge.

West Haven, *Kyleakin, Isle of Skye, IV41 8PH.*
This house is one hundred years old it used
to be a shepherd's house.
Open: Easter to Oct
01599 534476 Mrs MacAskill
D: £18.00 **S:** £18.00–£18.20
Beds: 1D 1T 1S **Baths:** 1 Sh
🛏 🅿 (6) 📺 🏲 🟦 🔲 🛎

16 Kyleside, *Kyleakin, Isle of Skye, IV41 8PW.*
A warm, friendly Highland welcome awaits
you at our guest house.
Open: All Year
01599 534468
Mrs Maclennan
D: £16.00–£20.00 **S:** £16.00–£20.00
Beds: 3D 1T 1S **Baths:** 1 En 2 Pr 2 Sh
🛏 🅿 📺 🏲 ✕ 🟦 🔲 ✳ 🛎

17 Kyleside, *Kyleakin, Isle of Skye, IV41 8PW.*
A warm welcome awaits you at our family-
run bed and breakfast situated on seafront.
Open: All Year
01599 534197
Mrs Macrae
D: £18.00–£19.00 **S:** £18.00–£19.00
Beds: 1D 1S **Baths:** 1 Pr 1 Sh
🛏 🅿 📺 🏲 🟦 🛎

SKYE Luib

NG5627 🔔 *Scouser Lodge Hotel, Claymore*
Restaurant

Luib House, *Luib, Broadford, Isle of Skye,*
IV49 9AN.
Open: All Year
01471 822724
Mrs Dobson
D: £18.00–£19.00 **S:** £25.00
Beds: 2D 1T **Baths:** 2 En 1 Pr
🛏 🅿 📺 🏲 ✕ 🟦 🛎
Luib House - Our home is your home and
make full use of the guest lounge, with
maps, books, games for the children. Make a
snack or meal in guests kitchen! Breakfast
an experience not to be missed.

SKYE Ord

NG6213

Fiordhem, *Ord, Sleat, Isle of Skye, IV44 8RN.*
Fiordhem, our home, is a unique stone
cottage idyllically situated 20 feet from
lochside.
Open: Easter to Oct
01471 855226
Mrs La Trobe
D: £22.00–£26.00
Beds: 2D 1T **Baths:** 3 En
🅿 (5) ✄ 📺 ✕ 🟦 🛎 cc

SKYE Portnalong

NG348353 🔔 *Taigh Ailean*

Taigh Ailean Hotel, *Portnalong, Carbost,*
Isle of Skye, IV47 8SL.
Superb lochside location with sea and
mountain views.
Open: All Year
01478 640271 (also fax)
Mr & Mrs Anslow
call@taighaileanhotel.demon.co.uk
D: £20.00–£25.00 **S:** £28.00
Beds: 2F 2D 1T 1S **Baths:** 3 Pr
🛏 🅿 (6) ✄ 📺 🏲 ✕ 🟦 🔲 ✳ 🛎 cc

SKYE Portree

NG4843 ◀ *Bosville Hotel, Ishes Inn, Cuillin Hills Hotel, Skeabost House Hotel, Portree House*

Creag An Fhithich, *10 Achachork, Achachork, Portree, Isle of Skye, IV51 9HT.*
Open: Easter to Nov
01478 612213 (also fax)
Mrs MacDonald
D: £16.50 **S:** £16.50
Beds: 1F 1D 1T 1S **Baths:** 1 En 2 Sh
⛺ 🅿 (6) 📺 🛏 📶 ▣ ⚓
Modern farmhouse with panoramic views, situated 2 miles north of Portree on A855 Staffin Road. Ideal for touring North and West of Island. TV lounge for guests use, full Scottish breakfast. Warm welcome.

Myrtlebank, *Achachork, Portree, Isle of Skye, IV51 9HT.*
Modern croft house overlooking Portree. Panoramic view towards Cuillin Mountains.
Open: May-Aug
01478 612597 (also fax)
Mrs Gilmour
skye.gilmour@lineone.net
D: £16.00 **S:** £16.00
Beds: 2F 1D 1S **Baths:** 2 En 1 Sh
⛺ 🅿 (5) 📺 🛏 ▣ ⚓

12 Stormyhill Road, *Portree, Isle of Skye, IV51 9DY.*
Centrally located in Portree village, within five minutes walking distance to shop, restaurants. **Open:** All Year
01478 613165 Mrs Nicolson
audrey-nicolson3@yahoo.co.uk
D: £17.50–£20.00 **S:** £20.00–£25.00
Beds: 1F 1T 2D **Baths:** 1 Pr 1 Sh
⛺ 🅿 (3) ✒ 📺 📶 ⚓

Cnoc Iain, *3 Sluggans, Portree, Isle of Skye, IV51 9EQ.*
Modern home with friendly atmosphere; good Scottish breakfast, panoramic views.
Open: Mar to Oct
Grades: STB 3 Star
01478 612143 Mrs MacSween
D: £19.00–£25.00 **S:** £30.00–£42.00
Beds: 2D 1T **Baths:** 3 En
⛺ 🅿 (3) 📺 🛏 📶 ▣ ⚓

Glendale, *2 Carn Dearg Place, Portree, Isle of Skye, IV51 9PZ.*
Friendly family home, single guests welcome. Central for touring Skye.
Open: All Year
Grades: STB 3 Star
01478 613149 (also fax)
Mrs Algie
D: £20.00–£30.00 **S:** £25.00–£35.00
Beds: 2T 1D 1S **Baths:** 2 En 2 Sh
⛺ 🅿 (3) ✒ 📺 📶 ▣ ♿ ⚓

brenitote, *9 Martin Crescent, Portree, Isle of Skye, IV51 9DW.*
Family B&B 5 mins walk from Portree village. Sun lounge and ensuite facilities.
Open: All Year
Grades: STB 3 Star
01478 612808 Mrs Matheson
D: £16.00–£18.00
Beds: 1T 1D **Baths:** 2 En
🅿 📺 📶 ▣ ⚓

12 Fraser Crescent, *Portree, Isle of Skye, IV51 9PH.*
Family-run Bed & Breakfast, offering clean, comfortable accommodation, 5 mins from bus.
Open: Apr to Oct
Grades: STB 3 Star
01478 612529 Mr Speed
D: £19.00–£20.00 **S:** £19.00–£20.00
Beds: 1T 1D **Baths:** 1 Pr
🅿 (2) 📺 🛏 📶 ▣ ⚓

Easdale Bridge Road, *Portree, Isle of Skye, IV51 9ER.*
Centrally situated bungalow with view of Cuillins and warm welcome.
Open: Easter to Oct
Grades: STB 2 Star
01478 613244 Mrs Macdonald
D: £20.00–£25.00 **S:** £25.00–£30.00
Beds: 2D **Baths:** 2 En
⛺ 🅿 (2) 📺 📶 ▣ ⚓

Planning a longer stay?
Always ask for any special rates

Givendale Guest House, *Heron Place, Portree, Isle of Skye, IV51 9EU.*
Quiet location outstanding views quality food and accommodation.
Open: Easter to Oct
Grades: STB 3 Star GH
01478 612183 Mrs Rayner
trevor@givendale7.freeserve.co.uk
D: £20.00–£25.00 **S:** £25.00–£35.00
Beds: 2D 2T **Baths:** 3 En 1 Pr
ﾋ 🅿 (6) ✗ 📺 🕮 Ⅴ ♨ cc

9 Stormyhill Road, *Portree, Isle of Skye, IV51 9DY.*
In quiet location 3 minutes walk from village centre and harbour.
Open: All Year
Grades: STB 3 Star
01478 613332 S Campbell
sandra_campbell_B_B@yahoo.co.uk
D: £18.00–£25.00 **S:** £20.00–£28.00
Beds: 3D **Baths:** 3 En
🅿 (3) 📺 🕇 🕮 Ⅴ ♨

Larch Grove, *Treaslane, Portree, Isle of Skye, IV51 9NX.*
Larch Grove offers you your own private suite - sitting room, double bedroom, bathroom.
Open: Easter to October
01470 582212 Mrs Aitken
D: £20.00–£25.00
Beds: 1D **Baths:** 1 En
🅿 ✗ 📺 🕮 ♨

SKYE Staffin

NG4867 🍺 Glenview Inn, Flodigarry Hotel, Columba, Oystercatcher

Gracelands, *5 Glasphein, Staffin, Portree, Isle of Skye, IV51 9LZ.*
Fantastic sea and hill views. Boat/fishing trips. Hill walking.
Open: Apr to Nov
01470 562313 Mrs Nicolson
D: £15.00–£16.00 **S:** £15.00–£16.00
Beds: 1F 2D 1T 1S **Baths:** 2 Sh
ﾋ (4) 🅿 (3) 📺 🕮 ♨

Tigh Cilmartin, *Staffin, Portree, Isle of Skye, IV51 9JS.*
Comfortable bedrooms with mountain view. Good breakfasts with home-made bread and home-grown produce.
Open: All Year
01470 562331 Mrs Poole
D: £15.00–£19.00 **S:** £15.00–£25.00
Beds: 1F 1D 1T **Baths:** 1 En 1 Sh
ﾋ 🅿 (6) 📺 🕇 ✗ 🕮 Ⅴ ♨

2 Glasphein, *Staffin, Portree, Isle of Skye, IV51 9JZ.*
Quiet, traditional, croft house with spectacular views.
Open: Easter to Oct
01470 562268 Mrs Macdonald
D: £14.00 **S:** £14.00
Beds: 1F 1T **Baths:** 1 Sh
ﾋ (1) 🅿 (2) 📺 🕮 ♨

SKYE Stenscholl

NG4868 🍺 Flodigarry Hotel, Glenview Inn

Quiraing Lodge, *Stenscholl, Staffin, Portree, Isle of Skye, IV51 9JS.*
Victorian hunting lodge. Dramatically situated in acre of garden. Quiet, seaside location.
Open: All Year
01470 562330 Mr Gardener
D: £21.00 **S:** £21.00–£30.00
Beds: 1F 4T 2D 1S **Baths:** 3 Sh
ﾋ 🅿 (10) ✗ ✗ 🕮 Ⅴ ♨

Achtalean, *Stenscholl, Staffin, Portree, Isle of Skye, IV51 9JS.*
Working croft, views over sea & the Quinag. Home baking and a cosy peat fire.
Open: Easter to Oct
01470 562723 Mrs Gillies
achtalean.b.b@talk21.com
D: £16.00–£18.00
Beds: 1F 1D 1T **Baths:** 1 En 1 Sh
ﾋ 🅿 (6) ✗ 📺 ✗ 🕮 Ⅴ ♨

Bringing children with you?
Always ask for any special rates

SKYE Strathaird

NG5317   ◀ *The Hayloft*

Strathaird House, *Strathaird, Broadford, Isle of Skye, IV49 9AX.*
Open: Easter to Sep
Grades: STB 1 Star GH
01471 866269 Mr Kubale
Fax: 01471 866320
straithairdhouse.skye.co.uk
D: £25.00–£30.00 **S:** £25.00–£30.00
Beds: 4F 1D 2S **Baths:** 1 En 1 Pr 3 Sh
🛇 🅿 (6) 🛏 ▥ ♨ cc
Family-run guest house above Kilmarie Bay on the Elgol Road. Ideal for walks to Camasunary Bay, Blaven, the Cuillins, seashore exploring & boat trips to Loch Coruisk. Rambling house with glorious views. Licensed 'Hayloft Restaurant', fireside library, drying room & garden.

SKYE Struan

NG3438   ◀ *Munro Tables, Ullinish Lodge Hotel*

Ard-Bhealaidh, *Balgown, Struan, Isle of Skye, IV56 8FA.*
Scenic lochside view, and a warm Highland welcome, await all who stay.
Open: Easter to Oct
Grades: STB 3 Star
01470 572334 (also fax)
Mr MacKay
ard-bhealaidh@uk-bedandbreakfasts.com
D: £16.00 **S:** £16.00
Beds: 1F 1D 1S **Baths:** 1 En 1 Sh
🛇 🅿 (5) ▥ 🛏 ♨

Glenside, *4 Totarder , Struan, Isle of Skye, IV56 8FW.*
Situated on working croft in lovely valley. Warm welcome assured.
Open: Easter to Oct
Grades: STB 3 Star
01470 572253 Mrs MacCusbic
D: £17.00–£20.00 **S:** £20.00–£22.00
Beds: 1D 1T **Baths:** 1 En 1 Pr
🛇 (12) 🅿 (3) ⅍ ▣ ✻ cc

The Anchorage, *9 Eabost West, Struan, Isle of Skye, IV56 8FE.*
Modern comfortable bungalow with panoramic sea and mountain views.
Open: All Year **Grades:** STB 3 Star
01470 572206 Mrs Campbell
eabost@aol.com
D: £18.00–£20.00 **S:** £20.00
Beds: 2D 1T **Baths:** 2 En 1 Pr
🛇 🅿 (3) ▣ 🛏 ✕ ▥ ▣ ♨ cc

Seaforth, *Coillore, Struan, Isle of Skye, IV56 8FX.*
Comfortable accommodation with panoramic views, ideally situated for touring.
Open: Oct
01470 572230 Mrs Mackinnon
D: £17.00–£19.00
Beds: 1D 2T **Baths:** 2 Sh
🛇 🅿 (4) ▣ ▥ ♨

SKYE The Braes

NG5234   ◀ *Portree House*

Tianavaig, *Camustianavaig, The Braes, Portree, Isle of Skye, IV51 9LQ.*
A pretty rural seashore location magnificent sea and mountain views.
Open: All Year (not Xmas)
Grades: STB 3 Star
01478 650325 Mrs Corry
D: £17.50–£20.00 **S:** £17.50–£20.00
Beds: 2D **Baths:** 1 En 1 Pr
🛇 🅿 (2) ⅍ ▣ 🛏 ▥ ♨

Cnoc Donn, *Achnahanaid, The Braes, Portree, Isle of Skye, IV51 9LH.*
Located on a working croft lovely sea and mountain views.
Open: All Year (not Xmas)
01478 650327 Mrs Macpherson
D: £17.50 **S:** £17.50
Beds: 2D **Baths:** 1 Sh
🛇 🅿 (2) ⅍ ▣ ▥ ♨

High season, bank holidays
and special events mean low
availability anywhere

SKYE   Uig (Uig Bay)
NG3963

Ard-na-mara, *11 Idrigill, Uig, Portree, Isle of Skye, IV51 9XU.*
Modern bungalow in a quiet location with half acre garden. **Open:** All Year
01470 542281 Fax: 01470 542289
D: £18.00–£25.00
Beds: 3D 1F **Baths:** 4 En
🛏 (14) 🅿 (4) 📺 🐕 🛢. ♨

13 Earlish, *Uig, Portree, Isle of Skye, IV51 9XL.*
Comfortable modern house on working croft. Extensive views over Loch Snizort to Black Cuillins. **Open:** All Year
01470 542361 (also fax) Mr & Mrs Pritcard
D: £14.00–£16.00 **S:** £14.00–£16.00
Beds: 2D 1T **Baths:** 2 Sh
🛏 🅿 (5) ✆ 📺 🐕 ✕ 🛢. 📹 ❀ ♨

SKYE   Uigshader
NG4346

Torwood, *1 Peiness, Uigshader, Portree, Isle of Skye, IV51 9LW.*
Open: Easter to Oct **Grades:** STB 3 Star
01470 532479 Mrs Gillies anne@selma.co.uk
D: £16.00–£20.00
Beds: 1F 1D 1T **Baths:** 2 En 1 Pr
🛏 (1) 🅿 (4) ✆ 📺 🛢. 📹 ♨
Torwood is a modern home offering warm, comfortable accommodation situated in the countryside yet only 10 minutes from Portree. An ideal base for touring or relaxing. Pony trekking, golf & fishing nearby. A warm highland welcome awaits you.

SKYE   Vatten
NG2843   🍴 *Dunvegan Hotel*

Sea View, *3 Herebost, Vatten, Dunvegan, Isle of Skye, Isle Of Skye, IV55 8GZ.*
Modern bungalow with sea views, near the famous Dunvegan castle.
Open: Easter to Oct
Grades: STB 3 Star
01470 521705 Mrs Campbell
D: £16.00–£17.50
Beds: 1D 1T **Baths:** 1 En 1 Pr
🅿 (2) ✆ 📺 🛢. ♨

SKYE   Waternish
NG2658   🍴 *Lochbay Rest, Stein Inn*

Lusta Cottage, *11-12 Lochbay, Waternish, Isle of Skye, IV55 8GD.*
Modern cottage set in 18 acre croft with waterfalls to shore of Loch Bay.
Open: May to Oct
Grades: STB 3 Star
01470 592263 Mrs Smith
lustacottage@supanet.com
D: £20.00 **S:** £20.00
Beds: 1D 1T **Baths:** 1 En 1 Pr
🅿 (8) ✆ 📺 🛢. ♨

34 Lochbay, *Waternish, Isle of Skye, IV55 8GD.*
Newly built croft house with spectacular views to Outer Hebrides.
Open: Easter to Oct
01470 592372 Mrs Broughton
D: £20.00–£25.00 **S:** £25.00–£27.00
Beds: 1D 1T **Baths:** 2 En
🛏 (10) 🅿 (4) ✆ 📺 🐕 🛢. ♨

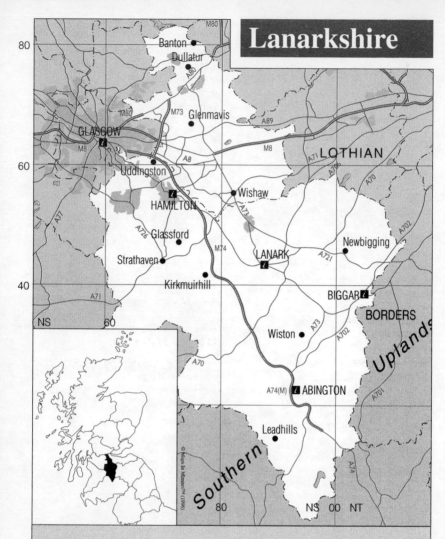

Lanarkshire

BUS 🚌

Scottish Citylink, tel. 08705 505050,
National Express, tel. 0141 226 4826.

RAIL 🚄

For rail information, telephone the National
Rail Enquiries line, on 08457 484950. For
the Minicom service for the deaf and hard
of hearing, tel. 0845 605 0600.

TOURIST INFORMATION OFFICES 🅸

Little Chef Service Area, A74 North,
Abington, Biggar, Lanarkshire, ML12 6SD,
01864 502436 (Easter to Oct).

155 High Street, **Biggar**, Lanarkshire,
ML12 6DL, 01899 221066 (Easter to Oct).

Road Chef Services, M74 (North), **Hamilton**,
Lanarkshire, ML3 6JW, 01698 285590.

Horsemarket, Ladyacre Road, **Lanark**,
ML11 7LQ, 01555 661661.

Banton

NS7579 🍺 *Swan Inn, Coachman Hotel*

Auchenrivoch Farm, *Banton, Kilsyth, Glasgow, G65 0OZ.*
Beautifully situated, south facing farmhouse. Large garden and views of Kelvin Valley.
Open: All Year
01236 822113 Mrs Henderson
D: £18.00–£21.00 **S:** £20.00–£22.00
Beds: 2T
🛏 🅿 📺 ▥ ▣ ♨

Biggar

NT0437 🍺 *Elphinstone Hotel*

Lindsaylands, *Biggar, Lanarkshire, ML12 6EQ.*
Beautiful country house, peaceful setting, local touring, Edinburgh/Glasgow borders.
Open: Easter to Nov
Grades: STB 4 Star
01899 220033
Mrs Stott
Fax: 01899 221009
elspeth@lindsaylands.co.uk
D: £24.00–£28.00 **S:** £28.00–£30.00
Beds: 2D 1T **Baths:** 2 En 1 Pr
🛏 🅿 (8) 📺 ✕ ▥ ▣ ♨

Cultershogle, *12 Langvout Gate, Biggar, Lanarkshire, ML12 6UF.*
Beautiful outlook from very comfortable bungalow; quiet location, home cooking.
Open: All Year (not Xmas)
01899 221702
Mr & Mrs Tennant
D: £18.00–£19.00 **S:** £20.00
Beds: 2T **Baths:** 2 En
🛏 🅿 (3) � 📺 ♀ ▥ ♨

RATES

D = Price range per person sharing in a double room

S = Price range for a single room

Cormiston Cottage, *Cormiston Road, Biggar, ML12 6NS.*
Open: All Year **Grades:** STB 3 Star
01899 220 200 Mrs Wales **Fax: 0131 440 0272**
jwales4453@aol.com
D: £20.00–£25.00 **S:** £25.00–£30.00
Beds: 1F 1T **Baths:** 1 En
🛏 (3) 🅿 (2) 📺 ✕ ▥ ▣ ♨ ♿
Delightful country cottage with beautiful views over the fields and hills beyond. The accommodation is on one floor and offers guests complete privacy. Spacious twin bedded room with ensuite facilities. There are bunk beds in the adjoining offering family accommodation.

Woodgill, *12 Edinburgh Road, Biggar, Lanarkshire, ML12 6AX.*
Friendly and welcoming family home in historic country town. **Open:** Easter to Oct
01899 220324 Mrs Brown
D: £18.00 **S:** £16.00
Beds: 1D 1T 1S **Baths:** 1 Sh
🛏 🅿 (4) ダ 📺 ▥ ▣ ♨

Dullatur

NS7476 🍺 *Castlecarry House Hotel, Craigmarloch Inn*

Dullatur House, *Dullatur, Glasgow, G68 0AW.*
Georgian mansion house circa 1740.
Open: All Year
01236 738855 (also fax) Mrs Moore
mooread@global.com
D: £19.50–£23.50 **S:** £21.50–£25.00
Beds: 1F 2T **Baths:** 2 En 1 Pr
🛏 🅿 (4) 📺 ♀ ✕ ▥ ▣ ♨

Glassford

NS7247 🍺 *Glassford Inn*

Avonlea, *46 Millar Street, Glassford, Strathaven, Lanarkshire, ML10 6TD.*
Comfortable homely accommodation country village near M74 junction 8. Rear garden. **Open:** Jan to Nov
Grades: STB 3 Star, AA 2 Diamond
01357 521748 Miss Rankin
D: £18.00–£20.00 **S:** £22.00–£25.00
Beds: 2T **Baths:** 1 Sh
🛏 (7) ダ 📺 ▥ ♨

RATES

D = Price range per person sharing in a double room
S = Price range for a single room

Glenmavis

NS7567   🍺 *Kirkstyle Inn*

Rowan Lodge, 23 Condorrat Road, *Glenmavis, Airdrie, Lanarkshire, ML6 0NS.* Excellent bungalow accommodation opposite village church. Ideal for touring.
Open: All Year **Grades:** STB 3 Star
01236 753934 june@rowanlodge.co.uk
D: £20.00–£30.00 **S:** £20.00–£30.00
Beds: 1T 1D 1S **Baths:** 3 En
🅿 (4) ⅍ 📺 🆖 Ⓥ 🍴 CC

Hamilton

NS7255   🍺 *Gults Bar, Harveys Bar, Hamilton Town Hotel*

57 Townhill Road, *Hamilton, Lanarkshire, ML3 9RH.*
Family house country view to rear, 5 minutes from M74. **Open:** All Year (not Xmas)
01698 824174 Mrs Reddy
Fax: 01698 327018
p.j.reddy.ltd@cableinet.co.uk
D: £16.00–£18.00 **S:** £16.00–£18.00
Beds: 2T **Baths:** 2 Sh
🐕 (2) 🅿 (2) 📺 🆖 🍴

Kirkmuirhill

NS7943   🍺 *The Poachers*

Dykecroft Farm, *Kirkmuirhill, Lesmahagow, Lanark, ML11 0JQ.*
Convenient for Glasgow and airports. Tea-making facilities. Good breakfast.
Open: All Year
01555 892226 Mrs McInally
D: £18.50–£20.00 **S:** £20.00–£22.00
Beds: 2D 1T **Baths:** 2 Sh
🐕 🅿 (4) 📺 🐾 🆖 Ⓥ 🍴 ♿ 1

Lanark

NS8843   🍺 *Crown Tavern, Lovejoys*

Roselea, 9 Cleghorn Road, Lanark, ML11 7QT. Edwardian House, original features. Close to New Lanark. Golf, fishing, riding and genealogy.
Open: All Year
Grades: STB 3 Star
01555 662540
Mrs Allen
margaretallen2@tesco.net
D: £18.00–£20.00 **S:** £17.00–£26.00
Beds: 1F 1D 1S **Baths:** 1 En 1 Sh
🐕 🅿 (2) 📺 🐾 🆖 Ⓥ ❀ 🍴

5 Hardacres, *Lanark, ML11 7QP.*
Home form Home. Well-appointed bungalow, 25 miles Edinburgh-Glasgow.
Open: All Year (not Xmas)
Grades: STB 3 Star
01555 661002
Mrs Buchanan
D: £16.00–£18.00 **S:** £17.00–£18.00
Beds: 2D 1T **Baths:** 1 En 1 Sh
🅿 (1) ⅍ 📺 🆖 🍴

Leadhills

NS8815   🍺 *Colebrook Arms, Hopetown Arms*

Meadowfoot Cottage, Gowanbank, *Leadhills, Biggar, Lanarkshire, ML12 6YB.*
Open: All Year (not Xmas)
Grades: STB 3 Star
01659 74369
Mrs Ledger
enquiries@meadowfootcottage.co.uk
D: £18.50–£20.00
S: £20.00–£25.00
Beds: 1F 1T **Baths:** 1 En 1 Sh
🐕 🅿 (4) ⅍ 📺 ✕ 🆖 Ⓥ 🍴
Blending history and modern amenities with the warmest welcome and delicious home cooking makes your stay a real highlight. Ideal for hill walking, Southern Upland Way, gold-panning, visiting Museum of Lead mining, Edinburgh, Glasgow, the beautiful Clyde Valley. Peaceful stopover just six miles from M74.

Newbigging

NT0145

Nestlers Hotel, *Newbigging, Lanark, ML11 8NA.*
Small intimate family run hotel in rural South Lanarkshire.
Open: All Year
Grades: STB 2 Star
01555 840680 Mr Anderson
nestlers@hotel98.freeserve.co.uk
D: £23.50–£27.50 **S:** £28.50–£35.00
Beds: 1F 2T 1D **Baths:** 4 En
🛏 🅿 (9) ⚊ 📺 �🛏 ✕ 🖳 🆅 🎇 👤 ⚻ cc

Strathaven

NS7044 🍺 *Glassford Inn, Waterside, Strathaven Hotel*

Avonlea, *46 Millar Street, Glassford, Strathaven, Lanarkshire, ML10 6TD.*
Comfortable homely accommodation country village near M74 junction 8. Rear garden. **Open:** Jan to Nov
Grades: STB 3 Star, AA 2 Diamond
01357 521748 Miss Rankin
D: £18.00–£20.00 **S:** £22.00–£25.00
Beds: 2T **Baths:** 1 Sh
🛏 (7) ⚊ 📺 🖳 👤

Kypemhor, *West Kype Farm, Strathaven, Lanarkshire, ML10 6PR.*
Bungalow with scenic rural views, 3 miles from busy market town.
Open: All Year **Grades:** STB 2 Star
01357 529831 Mrs Anderson
D: £17.00–£20.00 **S:** £18.00–£22.00
Beds: 1D 1T **Baths:** 1 Sh
🛏 🅿 (12) 📺 �🛏 ✕ 🖳 🆅 👤 ⚻

Haroldslea, *3 Kirkhill Road, Strathaven, Lanarkshire, ML10 6HN.*
Modern detached villa with garden in quiet residential area near village centre.
Open: All Year (not Xmas/New Year)
Grades: STB Listed, Approv
01357 520617 Mrs Goodwillie
D: £20.00 **S:** £20.00
Beds: 1F 1D **Baths:** 2 Sh
🛏 🅿 (2) ⚊ 📺 �🛏 🖳 🆅 👤

Uddingston

NS6960 🍺 *Windmill, Redstones*

Phoenix Lodge Guest House, *4 Girdons Way, Uddingston, Glasgow, G71 7ED.*
Open: All Year
Grades: STB 2 Star
01698 815296
Mr Boyce
Fax: 01698 267567
D: £19.00–£22.00 **S:** £23.00–£25.00
Beds: 6F 1T 1D **Baths:** 3 En 2 Sh
🛏 🅿 (8) 📺 ⛾ ✕ 🖳 🆅 🎇 👤 ⚻ cc
Modern building, close to motorways north & south, rail station, lots of tourist attractions locally, walks, close to swimming pool, tenpin bowling, cinemas, parks, gymnasium, lots of pubs, clubs, various eating places, e.g. Indian, Italian, Chinese. Close to Glasgow Zoo.

Northcote Guest House, *2 Holmbrae Avenue, Uddingston, Glasgow, G71 6AL.*
Large Victorian private house, quiet locality. Easily accessible.
Open: All Year (not Xmas)
01698 813319 (also fax)
Mrs Meggs
meggs@accanet.com
D: £16.00–£17.00 **S:** £16.00–£17.00
Beds: 1F 1D 1S **Baths:** 1 Sh
🛏 🅿 (3) 📺 🖳 🆅

Wishaw

NS7954 🍺 *Chardonnay*

The Mill House, *Garrion Bridge, Wishaw, Lanarkshire, ML2 0RR.*
Mill House, built 1907 with delightful garden, comfortable warm home.
Open: All Year
01698 881166
Mrs Pinkerton
Fax: 01698 886874
alanphotog@aol.com
D: £15.00–£18.00 **S:** £22.50–£27.50
Beds: 1F 1D 1T **Baths:** 1 En 1 Sh
🅿 (6) ⚊ 📺 🖳 👤

Lothian & Falkirk

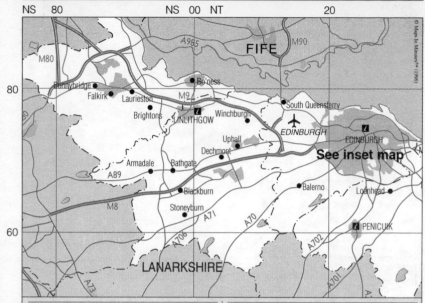

NS 80 NS 00 NT 20

AIRPORTS ⊕

Edinburgh Airport, tel. 0131 333 1000.

AIR SERVICES & AIRLINES ✈

British Airways: *Edinburgh to Bristol, Birmingham, Kirkwall (Orkney), London (Heathrow), Manchester, Sumburgh (Shetland), Wick.*
Tel. (local rate): 0345 222111.

KLM UK: *Edinburgh to East Midland, Bradford, London (Gatwick & Stansted), Norwich.*
Tel. (local rate): 08705 074074.

RAIL ⇌

For rail information, telephone the National Rail Enquiries line, on 08457 484950. For the Minicom service for the deaf and hard of hearing, tel. 0845 605 0600.

BUS 🚌

Scottish Citylink, tel. 08705 505050,
National Express, tel. 0141 226 4826.

TOURIST INFORMATION OFFICES ℹ

Hamilton's Cottage, **Bo'ness**, West Lothian, EH51 0NG, 01506 826626 (Easter to Oct).

143 High Street, **Dunbar**, East Lothian, EH42 1ES, 01368 863353.

3 Princes St, **Edinburgh**, EH2 2AN, 0131 473 3800.

2-4 Glebe Street, **Falkirk**, FK1 1HX, 01324 620244.

Burgh Halls, The Cross, **Linlithgow**, West Lothian, EH49 7AH, 01506 844600.

Scottish Mining Museum, Lady Victoria Colliery, **Newtongrange**, Dalkeith, Midlothian, 0131 663 4262 (Easter to Oct).

Quality Street, **North Berwick**, East Lothian, EH39 4HJ, 01620 892197.

Granada Service Area, A1, **Old Craighall**, Musselburgh, East Lothian, EH21 8RE, 0131 653 6172.

Edinburgh Crystal Visitor Centre, Eastfield Industrial Estate, **Penicuik**, Midlothian, EH26 8HB, 01968 673846 (Easter to Oct).

Edinburgh Airport, **Turnhouse**, Edinburgh, 0131 473 3800.

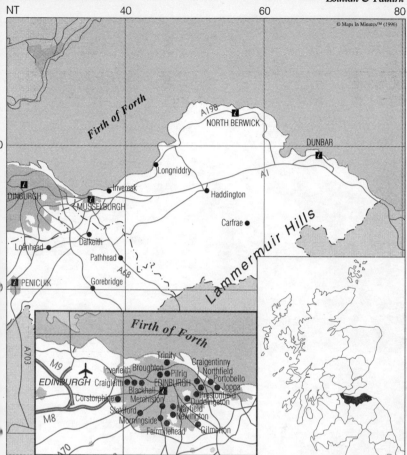

© Maps In Minutes™ (1996)

Armadale

NS9368

Tarrareoch Farm, *Armadale, Bathgate, W Lothian, EH48 3BJ.*
C17th farmhouse all on one level. Midway Edinburgh/Glasgow. Beautiful countryside.
Open: All Year
Grades: STB 3 Star
01501 730404 (also fax)
Mrs Gibb
D: £16.00–£20.00 **S:** £20.00–£26.00
Beds: 1F 2T **Baths:** 1 En 1 Sh
☼ 🅿 (10) 📺 🛏 🏠 Ⓥ ♨

Balerno

NT1666   🍴 *Tanners, Kestrel*

Newmills Cottage, *472 Lanark Road West, Balerno, EH14 5AE.*
Delightful house set in own grounds with ample private off-road parking.
Open: All Year
Grades: STB 4 Star, AA 4 Diamond
0131 449 4300 (also fax)
Mrs Linn
newmillscottage@blueyonder.co.uk
D: £20.00–£27.50 **S:** £25.00–£35.00
Beds: 2T **Baths:** 1 En 1 Pr
🅿 ⚜ 📺 🏠 Ⓥ ♨

Bathgate

NS9769   🛏 *Kaim Park*

Hillview, *35 The Green, Bathgate, W Lothian, EH48 4DA.*
Quality and friendly accommodation with spectacular views of West Lothian.
Open: All Year (not Xmas)
Grades: STB 2 Star
01506 654830 (also fax)
Mrs Connell
D: £15.00–£16.00 **S:** £20.00–£22.00
Beds: 1F 1T **Baths:** 1 Sh
🐎 ⅍ 📺 🐕 🛏, Ⅴ ⚓

Blackburn

NS9865

Cruachan Guest House, *78 East Main Street, Blackburn, Bathgate, West Lothian, EH47 7QS.*
Relaxed, friendly, high-quality. Airport nearby, rail service to Edinburgh.
Open: All Year (not Xmas)
Grades: STB 3 Star
01506 655221
Mr Harkins
Fax: 01506 652395
cruachan.bb@virgin.net
D: £20.00–£23.00 **S:** £25.00–£30.00
Beds: 1F 3D **Baths:** 3 En 1 Pr
🐎 🅿 (5) ⅍ 📺 🛏, Ⅴ ⚓

Bo'ness

NS9981   🛏 *Richmond Park Hotel*

Haypark, *28 Grange Terrace, Bo'ness, EH51 9DS.*
Attractive stone built house overlooking the Forth, convenient for Edinburgh and Stirling.
Open: May to September
Grades: STB 2 Star
01506 823193 (also fax)
Mrs Croxford
D: £20.00–£25.00 **S:** £25.00
Beds: 1T 1D **Baths:** 1 Sh
⅍ 📺 🛏, ☕ ⚓

Bonnybridge

NS8380   🛏 *Castrechery House*

Bandominie Farm, *Walton Road, Bonnybridge, Stirlingshire, FK4 2HP.*
Farmhouse friendly atmosphere. 2 miles from A80, Castle Cary, B816.
Open: All Year (not Xmas/New Year)
Grades: STB 2 Star
01324 840284
Mrs Forrester
D: £17.00–£18.00 **S:** £17.00–£18.00
Beds: 1D 1T 1S **Baths:** 1 Sh
🐎 🅿 (3) ⅍ 📺 🐕 🛏, ⚓

Brightons

NS9377   🛏 *Whyteside Hotel*

Chez Nous, *Sunnyside Road, Brightons, Falkirk, FK2 0SA.*
Detached property with large car park equidistant Edinburgh-Glasgow, convenient for M9, M8.
Open: All Year (not Xmas)
01324 712836 (also fax)
Mr & Mrs Hunter
D: £18.00–£25.00 **S:** £18.00–£25.00
Beds: 2D 2T 2S **Baths:** 1 En 2 Sh
🐎 (9) 🅿 (8) ⅍ 📺 🛏, Ⅴ ⚓

Carfrae

NT5769   🛏 *Goblin Ha Hotel, Tweedale Arms Hotel*

Carfrae Farm, *Carfrae, Haddington, E Lothian, EH41 4LP.*
Peaceful farmhouse overlooking lovely gardens. Edinburgh, The Borders, Golf nearby.
Open: Apr to Oct
Grades: STB 4 Star
01620 830242
Mrs Gibson
Fax: 01620 830320
dgcarfrae@aol.com
D: £25.00–£27.00 **S:** £35.00–£40.00
Beds: 2D 1T **Baths:** 2 En 1 Pr
🐎 (10) 🅿 (6) ⅍ 📺 🛏, ⚓

Dalkeith

NT3467 🍴 *Justinlees Inn, County Hotel*

Belmont, *47 Eskbank Road, Dalkeith, Midlothian, EH22 3BH.*
Spacious Victorian family house with lovely large garden.
Open: All Year (not Xmas/New Year)
0131 663 8676 (also fax)
Mrs Jarvis
D: £21.00–£23.00 **S:** £25.00–£30.00
Beds: 2D 1T **Baths:** 1 En 2 Sh
🛏 🅿 (8) ⅄ 📺 🐾 🏛 Ⅴ cc

Dechmont

NT0370 🍴 *Beecraigs Restaurant*

Bankhead Farm, *Dechmont, Broxburn, EH52 6NB.*
Panoramic views of beautiful countryside yet easy access to Edinburgh airport.
Open: All Year (not Xmas)
Grades: STB 3 Star
01506 811209
H Warnock
Fax: 07970 691318
bankheadbb@aol.com
D: £20.00–£25.00 **S:** £25.00–£35.00
Beds: 2F 2D 1T 2S **Baths:** 7 En
🛏 🅿 ⅄ 📺 🏛 Ⅴ ☕ cc

Dunbar

NT6779 🍴 *Craig En Gelt, Bayswell Hotel, Hillside Hotel, Starfish Restaurant*

Overcliffe Guest House, *11 Bayswell Park, Dunbar, E Lothian, EH42 1AE.*
Family-run, perfect for touring East Lothian's golf courses beaches.
Open: All Year
Grades: STB 2 Star, AA 3 Diamond
01368 864004
Mrs Bower
Fax: 01368 865995
overcliffe@aol.com
D: £20.00–£35.00 **S:** £25.00–£35.00
Beds: 3F 2T **Baths:** 3 En 2 Sh
🛏 (1) 🅿 (2) ⅄ 📺 🐾 🏛 ☕

Cruachan Guest House, *East Links Road, Dunbar, E Lothian, EH42 1LT.*
125 year old spacious roomed, family home on beach.
Open: All Year **Grades:** STB 2 Star
01368 863006 Mr & Mrs McVicar
D: £20.00–£28.00 **S:** £20.00
Beds: 2F 1D 1T 1S **Baths:** 2 En 1 Pr
🛏 🅿 (5) 📺 🐾 ✕ 🏛 Ⅴ ☕ ♿

Battleblent Hotel, *West Barns, Dunbar, E Lothian, EH42 1TS.*
Elevated castle-like country house hotel facing the Belhaven Bay. **Open:** All Year
01368 862234 (also fax) Mr Ferguson
battleblent. dunbar@tinyworld.co.uk
D: £25.00–£35.00 **S:** £25.00–£35.00
Beds: 1F 1D 3T 2S **Baths:** 7 En 1 Pr
🛏 🅿 (20) 📺 🐾 ✕ 🏛 Ⅴ ☕ cc

EDINBURGH   Blackhall

NT2174

Sandilands House, *25 Queensferry Road, Edinburgh, EH4 3HB.*
1930's bungalow with many art deco features. Near Murrayfield Stadium.
Open: All Year **Grades:** STB 4 Star
0131 332 2057 Mrs Sandilands
Fax: 0131 315 4476
D: £20.00–£34.00 **S:** £25.00–£45.00
Beds: 1F 1D 1T **Baths:** 3 En
🛏 🅿 ⅄ 📺 🏛 Ⅴ ☕ cc

EDINBURGH   Broughton

NT2575 🍴 *Clarmont Bar*

Ben Cruachan, *17 Mcdonald Road, Edinburgh, EH7 4LX.*
Open: April to Oct **Grades:** STB 3 Star
0131 556 3709 N Stark
D: £25.00–£35.00
Beds: 1F 1T 1D **Baths:** 3 En
🛏 (10) 🅿 ⅄ 📺 🏛 Ⅴ ☕
Be assured of a very warm welcome at our family-run centrally situated guesthouse within walking distance of all main attractions. Bedrooms are fully equipped with your every comfort in mind. Excellent breakfast served. Free street parking.

Elas Guest House, *10 Claremont Crescent, Edinburgh, EH7 4HX.*
Georgian house, central Edinburgh. Free street parking. Traditional Scottish breakfasts. Groups - families welcome.
Open: All Year **Grades:** STB 2 Star
0131 556 1929 Mrs Elas
D: £20.00–£30.00 **S:** £20.00–£30.00
Beds: 3F 2D 2T 1S **Baths:** 8 En
📺 🛏 ✕ 🖥 📶 🖳

Brodies Guest House, *22 East Claremont Street, Edinburgh, EH7 4JP.*
A warm Scottish welcome awaits you at our Victorian town house.
Open: All Year (not Xmas)
0131 556 4032 Mrs Olbert **Fax: 0131 556 9739**
rose.olbert@saqnet.co.uk
D: £22.00–£35.00 **S:** £22.00–£30.00
Beds: 1F 1D 1T 1S **Baths:** 2 Pr 1 Sh
📺 🖥 📶 🖳

EDINBURGH   Central

NT2573   ⬤ *Golf Tavern, Bennets Bar, Minto Hotel, Navaar Hotel, Allison Hotel, Seahaven Hotel*

Rothesay Hotel, *8 Rothesay Place, Edinburgh, EH3 7SL.*
Heart of Edinburgh's Georgian new town in the city centre, short walk Princes Street.
Open: All Year
Grades: STB 2 Star, AA 3 Diamond
0131 225 4125 Mr Borland
info@rothesay-hotel.demon.co.uk
D: £25.00–£45.00 **S:** £38.00–£65.00
Beds: 2F 4D 18T 12S **Baths:** 36 Pr
📺 🛏 ✕ 🖥

Averon Guest House, *44 Gilmore Place, Edinburgh, EH3 9NQ.*
Open: All Year **Grades:** STB 1 Star, AA 2 Diamond, RAC 3 Diamond
0131 229 9932 Mr Cran
D: £18.00–£38.00 **S:** £25.00–£38.00
Beds: 3F 2D 3T 1S **Baths:** 6 Pr
📺 🅿 (10) 📺 📶 🖳 cc
Fully restored Georgian town house, built in 1770. Central Edinburgh with car park. Standard and ensuite rooms available. STB, AA, RAC, Les Routiers recommended. 10 minute walk to Castle and Princes Street.

6 Dean Park Crescent, *Edinburgh, EH4 1PN.*
Warm friendly home. Large rooms. 10 mins walk to centre.
Open: Easter to Oct
Grades: STB 3 Star B&B
0131 332 5017 Mrs Kirkland
kirkland.b&b@cableinet.co.uk
D: £22.00–£29.00 **S:** £40.00–£55.00
Beds: 1F 1D 1T **Baths:** 1 En 1 Pr 1 Sh
📺 ⚜ 📺 📶 🖳 ♿

Amaryllis Guest House, *21 Upper Gilmore Place, Edinburgh, EH3 9NL.*
Warm, comfortable, friendly, central all attractions. Walkable but quietly situated.
Open: All Year (not Xmas)
Grades: STB 2 Star
0131 229 3293 (also fax)
L Melrose
ghamaryllis@aol.com
D: £18.00–£30.00 **S:** £25.00–£40.00
Beds: 3F 1D 1T **Baths:** 4 En 1 Pr
📺 (10) 🅿 (2) 📺 📶 🖳 cc

17 Hope Park Terrace, *Edinburgh, EH8 9LZ.*
Fifteen minutes' walk city centre. H&C in bedrooms.
Open: All Year
Grades: STB 1 Star
0131 667 7963 Mrs Frackelton
D: £25.00 **S:** £25.00
Beds: 2D **Baths:** 1 Sh
📺 (10) ⚜ 📶 🖳 🖳

28 London Street, *Edinburgh, EH3 6NA.*
Central Georgian 1st flat 5 minutes walk from station.
Open: Easter to Oct **Grades:** STB 2 Star
0131 556 4641 Mr & Mrs Campbell
D: £18.00–£25.00 **S:** £20.00–£27.00
Beds: 1F 1T 1D 1S **Baths:** 3 Sh
📺 (5) 🅿 (1) 📺 📶

BATHROOMS
Pr - Private
Sh - Shared
En - Ensuite

All details shown are as
supplied by B&B owners in
Autumn 2000

Ailsa Craig Hotel, 24 Royal Terrace,
Edinburgh, EH7 5AH.
Elegant city centre Georgian town house
hotel. Walking distance major attractions.
Open: All Year
Grades: STB 3 Star
0131 556 1022 Fax: 0131 556 6055
ailsacraighotel@ednet.co.uk
D: £25.00–£45.00 **S:** £25.00–£60.00
Beds: 5F 5D 3T 4S **Baths:** 14 En 1 Pr 2 Sh
❄ 📺 ✕ 📖 Ⓥ ⚲ cc

Castle Park Guest House, 75 Gilmore
Place, *Edinburgh, EH3 9NU.*
Charming Victorian guest house ideally
situated close to King Theatre & city centre.
Open: All Year
Grades: STB 2 Star
0131 229 1215 Fax: 0131 229 1223
D: £17.50–£25.00 **S:** £17.50–£22.50
Beds: 1F 4D 1T 2S **Baths:** 4 En 2 Sh
❄ 📵 (4) 📺 🐾 📖 ⚲ cc

37 Howe Street, Edinburgh, EH3 6TF.
Listed building the the heart of Edinburgh in
historic New Town.
Open: Easter to Oct
Grades: STB 2 Star
0131 557 3487 (also fax)
Mrs Collie
D: £20.00
Beds: 1D **Baths:** 1 Sh
📺 📖 Ⓥ ⚲ ♿

Aries Guest House, 5 Upper Gilmore
Place, *Edinburgh, EH3 9NW.*
Small central friendly, all attractions
walkable. TV, tea in rooms.
Open: All Year (not Xmas)
0131 229 4669 Mrs Robertson
D: £17.00–£28.00 **S:** £25.00–£35.00
Beds: 1F 2D 2T **Baths:** 2 Sh
❄ 📺 🐾 📖 ⚲ ♿ cc

EDINBURGH   Corstorphine
NT1972

Zetland Guest House, 186 St Johns Road,
Edinburgh, EH12 8SG.
A splendid Victorian house situated on the
west side of Edinburgh.
Open: All Year
Grades: STB 3 Star GH, AA 4 Diamond
0131 334 3898 (also fax)
Mr Stein
zetland@dial.pipex.com
D: £20.00–£27.50 **S:** £20.00–£50.00
Beds: 1F 2D 4T 1S **Baths:** 4 En 2 Sh
❄ 📵 (7) 📺 📖 Ⓥ ⚲

EDINBURGH   Craigentinny
NT2974

Glenfarrer House, 36 Farrer Terrace,
Edinburgh, EH7 6SG.
Chalet bungalow close to excellent bus
services. City centre 2 miles.
Open: Easter to Oct
0131 669 1265 Mrs Smith
D: £21.00 **S:** £17.00
Beds: 1D 1T 2S **Baths:** 2 En 1 Sh
📵 (2) ⅌ 📺 📖 Ⓥ ⚲

EDINBURGH   Craigleith
NT2374

St Bernards Guest House, 22 St
Bernards Crescent, *Edinburgh, EH4 1NS.*
Victorian town house. 15 minute walk from
city centre. Quiet location.
Open: All Year
0131 332 2339 Mr & Mrs Alsop
D: £22.50–£30.00 **S:** £25.00–£30.00
Beds: 3D 4T 1S **Baths:** 4 En 2 Sh
⅌ 📺 📖 Ⓥ ⚲

High season, bank holidays
and special events mean low
availability anywhere

EDINBURGH Duddingston

NT2973 ◀ *Sheeps Heid Inn*

Sure & Steadfast, *76 Milton Road West, Duddingston, Edinburgh, EH15 1QV.*
Open: Easter to Sep
Grades: STB 3 Star B&B
0131 657 1189
Mr & Mrs Taylor
a_t_taylor@ednet.co.uk
D: £16.50–£22.00 **S:** £20.00–£44.00
Beds: 2D 1T **Baths:** 3 Sh
ॐ ℙ (3) ⅍ ⊤⊽ ▥ ⊻ ♨ **cc**
Small, family-run 3 star B&B situated about 2 miles from the city centre. The property is located on the main bus route and can be easily reached by taxi or bus from the railway station or airport.

EDINBURGH Fairmilehead

NT2468 ◀ *Steading*

Valhalla, *35 Comiston View, Edinburgh, EH10 6LP.*
Modern detached property; quiet; golf, full breakfast. Warm welcome guaranteed.
Open: All Year
Grades: STB 2 Star
0131 445 5354
Mrs Stevenson-Renwick
D: £20.00–£32.00 **S:** £25.00–£35.00
Beds: 1D 1T 1S **Baths:** 2 En 1 Pr
ॐ ℙ (2) ⅍ ⊤⊽ ▥ ⊻ ♨

EDINBURGH Gilmerton

NT2968

Emerald Guest House, *3 Drum Street, Gilmerton, Edinburgh, EH17 8QQ.*
Victorian villa situated on bus route to city centre.
Open: All Year (not Xmas/New Year)
Grades: STB 2 Star
0131 664 5918
Mrs O'Connor
D: £20.00–£31.00 **S:** £35.00
Beds: 1F 2T 2D **Baths:** 3 En 1 Sh
ॐ (4) ℙ (5) ⊤⊽ ✕ ▥ ⊻ ♨

EDINBURGH Inverleith

NT2475 ◀ *Golf Tavern, Bennets Bar, Tapas Ole, Minto Hotel, Navaar Hotel, Allison Hotel, Grannies Attic, Seahaven Hotel*

The Inverleith Hotel, *5 Inverleith Terrace, Edinburgh, EH3 5NS.*
Licensed Victorian Hotel, city centre, adjacent botanic gardens, groups accepted.
Open: All Year (not Xmas)
0131 556 2745
Mr & Mrs Case
Fax: 0131 557 0433
hotel@inverleith.freeserve.co.uk
D: £25.00–£50.00 **S:** £30.00–£50.00
Beds: 2F 2D 2T 2S **Baths:** 8 En
ॐ ⅍ ⊤⊽ ♔ ✕ ▥ ⊻ ♨ **cc**

EDINBURGH Joppa

NT3173 ◀ *Bedford House Hotel*

Joppa Turrets Guest House, *1 Lower Joppa, Beach End of Morton Street, Edinburgh, EH15 2ER.*
Quiet, fine sea views, sandy beach, unrestricted parking, frequent buses, 3.5 miles to city.
Open: All Year (not Xmas)
0131 669 5806 (also fax)
Mr & Mrs Stanley
stanley@joppaturrets.demon.co.uk
D: £18.00–£35.00 **S:** £18.00–£35.00
Beds: 1F 4D **Baths:** 3 En 2 Sh
ॐ (3) ⅍ ⊤⊽ ▥ ⊻ ♨

Buchanan Guest House, *97 Joppa Road, Edinburgh, EH15 9HB.*
Comfortable friendly family-run guest house overlooking beach and Firth of Forth.
Open: All Year (not Xmas)
0131 657 4117
Mr Buchanan
Fax: 0131 669 9353
buchananhouse@bigfoot.com
D: £18.00–£25.00 **S:** £18.00–£25.00
Beds: 1F 1D 2T **Baths:** 1 En 2 Sh
ॐ ⊤⊽ ▥ ⊻ ♨ **cc**

EDINBURGH Mayfield

NT2672   🕮 *Braidburn Inn, Leasley, La Campana, Old Bell Inn*

The International, *37 Mayfield Gardens, Edinburgh, EH9 2BX.*
Open: All Year
Grades: STB 4 Star, AA 4 Diamond
0131 667 2511 Mrs Niven
Fax: 0131 667 1112
intergh@easynet.co.uk
D: £20.00–£40.00 **S:** £25.00–£45.00
Beds: 2F 2D 2T 3S **Baths:** 9 Pr
🛏 📺 🏛 🆅 ✻ 🏊 ♿
An attractive stone built Victorian house situated 1.5 miles south of Princes Street. Lying on main bus route, access to city centre is easy. The decor is outstanding, some rooms enjoy magnificent views across to the extinct Arthur's Seat volcano. Direct dial telephones.

Hopetoun Guest House, *15 Mayfield Road, Edinburgh, EH9 2NG.*
Open: All Year (not Xmas)
Grades: STB 3 Star
0131 667 7691 Mrs Mitchell
Fax: 0131 466 1691
hopetoun@aol.com
D: £20.00–£27.00 **S:** £25.00–£40.00
Beds: 1F 1D 1T **Baths:** 1 En 1 Pr 1 Sh
🛏 (6) 📦 (2) ✂ 📺 🏛 🆅 🏊 cc
Completely non-smoking. Small, friendly, family-run guest house, close to Edinburgh University. Excellent bus service. Royal Mile/Castle 25 mins, on foot. Personal attention in a relaxed, informal atmosphere. Good choice of breakfast. Owner a fund of local information! Which? Books B&B Guide.

RATES

D = Price range per person sharing in a double room
S = Price range for a single room

Lauderville Guest House, *52 Mayfield Road, Edinburgh, EH9 2NH.*
Open: All Year
Grades: STB 4 Star
0131 667 7788 Mrs Marriott
Fax: 0131 667 2636
res@laudervilleguesthouse.co.uk
D: £25.00–£40.00 **S:** £28.00–£48.00
Beds: 1F 6D 2T 1S **Baths:** 10 En
🛏 📦 (6) ✂ 📺 ✗ 🏛 🆅 cc
Restored Victorian town house minutes from the city sights, Royal Mile, Castle, Princes St. Elegant non-smoking bedrooms and excellent breakfast awaits, with varied menu including vegetarian. Secluded garden and secure car park. Traditional Pubs and quality Restaurants nearby.

Ivy Guest House, *7 Mayfield Gardens, Edinburgh, EH9 2AX.*
Open: All Year
Grades: STB 3 Star, AA 3 Diamond, RAC 4 Diamond
0131 667 3411 Mr Green
Fax: 0131 620 1422
don@ivyguesthouse.com
D: £17.00–£35.00 **S:** £17.00–£65.00
Beds: 2F 3D 2T 1S **Baths:** 6 En 2 Pr
🛏 📦 (7) 📺 🐾 🏛 🏊
Quiet, family-run Victorian villa guest house, many local restaurants, close to all Edinburgh's major cultural attractions, golf courses, Commonwealth swimming pool and university. A hearty Scottish breakfast and a warm welcome is assured.

Glenalmond Guest House, *25 Mayfield Gardens, Edinburgh, EH9 2BX.*
Open: All Year (not Xmas)
Grades: STB 4 Star
0131 668 2392 (also fax)
Mr & Mrs Fraser
glen@almond25.freeserve.co.uk
D: £20.00–£35.00 **S:** £25.00–£40.00
Beds: 3F 4D 2T 1S **Baths:** 10 En
🛏 (5) 📺 🏛 🆅 🏊 ♿
Deb & Dave warmly welcome you to their superb accommodation. Ground, four poster, en-suite rooms available. Close to Waverley Station. Varied breakfast served daily with home-made scones.

Lorne Villa Guest House, *9 East*
Mayfield, Edinburgh, EH9 1SD.
Festival city residence, serving fine Scottish
cuisine with Scottish hospitality.
Open: All Year
Grades: STB 3 Star
0131 667 7159 (also fax)
Mr McCulloch
lornevilla@cableinet.co.uk
D: £18.00–£32.00 **S:** £18.00–£32.00
Beds: 1F 2D 3T 1S **Baths:** 3 En 1 Pr 3 Sh
ॐ ▣ (6) 📺 �)(✕ ▥ Ⅴ 🍴

Ben Doran Guest House, *11 Mayfield*
Gardens, Edinburgh , EH9 2AX.
Beautiful refurbished Georgian house.
Elegant, cosy, comfortable, central. Family
run hotel.
Open: All Year
Grades: STB 4 Star, AA 4 Diamond,
RAC 4 Diamond, Sparkling
0131 667 8488 Dr Labaki
Fax: 0131 667 0076
info@bendoran.com
D: £25.00–£60.00 **S:** £25.00–£60.00
Beds: 4F 3D 2T 1S **Baths:** 6 En 4 Sh
ॐ ▣ (17) ⅙ 📺 ✕ ▥ Ⅴ 🍴 cc

Crion Guest House, *33 Minto Street,*
Edinburgh, EH9 2BT.
Family run guest house near city centre.
Most tourist attractions.
Open: All Year
Grades: STB Approv
0131 667 2708 Fax: 0131 662 1946
w.cheape@gilmourhouse.freeserve.co.uk
D: £20.00–£27.00 **S:** £20.00–£27.00
Beds: 1D 2T 1S **Baths:** 1 Sh
ॐ ▣ (2) 📺 ▥ Ⅴ ✳ 🍴 cc

Tania Guest House, *19 Minto Street,*
Edinburgh, EH9 1RQ.
Comfortable Georgian guest house, very
good bus route, Italian spoken.
Open: All Year (not Xmas)
Grades: STB 1 Star
0131 667 4144 Mrs Roscilli
D: £18.00–£25.00 **S:** £20.00–£27.50
Beds: 3F 1D 1T 1S **Baths:** 2 En
ॐ 🐾 ▣ 📺 ▥ Ⅴ 🍴

Parklands Guest House, *20 Mayfield*
Gardens, Edinburgh, EH9 2BZ.
Comfortable well maintained Victorian guest
house near city centre.
Open: All Year
Grades: STB 3 Star, AA 3 Diamond
0131 667 7184 Mr Drummond
Fax: 0131 667 2011
parklands_guesthouse@yahoo.com
D: £22.00–£30.00 **S:** £25.00–£40.00
Beds: 1F 2D 2T 1S **Baths:** 5 En 1 Pr
ॐ ▣ (1) 📺 ▥ Ⅴ 🍴

Sylvern Guest House, *22 West Mayfield,*
Edinburgh, EH9 1TQ.
Situated near the city centre. Good bus
routes, car park.
Open: All Year
Grades: STB 2 Star
0131 667 1241 (also fax)
Mr & Mrs Livornese
D: £17.00–£24.00
Beds: 2F 2T 2D **Baths:** 4 En 2 Sh
ॐ ▣ (8) ⅙ 📺 ▥ 🍴

Fairholme Guest House, *13 Moston*
Terrace, Edinburgh, EH9 2DE.
Nestled away from noisy traffic, yet only 1.5
miles from Castle.
Open: All Year
Grades: STB 3 Star
0131 667 8645 Mrs Blows
Fax: 0131 668 2435
stilwell@fairholme.co.uk
D: £23.00–£35.00 **S:** £25.00–£40.00
Beds: 1F 1D 1T 1S **Baths:** 3 En 1 Pr
ॐ ▣ (1) ⅙ 📺 🐾 ✕ ▥ Ⅴ 🍴 cc

St Conan's Guest House, *30 Minto*
Street, Edinburgh, EH9 1SB.
A handsome, stone-built, Listed, end-terrace
Georgian town house on three floors.
Open: All Year
0131 667 8393 (also fax)
Mr Bryce
st.conans@virgin.net
D: £20.00–£27.00 **S:** £20.00–£30.00
Beds: 3F 1D 3T **Baths:** 1 En 4 Pr 1 Sh
ॐ ▣ (7) 📺 🐾 ▥ Ⅴ 🍴

EDINBURGH Merchiston

NT2472 ◀ *Allison Hotel, Backstage Bistro, Belfry, Bennets Bar, Cafe Royal, Grannies Attic, Kings Wark, March Hall Hotel, Minto Hotel, Navaar House, Railto Restaurant, Seahaven Hotel, Suffolk Hall Hotel, Tatlers Golf Tavern, Tapas Ole*

Villa Nina Guest House, *39 Leamington Terrace, Edinburgh, EH10 4JS.*
Open: All Year (not Xmas/New Year)
Grades: STB 1 Star
0131 229 2644 (also fax) Mr Cecco
villanina@amserve.net
D: £18.00–£24.00
Beds: 1F 2D 2T **Baths:** 2 Sh
Ⓟ ▣ ▥ Ⓥ ♨
Very comfortable Victorian terrace house situated in quiet residential part of city yet 15 minutes' walk Princes Street, Castle, theatres. TV in all rooms. Private showers. Full cooked breakfast.

Granville Guest House, *13 Granville Terrace, Edinburgh, EH10 4PQ.*
Open: All Year (not Xmas)
Grades: STB 1 Star
0131 229 1676 B Oussellam
Fax: 0131 227 4633
granvilleguesthouse@tinyworld.co.uk
D: £19.00–£30.00 **S:** £20.00–£30.00
Beds: 2F 1T 3D 1S **Baths:** 2 En 2 Sh
▷ Ⓟ (2) ⏣ ▣ ▥ ♨
A family run guest house situated centrally in Edinburgh, all local amenities are nearby - not to mention the Kings Theatre and a newly built leisure complex. We are around a ten minute walk from the city centre and the historic Edinburgh Castle.

Leamington Guest House, *57 Leamington Terrace, Edinburgh, EH10 4JS.*
Elegant Victorian town house close to city centre. Warm welcome assured.
Open: All Year
Grades: STB 3 Star, AA 3 Diamond
0131 228 3879 Ms Stewart
Fax: 0131 221 1022
lemgh@globalnet.co.uk
D: £25.00–£40.00 **S:** £25.00–£40.00
Beds: 3F 2D 1T 2S **Baths:** 4 En 2 Sh
▷ ⏣ ▣ ⏣ ▥ Ⓥ ♨ cc

Kariba Guest House, *10 Granville Terrace, Edinburgh, EH10 4BQ.*
Victorian townhouse 15 minutes walk to city centre. Private parking.
Open: All Year
Grades: AA 2 Diamond, RAC 2 Diamond
0131 229 3773 Mrs Holligan
Fax: 0131 229 4968
karibaguesthouse@hotmail.com
D: £18.00–£28.00 **S:** £25.00–£50.00
Beds: 2F 4D 3T **Baths:** 2 En
▷ (1) ▣ ⏣ ▥ Ⓥ ♨ ⓖ cc

EDINBURGH Morningside

NT2471 ◀ *Montpeliers*

Dunedin, *21-23 Colinton Road, Edinburgh, EH10 5DR.*
Victorian terraced villa, furnished in period-style. Princess street, 15 mins.
Open: All Year (not Xmas)
0131 447 0679 Mr Fortune
Fax: 0131 446 9358
h.fort10560@aol.com
D: £20.00–£30.00 **S:** £20.00–£30.00
Beds: 4F 2D 1T 2S **Baths:** 6 En 1 Pr 2 Sh
▷ ⏧ ▣ ▥ ♨ ⓖ cc

EDINBURGH Newington

NT2671 ◀ *Old Bell Inn, Suffolk Hall Hotel, Cragg, Braidburn Inn*

Rowan Guest House, *13 Glenorchy Terrace, Edinburgh, EH9 2DQ.*
Open: All Year (not Xmas)
Grades: STB 3 Star, AA 3 Diamond
0131 667 2463 (also fax)
Mr & Mrs Vidler
rowanhouse@hotmail.com
D: £23.00–£32.00 **S:** £24.00–£29.00
Beds: 1F 3D 2T 3S **Baths:** 3 En 3 Sh
▷ (2) Ⓟ (2) ▣ ▥ ♨ cc
Comfortable Victorian home in quiet, leafy, conservation area, a mile and a half from city centre, castle and Royal Mile. Delicious breakfast, including porridge and freshly baked scones. A warm welcome and personal service from Alan and Angela. Free parking.

Ascot Guest House, *98 Dalkeith Road,*
Edinburgh, EH16 5AF.
Comfortable family-run guest house close to
all attractions.
Open: All Year
0131 667 1500
J Williams
ascotedinburgh@btinternet.com
D: £18.00–£30.00 **S:** £20.00–£40.00
Beds: 2F 2T 2D 1S **Baths:** 2 En 2 Pr 2 Sh
🛏 (10) 🅿 (3) 📺 🛏 🛏️ 📺 🔌

Gifford House, *103 Dalkeith Road,*
Edinburgh, EH16 5AJ.
Elegant Victorian house. Superior rooms
with Edinburgh's attractions within easy
reach.
Open: All Year
Grades: STB 4 Star
0131 667 4688 (also fax)
Mrs Dow
giffordhotel@btinternet.com
D: £20.00–£38.00 **S:** £23.00–£50.00
Beds: 2F 2D 2T 1S **Baths:** 7 En
🛏 ⚡ 📺 🛏 🛏️ 📺 ❄ 🔌 cc

17 Crawfurd Road, *Edinburgh, EH16 5PQ.*
Victorian family home, friendly welcome -
easy access to city centre.
Open: May to Sep
Grades: STB 2 Star
0131 667 1191
Ms Simpson
D: £17.50–£25.00 **S:** £17.50–£25.00
Beds: 1D 1T 1S **Baths:** 2 Sh
🛏 🅿 (1) ⚡ 📺 🛏️ 🔌

Kingsley Guest House, *30 Craigmillar*
Park, Edinburgh, EH16 5PS.
Friendly family run house on excellent bus
route for sightseeing.
Open: All Year
Grades: STB 3 Star, AA 3 Diamond
0131 667 8439 (also fax)
D: £20.00–£35.00
S: £25.00–£40.00
Beds: 1F 2T 3D **Baths:** 3 En 2 Pr
🛏 (3) 🅿 (5) ⚡ 📺 🛏️ 🍵 🔌

EDINBURGH   Northfield

NT2973 🍺 *Golf Tavern, Bennets Bar, Tapas Ole,*
Minto Hotel, Navaar Hotel, Allison Hotel, Grannies
Attic, Seahaven Hotel

Brae Guest House, *119 Willowbrae Road,*
Edinburgh, EH8 7HN.
Friendly guest house. Meadowbank, Holyrood
Palace, on main bus route. **Open:** All Year
Grades: STB 3 Star, AA 3 Diamond
0131 661 0170 Mrs Walker
braeguesthouse@tinyworld.co.uk
D: £18.00–£40.00 **S:** £18.00–£40.00
Beds: 1F 1T 1D 1S **Baths:** 3 En 1 Pr
🛏 📺 🛏 🛏️ 📺 🔌

EDINBURGH   Pilrig

NT2675 🍺 *Oyster Bar*

Claymore Guest House, *68 Pilrig Street,*
Edinburgh, EH6 5AS.
Warm, welcoming, personally run, centrally
situated, close to all attractions.
Open: All Year (not Xmas)
Grades: STB 2 Star GH
0131 554 2500 (also fax) Mrs Dorrian
D: £18.00–£30.00 **S:** £22.00
Beds: 2F 2D 2T **Baths:** 3 En 1 Pr 2 Sh
🛏 ⚡ 📺 🛏 🛏️ 📺 🔌

Sunnyside Guest House, *13 Pilrig Street,*
Edinburgh, EH6 5AN.
Beautiful Georgian family-run guest house.
An easy atmosphere and ample breakfast.
Open: All Year (not Xmas) **Grades:** STB 2 Star
0131 553 2084 Mr Wheelaghan
sunnyside.guesthouse@talk21.com
D: £17.00–£30.00 **S:** £17.00–£30.00
Beds: 2F 4D 2T 1S **Baths:** 4 En 1 Pr 1 Sh
🛏 🅿 ⚡ 📺 🛏️ 📺 🔌

Glenburn Guest House, *22 Pilrig Street,*
Edinburgh, EH6 5AJ.
Clean, welcoming, budget accommodation.
15 minutes from the city centre.
Open: All Year (not Xmas)
0131 554 9818 (also fax) Mrs McVeigh
glenburn@lineone.net
D: £19.00–£26.00 **S:** £20.00–£36.00
Beds: 3F 3D 4T 3S **Baths:** 1 En 6 Sh
📺 🛏️ 🔌

EDINBURGH Portobello

NT3074 🍺 *Peacock Inn*

Hopebank, *33 Hope Lane North, Portobello,*
Edinburgh, EH15 2PZ.
Open: Easter to Oct
0131 657 1149
Ms Williamson
D: £20.00 **S:** £20.00
Beds: 2D 1T **Baths:** 3 Pr 1 Sh
🛏 🅿 ⅃ 📺 🛏 🖂 ⅂

Victorian terraced villa, two minutes sea -
beautiful promenade, 20 minutes city centre.
Good food, Scottish hospitality, inexpensive
bus service to centre. Non smoking, showers
ensuite, TV in all rooms. Many golf courses
nearby, good touring centre.

Cruachan, *6 Pittville Street, Edinburgh,*
EH15 2BY.
Elegant Georgian villa adjacent to beach,
promenade, city centre 2.5 miles. Good
parking.
Open: Easter to Oct
Grades: STB 2 Star B&B
0131 669 2195
Mrs Thom
D: £20.00–£22.00 **S:** £19.00–£21.00
Beds: 2D 1T 1S **Baths:** 2 Sh
🛏 (12) 🅿 (3) ⅃ 📺 🐾 🖂 ⅂

EDINBURGH Prestonfield

NT2771 🍺 *Golf Tavern, Bennets Bar, Tapas Ole,*
Minto Hotel, Navaar Hotel, Allison Hotel, Grannies
Attic, Seahaven Hotel, Hotel Ceilidhonia

Airdenair, *29 Kilmaurs Road, Edinburgh,*
EH16 5DB.
Fabulous views of Edinburgh. Recently
refurbished, family run. Quiet location.
Open: All Year
Grades: STB 3 Star
0131 668 2336
Mrs Mclennan
airdenair@tinyonline.co.uk
D: £22.00–£30.00 **S:** £30.00–£40.00
Beds: 2T 2D 2S **Baths:** 5 En
🅿 ⅃ 📺 🛏 🖂 ⅂ cc

Cameron Toll Guest House, *299*
Dalkeith Road, Edinburgh, EH16 5JX.
Eco-friendly family guest house on A7, 10
minutes from city centre.
Open: All Year
Grades: STB 4 Star
0131 667 2950 M Deans
Fax: 0131 662 1987
stil@edinburghguesthouse.co.uk
D: £20.00–£35.00 **S:** £25.00–£37.00
Beds: 3F 2T 3D 3S **Baths:** 10 En 1 Pr
🛏 🅿 (4) ⅃ 📺 ✕ 🖂 ⅂ ⅂ ⅂ cc

EDINBURGH Slateford

NT2271 🍺 *Dell Inn, Tickled Trout*

13 Moat Street, *Edinburgh, EH14 1PE.*
Comfortable accommodation, colour TV,
each room.
Open: Easter to Mar
Grades: STB 2 Star
0131 443 8266 Mrs Hume
D: £15.00–£20.00 **S:** £18.00–£20.00
Beds: 1D 1T
🛏 🅿 📺 🖂 ⅂ ⅂

Doocote House, *15 Moat Street,*
Edinburgh, EH14 1PE.
Victorian terraced house 2 miles from city
centre, unrestricted parking.
Open: All Year
Grades: STB 2 Star
0131 443 5455 Mr Manson
D: £18.00–£20.00 **S:** £20.00–£30.00
Beds: 1F 1D 1T **Baths:** 2 Sh
🛏 🅿 📺 🐾 🖂 ⅂

EDINBURGH Trinity

NT2476 🍺 *Peacock Inn*

Falcon Crest, *70 South Trinity Road,*
Edinburgh, EH5 3NX.
Victorian family home, 2 miles north of
Edinburgh Castle.
Open: All Year (not Xmas)
Grades: STB 1 Star
0131 552 5294 Mrs Clark
D: £15.00–£26.00 **S:** £16.00–£26.00
Beds: 1F 2D 2T 1S **Baths:** 3 En 2 Sh
🛏 🅿 (2) ⅃ 📺 🐾 ✕ 🖂 ⅂ ⅂ cc

Falkirk

NS8680   ◀ *Copper Top*

Denecroft, *8 Lochgreen Road, Falkirk,*
FK1 5NJ.
1.5 miles from town centre, near railway
station and hospital.
Open: All Year
01324 629258 (also fax)
Mrs Stewart
D: £22.00–£26.00 **S:** £25.00–£30.00
Beds: 2T 1D 1S **Baths:** 3 En 1 Sh
🅿 (6) ⚡ 📺 🛏 ▥ ⚓ cc

Gorebridge

NT3460   ◀ *Coronation Inn*

Ivory House, *14 Vogrie Road, Gorebridge,*
EH23 4HH.
Secluded Victorian house, 10 miles
Edinburgh. Ideal base Borders/Coast.
Open: All Year
Grades: STB 4 Star
01875 820755 Mrs Maton
ivory.house@talk21.com
D: £25.00–£35.00 **S:** £27.50–£40.00
Beds: 1F 1D 1T **Baths:** 3 En
🐕 🅿 (6) ⚡ 📺 ▥ Ⓥ ⚓ ♿ cc

Haddington

NT5173   ◀ *George Hotel, Waterside Hotel, Plough Inn, Goblin Ha', Tweedale Arms*

28 Market Street, *Haddington, E Lothian,*
EH41 3JE.
Open: All Year
Grades: STB 3 Star
01620 822465 Mrs Hamilton
Fax: 01620 825613
D: £20.00–£26.00 **S:** £18.00–£22.00
Beds: 1F 1D 2T 1S **Baths:** 2 En 1 Pr 2 Sh
🐕 ⚡ 📺 ▥ Ⓥ ⚓
Victorian building in centre of picturesque
Haddington on Edinburgh (17 miles) bus
route. Ideal base for golf. Walkers and
cyclists welcome. Meals available within
walking distance.

Eaglescairnie Mains, *Haddington, E Lothian, EH41 4HN.*
Superb farmhouse with wonderful views
over conservation award-winning farm.
Open: All Year (not Xmas)
Grades: STB 4 Star
01620 810491 (also fax)
Mrs Williams
williams.eagles@btinternet.com
D: £20.00–£27.00 **S:** £25.00–£35.00
Beds: 1D 1T 2S **Baths:** 2 En 1 Sh
🐕 🅿 (6) ⚡ 📺 🛏 ▥ ⚓ cc

The Farmhouse, *Upper Bolton, Haddington, EH41 4HW.*
A warm welcome awaits you at our
traditional farm house.
Open: All Year (not Xmas)
Grades: STB 3 Star
01620 810476
Mrs Clark
boltontoad@yahoo.co.uk
D: £17.00–£20.00 **S:** £18.00
Beds: 1D 1T **Baths:** 1 Sh
🐕 🅿 (4) 🛏 ▥ ⚓

Inveresk

NT3572   ◀ *Dolphin*

Delta House, *16 Carberry Road, Inveresk, Musselburgh, E Lothian, EH21 7TN.*
A beautiful Victorian house 7 miles east of
central Edinburgh overlooking fields.
Open: All Year (not Xmas)
Grades: STB 3 Star
0131 665 2107 (also fax)
D: £20.00–£27.50
S: £30.00–£50.00
Beds: 1F 3D **Baths:** 2 En 1 Pr
🐕 (5) 🅿 (3) ⚡ 📺 ▥ Ⓥ ⚓

RATES

D = Price range per person
sharing in a double room
S = Price range for a
single room

Laurieston

NS9079 ◀ *Lawries, Beancross Restaurant*

Oaklands, *32 Polmont Road, Laurieston, Falkirk, FK2 9QT.*
Open: All Year (not Xmas)
Grades: STB 4 Star
01324 610671 (also fax)
Mrs Fattori
b-and-b@oaklands.ndirect.co.uk
D: £25.00–£35.00 **S:** £35.00
Beds: 1D 2T **Baths:** 3 En
🛇 🅿 (4) ⌇ 📺 🖾 Ⅴ ☕ **cc**
Edwardian house, 1.5 miles Falkirk, situated 5 mins M9 (J5), taking you to Edinburgh (east), Glasgow, Stirling (west). 20 mins by road to Edinburgh Airport. Near 2 mainline rail stations, frequent service to Edinburgh/Glasgow (approx 20 mins each way).

Linlithgow

NS9977 ◀ *Blackness Inn, Bridge Inn, Four Marys, Torphichin Inn*

Woodcockdale Farm, *Lanark Road, Linlithgow, W Lothian, EH49 6QE.*
Look no further. Easy access to airport, Edinburgh, Stirling. Phone now.
Open: All Year
01506 842088 (also fax)
Mrs Erskine
arn-guest-house@euphony.net
D: £18.00–£25.00 **S:** £18.00–£25.00
Beds: 3F 2D 1T 1S **Baths:** 4 En 1 Pr 2 Sh
🛇 🅿 ⌇ 📺 🐕 🖾 Ⅴ ☕ ♿

Wester William Craigs, *Linlithgow, W Lothian, EH49 6QF.*
Modern country house, quiet location, 2 miles from historic Linlithgow.
Open: All Year (not Xmas/New Year)
01506 845470
Mrs Millar
Fax: 01506 876166
info@craiglodges.freeserve.co.uk
D: £20.00–£22.50 **S:** £20.00–£25.00
Beds: 1D 1T **Baths:** 1 En 1 Pr
🅿 ⌇ 📺 🖾 Ⅴ ☕

Loanhead

NT2765 ◀ *Countryside Inn*

Aaron Glen, *7 Nivensknowe Road, Loanhead, Edinburgh, EH20 9AU.*
Hotel quality accommodation at B&B prices.
Open: All Year
Grades: STB 3 Star, AA 3 Star
0131 440 1293 Mrs Davidson
Fax: 0131 440 2155
aaronglen1@aol.com
D: £20.00–£30.00 **S:** £25.00–£60.00
Beds: 1F 3D 1T **Baths:** 5 En
🛇 🅿 (8) ⌇ 📺 🐕 🖾 Ⅴ ☕ ♿ **3 cc**

Inveravon House Hotel, *9 Inveravon Road, Loanhead, Midlothian, EH20 9EF.*
Large Victorian house.
Open: All Year
0131 440 0124 Mr Potter
D: £20.00–£25.00 **S:** £25.00
Beds: 5F 5D 1T 3S **Baths:** 13 En
🛇 🅿 (20) 📺 🐕 ✗ 🖾 Ⅴ ❉ ☕ ♿ **cc**

Longniddry

NT4476 ◀ *Longniddry Inn*

13 Glassel Park Road, *Longniddry, EH32 0NY.*
20 minutes by train to Edinburgh. Easy access to golf courses.
Open: Easter to Sep
Grades: STB 3 Star
01875 852333
Mrs Morrison
D: £18.00–£20.00 **S:** £25.00
Beds: 1D 1T **Baths:** 2 Pr
🛇 (8) 🅿 (2) ⌇ 📺 🖾 ☕

The Spinney, *Old School Lane, Longniddry, E Lothian, EH32 0NQ.*
Bungalow, secluded position, near shops, bus and train to Edinburgh.
Open: Feb to Nov
Grades: STB 2 Star
01875 853325 Mr & Mrs Playfair
D: £18.00–£20.00 **S:** £20.00–£22.00
Beds: 2D 1T **Baths:** 1 En 1 Sh
🛇 🅿 (3) ⌇ 📺 🖾 Ⅴ ☕

Musselburgh

NT3573 🍺 *Musselburgh, Volunteer Arms, Woodside Hotel, Foreman's, Ravelston House Hotel, The Burgh*

18 Woodside Gardens, *Musselburgh, Midlothian, EH21 7LJ.*
Quiet bungalow, easy access Edinburgh, seaside, countryside and golf parking.
Open: All Year
Grades: STB 2 Star
0131 665 3170 Mrs Aitken
D: £17.00–£19.00 **S:** £17.00–£19.00
Beds: 1F 1D 1T **Baths:** 2 Sh
ᵇ 🄿 (4) 📺 🛏 🛋 Ⓥ ♨ &

Craigesk, *10 Albert Terrace, Musselburgh, Midlothian, EH21 7LR.*
Terraced villa overlooking golf and racecourse. Bus/railway close by.
Open: All Year
Grades: STB 2 Star
0131 665 3344 (also fax)
Miss Mitchell
D: £17.00 **S:** £18.00
Beds: 2F 1D 1T 1S **Baths:** 2 Sh
ᵇ 🄿 (4) 📺 🛏 🛋 Ⓥ ♨

Eildon B&B, *109 Newbigging Road, Musselburgh, EH21 7AS.*
Georgian townhouse. Frequent buses to city centre(20 minutes). Parking.
Open: All Year
Grades: STB 3 Star
0131 665 3981 Mrs Roache
eve@stayinscotland.net
D: £16.00–£25.00 **S:** £25.00–£35.00
Beds: 1F 1D 1T **Baths:** 1 En 1 Sh
⌇ 📺 🛋 ♨ cc

Arden House, *26 Linkfield Road, Musselburgh, Midlothian, EH21 7LL.*
A warm and friendly welcome awaits you at Arden House.
Open: All Year
Grades: STB 4 Star, AA 4 Diamond
0131 665 0663 (also fax) Mr Pringle
ardenhouse@talk21.com
D: £18.00–£27.00 **S:** £25.00–£35.00
Beds: 2F 3T 2D **Baths:** 4 En 2 Sh
ᵇ ⌇ 📺 🛏 ✕ 🛋 Ⓥ ❋ ♨ cc

North Berwick

NT5585 🍺 *Blenheim House Hotel, Castle Inn, Dalrymple Hotel, Nether Abbey Hotel, Pointgarry Hotel, Tantallon Inn*

Troon, *Dirleton Road, North Berwick, E Lothian, EH39 5DF.*
Comfortable pleasant bungalow, large garden. Outskirts of town, coastal view.
Open: Apr to Oct
Grades: STB 3 Star
01620 893555 Mrs Dixon
D: £16.00–£25.00
Beds: 1D **Baths:** 1 En
🄿 (1) ⌇ 📺 🛋 ♨

The Belhaven Hotel, *28 Westgate, North Berwick, E Lothian, EH39 4AH.*
Overlooking golf course and sea; convenient for town centre and railway station.
Open: Dec to Oct
Grades: STB 2 Star Hotel
01620 893009 M Free
D: £19.00–£26.00 **S:** £20.00–£35.00
Beds: 2F 5T 2S **Baths:** 5 En 4 Sh
ᵇ (9) 📺 ✕ 🛋 Ⓥ ♨

Golf Hotel, *34 Dirleton Avenue, North Berwick, E Lothian, EH39 4BH.*
Family run hotel in seaside town close to golf courses.
Open: All Year
Grades: STB 1 Star
01620 892202 Mr Searle
Fax: 01620 892290
D: £26.00–£65.00 **S:** £26.00–£50.00
Beds: 5F 1D 3T 2S **Baths:** 10 Pr 1 Sh
ᵇ 🄿 (20) ⌇ 📺 ✕ 🛋 Ⓥ ♨ &

Beehive Cottage, *12 Kingston, North Berwick, EH39 5JE.*
Country cottage, own entrance, lovely garden, views, homemade honey/jams.
Open: Apr to Oct
Grades: STB 3 Star
01620 894785 Mrs Fife
D: £20.00–£24.00 **S:** £25.00–£27.00
Beds: 1D **Baths:** 1 En
ᵇ 🄿 (1) ⌇ 📺 🛏 🛋 Ⓥ ♨

Pathhead

NT3964 ◖ *Forresters*

The Old Farm House, *47 Main Street,*
Pathhead, Midlothian, EH37 5PZ.
Comfortable, C Listed B&B. 12 miles south of
Edinburgh on the A68.
Open: All Year
01875 320100 Mr Reid
Fax: 01875 320501
oldfarmhouse@tinyworld.co.uk
D: £16.00–£18.00 **S:** £20.00–£25.00
Beds: 1F 1T 1D **Baths:** 2 En 1 Pr
ॐ 🅿 (3) 📺 ⊁ ▥ ♨ cc

Penicuik

NT2360 ◖ *Howgate*

Loanstone House, *Loanstone, Penicuik,*
EH26 8PH.
A Victorian family house in peaceful country
surroundings.
Open: Easter to Oct
Grades: STB 3 Star
01968 672449 Mrs Patch
the.patches@btinternet.com
D: £17.50 **S:** £20.00
Beds: 1D **Baths:** 1 Sh
ॐ 🅿 (2) ⊬ 📺 ⊁ ▥ ♨

South Queensferry

NT1277

Priory Lodge, *8 The Loan, South*
Queensferry, EH30 9NS.
Beautiful guest house in a tranquil village,
twenty minutes from Edinburgh.
Open: All Year (not Xmas)
Grades: STB 4 Star, AA 4 Diamond
0131 331 4345 (also fax)
C C Lamb
calmyn@aol.com
D: £25.00–£30.00 **S:** £35.00–£50.00
Beds: 3F 1D 1T **Baths:** 5 En
ॐ 🅿 ⊬ 📺 ▥ ♨ cc

Stoneyburn

NS9762 ◖ *Croftmalloch Inn*

Eisenach, *1 Cannop Crescent, Stoneyburn,*
Bathgate, W Lothian, EH47 8EF.
Large detached countryside villa.
Open: All Year
01501 762659
Mrs Gray
cagray@eisenach.demon.co.uk
D: £15.00 **S:** £20.00
Beds: 1F 1D 1T 1S **Baths:** 1 Pr
ॐ 🅿 (3) ⊬ 📺 ✕ ▥ Ⓥ

Uphall

NT0572 ◖ *Beefeater*

20 Houston Mains Holdings, *Uphall,*
Broxburn, EH52 6PA.
Charming guest house eleven miles from
Edinburgh. Railway link nearby.
Open: All Year
Grades: STB 3 Star
01506 854044
Mr Fisher
Fax: 01506 855118
michaelfisher@cmgh.freeserve.co.uk
D: £23.00–£25.00 **S:** £35.00–£37.00
Beds: 1F 1T 4D **Baths:** 6 En

Winchburgh

NT0875

Turnlea, *123 Main Street, Winchburgh,*
Broxburn, EH52 6QP.
All bedrooms refurbished 1999. Edinburgh 12
miles, airport 6 miles and Linlithgow 6 miles.
Open: All Year (not Xmas)
Grades: STB 3 Star B&B
01506 890124
R W Redwood
royturnlea@hotmail.com
D: £22.00–£25.00 **S:** £25.00–£30.00
Beds: 1D 2T **Baths:** 3 En
ॐ 🅿 (3) ⊬ 📺 ▥ ♨ cc

Orkney

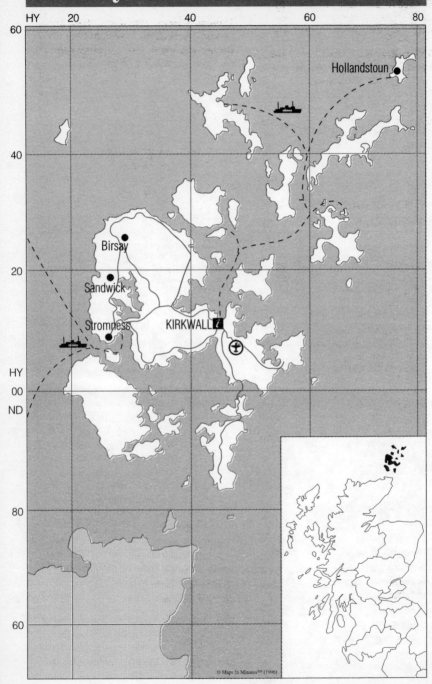

AIRPORTS ⊕

Kirkwall Airport, tel. 01856 872421.

AIR SERVICES & AIRLINES ✈

British Airways: *Kirkwall to Aberdeen, Edinburgh, Glasgow, Inverness, Sumburgh (Shetland), Wick*.
Tel. (local rate): 0345 222111.
There also interisland flights between
Kirkwall and *Eday, North Ronaldsay, Papa Westray, Sanday, Stronsay* and *Westray*.

FERRIES ⚓

P&O Scottish Ferries: *Stromness to Aberdeen* - 8 hrs; *Stromness to*

Scrabster (near Thurso) - 50 mins;
Stromness to Lerwick (Shetland)
- 8 hrs. Tel. 01224 572615.

Thomas & Bews: *Burwick to John o' Groats* - 45 mins. Tel. 01955 611353.
Orkney Islands Shipping operate ferries between the islands themselves.
Tel. 01856 872044.

TOURIST INFORMATION OFFICES ℹ

6 Broad Street, **Kirkwall**, Isles of Orkney, KW15 1NX, 01856 872856.

Ferry Terminal Road, The Pierhead, **Stromness**, Isles of Orkney, KW16 3AE, 01856 850716.

MAINLAND Birsay

HY2527 ⚐ *Barony Hotel, Smithfield Hotel, Merkister Hotel*

Heatherlea, *Birsay, Orkney, KW17 2LR.*
Modern bungalow overlooking trout-fishing loch, wild birds, numerous archaeological sites.
Open: Easter to Oct
Grades: STB 1 Star
01856 721382 (also fax)
Mrs Balderstone
D: £17.00 **S:** £17.00
Beds: 1D 1T **Baths:** 1 Sh
❧ (6) 🅿 (2) ⅟ 📺 📖.

Primrose Cottage, *Birsay, Orkney, KW17 2NB.*
Quiet country cottage overlooking Marwick Bay. Close RSPB reserves, the Loons and Marwick Head.
Open: All Year (not Xmas)
01856 721384 (also fax)
Mrs Clouston
D: £14.50–£19.00
S: £14.50–£19.00
Beds: 1D 1T 1S **Baths:** 2 En 1 Sh
❧ 🅿 (4) ⅟ 📺 ✗ 📖. 📺 ♨

MAINLAND Kirkwall

HY4510 ⚐ *Queen's Hotel, Royal Hotel, West End Hotel*

7 Matches Square, *Kirkwall, Orkney, KW15 1AU.*
Personally run neighbouring houses. Centrally situated, shops, buses, ferries nearby.
Open: All Year
Grades: STB 1 Star
01856 872440 Mrs Parkins
D: £15.00–£17.00 **S:** £16.00–£18.00
Beds: 2T 1D 2S **Baths:** 1 En 2 Sh
❧ 🅿 (2) 📺 ♚ 📖. 📺 ♨

Elderwood, 4 Park Loan, *Kirkwall, Orkney, KW15 1PU.*
Modern bungalow in quiet cul-de-sac.
Open: All Year
01856 872657 Mrs Omand
D: £15.00 **S:** £15.00
Beds: 1D 1T **Baths:** 2 Sh
🅿 (2) ⅟ 📺 📖. ♨

Planning a longer stay?
Always ask for any special rates

Polrudden Guest House, *Peerie Sea*
Loan, Kirkwall, Orkney, KW15 1UH.
Peaceful location, ten minutes walk from
town centre. Stunning view.
Open: All Year (not Xmas)
Grades: STB 3 Star
01856 874761
Mrs Thornton
Fax: 01856 870950
linda@scapaflow.com
D: £22.00 **S:** £30.00
Beds: 2F 5T **Baths:** 7 En
ऊ P (7) 🖵 ✕ 🎞 V ⚓ cc

Lav'rockha Guest House, *Inganess Road,*
Kirkwall, Orkney, KW15 1SP.
Superior accommodation at an affordable
price, Finalist - 1999 Orkney Food awards.
Open: All Year
Grades: STB 4 Star
01856 876103 (also fax)
J Webster
lavrockha@orkney.com
D: £20.00–£24.00 **S:** £24.00–£30.00
Beds: 1F 2T 2D **Baths:** 5 En
ऊ P ⌇ 🖵 ⌇ ✕ 🎞 V ❋ ⚓ ⅄ cc

Shearwood, *Muddiesdale Road*
off Pickaquoy Road, Kirkwall, Orkney, KW15 1RR.
Quiet country location, 10 mins walk town
centre. Wonderful archaeology nearby.
Open: All Year
Grades: STB 2 Star
01856 873494
Mrs Braun
D: £15.00–£17.00 **S:** £17.00
Beds: 2T 1D **Baths:** 2 Sh
ऊ (12) P ⌇ 🖵 🎞 V ⚓ ⅄

Leikanger, *Old Scapa Road, Kirkwall,*
Orkney, KW15 1BB.
15 minutes walk from centre of Kirkwall
house on outskirts of town.
Open: All Year (not Xmas/New Year)
Grades: STB Listed, Comm
01856 872006
Mr & Mrs Linklater
D: £15.00–£16.00 **S:** £16.00–£17.00
Beds: 1D 1T 1S **Baths:** 2 Sh
ऊ P (2) 🖵 ⌇ 🎞 V ⚓

MAINLAND Sandwich
HY2519   ◀ *Smithfield Hotel*

Netherstove, *Sandwich, Stromness,*
Orkney, KW16 3LS.
Farmhouse B&B, overlooking the Bay of
Skaill. Near Skara - Bare.
Open: Easter to Nov
Grades: STB 3 Star
01856 841625 (also fax)
Mrs Poke
ann.poke@virgin.net
D: £16.00–£18.50 **S:** £16.00–£18.50
Beds: 1D 1T **Baths:** 2 Sh
ऊ P ⌇ 🖵 ✕ 🎞 V ⚓

MAINLAND Stromness
HY2509   ◀ *Ferry Inn*

Lindisfarne, *Stromness, Orkney, KW16 3LL.*
Open: Jan to Dec
Grades: STB 3 Star
01856 850828
Mrs Worthington
Fax: 01856 850805
eprworthington@hotmail.com
D: £20.00–£22.00
Beds: 1F 4T **Baths:** 5 En
P 🖵 🎞 V ⚓
Modern detached house, set in a elevated
rural location, overlooking the town of
Stromness views of Scapa Flow, the island
of Gramsay, Hoy Hills and the island of Hoy
also Stromness harbour.

Miller's House and Harbourside Guest
House, *John Street, Stromness, Orkney,*
KW16 3AD.
Breakfast in the oldest house in Stromness
(1716). Centrally situated.
Open: Easter to Nov
Grades: STB 3 Star
01856 851969
Mrs Dennison
Fax: 01856 851967
millershouse@orkney.com
D: £20.00 **S:** £25.00
Beds: 4F 2D 2T **Baths:** 13 Pr 1 Sh
ऊ P ⌇ 🖵 ⌇ ✕ 🎞 V ⚓

Oakleigh Hotel, *76 Victoria Street,*
Stromness, Orkney, KW16 3BS.
Small family-run guest house.
Open: All Year (not Xmas)
Grades: STB 2 Star
01856 850447 Ms Woodford
D: £20.00–£25.00 **S:** £20.00–£25.00
Beds: 2D 4T **Baths:** 6 En
🛏 🅿 (1) 📺 ✟ ✗ 🛏 Ⅴ 🛁

All details shown are as
supplied by B&B owners in
Autumn 2000

NORTH RONALDSAY
Hollandstoun

HY7553

North Ronaldsay Bird Observatory,
North Ronaldsay, Orkney, KW17 2BE.
Comfortable island guest accommodation.
Solar and wind powered.
Open: All Year (not Xmas/New Year)
Grades: STB 2 Star
01857 633200 A E Duncan
Fax: 01857 633207
alison@nrbo.prestel.co.uk
D: £18.00 **S:** £23.00
Beds: 2D 2T **Baths:** 4 En
🛏 🅿 ⅍ 📺 ✗ 🛏 Ⅴ 🛁 ♿ 2 cc

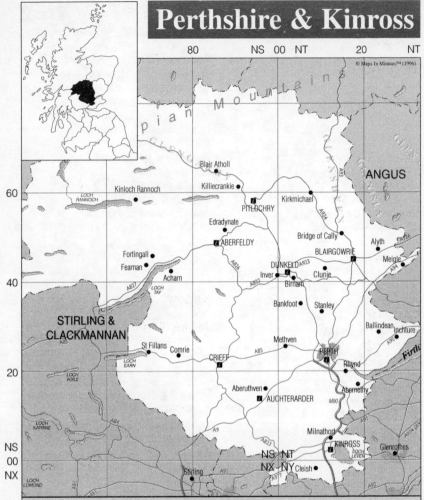

© Maps In Minutes™ (1996)

RAIL

For rail information, telephone the National Rail Enquiries line, on 08457 484950. For the Minicom service for the deaf and hard of hearing, tel. 0845 605 0600.

BUS

Scottish Citylink, tel. 08705 505050, **National Express**, tel. 0141 226 4826.

TOURIST INFORMATION OFFICES

The Square, **Aberfeldy**, Perthshire, PH15 2DD, 01887 820276.

90 High Street, **Auchterarder**, Perthshire, PH3 1BJ, 01764 663450.

26 Wellmeadow, **Blairgowrie**, Perthshire, PH10 6AS, 01250 872960.

Town Hall, High Street, **Crieff**, Perthshire, PH7 3HU, 01764 652578.

The Cross, **Dunkeld**, Perthshire, PH8 0AN, 01350 727688.

Kinross Service Area, Junction 6, M90, **Kinross**, KY13 7BE, 01577 863680.

45 High Street, **Perth**, PH1 5TJ, 01738 450600.

Caithness Glass Car Park, A9 Western City By-pass, Inveralmond, **Perth**, 01738 638481.

22 Atholl Street, **Pitlochry**, Perthshire, PH16 5BX, 01796 472215.

Aberfeldy

NN8549 ◀ *Black Watch, Aileen Chraggan Hotel, Coshieville Hotel*

Ardtornish, *Kenmore Street, Aberfeldy, PH15 2BL.*
In beautiful friendly Highland Perthshire with walking, golf, cycling, water sports and more.
Open: All Year (not Xmas/New Year)
Grades: STB 3 Star
01887 820629 Mrs Ross
ardtornish@talk21.com
D: £16.00–£19.00 **S:** £16.00–£19.00
Beds: 1D 1T 1D/F **Baths:** 1 En 1 Sh
🅿 (3) ⅙ 📺 ▥ 🎦 ⬥

Tomvale, *Tom of Cluny Farm, Aberfeldy, Perthshire, PH15 2JT.*
Modern farmhouse with outstanding views of the Upper Tay Valley.
Open: All Year (not Xmas)
01887 820171 (also fax)
Mrs Kennedy
dken301762@aol.com
D: £17.00 **S:** £18.00
Beds: 1F 1D **Baths:** 1 Sh
🕿 🅿 📺 🐾 ✗ ▥ 🎦 ⬥

Carn Dris, *Aberfeldy, Perthshire, PH15 2LB.*
Large Edwardian private house, ex manse, overlooking Aberfeldy golf course.
Open: Easter to Oct
01887 820250
Mrs Bell Campbell
D: £20.00–£25.00 **S:** £20.00–£25.00
Beds: 2D 1T **Baths:** 1 En 1 Sh
🕿 (10) 🅿 (4) 📺 🐾 ▥

Novar, *2 Home Street, Aberfeldy, Perthshire, PH15 2AJ.*
Novar is a comfortable stone house near golf course; good walks.
Open: All Year (not Xmas)
01887 820779
Mrs Malcolm
D: £17.00–£19.00 **S:** £25.00
Beds: 1F 1D 1T **Baths:** 2 En 5 Pr 1 Sh
🕿 🅿 (3) ⅙ 📺 🐾 ▥ 🎦 ⬥ ⬥

Abernethy

NO1816

Gattaway Farm, *Abernethy, Perth, Perthshire & Kinross, PH2 9LQ.*
Large Georgian/Victorian farmhouse; excellent views, excellent food. Recommended.
Open: All Year
Grades: STB 3 Star
01738 850746 Mrs Dawson
Fax: 01738 850925
tarduff@aol.com
D: £19.00–£20.00 **S:** £20.00–£25.00
Beds: 2D 1T **Baths:** 3 En
🕿 🅿 (4) ⅙ 📺 🐾 ✗ ▥ 🎦 ⬥ ♿ 1

Aberuthven

NN9815 ◀ *Kirkstyle Inn*

Craiginver, *Aberuthven, Auchterarder, PH3 1HE.*
Open: April to Oct
Grades: STB 3 Star
01764 662411 J M Smith
jms@craiginver.freeserve.co.uk
D: £18.50–£19.50 **S:** £19.50–£20.50
Beds: 2T **Baths:** 1 En 1 Pr
🅿 (8) ⅙ 📺 ▥ 🎦 ⬥
Grade C Listed Victorian former manse (rectory) set in large garden with views over the earn valley towards the Ochils. Ample private off-street parking. comfortable beds and good Scottish breakfasts. Easy access to the main cities of Scotland.

Acharn

NN7543 ◀ *Croft-na-caber Hotel*

12 Ballinlaggan, *Acharn, Aberfeldy, Perthshire, PH15 2HT.*
Warm welcome awaits in quiet lochside village of Acharn, surrounded by beautiful scenery.
Open: All Year
01887 830409 Mrs Spiers
BandB.acharn@virgin.net
D: £16.00 **S:** £16.00
Beds: 1T 1S **Baths:** 1 Sh
🕿 🅿 (2) ⅙ 📺 ✗ ▥ 🎦 ⬥ ⬥

Alyth

NO2448   ◄ *Lands of Loyal Hotel, Drummacree Oven Bistro*

Mona Gowan, *3 Strathmore Terrace, Alyth, Blairgowrie, Perthshire, PH11 8DP.*
Open: All Year (not Xmas/New Year)
Grades: STB 4 Star
01828 632489 (also fax)
lynne@monagowan.freeserve.co.uk
D: £20.00–£22.50 **S:** £20.00–£22.50
Beds: 1T 1D 1F **Baths:** 3 En
🛏 🅿 (3) ⅋ 📺 🛍 🖂 Ⓥ ♨
Fine detached Victorian Villa with traditional coach house. Quietly situated at the foot of Glen Isla and North of historical Alyth. All bedrooms and sun lounge are south facing with superb uninterrupted views over large tiered gardens, the Vale of Strathmore and the Sidlaw Hills.

Auchterarder

NN9412   ◄ *Golf Inn, Collearn Hotel, Cairn Lodge, Cafe Cento*

Nether Coul, *Auchterarder, Perthshire, PH3 1ET.*
Substantial renovated cottage in rural location.
Open: All Year
Grades: STB 3 Star
01764 663119 (also fax)
Mr & Mrs Robertson
nethercoul@talk21.com
D: £17.00–£19.00 **S:** £20.00–£25.00
Beds: 1F 1T **Baths:** 2 Pr
🛏 🅿 (5) ⅋ 📺 🛊 ✕ 🛍 Ⓥ ♨

The Auld Nick, *89 The Feus, Auchterarder, Perthshire, PH3 1DG.*
Recently renovated former town police station, located on main street.
Open: All Year (not Xmas)
Grades: STB 3 Star
01764 662916 (also fax)
auldnick.langtoon@virgin.net
D: £20.00–£25.00 **S:** £16.00–£20.00
Beds: 1F 1D 1T 1S **Baths:** 3 En 1 Sh
🛏 🅿 (4) ⅋ 📺 🛊 🛍 Ⓥ ♨

10 The Grove, Collearn, *Auchterarder, Perthshire, PH3 1PT.*
Private house in quiet estate with off-street parking. **Open:** Jan to Dec
Grades: STB 2 Star
01764 662036 Mrs McFarlane
D: £17.50–£18.50 **S:** £18.00–£20.00
Beds: 1T **Baths:** 1 Sh
🛏 (3) 🅿 (1) ⅋ 📺 🛊 🛍 Ⓥ ♨ ♿

Ballindean

NO2529

The Orchard, *Easter Ballindean, Inchture, Perth, PH14 9QS.*
Characterful cottage in lovely rural setting. Magnificent views. Sunny conservatory.
Open: April to Oct
Grades: STB 3 Star
01828 686318 J.D Burrowes
theorchard@exl.co.uk
D: £22.00 **S:** £25.00–£27.00
Beds: 1T 2D **Baths:** 2 En 1 Pr
🛏 🅿 (4) ⅋ 📺 🛊 🛍 Ⓥ ♨ ♿

Balloch

NO2828   ◄ *Inchture Hotel*

Old School House, *Main Street, Inchture, Perth, PH14 9RN.*
Listed old school house.
Open: All Year (not Xmas/New Year)
01828 686275 Mrs Howard
D: £17.00 **S:** £17.00
Beds: 2D 1T **Baths:** 1 En 1 Pr
🛏 🅿 (1) 📺 🛊 🛍 Ⓥ ♨

Bankfoot

NO0635   ◄ *Spiral Restaurant*

Blair House, *Main Street, Bankfoot, Perth, PH1 4AB.*
Gateway to Highlands. Ideal touring spot, golfing, fishing, castles etc.
Open: All Year
Grades: STB 2 Star
01738 787338 (also fax) Mrs McKay
D: £18.00 **S:** £22.50
Beds: 2D 1T **Baths:** 2 En 1 Pr
🛏 🅿 (3) 📺 🛊 🛍 ♨

Birnam

NO0341   *Birnam Hotel, Atholl Arms*

The Waterbury Guest House, *Murthly Terrace, Birnam, Dunkeld, Perthshire, PH8 0BG.*
Listed Victorian home with modern comforts next to Beatrix Potter garden.
Open: All Year
01350 727324 Mrs Neil
bneil@waterbury.demon.co.uk
D: £18.00–£22.00 **S:** £18.00–£22.00
Beds: 2F 3D 1T 2S **Baths:** 6 En 1 Sh
🛇 🅿 (4) 📺 🛏 ✕ 🛏. 🖳 ♨ cc

Blair Atholl

NN8764   *Tilt Hotel, The Roundhouse*

Dalgreine, *off St Andrews Crescent, Blair Atholl, Pitlochry, Perthshire, PH18 5SX.*
Attractive comfortable guest house, set in beautiful surroundings near Blair Castle.
Open: All Year
Grades: STB 3 Star, AA 4 Diamond
01796 481276
Mr & Mrs Pywell & Mrs F Hardie
D: £16.00–£20.00 **S:** £17.00–£20.00
Beds: 1F 2D 2T 1S **Baths:** 2 En 1 Pr 1 Sh
🛇 🅿 (6) ⌫ 📺 ✕ 🛏. 🖳 ♨

Blairgowrie

NO1745   *Angus Hotel Bar, Brig O'Blair, Burrelton Park Inn, Victoria Hotel, Woodside Inn*

The Laurels Guest House, *Golf Course Road, Rosemount, Blairgowrie, Perthshire, PH10 6LH.*
Open: Jan to Dec
Grades: STB 3 Star
01250 874920 (also fax)
Mr & Mrs McPherson
D: £19.50–£20.00 **S:** £20.00–£30.00
Beds: 2D 3T 1S **Baths:** 4 En
🛇 🅿 (8) ⌫ 📺 ✕ 🛏. ♨ cc
Converted C18th farmhouse. First class cooking, licensed. Our bedrooms are very well-equipped with power showers in ensuite rooms and bathroom.

Ridgeway, *Wester Essendy, Blairgowrie, Perthshire, PH10 6RA.*
Bungalow overlooking loch and hills. Friendly, comfortable accommodation, large garden.
Open: All Year (not Xmas)
Grades: STB 3 Star
01250 884734 Mrs Mathews
Fax: 01250 884735
pam.mathews@btinternet.com
D: £22.00 **S:** £22.00
Beds: 1D 1T **Baths:** 2 En
🛇 🅿 (8) ⌫ 📺 🛏. ♨

Garfield House, *Perth Road, Blairgowrie, Perthshire, PH10 6ED.*
Attractive detached Victorian house. Quiet and comfortable with lovely homely atmosphere.
Open: Jan to Dec
Grades: STB 3 Star
01250 872999 Mrs Safsaf
D: £17.00–£20.00 **S:** £17.00–£20.00
Beds: 1D 1T 1S **Baths:** 2 En 1 Pr
🛇 🅿 (4) ⌫ 📺 🛏. ♨

Eildon Bank, *Perth Road, Blairgowrie, Perthshire, PH10 6ED.*
Victorian detached house. Shops, walking, ski-ing available in area.
Open: All Year (not Xmas)
Grades: STB 3 Star
01250 873648 (also fax)
Mrs Murray
D: £16.00–£18.00 **S:** £20.00–£22.00
Beds: 2D 1T
🛇 🅿 (4) 📺 🛏 🛏. ♨

Bridge of Cally

NO1351   *Bridge Of Cully Hotel, The Corriefodly*

Bridge Of Cally Hotel, *Bridge of Cally, Blairgowrie, Perthshire, PH10 7JJ.*
Small family hotel. Cooking award. Walk over 2000 acres.
Open: All Year (not Xmas)
Grades: STB 2 Star
01250 886231 Mr McCosh
D: £20.00–£27.50 **S:** £20.00–£27.50
Beds: 1F 3D 4T 1S **Baths:** 7 En 2 Pr
🛇 🅿 📺 🛏 ✕ 🛏. 🖳 ♨

Cleish

NT0998   🏠 *Tormaukin Inn, Balgeddie Toll*

Mawmill House, *Cleish, Kinross, KY13 7LN.*
Open: Easter to Oct
01577 850249
Mrs Whitehead
andrewmawmill@tinyworld.co.uk
D: £20.00 **S:** £25.00
Beds: 2D 1S **Baths:** 1 Pr
🛏 🅿 (4) ⅍ 📺 🎞 Ⅴ ☕

Peaceful spacious C18th farmhouse in the
Cleish Valley. Convenient for Edinburgh,
Perth, St Andrews, Stirling & routes to the
Highlands. Private sitting room. Traditional
breakfast. Warmest welcome. Perfect base
for walking, fishing, golf & sightseeing.

Clunie

NO1043

Bankhead, *Clunie, Blairgowrie, Perthshire,*
PH10 6SG.
Quiet house on small farm, golfing, fishing,
walking nearby.
Open: All Year
Grades: STB 3 Star
01250 884281 (also fax)
Mrs Wightman
ian@iwwightman.freeserve.co.uk
D: £18.00 **S:** £20.00–£21.00
Beds: 1F 1T **Baths:** 2 En
🛏 🅿 (3) ⅍ 📺 🐾 ✕ 🎞 Ⅴ ☕

Comrie

NN7722   🏠 *Comrie Hotel, Royal Hotel, Deil's*
Cauldron, Achray House

St Margarets, *Braco Road, Comrie, Crieff,*
Perthshire, PH6 2HP.
Attractive Victorian family house, good
fishing, golfing, walking, horse riding.
Open: Mar to Nov
Grades: STB 3 Star B&B
01764 670413
Mr & Mrs Paterson
D: £17.00–£20.00 **S:** £17.00–£20.00
Beds: 1D 2T **Baths:** 1 En 1 Sh
🛏 (3) 🅿 (4) ⅍ 📺 🎞 Ⅴ ☕ ♿

Millersfield, *Dalginross, Comrie, Crieff,*
Perthshire, PH6 2HE.
Modern centrally heated bungalow. Peaceful
location, attractive garden and warm
welcome. **Open:** All Year (not Xmas/New Year)
01764 670073 Mrs Rae
D: £19.00–£20.00 **S:** £19.00–£20.00
Beds: 1D 1T
🛏 (12) 🅿 (3) ⅍ 📺 🎞 Ⅴ ☕ ♿

Crieff

NN8621   🏠 *Oakbank, Glenturret Distillery,*
Arouthie Hotel, Locke's Acre

Merlindale, *Perth Road, Crieff, PH7 3EQ.*
Open: Feb to Dec
Grades: STB 4 Star
01764 655205 (also fax) Mr & Mrs Clifford
merlin.dale@virgin.net
D: £22.50–£27.00 **S:** £25.00–£35.00
Beds: 1F 1T **Baths:** 2 En
🛏 🅿 ⅍ 📺 ✕ 🎞 ☕

Luxury Georgian house, all bedrooms
ensuite with tea/coffee making facilities. We
have a Jacuzzi bath, garden, ample off-road
parking, satellite television, and extensive
library. Cordon Bleu cooking is our
speciality. A warm welcome awaits you in
this non-smoking house.

Somerton House, *Turret Bank, Crieff,*
Perthshire, PH7 4JN.
Quietly situated in own grounds, large
detached modern private house.
Open: All Year (not Xmas)
01764 653513 Mrs Sloan
Fax: 01764 655028
katie@turretbank7.freeserve.co.uk
D: £15.00–£19.00 **S:** £19.00–£23.00
Beds: 1F 1D 1T **Baths:** 3 En
🛏 🅿 (6) ⅍ 📺 🐾 🎞 Ⅴ ☕

5 Duchlage Terrace, *Crieff, Perthshire,*
PH7 3AS.
Peaceful and gracious rooms, superb food,
magnificent scenery, golf and fishing.
Open: All Year
01764 653516 (also fax) Ms Coutts
D: £18.00–£20.00 **S:** £20.00–£25.00
Beds: 1F 1T **Baths:** 1 En 1 Pr
🛏 (2) 🅿 (2) ⅍ 📺 🐾 ✕ 🎞 Ⅴ ☕

11 Galloway Crescent, *Crieff, PH7 4LG.*
Bungalow in quiet location close to public
parks and distillery. **Open:** Easter to Oct
01764 655276 Mrs Cooper
D: £15.00–£18.00 **S:** £15.00–£18.00
Beds: 1T 1S
P (2) ⌧ ⊡ Ⅲ. ⚿

Dunkeld

NO0243

Taybank Hotel, *Tay Terrace, Dunkeld,*
Perthshire, PH8 0AQ.
Friendly music bar, spontaneous sessions,
beautiful location, tasteful rooms.
Open: All Year
01350 727340 Mr Close
Fax: 01350 728606
admin@dunkeld.co.uk
D: £17.50 **S:** £17.50–£22.50
Beds: 2F 1T 1D 1S **Baths:** 2 Sh
⛺ **P** ✕ cc

Edradynate

NN8852

Lurgan Farm, *Edradynate, Aberfeldy,*
Perthshire, PH15 2JX.
Traditional working farm, with stunning
views over the Tay Valley.
Open: All Year (not Xmas)
01887 840451 Mrs Kennedy
D: £17.00–£22.00 **S:** £17.00–£22.00
Beds: 1F **Baths:** 1 En
⛺ **P** ⌧ ⊡ ⤬ Ⅲ. Ⅴ ⚿

Fearnan

NN7244

Tigh An Loan Hotel, *Fearnan, Aberfeldy,*
Perthshire, PH15 2PF.
Old inn built in C19th; beautifully situated
overlooking Loch Tay.
Open: Easter to Oct
Grades: STB 1 Star
01887 830249 Mr Kelloe
D: £29.00–£31.00 **S:** £29.00–£31.00
Beds: 1F 3S **Baths:** 3 En 2 Sh
⛺ **P** (25) ⊡ ⤬ ✕ Ⅴ ⚿ cc

Fortingall

NN7347 ⚐ *Fortingall Hotel*

Kinnighallen Farm, *Duneaves Road,*
Fortingall, Aberfeldy, Perthshire, PH15 2LR.
Come and have a relaxing stay in this sleepy,
rural backwater where wildlife abounds.
Open: May to Oct
Grades: STB 1 Star
01887 830619 Mrs Kininmonth
a.kininmonth@talk21.com
D: £15.00 **S:** £15.00
Beds: 1D 1T 1S **Baths:** 1 Sh
⛺ (2) **P** (5) ⤬ Ⅲ. Ⅴ

Inver

NO0142 ⚐ *Taybank, Macleans*

3 Knockard Road, *Pitlochry, Perthshire,*
PH16 5JE.
Birthplace of C18th Fiddler. Large secluded
garden. Open views.
Open: Easter to Oct
01796 472157 Mr & Mrs Gardiner
D: £14.00–£15.00
Beds: 1T 1D **Baths:** 1 Sh
P (3) ⊡ Ⅲ. ⚿

Killiecrankie

NN9162 ⚐ *Killiecrankie Hotel*

Tighdornie, *Killiecrankie, Pitlochry,*
Perthshire, PH16 5LR.
Modern house in historic Killiecrankie. 2.5
miles from Blair Castle.
Open: All Year
Grades: STB 3 Star
01796 473276 (also fax)
Mrs Sanderson
tigh-dornie@btinternet.com
D: £22.00–£24.00 **S:** £27.00
Beds: 1T 2D **Baths:** 3 En
⛺ (12) **P** (4) ⤬ ⊡ Ⅲ. Ⅴ ⚿

High season, bank holidays
and special events mean low
availability anywhere

Kinloch Rannoch

NN6658

Dunalastair Hotel, *Kinloch Rannoch,*
Pitlochry, Perthshire, PH16 5PW.
Open: All Year
Grades: STB 3 Star, AA 2 Star
01882 632323 Paul Edwards
Fax: 01882 632371
reservations@dunalastair.co.uk
D: £27.50 **S:** £27.50
Beds: 2F 10D 10T 1S **Baths:** 25 En
🐾 🅿 ⊁ ✕ ▥ ⛉ ❄ ♨ ♿ cc
Romantically situated in the heart of
Highland Perthshire, Dunalastair is a C18th
former shooting lodge, now a wonderful
hotel with luxurious rooms. Cosy lounge and
baronial dining areas. Perfect base for
exploring Scotland. This is a genuine
discount, come and see for yourself.

Bunrannoch House, *Kinloch Rannoch,*
Pitlochry, Perthshire, PH16 5QB.
Lovely country house, beautiful views, open
fires. Warm welcome and excellent food.
Open: All Year (not Xmas/New Year)
Grades: STB 2 Star
01882 632407 (also fax)
Mrs Skeaping
bun.house@tesco.net
D: £22.00–£24.00 **S:** £22.00–£24.00
Beds: 2F 3D 2T **Baths:** 5 Pr 2 Sh
🐾 🅿 (10) ⊁ ✕ ▥ ⛉ ♨ cc

Kinross

NO1102   ◀ *Carlin Maggies*

Lochleven Inn, *6 Swansacre, Kinross, Fife,*
KY13 7TE.
Local friendly inn (public bar).
Open: All Year
01577 864185 Mr McGregor
D: £18.00 **S:** £18.00
Beds: 1F 1T 1D **Baths:** 2 Pr
🐾 🅿 (2) ▥ ✕ ▥ ⛉ ♨

Bringing children with you?
Always ask for any special rates

The Roxburghe Guest House, *126 High*
Street, Kinross, Fife, KY13 8DA.
Family-run guest house. Ideal base in the
heart of Scotland, for fishing.
Open: All Year
01577 862498 Mrs Robertson
D: £16.00–£18.00 **S:** £16.00–£18.00
Beds: 2F 1D 2T **Baths:** 2 Sh
🐾 🅿 (5) ▥ ⊁ ✕ ▥ ⛉ ♨

Kirkmichael

NO0860   ◀ *Strathardle Inn, Log Cabin Hotel*

Curran House, *Kirkmichael, Blairgowrie,*
Perthshire, PH10 7NA.
Traditional Scottish house. Log fire. Home
baking on arrival.
Open: Jan to Sept **Grades:** STB 4 Star
01250 881229 Mr & Mrs Van der Veldt
Fax: 01250 881448
a.m.vanderveldt@tesco.net
D: £18.00–£36.00
Beds: 2D 1T **Baths:** 1 Pr 1 Sh
🐾 🅿 ⊁ ▥ ⛉ ♨

Meigle

NO2844   ◀ *Belmount Arms*

Loanhead House, *Dundee Road, Meigle,*
Blairgowrie, PH12 8SF.
Superb accommodation and food in edge of
castle estate location.
Open: All Year (not Xmas/New Year)
Grades: STB 4 Star
01828 640358 Mr Taylor
Fax: 0870 132 9749
gill@loanheadhouse.co.uk
D: £20.00–£24.00 **S:** £20.00–£28.00
Beds: 1D 1T **Baths:** 1 En 1 Pr
🐾 🅿 (4) ⊁ ▥ ⛉ ♨

Cardean Water Mill, *Meigle, Blairgowrie,*
Perthshire, PH12 8RB.
An 1840 watermill offers peace, free fishing
and beautiful gardens. **Open:** All Year
01828 640633 Mr Wares
Fax: 01828 640741
D: £20.00 **S:** £20.00
Beds: 1T **Baths:** 1 Pr
🅿 (2) ▥ ⛉ ♨

Methven

NO0226   *Almondbank*

Lismore, *1 Rorrie Terrace, Methven, Perth, PH1 3PL.*
Traditional Scottish hospitality in friendly family home. Ideal touring base, 5 miles from Perth.
Open: All Year
01738 840441 (also fax)
Mr Comrie
D: £14.50–£15.50 **S:** £17.50–£25.00
Beds: 1T 1D
🛇 (8) 🅿 (2) ⅋ 📺 ⊞, 📺 cc

Milnathort

NO1204   *Balgeddie Toll, Lamond Inn, Thistle Hotel*

Hattonburn Farmhouse, *Milnathort, Kinross, Fife, KY13 0SA.*
Modernised C19th sandstone farmhouse, close by M90. Edinburgh 35 mins, Perth 15 mins. **Open:** All Year (not Xmas)
01577 862362 Mrs Todrick
D: £20.00–£25.00 **S:** £20.00–£25.00
Beds: 1D 1T **Baths:** 2 Pr
🛇 🅿 (8) 📺 🐾 ✕ ⊞, 📺 ♨

Perth

NO1123   *Isle Of Skye Hotel, Huntingtower Hotel, Letham Farmhouse Hotel, Lovat Hotel, Moncrieff Hotel, Paco's, Royal George Hotel, Silver Broom, Wheel*

Huntingtower House, *Crieff Road, Perth, PH1 3JJ.*
Open: Feb to Dec
Grades: STB 3 Star
01738 624681 Mrs Lindsay
dlindsay@btinternet.com
D: £18.00–£21.00 **S:** £18.00–£21.00
Beds: 1D 2T **Baths:** 1 Pr 1 Sh
🛇 (11) 🅿 (3) ⅋ 📺 ⊞, 📺
Situated on the western outskirts of Perth, this charming country house with large, secluded garden nestles beside historic Huntingtower Castle. There is easy access to Perth & all main routes throughout Scotland. A friendly welcome & delicious breakfast are assured.

Aberdeen Guest House, *Pitcullen Crescent, Perth, PH2 7HT.*
Beautiful Victorian house where comfort and care is paramount.
Open: All Year
Grades: STB 4 Star
01738 633183 (also fax)
Mrs Buchan
buchan@aberdeenguesthouse.fsnet.co.uk
D: £18.00–£22.00 **S:** £18.00–£25.00
Beds: 2D 1T **Baths:** 1 En 2 Sh
🛇 🅿 (4) 📺 ⊞, 📺 ♨

Beeches, *2 Comely Bank, Perth, PH2 7HU.*
Home from home Victorian house. Friendly, relaxing, check web details!
Open: All Year
Grades: STB 3 Star
01738 624486 Mrs Smith
Fax: 01738 643382
enquiries@beeches-guest-house.co.uk
D: £18.00–£20.00 **S:** £18.00–£20.00
Beds: 1D 1T 2S **Baths:** 4 En
🛇 🅿 (4) ⅋ 📺 🐾 ✕ ⊞, ♨ cc

Dunallan Guest House, *10 Pitcullen Crescent, Perth, PH2 7HT.*
Well-appointed Victorian villa within walking distance Perth City Centre.
Open: All Year
Grades: STB 3 Star
01738 622551 (also fax)
Mrs Brown
D: £20.00–£22.00 **S:** £21.50–£23.00
Beds: 1F 1D 2T 3S **Baths:** 7 En
🛇 🅿 (7) ⅋ 📺 🐾 ✕ ⊞, 📺 ♨ & cc

Arisaig Guest House, *4 Pitcullen Crescent, Perth, Perthshire & Kinross, PH2 7HT.*
Late-Victorian family run guest house situated on the A94.
Open: All Year
Grades: STB 4 Star
01738 628240 (also fax)
Stewart & Wilma Bousie
reservations@arsaig.demon.co.uk
D: £20.00–£22.50 **S:** £25.00–£30.00
Beds: 1F 2D 1T 1S **Baths:** 5 En
🛇 🅿 (5) ⅋ 📺 ⊞, ♨ cc

The Darroch Guest House, 9 Pitcullen
Crescent, Perth, PH2 7HT.
Victorian semi, friendly relaxed atmosphere,
ideal base for touring.
Open: All Year
Grades: STB 2 Star
01738 636893 (also fax)
Mr & Mrs Hirst
D: £16.00–£21.00 **S:** £16.00–£25.00
Beds: 1F 1D 2T 2S **Baths:** 3 En 1 Sh
ʊ P (8) ⊡ ⋔ ✗ ⊞ ⩒ ⅃

Parkview Guest House, 22 Marshall
Place, Perth, PH2 8AG.
Listed Georgian town house. Very central,
overlooking park.
Open: All Year
01738 620297 (also fax)
Mr Farquharson
fiona.farquharson@btinternet.com
D: £16.00–£19.00 **S:** £18.00–£20.00
Beds: 4F 1T **Baths:** 3 En 1 Sh
ʊ P (4) ⊡ ⋔ ⊞ ⩒ ⅃

Comely Bank Cottage, 19 Pitcullen Cres,
Perth, Perthshire, PH2 7HT.
Enjoy true Scottish hospitality in
comfortable family home, 10 minutes walk
city centre.
Open: All Year (not Xmas)
Grades: STB 3 Star
01738 631118
Mrs Marshall
Fax: 01738 571245
comelybankcott@hotmail.com
D: £18.00–£22.00 **S:** £22.00–£30.00
Beds: 1F 1D 1T **Baths:** 2 En 1 Pr
ʊ P (3) ⊡ ⋔ ⊞ ⩒ ⅃ cc

Brae Lodge, 140 Glasgow Road, Perth,
PH2 0LX.
Small and friendly with lots of advice on
locality/tours.
Open: All Year (not Xmas/New Year)
01738 628473
Mr Muir
D: £16.00–£18.00 **S:** £20.00–£25.00
Beds: 2F 1D **Baths:** 2 Sh
ʊ P (2) ⅍ ⊡ ⋔ ⊞ ⅃

Heidl Guest House, 43 York Place, Perth,
Perthshire & Kinross, PH2 8EH.
Family run, central location, close to bus and
railway stations.
Open: All Year (not Xmas/New Year)
Grades: STB 2 Star
01738 635031 Mr & Mrs McMahon
Fax: 01738 643710
B&B@heidl.co.uk
D: £15.00–£22.00 **S:** £18.00–£26.00
Beds: 1F 2D 3T 2S **Baths:** 1 Pr 2 Sh
ʊ P (3) ⊡ ⋔ ⊞ ⅃

Pitlochry

NN9458 ⚑ *Acarsaid Hotel, Pine Trees Hotel,
Atholl Arms Hotel, Old Smithy, Old Armoury, Port-
na-Craig Inn, Moulin Hotel, Westlands, Mill,
McKay's, Ballinling Inn*

Auchlatt Steading, Kinnaird, Pitlochry,
Perthshire, PH16 5JL.
Open: Easter to Nov
01796 472661 Miss Elkins
Fax: 01796 472661
D: £17.00 **S:** £17.00
Beds: 1T 1D **Baths:** All En
P (2) ⅍ ⊡ ⋔ ⊞
Newly converted Scottish barn comfortable
beds and a good honest breakfast
overlooking Pitlochry and surrounding
beautiful countryside close Edradour and
Scotland smallest distillery good hill walking
and fishing, also the theatre and much
historic interest.

Atholl Villa, 29 Atholl Road, Pitlochry,
Perthshire, PH16 5BX.
Open: All Year
Grades: STB 3 Star
01796 473820 Mrs Bruce
atholluilla@aol.com
D: £17.50–£25.00 **S:** £17.50–£25.00
Beds: 3F 2T 2D **Baths:** 7 En
ʊ P (10) ⅍ ⊡ ⋔ ✗ ⊞ ⩒ ❋ ⅃ ⅙ cc
This 10 bedroom Victorian detached stone
house of typical highland construction, built
150 years ago is situated right at the edge of
town, close to rail and bus stations, an
abundance of restaurants, shops and the
most famous Festival Theatre.

Wellwood House, West Moulin Road, Pitlochry, Perthshire, PH16 5EA.
Open: March to Nov
Grades: STB 2 Star, AA 3 Diamond
01796 474288 Ms Herd
Fax: 01796 474299
wellwood@ukonline.co.uk
D: £19.50–£25.00 **S:** £25.00–£35.00
Beds: 1F 5D 4T **Baths:** 8 En 2 Sh
ᗡ 🅿 (25) 📺 🚻 🛏. 👤
The Wellwood is a Victorian mansion house set in 2 acres of splendid gardens, yet only a 5 minute walk from town centre, comfortable rooms, glorious views, secure open car park.

Balrobin Hotel, Higher Oakfield, Pitlochry, Perthshire, PH16 5HT.
Quality accommodation with panoramic views at affordable prices.
Open: Apr to Oct
Grades: STB 3 Star, AA 2 Star, RAC 2 Star
01796 472901 Mr Hohman
Fax: 01796 474200
info@balrobin.co.uk
D: £25.00–£33.00 **S:** £25.00–£39.00
Beds: 1F 10D 3T 1S **Baths:** 15 En
ᗡ (5) 🅿 (15) 🕊 📺 🛏 ✕ 🛏. �V 👤 cc

Easter Dunfallandy Country House B&B, Pitlochry, Perthshire, PH16 5NA.
Beautifully presented country house with fine views and gourmet breakfast.
Open: All Year (not Xmas/New Year)
Grades: STB 4 Star
01796 474128 Mr Mathieson
Fax: 01796 473994
sue@dunfallandy.co.uk
D: £28.00 **S:** £38.00
Beds: 1D 2T **Baths:** 3 En
ᗡ (12) 🅿 (6) 🕊 📺 🛏. �V

Pooltiel, Lettoch Road, Pitlochry, PH16 5AZ.
Quiet scenic location in Perthshire Highlands with panoramic views.
Open: Easter to Oct
Grades: STB 3 Star
01796 472184 Mrs Sandison
ajs@pooltiel.freeserve.co.uk
D: £17.00–£18.00 **S:** £17.00–£18.00
Beds: 1F 1T 1D **Baths:** 1 Sh
ᗡ 🅿 🕊 📺 🛏 🛏. 👤

Lynedoch, 9 Lettoch Terrace, Pitlochry, Perthshire, PH16 5BA.
Open: Easter to Oct
01796 472119 Mrs Williamson
iwilliamson@talk21.com
D: £16.00–£18.00 **S:** £16.00–£18.00
Beds: 2D 1T **Baths:** 2 Sh
🅿 (3) 🕊 📺 🛏 🛏. 👤
Stone-built semi-detached villa in beautiful Highland Perthshire, ideally situated for walking, golf, fishing etc. Close by are hydroelectric dam, fish ladder, world famous festival theatre, and whisky distilleries. Views of Ben Vrackie and the Fonab Hills.

8 Darach Road, Pitlochry, Perthshire, PH16 5HR.
Semi detached house. Hill walking, theatre, various walks, central to cities.
Open: All Year (not Xmas/New Year)
01796 472074 Mrs Weyda-Wernick
weydawernick@aol.com
D: £15.00 **S:** £18.00
Beds: 1D **Baths:** 2 Sh
ᗡ 🅿 (2) 📺 🛏 🛏. �V

Carra Beag Guest House, 16 Toberargan Road, Pitlochry, Perthshire, PH16 5HG.
Magnificent views; central location; breakfast cooked to order; period features.
Open: All Year
Grades: STB 3 Star
01796 472835 (also fax)
Mr Stone
D: £13.00–£23.00 **S:** £13.00–£23.00
Beds: 2F 3D 3T 2S **Baths:** 9 Pr 1 Sh
ᗡ 🅿 (9) 🕊 📺 🛏 ✕ 🛏. �V ✳ 👤

Ferrymans Cottage, Port-na-Craig, Pitlochry, Perthshire, PH16 5ND.
Cosy riverside cottage below Festival Theatre or stroll into town.
Open: Easter to Nov
Grades: STB 3 Star
01796 473681 (also fax)
Mrs Sanderson
D: £19.00–£24.00
Beds: 2F **Baths:** 1 Pr 1 En
ᗡ 🅿 (6) 🕊 📺 🛏. �V 👤

Rhynd

NO1520 ◀ *Baiglie Inn*

Fingask Farm, *Rhynd, Perth, Perthshire & Kinross, PH2 8QF.*
Spacious accommodation in well-appointed farmhouse in a peaceful part of central Perthshire.
Open: Easter to Oct **Grades:** STB 4 Star
01738 812220 Mrs Stirrat **Fax: 01738 813325**
libby@agstirrat.sol.co.uk
D: £19.00–£21.00 **S:** £19.00–£21.00
Beds: 1D 1T 1S **Baths:** 2 Pr
🛏 (10) **P** (3) ⅍ 📺 ✕ ▥ 🍴 **cc**

St Fillans

NN6924

Earngrove Cottage, *St Fillans, Crieff, Perthshire, PH6 2ND.*
Modernised traditional cottage amidst mountain loch scenery; golfing, hillwalking, fishing. **Open:** Mar to Nov
01764 685224 (also fax) Mrs Ross
D: £15.00 **S:** £18.00–£20.00
Beds: 2T **Baths:** 2 Sh
P (4) ⅍ 📺 🐾 ✕ ▥ 📺 🍴

Stanley

NO1133 ◀ *The Spiral*

Beechlea, *Stanley, Perth, Perthshire, PH1 4PS.*
Luxury comfortable B&B, beautiful quiet countryside, excellent location off A9.
Open: All Year (not Xmas)
Grades: STB 4 Star
01738 828715
Mrs Lindsay
chaslizlin@aol.com
D: £20.00–£27.00 **S:** £25.00–£27.00
Beds: 1F 1D 1T
Baths: 3 En
🛏 (10) **P** (6) ⅍ 📺 ▥ 🍴 **cc**

The Linn, *3 Duchess Street, Stanley, Perth, PH1 4NF.*
Friendly hosts; rooms prettily furnished and decorated for your comfort.
Open: All Year (not Xmas)
01738 828293
Mrs Lundie
D: £20.00 **S:** £25.00–£30.00
Beds: 2F 1T
Baths: 2 En 1 Pr
🛏 **P** (20) 📺 ✕ ▥ 📺 🍴

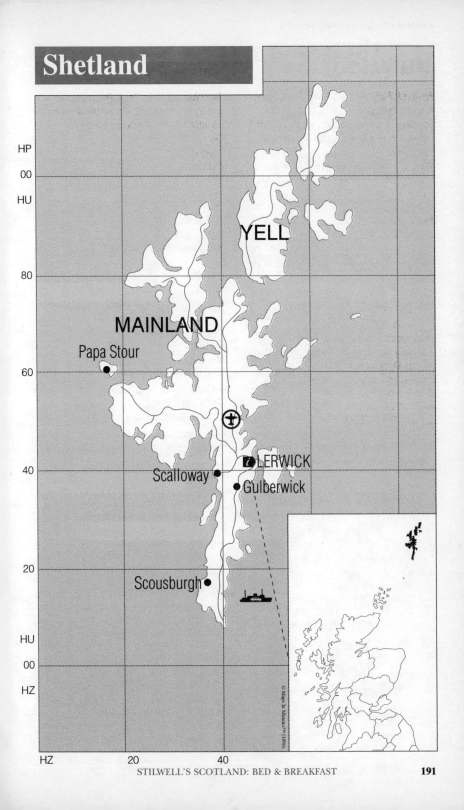

Shetland

AIRPORTS ⊕
Sumburgh Airport, tel. 01950 460654.

AIR SERVICES & AIRLINES ✈

British Airways: *Sumburgh to Aberdeen, Edinburgh, Glasgow, Inverness, Kirkwall (Orkney), Lerwick, Unst, Wick*. Tel. (local rate): 0345 222111.

FERRIES 🛳

P&O Scottish Ferries: *Lerwick to Aberdeen* - 14 hrs;

Lerwick to Stromness (Orkney) - 8 hrs. Tel. 01224 572615.

The **Shetland Islands Council** operate ferries between the islands themselves. Tel. 01595 693434.

TOURIST INFORMATION OFFICE 🅸

Market Cross, **Lerwick**, Shetland Islands, ZE1 0JP, 01595 693434·

FAIR ISLE   Fair Isle

HZ2271

Upper Leogh, *Fair Isle, Shetland, ZE2 9JU.*
Working croft, hand spinning demonstration/tuition available. Local crafts nearby.
Open: All Year
Grades: STB 2 Star
01595 760248 Mrs Coull
kathleen.coull@lineone.net
D: £20.00–£22.00 **S:** £20.00–£22.00
Beds: 1T 1D 1S
🛏 🅿 (3) ⅙ 📺 ✕ Ⓥ 🍴

MAINLAND   Gulberwick

HU4438

Virdafjell, *Shurton Brae, Gulberwick, Shetland, ZE2 9TX.*
Peaceful Nordic home overlooking bay. Walks, ponies, bird watching, good touring base.
Open: All Year **Grades:** STB 3 Star
01595 694336 Mrs Stove
Fax: 01595 696252
d.stove@talk21.com
D: £20.00–£25.00 **S:** £22.00–£30.00
Beds: 2T 1D **Baths:** 1 En 1 Sh
🛏 🅿 (6) ⅙ 📺 ✕ 🖾 Ⓥ 🍴

Bringing children with you?
Always ask for any special rates

MAINLAND   Lerwick

HU4741   ⌕ *Candlestick Maker, Queen's Hotel, Lerwick Hotel*

Breiview, *43 Kantersted Road, Lerwick, Shetland, ZE1 0RJ.*
Friendly modern accommodation in quiet location overlooks bay and Bressay.
Open: All Year (not Xmas/New Year)
Grades: STB 3 Star
01595 695956 Mr Glaser
Fax: 01595 365956
D: £25.00–£30.00 **S:** £30.00–£35.00
Beds: 1F 2D 3T **Baths:** 6 En
🛏 🅿 (6) 📺 ✕ 🖾 🍴

Woosung, *43 St Olaf Street, Lerwick, Shetland, ZE1 0EN.*
Central, close to all amenities - street parking.
Open: All Year
01595 693687 Mrs Conroy
D: £17.00 **S:** £20.00
Beds: 3T 1S **Baths:** 2 Sh
🛏 📺 🐾 ✕ 🖾 Ⓥ 🍴

Whinrig, *12 Burgh Road, Lerwick, Shetland, ZE1 0LB.*
Private bungalow centrally heated neat community centre museum town parks.
Open: Jan to Dec
01595 693554 Mrs Gifford
c.gifford@btinternet.com
D: £19.00–£20.00 **S:** £20.00
Beds: 3F 1D 1T **Baths:** 1 En 1 Pr
🅿 (3) ⅙ 📺 🖾 Ⓥ 🍴 ♿ 3

MAINLAND Scalloway

HU4039

Broch Guest House, *Scalloway, Lerwick, Shetland, ZE1 0UP.*
Comfortable guest house.
Open: All Year (not Xmas)
01595 880767 Mrs Young
D: £17.00 **S:** £19.00
Beds: 3D **Baths:** 3 En
⏰ 🅿 (3) 📺 🏠 Ⓥ 🍴

MAINLAND Scousburgh

HU3717

Spiggie Lodge, *Scousburgh, Shetland, ZE2 9JE.*
Overlooking Spiggie Loch and bird reserve.
Ten minutes Sumburgh Airport.
Open: All Year **Grades:** STB 2 Star
01950 460563 Mr Wilkins
nina.wilkins@zetnet.co.uk
D: £20.00–£22.00 **S:** £18.00–£20.00
Beds: 1T 1D 1S **Baths:** 2 En 1 Sh
⏰ 🅿 (6) ✂ 📺 ✕ 🏠 Ⓥ 🍴

PAPA STOUR Papa Stour

HU1660

Northouse, *Papa Stour, Shetland, ZE2 9PW.*
Working island croft, marine conservation area, spectacular coastline, recreation/sitting room.
Open: All Year
01595 873238
Mrs Holt-Brook
D: £18.00–£19.00 **S:** £18.00–£20.00
Beds: 1F 1D 1T 1S **Baths:** 1 En 1 Sh
⏰ ✂ 📺 🐾 ✕ 🏠 Ⓥ 🍴

RATES

D = Price range per person sharing in a double room

S = Price range for a single room

Stirling & the Trossachs

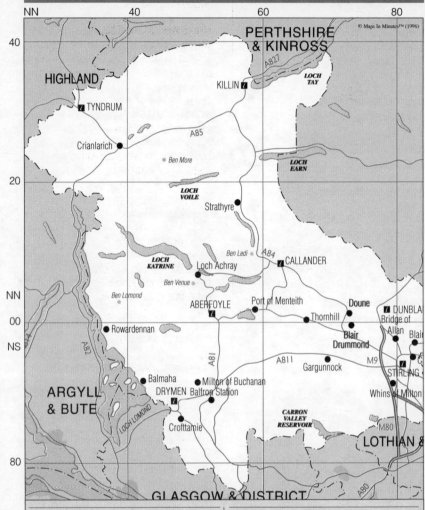

© Maps In Minutes™ (1996)

RAIL ≋

For rail information, telephone the National Rail Enquiries line, on 08457 484950. For the Minicom service for the deaf and hard of hearing, tel. 0845 605 0600.

BUS 🚌

Scottish Citylink, tel. 08705 505050, **National Express**, tel. 0141 226 4826.

TOURIST INFORMATION OFFICES *i*

Main Street, **Aberfoyle**, Stirling, FK8 3UG, 01877 382352 (Easter to Oct).

Alva Mill Trail Visitor Centre, West Stirling Street, **Alva**, Clackmannanshire, FK12 5EN, 01259 769696.

Rob Roy & The Trossachs Visitor Centre, Ancaster Square, **Callander**, Perthshire, FK17 8AD, 01877 330342.

Drymen Library, **Drymen**, Glasgow, G63 0AA, 01360 660068 (Easter to Oct).

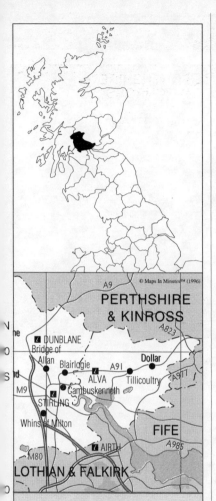

Stirling Rd, **Dunblane**, Perthshire,
FK15 9EY, 01786 824428
(Easter to Oct).

Main Street, **Killin**, Perthshire,
FK21 8UH, 01567 820254
(Easter to Oct).

41 Dumbarton Road, **Stirling**, FK8 2QJ,
01786 475019.

Royal Stirling Visitor Centre, The
Esplanade, **Stirling**, 01786 479901.

Motorway Service Area (M9/M80 J9),
Stirling, 01786 814111 (Easter to Oct).

Main Street, **Tyndrum**, Crianlarich,
Perthshire, FK20 8RY, 01838 400246
(Easter to Oct).

Aberfoyle

NN5200 *Black Bull, Byre, Old Coach House,
Inverard Hotel, Forth Inn*

Creag Ard House B&B, *Aberfoyle,
Stirling, FK8 3TQ.*
A beautiful Victorian house with extensive
and colourful gardens, set in magnificent
scenery.
Open: All Year
Grades: STB 4 Star
01877 382297 Mrs Wilson
creag-ard@tinyonline.co.uk
D: £27.00–£40.00 **S:** £35.00–£70.00
Beds: 4D 2T **Baths:** 6 En
🛏 🅿 (7) ⅟ ♔ ✗ 🍽 Ⓥ 🚲 cc

Mayfield, *Main Street, Aberfoyle, Stirling,
FK8 3UQ.*
Large Victorian private house in centre of
Aberfoyle.
Open: All Year (not Xmas/New Year)
Grades: STB Listed, Comm
01877 382845 Mrs Oldham
D: £18.50–£22.00 **S:** £20.00–£25.00
Beds: 2D 1T 1S **Baths:** 3 En 1 Pr
🛏 🅿 (4) 📺 ♔ 🍽 Ⓥ 🚲 ♿

Oak Royal Guest House, *Aberfoyle,
Stirling, FK8 3UX.*
Beautiful Trossachs countryside. Ideal base
for touring & outdoor enthusiasts.
Open: All Year
01877 382633 (also fax)
D: £20.00–£22.50 **S:** £25.00–£30.00
Beds: 2D 1T **Baths:** 2 En 1 Sh
🛏 🅿 (6) ⅟ 📺 ♔ 🍽 Ⓥ 🚲

Alva

NS8897

Johnstone Arms Hotel, *48 Stirling Street,
Alva, Clackmannanshire, FK12 5EA.*
100-year-old coaching house extensively
refurbished, nestling at the foot of the Ochil
Hills. **Open:** All Year
01259 762884 Mr Cairns
D: £18.00–£20.00 **S:** £18.00–£20.00
Beds: 1F 2T 3S **Baths:** 2 En 1 Sh
🛏 (14) 🅿 (8) ⅟ 📺 ✗ 🍽 Ⓥ ❉ 🚲

Balfron Station

NS5289   🍺 *Clachan, Pottery*

Easter Balfunning Farm, *Drymen, Glasgow, G63 0NF.*
A warm welcome awaits you in our attractive farmhouse idyllically situated.
Open: All Year
Grades: STB 3 Star
01360 440755 Ms Black
D: £18.00–£21.00 **S:** £21.00–£27.00
Beds: 1D 1F **Baths:** 1 Pr 1 En
🐾 ₽ (4) ⊁ ⊠ ↟ ▥ Ⓥ ♨ ♿

Balmaha

NS4290   🍺 *Oak Tree, Clachan Inn*

Critreoch, *Rowardennan Road, Balmaha, Glasgow, G63 0AW.*
Family home quiet location beautiful view over garden to Loch. **Open:** May to Sept
Grades: STB 3 Star
01360 870309 Mrs MacLuskie
D: £20.00–£22.00 **S:** £25.00–£30.00
Beds: 1D 1T **Baths:** 1 En 1 Pr
₽ (6) ⊁ ⊠ ↟ ▥ Ⓥ ♨

Mar Achlais, *Milton of Buchanan, Balmaha, Glasgow, G63 0JE.*
Rural setting near Loch Lomond. Excellent touring centre for Scotland.
Open: All Year (not Xmas)
Grades: STB 3 Star
01360 870300 Mr Nichols
Fax: 01360 870444
marachlais@dial.pipex.com
D: £18.50 **S:** £23.50–£28.50
Beds: 1F 1D **Baths:** 2 En
🐾 ₽ (2) ⊠ ↟ ✕ ▥ Ⓥ ♨ cc

Conic View Cottage, *Balmaha, Glasgow, G63 0JQ.*
Beautifully situated near Loch Lomond and the West Highland Way, surrounded by forest walks. **Open:** Mar to Nov
01360 870297 Mrs Cronin
jenny@balmaha32.freeserve.co.uk
D: £15.00–£20.00 **S:** £18.00–£20.00
Beds: 1D 1S **Baths:** 1 Sh
₽ (2) ⊁ ⊠ ▥ Ⓥ ♨

RATES

D = Price range per person sharing in a double room
S = Price range for a single room

Dunleen, *Balmaha, Glasgow, G63 0JE.*
Ranch-style house. Warm welcome, lovely garden, trout , east side of Loch Lomond. 'Which?' recommended.
Open: May to Oct
Grades: STB 4 Star
01360 870274 Mrs MacFadyen
D: £19.00–£20.00 **S:** £25.00
Beds: 1D 1T **Baths:** 1 Sh
🐾 ₽ (4) ⊁ ⊠ ▥ Ⓥ ♨

Blair Drummond

NS7299   🍺 *Cross Keys Hotel*

The Linns, *Kirk Lane, Blair Drummond, Stirling, FK9 4AN.*
Traditional cottage set in an exclusive rural location surrounded by hills & woodland.
Open: All Year (not Xmas)
01786 841679 (also fax)
Mr Darby
info@thelinns.co.uk
D: £18.50 **S:** £32.00
Beds: 1F 2D 1T **Baths:** 2 En
🐾 (2) ₽ (7) ⊠ ↟ ✕ ▥ Ⓥ ♨ ♿ cc

Blairlogie

NS8296   🍺 *Sword Hotel*

Blairmains Farm, *Manor Loan, Blairlogie, Stirling, FK9 5QA.*
Traditional stone farmhouse. working farm, beautiful country location. Warm Welcome.
Open: All Year (not Xmas/New Year)
Grades: STB 2 Star
01259 761338 Mrs Logan
D: £18.00–£20.00 **S:** £20.00–£23.00
Beds: 2T 1D **Baths:** 1 Sh
🐾 ₽ ⊁ ⊠ ▥ Ⓥ ♨

Bridge of Allan

NS7997 ◀ *Old Bridge, Westerton Arms*

Lorraine, 10 Chalton Road, Bridge of Allan, *Stirling, FK9 4DX.*
Listed building, off main road, lovely views, good walking country.
Open: All Year (not Xmas)
01786 832042
B Holliday
Fax: 01786 831066
101567.2041@compuserve.com
D: £17.00–£18.00 **S:** £17.00–£25.00
Beds: 1D 1T 1S **Baths:** 1 Sh
ॐ ⓟ (4) ⊬ 🆅 🎞 Ⓥ ॠ

Callander

NN6307 ◀ *Abbotsford Lodge Hotel, Myrtle Inn, Crags Hotel, Bracklin Fall, Bridge End, Byre*

Arden House , Bracklinn Road, Callander, *Perthshire, FK17 8EQ.*
Open: Easter to Nov
01877 330235 (also fax)
Mr Mitchell & Mr W Jackson
D: £27.50–£30.00 **S:** £30.00
Beds: 3D 2T 1S **Baths:** 6 En
ॐ (14) ⓟ (6) ⊬ 🆅 🎞 ॠ cc
Tranquillity in the Trossachs. Peaceful Victorian country house with stunning views. Home of BBC TVs 'Dr Finlay's Case Book'. Comfortable, Elegant Ensuite rooms with TV, tea/coffee and many thoughtful touches. Few minutes walk to village. Generous Breakfasts and genuine hospitality.

Campfield Cottage, 138 Main Street, *Callander, Perthshire, FK17 8BG.*
Open: All Year (not Xmas/New Year)
01877 330597
Mrs Hunter
D: £18.00 **S:** £18.00
Beds: 2D 1T 1S **Baths:** 1 Sh
ॐ ⓟ ⊬ 🆅 🕊 🎞 Ⓥ ॠ
Charming C18th cottage in the heart of Callander, down a quiet lane, for a good nights sleep. Highly recommended by people from all over the world, colour TVs in double rooms, washing facilities, tea/coffee, visitors lounge, conservatory, parking.

Glengarry Hotel, Stirling Road, Callander, *Perthshire, FK17 8DA.*
Open: All Year
01877 330216 info@glengarryhotel.com
D: £22.00–£25.00
Beds: 3F 1D **Baths:** 4 En
ॐ ⓟ (15) 🆅 🕊 ✕ 🎞 Ⓥ ॠ
Family-run hotel in its own grounds in the picturesque town of Callander where the Lowlands meet the Highlands. Large comfortable bedrooms. A warm welcome, a hearty breakfast, traditional home-cooked evening meals. Easy access.

Riverview House, Leny Road, Callander, *Perthshire, FK17 8AL.*
Open: All Year (not Xmas)
Grades: STB 3 Star
01877 330635 Mr Little
auldtoll@netscapeonline.co.uk
D: £21.00–£22.00 **S:** £22.00–£24.00
Beds: 3D 2T 1S **Baths:** 5 En
ⓟ (6) ⊬ 🆅 ✕ 🎞 Ⓥ ॠ
Attractive, stone-built villa in own grounds within easy walking of town centre and cycle/pathway. Good home cooking. We also offer self catering cottages in beautiful Trossachs area.

Linley Guest House, 139 Main Street, *Callander, Perthshire, FK17 8BH.*
Open: All Year
Grades: STB 3 Star
01877 330087 M McQuilton
linley_guesthouse@tinyworld.co.uk
D: £16.00–£18.50 **S:** £20.00–£25.00
Beds: 1F 1T 3D **Baths:** 2 En 2 Sh
ॐ ⓟ (4) 🆅 🎞 Ⓥ ॠ
Comfortable Victorian terraced house close to Callander busy centre. Ideal for overnight stop/touring base for the magnificent scenery of the Trossachs renowned for hill walking, fishing, cycling and water sports. Stirling 25 minutes drive, Glasgow and Edinburgh only 1 hour.

Bringing children with you?
Always ask for any special rates

Burnt Inn House, *Brig o' Turk, Callander,*
Perthshire, FK17 8HT.
Situated in the heart of the Trossachs. Quiet
rural location.
Open: All Year (not Xmas/New Year)
Grades: STB 3 Star
01877 376212
Mrs Trzebiatowski
Fax: 01877 376233
burntinnhouse@aol.com
D: £20.00–£25.00 **S:** £20.00–£25.00
Beds: 2T 1D **Baths:** 3 En
☒ (12) ▣ (3) ▥ ☖

East Mains House, *Bridgend, Callander,*
Perthshire, FK17 8AG.
C18th mansion house, mature garden.
Open: All Year
Grades: STB 3 Star
01877 330535 (also fax)
Ms Alexander
east.mains@tesco.net
D: £22.00–£24.00 **S:** £29.00
Beds: 2F 4D **Baths:** 4 En
☒ ▣ (6) ⸙ ▦ ⸱ ▥ ▽ ⸙ ☖ CC

Brook Linn Country House, *Callander,*
Perthshire, FK17 8AU.
Lovely comfortable Victorian house with
magnificent views and personal attention.
Open: Easter to Oct
Grades: STB 4 Star, AA 4 Diamond
01877 330103 (also fax)
Mrs House
derek@blinn.freeserve.co.uk
D: £23.00–£27.00 **S:** £23.00–£27.00
Beds: 1F 2D 2T 2S **Baths:** 6 En 1 Pr
☒ ▣ (8) ⸙ ▦ ⸱ ▥ ▽ ☖ CC

White Cottage, *Bracklinn Road, Callander,*
FK17 8EQ.
Situated in one acre garden. Magnificent
views of Ben Ledi.
Open: Apr to Nov
Grades: STB 3 Star
01877 330896
Mrs Hughes
D: £17.50–£19.00 **S:** £22.00–£25.00
Beds: 2D **Baths:** 1 Sh
▣ (3) ⸙ ▦ ▥ ▽ ☖

Roslin Cottage, *Lagrannoch, Callander,*
Perthshire, FK17 8LE.
Beautiful C18th stone cottage & garden on
outskirts of town.
Open: All Year
01877 330638 Mrs Ferguson
Fax: 01877 331448
alifer@msn.com
D: £15.50–£16.00 **S:** £18.50
Beds: 1D 1T 2S **Baths:** 1 Sh
☒ ▣ ▦ ⸱ ✕ ▥ ▽ ⸙ ☖

Lamorna, *Ancaster Road, Callander,*
Perthshire, FK17 8JJ.
Detached bungalow, panoramic views of
Callander and surrounding countryside,
quiet location, close all amenities.
Open: Easter to Oct
01877 330868 D: £18.00–£20.00
Beds: 1D 1T **Baths:** 1 Sh
▣ (2) ⸙ ▦ ▥ ▽ ☖

Cambuskenneth

NS8094   ◁ *Abbey Inn*

Carseview, *16 Ladysneuk Road,*
Cambuskenneth, Stirling, FK9 5NF.
Quiet conservation village, 15 mins' walk
Stirling town centre, panoramic views.
Open: All Year
Grades: STB 3 Star
01786 462235 (also fax) Mr & Mrs Seaton
D: £18.00 **S:** £18.00–£20.00
Beds: 2T 1S **Baths:** 1 Sh
☒ ▣ (34) ⸙ ▦ ⸱ ✕ ▥ ▽ ☖ CC

Crianlarich

NN3825   ◁ *Ben More, Rod & Reel*

Ben More Lodge Hotel, *Crianlarich,*
Perthshire, FK20 8QS.
Family-run lodge hotel with spectacular
setting beneath Ben More.
Open: All Year
01838 300210 Mr Goodale
Fax: 01838 300218
john@ben-more.demon.co.uk
D: £25.00 **S:** £28.00
Beds: 2F 8D 1T **Baths:** 11 En
☒ ▣ ▦ ⸱ ✕ ▥ ▽ ☖ ⸱

Craigbank Guest House, Crianlarich,
Perthshire, FK20 8QS.
Situated one hour's drive from Glen Coe,
Loch Lomond, the Trossachs.
Open: All Year (not Xmas)
01838 300279 Mr Flockhart
D: £17.00–£19.00 **S:** £25.00
Beds: 2F 1D 3T **Baths:** 2 En 2 Sh
➤ ▣ (6) ⏻ ☑ ⌨ ▥ ♨

The Lodge House, Crianlarich, Perthshire,
FK20 8RU.
Superbly located guest house, magnificent
views of Crianlarich hills.
Open: All Year
Grades: STB 4 Star, AA 4 Diamond
01838 300276 Mr Gaughan
admin@lodgehouse.co.uk
D: £25.00–£30.00 **S:** £35.00–£45.00
Beds: 1F 3D 2T **Baths:** 6 En
➤ ▣ (10) ☑ ⌨ ✕ ▥ ☑ ✳ ♨ cc

Tigh-na Struith, Crianlarich, Perthshire,
FK20 8RU.
90-year-old guest house surrounded by hills
nestling by the river.
Open: Mar to Nov
01838 300235 Mr & Mrs Chisholm
Fax: 01838 300268
chisholm-crianlarich@gofornet.co.uk
D: £16.00–£22.00 **S:** £20.00–£30.00
Beds: 2F 3D 1T **Baths:** 1 En 2 Sh
➤ ▣ (6) ⏻ ☑ ⌨ ▥ ☑ ♨

Croftamie

NS4786 ⌛ Clachan Inn, Wayfarers

Croftburn, Croftamie, Drymen, Glasgow,
G63 0HA.
Former gamekeeper's cottage in one acre of
beautiful gardens overlooking Strathendrick
Valley & Campsie Fells.
Open: All Year
Grades: STB 3 Star, AA 4 Diamond
01360 660796 Mrs Reid
Fax: 01360 661005
johnreid@croftbarn.fsnet.co.uk
D: £18.00–£22.00 **S:** £20.00–£25.00
Beds: 2D 1T **Baths:** 2 En 1 Pr
➤ (12) ▣ (20) ⏻ ☑ ⌨ ✕ ▥ ☑ ♨ cc

Dollar

NS9597

Strathallan Hotel, Chapel Place, Dollar,
Clackmannanshire, FK14 7DW.
Stylish accommodation in fully licensed inn
with creative home cooking.
Open: All Year
01259 742205
Mr Green
Fax: 01259 743720
nrgstrath@aol.com
D: £20.00–£25.00 **S:** £35.00–£45.00
Beds: 2D 1T **Baths:** 1 En 1 Sh
➤ ▣ (20) ⏻ ☑ ✕ ▥ ☑ ♨ cc

Doune

NN7301 ⌛ Red Lion Hotel, Highland Hotel,
Crown Hotel

The Red Lion Hotel, Balkerach Street,
Doune, FK16 6DF.
Old hotel (1692), family-run business, 30
mins Edinburgh and Glasgow. Backpackers
£8.50.
Open: All Year
01786 842066 D: £18.00–£20.00
Beds: 3D **Baths:** 1 En 1 Sh

Drymen

NS4788 ⌛ Buchanan Arms, Clachan Inn, Pottery,
Wayfarers, Winnock Hotel

Green Shadows, Buchanan Castle Estate,
Drymen, Glasgow, G63 0HX.
Open: All year (not Xmas)
01360 660289
Mrs Goodwin
D: £21.00 **S:** £24.00
Beds: 1F 1D 1S
Baths: 2 Sh
➤ ▣ (8) ⏻ ☑ ▥ ☑ ♨
Warm, friendly welcome in a beautiful
country house with spectacular views over
golf course and the Lomond Hills. Buchanan
Castle to the rear. 1 mile from Drymen
Centre, 2 miles from Loch Lomond. Glasgow
Airport 40 mins away.

Easter Balfunning Farm, Drymen,
Glasgow, G63 0NF.
Open: All Year
Grades: STB 3 Star
01360 440755 Ms Black
D: £18.00–£21.00 **S:** £21.00–£27.00
Beds: 1D 1F **Baths:** 1 Pr 1 En
⌂ �𝐏 (4) ⌿ ▥ ⍓ ▦ ⍓ ⎐

A warm welcome awaits you in our attractive
farmhouse idyllically situated with
panoramic views of the Campsie Fells. Guest
rooms look onto the garden towards the
Campsies. Comfortable beds and excellent
breakfasts. Convenient for Loch Lomond,
Stirling and the Trossachs.

Croftburn, Croftamie, Drymen, Glasgow,
G63 0HA.
Former gamekeeper's cottage in one acre of
beautiful gardens overlooking Strathendrick
Valley & Campsie Fells.
Open: All Year
Grades: STB 3 Star, AA 4 Diamond
01360 660796 Mrs Reid
Fax: 01360 661005
johnreid@croftbarn.fsnet.co.uk
D: £18.00–£22.00 **S:** £20.00–£25.00
Beds: 2D 1T **Baths:** 2 En 1 Pr
⌂ (12) � ⎙ (20) ⌿ ▥ ⍓ ✕ ▦ ⍓ ⎐ cc

Easter Drumquhassle Farm, Gartness
Road, Drymen, Glasgow, G63 0DN.
Traditional farmhouse, beautiful views, home
cooking, excellent base on the West
Highland Way.
Open: All Year
Grades: STB 3 Star, AA 3 Diamond
01360 660893 Mrs Cross
Fax: 01360 660282
juliamacx@aol.com
D: £18.00–£25.00 **S:** £25.00–£30.00
Beds: 1F 1D 1T **Baths:** 3 En
⌂ ⎙ (10) ⌿ ▥ ⍓ ✕ ▦ ⍓ ⎐

All details shown are as
supplied by B&B owners in
Autumn 2000

Ceardach, Gartness Road, Drymen,
Glasgow, G63 0BH.
Open: All Year (not Xmas)
01360 660596 (also fax)
Mrs Robb
D: £18.00–£20.00 **S:** £18.00–£20.00
Beds: 1D 1T **Baths:** 1 Sh
⌂ (1) ⎙ (3) ▥ ⍓ ▦ ⍓ ⎐

250 year old Coach house. Situated near the
shores of Loch Lomond large garden. Good
home cooking, a warm and friendly welcome
awaits you.

Glenava, Stirling Road, Drymen, Glasgow,
G63 0AA.
A Warm welcome, stunning scenery,
comfortable rooms, lovely local Walks.
Open: Easter to Oct
Grades: STB 3 Star
01360 660491 Ms Fraser
D: £18.00–£20.00 **S:** £30.00
Beds: 1D 1T **Baths:** 1 Sh
⌂ ⎙ (4) ⌿ ▥ ▦ ⍓ ⎐

17 Stirling Road, Drymen, Glasgow, G63
0BW.
Family home in village near West Highland
Way; lovely garden.
Open: All Year
01360 660273 (also fax)
Mrs Lander
david_lander@lineone.net
D: £15.00–£18.00 **S:** £18.00–£23.00
Beds: 1F 1T **Baths:** 1 Sh
⌂ ⎙ (1) ▥ ⍓ ⎐

Dunblane

NN7801   ⌇ Westlands Bar

Mossgiel, Doune Road, Dunblane,
Perthshire, FK15 9ND.
Charming well-equipped countryside house
offering guests a comfortable relaxing
holiday.
Open: March to October
01786 824325 Mrs Bennett
judy@mossgiel.com
D: £20.00–£22.00 **S:** £25.00
Beds: 2T 1D **Baths:** 2 En 1 Pr
⎙ (5) ⌿ ▥ ▦ ⍓ ⎐

Gargunnock

NS7094 🍺 *Gargunnock Inn*

East Lodge, *Leckie, Gargunnock, Stirling, FK8 3BN.*
Open: All Year (not Xmas)
Grades: STB 3 Star
01786 860605 Mrs Currie
janc123456@aol.com
D: £20.00–£22.00 **S:** £25.00–£28.00
Beds: 1D 1T **Baths:** 1 Pr 1 Sh
🛇 🅿 (3) ⅍ 📺 ⋔ 📖 ♨ ♿ ¶
C19th lodge house tastefully extended. In attractive woodland setting. Ideal base to visit Edinburgh, Glasgow, Loch Lomond and Trossachs. 'Comfortable, peaceful and elegant'.

Killin

NN5732 🍺 *Bridge Of Lochay, Coach House, Killin Hotel, Shutters*

Falls of Dochart Cottage, *Killin, Perthshire, FK21 8SW.*
Open: All Year (not Xmas)
Grades: STB 2 Star
01567 820363 Mr & Mrs Mudd
D: £16.00–£17.00 **S:** £17.00
Beds: 1D 1T 1S **Baths:** 2 Sh
🛇 (1) 🅿 (4) ⅍ 📺 ⋔ ✕ 📖 Ⓥ
C17th cottage, overlooking the falls and river - home cooking - comfortable and friendly atmosphere. Open all year: central to magnificent mountain area - renowned for hill walking.

Main Street, *Killin, Perthshire, FK21 8TP.*
Open: All Year
Grades: STB 2 Star
01567 820296 Mr & Mrs Garnier
Fax: 01567 820647
killinhotel@btinternet.com
D: £19.00–£35.00 **S:** £19.00–£35.00
Beds: 3F 6T 17D 6S **Baths:** 32 En
🛇 🅿 (20) ⅍ 📺 ⋔ ✕ 📖 Ⓥ ❋ ♨ ♿ cc
The setting is magnificent, overlooking the river Lochay, we have a bistro restaurant specialising in home cooked dishes, all rooms are ensuite, lounge bar with stock of malt Whiskies. A friendly welcome from the owners guaranteed.

Allt Fulieach, *Maragowan, Killin, Perthshire, FK21 8TN.*
Comfortable, modern house at the head of Loch Tay.
Open: All Year
01567 820962 Mr Judd
D: £19.00 **S:** £19.00
Beds: 2T 1D **Baths:** 3 En
🛇 🅿 (4) ⅍ 📺 📖 ♨

The Coach House Hotel, *Lochay Road, Killin, Perthshire, FK21 8TN.*
Family-run hotel surrounded by mountains overlooking the river.
Open: All Year
01567 820349 (also fax)
D: £20.00–£26.00 **S:** £20.00–£26.00
Beds: 1F 1D 2T **Baths:** 2 En 2 Sh
🛇 🅿 (40) ⅍ 📺 📖 Ⓥ ♨ cc

Drumfinn House, *Manse Road, Killin, Perthshire, FK21 8UY.*
Warm, friendly country house in the centre of the highland village of Killin.
Open: All Year (not Xmas)
01567 820900 (also fax)
Mrs Semple
drumfinnhouse@beeb.net
D: £16.00–£20.00
Beds: 1F 3D 2T **Baths:** 3 En 1 Sh
🛇 (12) 🅿 (6) ⅍ 📺 ⋔ 📖 ♨

Loch Achray

NN5106

Glenbruach Country House, *Loch Achray, Trossachs, Callander, Perthshire, FK17 8HX.*
Open: All Year
01877 376216 (also fax)
Mrs Lindsay
D: £22.00–£25.00 **S:** £22.00–£25.00
Beds: 2D 1T **Baths:** 2 En 1 Pr
🛇 (12) 🅿 (3) ⅍ ⋔ ✕ 📖 Ⓥ ♨
Unique country mansion in the heart of Rob Roy country. All rooms with Loch views. Interesting interior design and collections in this Scots-owned home.

Milton of Buchanan

NS4490

Mar Achlais, *Milton of Buchanan,*
Balmaha, Glasgow, G63 0JE.
Rural setting near Loch Lomond. Excellent
touring centre for Scotland.
Open: All Year (not Xmas)
Grades: STB 3 Star
01360 870300 Mr Nichols
Fax: 01360 870444
marachlais@dial.pipex.com
D: £18.50 **S:** £23.50–£28.50
Beds: 1F 1D **Baths:** 2 En
🛏 🅿 (2) 📺 ⭐ ✗ 🛋 Ⓥ ♨ cc

Ochtertyre

NS7497   ◀ *Leonardo's*

Broadford House, *Ochtertyre, Stirling, FK9*
4UN.
Open: Easter to Oct
Grades: STB 3 Star
01786 464674 Mrs Littlejohn
Fax: 01786 463256
simonlittlejohn@compuserve.com
D: £20.00–£23.00
Beds: 1T 1D **Baths:** 1 En 1 Pr
✗ 📺 🛋 Ⓥ ♨
Lovely country house set in 2.5 acres of
garden, adorned with 300 year old oak trees.
Enjoy the character and tranquillity of this
home in the country, yet only 5 minutes from
the centre of Stirling.

Port of Menteith

NN5801   ◀ *Crown Hotel, Cross Keys*

Collymoon Pendicle, *Port of Menteith,*
Perthshire, FK8 3JY.
Rural location beside river, good home
cooking, assured warm welcome.
Open: Easter to Oct
01360 850222
Mrs Tough
106773,3050@compuserve.com
D: £16.00–£18.00 **S:** £20.00–£22.00
Beds: 1F 1D **Baths:** 1 Sh
🛏 (5) 🅿 (4) ✗ 🛋 ♨

Rowardennan

NS3598

Anchorage Cottage, *Rowardennan,*
Drymen, Glasgow, G63 0AW.
Open: Easter to Oct
01360 870394 (also fax)
D: £26.00–£30.00 **S:** £36.00–£40.00
Beds: 2T 1D **Baths:** 2 En 1 Pr
🅿 (6) ✗ 📺 🛋 ♨
Welcome to our family home on the eastern
shore of Loch Lomond. Our accommodation
is of the highest standards. The house
commands unique magnificent views over
the loch and islands to Luss on the western
shore. Situated on the West Highland Way.

Stirling

NS7993   ◀ *Abbey Inn, Birds & Bees, Hog's Head,*
Hollybank, Porters, Silver Tassie, Terraces Hotel,
Whistlebinkies

Woodside Guest House, *4 Back Walk,*
Stirling, FK8 2QA.
Open: All Year
01786 475470 Mr Drummond
D: £16.00 **S:** £18.00
Beds: 1F 3D 2T 1S **Baths:** 2 En 2 Pr 2 Sh
🛏 🅿 ✗ 📺 ⭐ 🛋 Ⓥ ♨
Beautifully situated on the old historic Wall
of Stirling. Modern, comfortable, friendly,
central to all amenities. Five minutes' walk
from rail and bus stations. All rooms have
private showers.

Anderson House, *8 Melville Terrace,*
Stirling, FK8 2NE.
Open: All Year (not Xmas)
Grades: STB 3 Star
01786 465185 Mrs Piggott
D: £22.00–£24.00 **S:** £25.00–£30.00
Beds: 1F 1T 1D 1S **Baths:** 3 En 1 Sh
🛏 🅿 (5) 📺 ⭐ 🛋 Ⓥ ♨
Welcome to our 200 year old Georgian home
within 2 minutes walk of historic Stirling.
Large, bright rooms, antique furnishings,
refurbished ensuites, a friendly atmosphere
and and a great Scottish breakfast will make
your stay a memorable one.

27 King Street, *Stirling, FK8 1DN.*
Comfortable Edwardian town house,
convenient bus/rail stations, town centre.
Open: All Year
Grades: STB 2 Star
01786 471082 (also fax)
Mr & Mrs Macgregor
jennifer@sruighlea.demon.co.uk
D: £16.00–£20.00 **S:** £20.00–£25.00
Beds: 1F 1D 1T **Baths:** 2 Pr
🛏 (2) ⅍ 📺 ▥ Ⅴ ⚓

12 Princes Street, *Stirling, FK8 1HQ.*
Central for Stirling. Near to Castle and
Wallace's monument.
Open: All Year
01786 479228 (also fax)
Mrs Cairns
D: £18.00–£20.00 **S:** £18.00–£20.00
Beds: 1D 1T 2S **Baths:** 2 En 2 Sh
🛏 (3) 🅿 ⅍ 📺 🐾 ✕ ▥ Ⅴ ⚓

Tiroran, *45 Douglas Terrace, Stirling, FK7 9LW.*
Open: Easter to Oct
Grades: STB 4 Star
01786 464655 Mrs Thomson
D: £18.00–£19.00
Beds: 1D 1T **Baths:** 1 Sh
🛏 (9) 🅿 (2) ⅍ 📺 ▥ Ⅴ ⚓
Agnes ensures a warm Scottish welcome to
Tiroran. A modern house situated in quiet
residential area close to Kings Park Golf
Course. Five minutes drive to town centre,
railway station, castle and historic old town.
Best B&B Tourist Award Winner.

16 Riverside Drive, *Stirling, FK8 1XF.*
Our small family home in quiet area near to
town.
Open: All Year
01786 461105 Mrs Miller
D: £13.50–£14.50 **S:** £13.50–£14.00
Beds: 2S **Baths:** 1 Sh
⅍ 📺 ▥ ⚓

Planning a longer stay?
Always ask for any special rates

Ravenscroft, *21 Clarendon Place, Stirling, FK8 2QW.*
Beautiful Victorian house in conservation
area, views over to castle.
Open: All Year (not Xmas)
Grades: STB 4 Star
01786 473815
Mr & Mrs Dunbar
Fax: 01786 450990
dunbar@ravenscroft3.freeserve.co.uk
D: £23.50 **S:** £35.00
Beds: 1D 1T **Baths:** 1 En 1 Pr
🅿 (2) ⅍ 📺 ▥ Ⅴ ⚓

Linden Guest House, *22 Linden Avenue, Stirling, FK7 7PQ.*
Situated in a tree-lined avenue only few
minutes' walk to town centre.
Open: All Year
Grades: STB 2 Star
01786 448850 (also fax)
Miss McGuinness
D: £18.00–£20.00 **S:** £19.00–£21.00
Beds: 2F 1D 1T **Baths:** 1 Sh
🛏 🅿 (2) 📺 🐾 ✕ ▥ Ⅴ ⚓

Barnsdale House, *19 Barnsdale Road, St Ninians, Stirling, FK7 0PT.*
Comfortable Victorian villa. Convenient base
for touring central Scotland.
Open: All Year
Grades: STB 3 Star
01786 461729 (also fax)
Mrs Pain
barnsdalehouse@
painstirling.freeserve.co.uk
D: £16.00–£18.00 **S:** £20.00–£25.00
Beds: 1F 1D **Baths:** 1 En 1 Pr
🛏 🅿 (3) ⅍ 📺 ✕ ▥ Ⅴ ⚓

Hopeton, *28 Linden Avenue, Stirling, FK7 7PQ.*
Ground floor flat of large detached stone
building surrounded by attractive gardens.
Open: All Year
01786 473418
Mrs McDonald
D: £18.00 **S:** £20.00
Beds: 1F 1D 1T **Baths:** 1 Pr 1 Sh
🛏 🅿 📺 🐾 ▥ ⚓ &

Wellgreen Guest House, *8 Pit Terrace,*
Stirling, FK8 2EZ.
Family-run guest house close to town centre
& all its amenities.
Open: All Year
01786 472675 Mrs Mcphail
D: £18.00 **S:** £18.00
Beds: 2F 1T 1S **Baths:** 2 Sh
🛏 🄿 ⅍ 📺 🐕 🗄 Ⓥ ♨

Kerann, *110 Causewayhead Road, Stirling,*
FK9 5HJ.
A warm welcome and excellent breakfast
await you.
Open: All Year
Grades: STB 3 Star
01786 462432 (also fax)
Mrs Paterson
bookings@kerann.ndirect.co.uk
D: £19.00–£21.00
Beds: 1D 2T **Baths:** 3 En
🄿 (6) ⅍ 📺 🗄 Ⓥ ♨

Allandale, *98 Causewayhead Road, Stirling,*
FK9 5HJ.
Warm, friendly family home.
Open: All Year
01786 465643 Mr & Mrs McLaren
D: £17.00–£18.00
Beds: 1F 1T **Baths:** 1 Sh
🄿 (2) ⅍ 📺 🗄 Ⓥ ♨

NN5617   ◀ *Strathyre Inn, Ben Shian Hotel*

Coire Buidhe, *Strathyre, Callander,*
Perthshire, FK18 8NA.
Family Bed and Breakfast, centrally located
for Stirling, Trossachs.
Open: All Year (not Xmas)
01877 384288 Mr & Mrs Reid
coire.buidhe@talk21.com
D: £17.00–£20.00 **S:** £17.00–£20.00
Beds: 3F 1D 1T 1S **Baths:** 1 Pr 3 Sh
🛏 🄿 (6) ⅍ 📺 🐕 🗄 Ⓥ ♨

Planning a longer stay?
Always ask for any special rates

Dochfour, *Strathyre, Callander, FK18 8NA.*
Award-winning B&B in scenic glen,
specialising in being the best!
Open: All Year
Grades: STB 3 Star
01877 384256 (also fax)
Mr & Mrs Ffinch
tony.ffinch@tesco.net
D: £17.00–£20.00 **S:** £23.00–£26.00
Beds: 2D 1T **Baths:** 2 En 1 Pr
🛏 🄿 (6) 📺 ✗ 🗄 Ⓥ ☀ ♨ cc

Rosebank House, *Strathyre, Callander,*
Perthshire, FK18 8NA.
Rosebank house is a fine example of
Victorian architecture.
Open: Mar to Dec
01877 384208 Mr & Mrs Moor
Fax: 01877 384201
D: £18.00–£20.00 **S:** £18.00–£25.00
Beds: 1F 2D 1T 1S **Baths:** 2 En 1 Pr
🛏 🄿 (3) ⅍ 📺 🐕 ✗ 🗄 Ⓥ ☀ ♨ cc

NS6699   ◀ *Lion & Unicorn, Crown Hotel*

The Granary, *West Moss Side, Thornhill,*
Stirling, FK8 3QJ.
Open: All Year (not Xmas)
Grades: STB 4 Star
01786 850310 Mrs Cumming
D: £20.00–£22.00 **S:** £25.00
Beds: 2D 1S **Baths:** 2 En 1 Sh
🛏 🄿 (6) ⅍ 📺 🗄 Ⓥ ☀ ♨ ♿
Recently converted granary. Rooms
overlooking gardens with spectacular views.
Luxury ground floor suite (with log fire).
Walk in the beautiful Trossachs or relax by
the lochs. 10 miles west of Stirling. Fast half
hourly train to Edinburgh.

Cairnsaigh, *Doig Street, Thornhill, Stirling,*
FK8 3PZ.
Spacious modern bungalow 10 miles west of
Stirling and 6 miles south of Callander.
Open: All Year
01786 850413 (also fax) Mr & Mrs Boswell
boswell@cairnsaigh.freeserve.co.uk
D: £24.00–£27.50
Beds: 2D 1T **Baths:** 3 En
🛏 🄿 (3) ⅍ 📺 🐕 ✗ 🗄 Ⓥ ☀ ♨ ♿ cc

Tillicoultry

NS9197

Wyvis, *70 Stirling Street, Tillicoultry,*
Clackmannanshire, FK13 6EA.
Converted mill worker's cottage with views
to the Ochil Hills.
Open: All Year (not Xmas/New Year)
Grades: STB 4 Star
01259 751513 Mrs Goddard
terrygoddard@netscapeonline.co.uk
D: £21.00–£28.00 **S:** £25.00–£28.00
Beds: 1T 1D **Baths:** 1 Pr 1 En
🏃 ⅍ 📺 🍴 ✗ 📖 Ⓥ ♨

Tyndrum

NN3330

Glengarry Guest House, *Tyndrum,*
Crianlarich, Perthshire, FK20 8RY.
Ideal base for touring and outdoor activities.
Scottish welcome awaits.
Open: All Year
Grades: STB 2 Star
01838 400224 Mr & Mrs Mailer
glengarry@altavista.net
D: £18.00–£22.00 **S:** £25.00
Beds: 1F 1T 1D **Baths:** 2 En 1 Pr
🏃 (2) 🅿 (4) ⅍ 🍴 ✗ 📖 Ⓥ ♨

Whins of Milton

NS7990 🛏 *Holly Bank Hotel*

Whinwell Cottage, *171 Glasgow Road,*
Whins of Milton, Stirling, FK7 0LH.
Immaculate, comfortable, accommodation,
close to many tourist attractions and
amenities.
Open: All Year
01786 818166
D: £18.00–£22.00 **S:** £20.00–£30.00
Beds: 1F 1T 1D **Baths:** 1 Sh
🏃 🅿 ⅍ 📺 📖 Ⓥ ♨

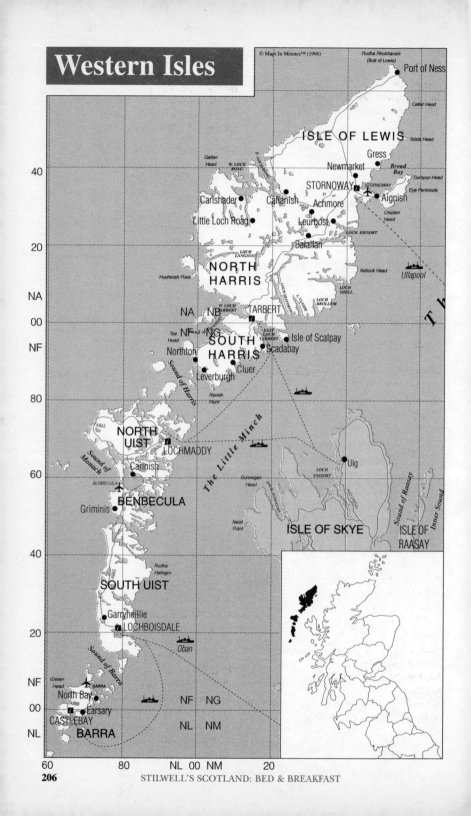

Western Isles

© Mags In Minutes™ (1996)

STILWELL'S SCOTLAND: BED & BREAKFAST

AIRPORTS ⊕
Isle of Barra, tel. 01871 890283,
Isle of Benbecula, tel. 01870 602051,
Stornoway, tel. 01851 702256.

AIR SERVICES & AIRLINES ✈

British Airways: *Barra to Glasgow; Benbecula to Glasgow; Stornoway to Glasgow* and *Inverness*. There are also inter-island flights between *Barra, Benbecula, Stornoway* and the *Isle of Tiree*. Tel. (local rate): 0345 222111.

FERRIES ⚓

Caledonian MacBrayne: *Castlebay to Oban* - 5 hrs; *Lochboisdale to Oban* - 6 hrs; *Lochmaddy to Uig (Skye)* - 45

mins; *Stornoway to Ullapool* - 3½ hrs; *Tarbert to Uig (Skye)* - 45 mins. Tel. 0990 650000.

TOURIST INFORMATION OFFICES 🇮

Main Street, **Castlebay**, Isle of Barra, HS9 5XD, 01871 810336 (Easter to Oct).

Pier Road, **Lochboisdale**, Isle of South Uist, HS8 5TH, 01878 700286 (Easter to Oct).

Pier Road, **Lochmaddy**, Isle of North Uist, HS6 5EU, 01876 500321 (Easter to Oct).

4 South Beach Street, **Stornoway**, Isle of Lewis, HS1 2XY, 01851 703088.

Pier Road, **Tarbert**, Isle of Harris, HS3 3BQ, 01859 502011.

BARRA Earsary
NL7099 ◀ *Craigard Hotel*

Gearadhmor, *123 Craigston, Earsary, Castlebay, Isle of Barra, HS9 5XS.*
Beautiful surroundings. Home cooking a speciality. Traditional Highland hospitality.
Open: All Year
Grades: STB 3 Star
01871 810688 Mrs Maclean
archie.b.maclean@tesco.net
D: £15.00–£18.00 **S:** £15.00–£20.00
Beds: 2F 2T **Baths:** 1 En 3 Sh
🛌 🅿 (6) 📺 🍴 ✕ 🖥 �📺 ⚲

BARRA North Bay
NF7203 ◀ *Castlebay Hotel*

Northbay House, *Balnabodach, North Bay, Castlebay, Isle of Barra, HS9 5UT.*
Attractive former school with comfortable and spacious accommodation. Warm hospitality.
Open: All Year (not Xmas/New Year)
Grades: STB 4 Star
01871 890255 (also fax)
Mrs Savory
northbayhouse@isleofbarra.com
D: £22.00–£26.00 **S:** £22.00–£26.00
Beds: 1T 1D **Baths:** 2 En
🅿 (4) ⚲ 📺 🖥 ⚲ 🕴 1

BENBECULA Griminis
NF7851

Creag Liath, *15 Griminis, Griminish, Isle of Benbecula, HS7 5QA.*
Rural working croft, ideal for birdwatching, fishing, cycling and beachcombing.
Open: All Year
01870 602992 Mrs MacDonald
creagliath@aol.com
D: £25.00 **S:** £25.00
Beds: 2F 1T 1D **Baths:** 2 En 2 Pr
🛌 🅿 (5) 📺 🍴 ✕ 🖥 ⚲ ⚲ 🕴 ♿

HARRIS Cluer
NG1490

Mount Cameron, *2 Cluer, Cluer, Isle of Harris, HS3 3EP.*
Open: All Year **Grades:** STB 3 Star
01859 530356 Mr Mackinnon
calmac2c@aol.com
D: £15.00–£20.00 **S:** £20.00
Beds: 2D **Baths:** 1 En 1 Pr 1 Sh
🛌 🅿 ⚲ 📺 ✕ 🕴
Mount Cameron is a seven apartment house. Situated within the scenic Bays of Harris. From the lounge and surrounding exterior of the house there are unparalleled views of the local bay across the Minch to Wester Ross and Skye.

HARRIS Isle of Scalpay

NG2395 Harris Hotel

Seafield, *Isle of Scalpay, Isle of Harris, HS4 3XZ.*
Fantastic sea views, homely atmosphere.
Free boat trip for two night stay.
Open: Easter to Nov **Grades:** STB 2 Star
01859 540250 Mrs Cunningham
roddy@mjg.sol.uk
D: £16.00–£18.00 **S:** £20.00–£22.00
Beds: 1F 2D **Baths:** 2 Sh
⌂ 🅿 (4) ✍ 📺 ✕ 🛏 ♨

HARRIS Leverburgh

NG0186

Garryknowe, *Ferry Road, Leverburgh, Isle
of Harris, HS5 3UA.*
Georgian house, scenic views. Good home-
cooking. A home from home.
Open: Easter to Oct
01895 520246 Mrs MacKenzie
D: £16.00–£18.00 **S:** £20.00–£25.00
Beds: 3F 2D 1T **Baths:** 1 En 1 Sh
⌂ 🅿 (1) 📺 ✕ 🛏 📺 ♨

HARRIS Northton

NF9989

39 Taobh Tuath, *Northton, Harris, HS3 3JA.*
Access to lovely secluded beaches. Dinner
served from 6-8.
Open: Mar to Oct
01859 520228 Mrs Morrison
D: £18.00 **S:** £18.00
Beds: 1F 1D 1T **Baths:** 2 Sh
⌂ (1) 🅿 (6) 📺 🐾 ✕ 🛏 📺

HARRIS Scadabay

NG1792

Hillhead, *Scadabay, Harris, HS3 3ED.*
Hillhead set in beautiful peaceful
surroundings, loch & sea fishing is available.
Open: Easter to Nov
01859 511226 Mrs MacLeod
D: £16.00–£17.00 **S:** £16.00
Beds: 1F 1D 1T 1S **Baths:** 1 En 2 Pr 1 Sh
⌂ (4) 🅿 (4) ✍ 📺 🐾 ✕ 🛏 📺 ♨

HARRIS Tarbert

NB1500 Harris Hotel

Avalon, *12 West Side, Tarbert, Isle of Harris,
HS3 3BG.*
Magnificent views, 3/4 mile ferry terminal.
Excellent base for touring Lewes & Hams.
Open: All Year
Grades: STB 4 Star
01859 502334 Mrs Morrison
info@avalonguesthouse.co.uk
D: £20.00
Beds: 2T 1D **Baths:** 2 En 1 Pr
⌂ 🅿 (4) ✍ 📺 🐾 ✕ 🛏 📺 ♨ ♿

Tigh Na Mara, *Tarbert, Harris, Isle of
Harris, HS3 3DB.*
Beautiful location, magnificent sea views,
hearty meals, near ferry terminal.
Open: All Year
01859 502270 Mrs Morrison
tighnamara@tarbert-harris.freeserve.co.uk
D: £16.00–£18.00 **S:** £16.00
Beds: 1F 1T 1S **Baths:** 1 En 1 Sh
⌂ 🅿 (3) ✍ 📺 ✕ 🛏 📺 ♨ cc

LEWIS Achmore

NB3128

Cleascro House, *Achmore, Isle of Lewis,
Western Isles, HS2 9DU.*
Open: All Year (not Xmas/New Year)
Grades: STB 4 Star
01851 860302 (also fax)
Mrs Murray
donnamurray@compuserve.com
D: £21.00–£25.00 **S:** £21.00–£25.00
Beds: 1T 2D **Baths:** 3 En
⌂ 🅿 📺 🐾 ✕ 🛏 📺 ♨
Ideal location for touring Lewis and Harris
with superb views of Uig and Harris hills. We
are within easy reach of ferries, Callanish
Stones and many places of interest. Superior
accommodation and excellent cuisine.
Featured in 'Which?' Good B&B Guide.

Bringing children with you?
Always ask for any special rates

High season, bank holidays
and special events mean low
availability anywhere

LEWIS   Aignish

NB4832

Ceol-Na-Mara, *1a, Aignish, Point, Isle of Lewis, Western Isles, HS2 0PB.*
Family home, very comfortable and welcoming, rural area near Stornaway.
Open: All Year
01851 870339 (also fax)
Ms MacDonald
lesmacd@globalnet.co.uk
D: £17.00–£19.00 **S:** £19.00–£21.00
Beds: 1F 1D 1T **Baths:** 1 Pr 1 Sh
ఠ ▣ (3) ⅍ ☑ ⋔ ✕ ▥ ☑ ⚓

LEWIS   Balallan

NB2920

Clearview, *44 Balallan, Balallan, Isle of Lewis, HS2 9PT.*
Modern house, peaceful elevated location giving panoramic views. Walkers/cyclists welcome.
Open: All Year (not Xmas/New Year)
Grades: STB 3 Star
01851 830472 Mr & Mrs Mackay
D: £18.00–£20.00 **S:** £18.00–£20.00
Beds: 1T 2D **Baths:** 2 En 1 Pr
ఠ ▣ (6) ⅍ ☑ ✕ ▥ ⚓

LEWIS   Callanish

NB2133

Eshcol Guest House, *21 Breascleit, Callanish, Isle of Lewis, Western Isles, HS2 9ED.*
Modern guest house, Callanish Stones 2 miles. Featured in Which? B&B.
Open: All Year (not Xmas)
01851 621357 Mrs MacArthur
donlewis@madasafish.com
D: £29.00–£31.00 **S:** £39.00–£41.00
Beds: 1D 2T **Baths:** 2 En 1 Pr
ఠ (8) ▣ (10) ⅍ ☑ ⋔ ✕ ▥ ☑ ⚓

LEWIS   Carishader

NB0933

1 Cairisiadar, *Carishader, Uig, Isle of Lewis, HS2 9ER.*
Comfortable crofthouse, traditional cooking, sea views, walks, friendly atmosphere.
Open: All Year
01851 672239 Mrs MacKay
D: £16.00 **S:** £16.00
Beds: 1D 1T **Baths:** 1 Sh
▣ (3) ☑ ✕ ▥ ☑

LEWIS   Gress

NB4941

Caladh, *44 Gress, Isle of Lewis, Western Isles, HS2 0NB.*
All rooms look overlook River and the sea, Even a talking Parrot.
Open: All Year
Grades: STB 3 Star
01851 820743 Mrs Evans
Eve@caladh.fsbusiness.co.uk
D: £17.00–£19.00 **S:** £18.00–£20.00
Beds: 2T **Baths:** 2 En
ఠ (0) ▣ (4) ⅍ ☑ ✕ ▥ ☑ ✿ ⚓

LEWIS   Leurbost

NB3725

Glen House, *77 Liurbost, Leurbost, Lochs, Isle of Lewis, HS2 9NL.*
Quiet country residence overlooking scenic sea loch, offering high standard of food and accommodation.
Open: All Year
Grades: STB 2 Star
01851 860241 Mrs Reid
glenhouse@talk21.com
D: £19.00 **S:** £20.00
Beds: 2F 1D 1T **Baths:** 2 En 1 Pr
ఠ (5) ▣ ⅍ ☑ ⋔ ✕ ▥ ☑ ⚓ ♿

All details shown are as
supplied by B&B owners in
Autumn 2000

LEWIS Little Loch Roag

NB1326

Scaliscro Lodge, *Little Loch Roag, Isle of Lewis, HS2 9EL.*
Private and secluded family run inn in spectacular sea front setting.
Open: Apr to Oct
01851 672325 Mr MacKenzie
Fax: 01851 672393
jimmy.mackenzie@easynet.co.uk
D: £18.75–£27.50 **S:** £22.50–£27.50
Beds: 1F 3T 3D 1S **Baths:** 3 En 3 Pr
☎ �ℙ (20) 📺 🍴 ✕ 🛏 Ⓥ ♨ cc

LEWIS Newmarket

NB4235

Lathamor, *Bakers Road, Newmarket, Isle of Lewis, HS2 0EA.*
Spacious family home, ideal for children, relaxed atmosphere, evening meals.
Open: All Year
01851 706093 (also fax) Mrs Ferguson
D: £18.00 **S:** £14.00–£18.00
Beds: 1F 1D 1T **Baths:** 1 Pr 1 Sh
☎ ⅋ (4) ✄ 📺 🍴 ✕ 🛏 Ⓥ ♨ cc

LEWIS Port of Ness

NB5363

Cliff House, *Port of Ness, Isle of Lewis, HS2 0XA.*
Cliff house situated above sandy beach and harbour. **Open:** Easter to Oct
01851 810278 Mrs Morrison
D: £18.00–£20.00 **S:** £18.00–£20.00
Beds: 1D 2T **Baths:** 1 Sh
☎ (5) ℙ (4) 📺 🍴 ✕ 🛏 Ⓥ ♨

RATES

D = Price range per person sharing in a double room
S = Price range for a single room

BATHROOMS

Pr - Private
Sh - Shared
En - Ensuite

LEWIS Stornoway

NB4232 🍴 *Crown Hotel, Caledonia Hotel, Seaforth Hotel, County Hotel*

Dunroamin, *18 Plantation Road, Stornoway, Isle of Lewis, HS1 2JS.*
Centrally located Victorian town house, warm welcome assured, hearty breakfasts.
Open: All Year
01851 704578 Mrs MacLeod
Fax: 01851 170578
D: £17.00–£20.00 **S:** £18.00–£25.00
Beds: 3F 1D 1T 1S **Baths:** 1 En 1 Sh
☎ 📺 🍴 ✕ 🛏 Ⓥ ♨

NORTH UIST Carinish

NF8259 🍴 *Carinish Inn, Westford Inn, Langash Lodge*

8 Cnoc Cuidehein, *Carinish, Lochmaddy, Isle of North Uist, HS6 5HW.*
A warm welcome and good food awaits you in our comfortable home.
Open: Easter to Nov
01876 580635 Mrs MacDonald
D: £15.00–£16.00 **S:** £19.00
Beds: 1F 1D 1T **Baths:** 1 Pr 1 Sh
☎ (5) ℙ (5) 📺 🍴 🛏 Ⓥ ♨

SOUTH UIST Garryheillie

NF7522 🍴 *Borrodale Hotel, Lochboisdale Hotel*

Clan Ranald, *247 Gearraidh Sheile, Garryheillie, Lochboisdale, Isle of South Uist, HS8 5SX.*
Working Croft 3 miles form ferry will collect form terminal. **Open:** April to end Dec
Grades: STB 3 Star
01878 700263 Mr & Mrs MacDonald
D: £23.00 **S:** £23.00
Beds: 1T 1D 1S **Baths:** 3 En
☎ ℙ 📺 🍴 ✕ 🛏 Ⓥ ♨

The Shieling, *238 Gearraidh Sheile, Garryheillie, Lochboisdale, Isle of South Uist, HS8 5SX.*
Modern croft house, walking and birdwatching. Situated near main road.
Open: Easter to Oct
01878 700504 Mrs Peteranna
D: £18.00–£20.00 **S:** £20.00–£25.00
Beds: 1D 2T **Baths:** 3 En 1 Sh
☼ (12) ₽ (6) ⅙ ⊡ ✕ Ⅷ. Ⓥ ♨

SOUTH UIST Lochboisdale

NF7919 **Riverside,** *Lochboisdale, Isle of South Uist, HS8 5TN.*
Riverside house on working croft near mountains and fishing lochs.
Open: Easter to Oct
01878 700250 Mrs MacLellan
anne@muir10.freeserve.co.uk
D: £14.00–£18.00 **S:** £10.00–£18.00
Beds: 1F 1T 1S **Baths:** 2 Sh
₽ (4) ⅙ ⊡ Ⅷ. ♨

Bayview, *Lochboisdale, Isle of South Uist, HS8 5TH.*
Adjacent to Lochboisdale ferry terminal and overlooking the Minch.
Open: All Year
01878 700329 Mrs MacLellan
D: £18.00–£20.00
Beds: 1D 1T **Baths:** 1 En 1 Sh
☼ ₽ ⅙ ⊡ ✕ Ⅷ. Ⓥ ❀ ♨

Location Index

The cities, towns, villages and hamlets listed in this index all have entries in **STILWELL'S: SCOTLAND BED & BREAKFAST** under their respective regional heading. If there is no listing for the place you wish to stay in, the section map for that particular region will show you somewhere else to stay close by.

A

Aberdeen *Aberdeen*	5
Aberdour *Fife*	85
Aberfeldy *Perth*	181
Aberfoyle *Stirling*	195
Aberlour *Aberdeen*	8
Abernethy *Perth*	181
Aberuthven *Perth*	181
Aboyne *Aberdeen*	8
Achachork *Skye, Inn Heb*	146
Acharn *Perth*	181
Achintee *Highland*	103
Achmore *Lewis, W Isles*	208
Aignish *Lewis, W Isles*	209
Aird of Sleat *Skye, Inn Heb*	147
Airlie *Angus*	22
Alcaig *Highland*	103
Alford *Aberdeen*	8
Allanton *Borders*	56
Alloway *Ayrshire*	43
Alness *Highland*	103
Altnaharra *Highland*	103
Alva *Stirling*	195
Alyth *Perth*	182
Annan *D & G*	67
Anstruther *Fife*	85
Appin *Argyll*	28
Arbroath *Angus*	22
Ardelve *Highland*	103
Arden *Argyll*	29
Ardfern *Argyll*	29
Arduaine *Argyll*	29
Ardwell *Ayrshire*	44
Arisaig *Highland*	103
Armadale *Lothian*	161
Arnisdale *Highland*	104
Arran, Isle of *Ayrshire*	44
Arrochar *Argyll*	29
Ashkirk *Borders*	56
Auchencairn *D & G*	68
Auchterarder *Perth*	182
Auchtermuchty *Fife*	85
Auchtertyre *Highland*	104
Aviemore *Highland*	104
Ayr *Ayrshire*	46

B

Badachro *Highland*	105
Badcall (Scourie) *Highland*	105
Baddidarroch *Highland*	105
Balallan *Lewis, W Isles*	209
Balerno *Lothian*	161
Balfron Station *Stirling*	196
Ballachulish *Highland*	106
Ballantrae *Ayrshire*	47
Ballater *Aberdeen*	8
Ballindean *Perth*	182
Balloch *Glasgow*	95

Balloch *Perth*	182
Balmaclellan *D & G*	68
Balmaha *Stirling*	196
Balnain *Highland*	106
Banavie *Highland*	106
Banchory *Aberdeen*	9
Banff *Aberdeen*	9
Bankfoot *Perth*	182
Banton *Lanarks*	157
Barassie *Ayrshire*	48
Barra, Isle of *W Isles*	207
Barrhill *Ayrshire*	48
Bathgate *Lothian*	162
Beattock *D & G*	68
Beauly *Highland*	107
Beeswing *D & G*	69
Beith *Ayrshire*	48
Benbecula, Isle of *W Isles*	207
Benderloch *Argyll*	30
Bernisdale *Skye, Inn Heb*	147
Berwick-upon-Tweed *Borders*	56
Bettyhill *Highland*	107
Biggar *Lanarks*	157
Birgham *Borders*	58
Birnam *Perth*	183
Birsay *Mainld, Orkney*	177
Blackburn *Lothian*	162
Blackhall *Edinburgh, Lothian*	163
Blair Atholl *Perth*	183
Blair Drummond *Stirling*	196
Blairgowrie *Perth*	183
Blairlogie *Stirling*	196
Blebocraigs *Fife*	85
Bo'ness *Lothian*	162
Boat of Garten *Highland*	107
Bonar Bridge *Highland*	108
Bonnybridge *Lothian*	162
Bowden *Borders*	58
Bowmore *Islay, Inn Heb*	143
Braemar *Aberdeen*	10
Braes of Ullapool *Highland*	108
Breakish *Skye, Inn Heb*	147
Bridge of Allan *Stirling*	197
Bridge of Cally *Perth*	183
Bridge of Orchy *Argyll*	30
Bridgend *Islay, Inn Heb*	143
Brightons *Lothian*	162
Broadford *Skye, Inn Heb*	147
Brodick *Arran*	44
Broomhill *Glasgow*	96
Brora *Highland*	108
Broughton *Edinburgh, Lothian*	163
Broughty Ferry *Angus*	22
Buckie (Spey Bay) *Aberdeen*	10
Bunessan *Mull, Inn Heb*	144
Burghead *Aberdeen*	10
Burnhervie *Aberdeen*	10
Burntisland *Fife*	86
Bute, Isle of *Argyll*	30

C

Cairnryan *D & G*	69
Callander *Stirling*	197
Callanish *Lewis, W Isles*	209
Calligarry *Skye, Inn Heb*	148
Cambuskenneth *Stirling*	198
Campbeltown *Argyll*	31
Camusteel *Highland*	109
Camustianavaig *Skye, Inn Heb*	148
Canisbay *Highland*	109
Canonbie *D & G*	69
Caol *Highland*	109
Carbost (Drynoch) *Skye, Inn Heb*	148
Cardross *Argyll*	31
Carfrae *Lothian*	162
Carinish *N Uist, W Isles*	210
Carishader *Lewis, W Isles*	209
Carnoustie *Angus*	23
Carradale *Argyll*	31
Carrbridge *Highland*	109
Castle Douglas *D & G*	69
Castle Kennedy *D & G*	70
Castletown (Thurso) *Highland*	110
Catacol *Arran*	45
Cawdor *Highland*	110
Chapel of Garioch *Aberdeen*	11
Clachan (Kintyre) *Argyll*	32
Clachan of Glendaruel *Argyll*	32
Cleish *Perth*	184
Cluer *Harris, W Isles*	207
Clunie *Perth*	184
Colbost *Skye, Inn Heb*	149
Coldingham *Borders*	58
Colintraive *Argyll*	32
Coll, Isle of *Inn Heb*	143
Comrie *Perth*	184
Connel *Argyll*	32
Conon Bridge *Highland*	110
Contin *Highland*	110
Corpach *Highland*	110
Corriecravie *Arran*	45
Corstorphine *Edinburgh, Lothian*	165
Cortachy *Angus*	23
Coxhill *D & G*	70
Coylton *Ayrshire*	48
Craigentinny *Edinburgh, Lothian*	165
Craigleith *Edinburgh, Lothian*	165
Craignure *Mull, Inn Heb*	144
Crail *Fife*	86
Craobh Haven *Argyll*	33
Crathie *Aberdeen*	11
Creebridge *D & G*	70
Creetown *D & G*	70
Crianlarich *Stirling*	198

Location Index

Crieff *Perth*	184
Croachy *Highland*	111
Crocketford *D & G*	71
Croftamie *Stirling*	199
Crossmichael *D & G*	71
Cullen *Aberdeen*	11
Culloden Moor *Highland*	111
Culross *Fife*	86
Cupar *Fife*	86

D

Dalbeattie *D & G*	71
Dalcross *Highland*	111
Dalkeith *Lothian*	163
Dalmally *Argyll*	33
Dalmuir *Glasgow*	97
Daviot *Highland*	111
Deargphort *Mull, Inn Heb*	144
Dechmont *Lothian*	163
Delny *Highland*	111
Dennistoun *Glasgow*	97
Dervaig *Mull, Inn Heb*	144
Dess *Aberdeen*	11
Diabaig *Highland*	112
Dollar *Stirling*	199
Dornie *Highland*	112
Dornoch *Highland*	112
Doune *Stirling*	199
Dowanhill *Glasgow*	97
Drumblade *Aberdeen*	11
Drumbreck *Glasgow*	97
Drumbuie *Highland*	113
Drumnadrochit *Highland*	113
Drumrack *Fife*	86
Drumsmittal *Highland*	113
Drymen *Stirling*	199
Duddingston *Edinburgh, Lothian*	166
Dufftown *Aberdeen*	12
Dullatur *Lanarks*	157
Dulnain Bridge *Highland*	114
Dumfries *D & G*	71
Dunbar *Lothian*	163
Dunblane *Stirling*	200
Dundee *Angus*	23
Dunfermline *Fife*	87
Dunkeld *Perth*	185
Dunoon *Argyll*	33
Duns *Borders*	59
Dunscore *D & G*	73
Dunure *Ayrshire*	48
Dunvegan *Skye, Inn Heb*	149
Durness *Highland*	114
Duthil *Highland*	114

E

Earsary *Barra, W Isles*	207
East Kilbride *Lanarks*	157
Ecclefechan *D & G*	73
Eckford *Borders*	59
Edinbane *Skye, Inn Heb*	150
Edinburgh *Lothian*	163
Edinburgh, Central *Lothian*	164
Ednam *Borders*	59
Edradynate *Perth*	185
Edzell *Angus*	24
Elgin *Aberdeen*	12

Elie *Fife*	87
Elliot *Angus*	24
Ellon *Aberdeen*	13
Embo *Highland*	115
Ettrick *Borders*	59
Eynort *Skye, Inn Heb*	150
Eyre *Skye, Inn Heb*	150

F

Fair Isle *Shetland*	192
Fairmilehead *Edinburgh, Lothian*	166
Fala *Lothian*	171
Falkirk *Lothian*	172
Falkland *Fife*	87
Fearnan *Perth*	185
Feshiebridge *Highland*	115
Finavon *Angus*	25
Fionnphort *Mull, Inn Heb*	144
Fordyce *Aberdeen*	13
Forfar *Angus*	25
Forres *Aberdeen*	13
Fort Augustus *Highland*	115
Fort William *Highland*	115
Fortingall *Perth*	185
Foyers *Highland*	118
Freuchie *Fife*	87

G

Gairloch *Highland*	118
Galashiels *Borders*	59
Gamrie *Aberdeen*	14
Gardenstown *Aberdeen*	14
Gargunnock *Stirling*	201
Garmouth *Aberdeen*	14
Garryheillie *S Uist, W Isles*	210
Gartocharn *Glasgow*	95
Garve *Highland*	118
Gatehead *Ayrshire*	49
Gattonside *Borders*	59
Gelston *D & G*	73
Giffnock *Glasgow*	96
Gilmerton *Edinburgh, Lothian*	166
Girvan *Ayrshire*	49
Glamis *Angus*	25
Glasgow *Glasgow*	96
Glasgow, Central *Glasgow*	96
Glassford *Lanarks*	157
Glenbarr *Argyll*	34
Glencoe *Highland*	118
Glenfinnan *Highland*	119
Glengolly *Highland*	119
Glenisla *Angus*	25
Glenkindie *Aberdeen*	14
Glenlivet *Aberdeen*	14
Glenluce *D & G*	73
Glenmavis *Lanarks*	158
Glenmore *Highland*	119
Glenmoriston *Highland*	119
Glenshiel *Highland*	119
Gorebridge *Lothian*	172
Govanhill *Glasgow*	98
Grantown-on-Spey *Highland*	119
Greenlaw *Borders*	60
Gress *Lewis, W Isles*	209
Gretna *D & G*	74
Gribun *Mull, Inn Heb*	145

Griminis *Benbecula, W Isles*	207
Guardbridge *Fife*	87
Gulberwick *Mainld, Shetland*	192

H

Haddington *Lothian*	172
Hamilton *Lanarks*	158
Harpsdale *Highland*	120
Harrapool *Skye, Inn Heb*	150
Harris, Isle of *W Isles*	207
Haugh of Urr *D & G*	74
Hawick *Borders*	60
Heiton *Borders*	60
Helensburgh *Argyll*	34
Helmsdale *Highland*	120
Heribusta *Skye, Inn Heb*	150
High Auchenlarie *D & G*	74
Hollandstoun *N Ronaldsay, Orkney*	179
Hollybush *Ayrshire*	49
Hopeman *Aberdeen*	14
Huntly *Aberdeen*	15

I

Inchree *Highland*	121
Innellan *Argyll*	36
Innerleithen *Borders*	60
Inver *Perth*	185
Inveralligin *Highland*	121
Inveraray *Argyll*	36
Inverarnan *Argyll*	36
Inverboyndie *Aberdeen*	15
Inveresk *Lothian*	172
Invergarry *Highland*	121
Invergordon *Highland*	121
Inverinate *Highland*	122
Inverkeithing *Fife*	88
Inverkip *Glasgow*	98
Inverleith *Edinburgh, Lothian*	166
Inverlochy *Highland*	122
Inverness *Highland*	122
Invershin *Highland*	125
Inverurie *Aberdeen*	15
Islay, Isle of *Inn Heb*	143

J

Jedburgh *Borders*	60
John O' Groats *Highland*	125
Johnshaven *Aberdeen*	16
Joppa *Edinburgh, Lothian*	166

K

Keiss *Highland*	125
Keith *Aberdeen*	16
Kelso *Borders*	61
Kentallen *Highland*	125
Kilbarchan *Glasgow*	98
Kilchrenan *Argyll*	36
Kilfinan *Argyll*	36
Killiecrankie *Perth*	185
Killin *Stirling*	201
Kilmacolm *Glasgow*	98
Kilmarnock *Ayrshire*	49
Kilmartin *Argyll*	37
Kilmore *Argyll*	37
Kilmuir (Uig) *Skye, Inn Heb*	150
Kilwinning *Ayrshire*	49

Kinbrace *Highland*	126
Kincraig *Highland*	126
Kinghorn *Fife*	88
Kingsbarns *Fife*	88
Kingussie *Highland*	126
Kinloch Rannoch *Perth*	186
Kinlochleven *Highland*	127
Kinross *Perth*	186
Kirk Yetholm *Borders*	62
Kirkcaldy *Fife*	88
Kirkcowan *D & G*	74
Kirkcudbright *D & G*	74
Kirkfieldbank *Lanarks*	158
Kirkmichael *Perth*	186
Kirkmuirhill *Lanarks*	158
Kirkton *D & G*	75
Kirkwall *Mainld, Orkney*	177
Kirriemuir *Angus*	25
Kyle of Lochalsh *Highland*	128
Kyleakin *Skye, Inn Heb*	151
Kylesku *Highland*	128

L

Ladybank *Fife*	89
Lagavulin *Islay, Inn Heb*	143
Laggan (Newtonmore)	
Highland	128
Laid *Highland*	129
Laide *Highland*	129
Lairg *Highland*	129
Lamlash *Arran*	45
Lanark *Lanarks*	158
Langholm *D & G*	75
Langlee *Borders*	62
Langshaw *Borders*	62
Largs *Ayrshire*	50
Larkhall *Lanarks*	158
Lassodie *Fife*	89
Lasswade *Lothian*	172
Latheron *Highland*	129
Lauder *Borders*	62
Laurieston *Lothian*	173
Leadhills *Lanarks*	158
Ledaig *Argyll*	37
Lendalfoot *Ayrshire*	50
Lerags *Argyll*	37
Lerwick *Mainld, Shetland*	192
Leswalt *D & G*	75
Letham *Angus*	26
Leuchars *Fife*	89
Leurbost *Lewis, W Isles*	209
Leven *Fife*	90
Leverburgh *Harris, W Isles*	208
Lewis, Isle of *W Isles*	208
Lewiston *Highland*	129
Linlithgow *Lothian*	173
Little Loch Roag	
Lewis, W Isles	210
Loanhead *Lothian*	173
Loch Achray *Stirling*	201
Locharbriggs *D & G*	75
Lochboisdale *S Uist, W Isles*	211
Lochcarron *Highland*	129
Lochfield *D & G*	75
Lochgilphead *Argyll*	37
Lochinver *Highland*	130
Lochluichart *Highland*	130

Lochmaben *D & G*	76
Lochranza *Arran*	46
Lochwinnoch *Glasgow*	98
Lockerbie *D & G*	76
Longformacus *Borders*	62
Longniddry *Lothian*	173
Lossiemouth *Aberdeen*	16
Luib *Skye, Inn Heb*	151
Luss *Argyll*	38
Luthrie *Fife*	90
Lybster (Wick) *Highland*	130

M

Mainland *Orkney*	177
Mainland *Shetland*	192
Mallaig *Highland*	130
Markinch *Fife*	90
Mauchline *Ayrshire*	50
Maud *Aberdeen*	17
Maybole *Ayrshire*	51
Mayfield (Edinburgh)	
Edinburgh, Lothian	167
Meigle *Perth*	186
Mellon Charles *Highland*	131
Melrose *Borders*	63
Melvich *Highland*	131
Merchiston	
Edinburgh, Lothian	169
Methlick *Aberdeen*	17
Methven *Perth*	187
Mey *Highland*	131
Milnathort *Perth*	187
Milngavie *Glasgow*	99
Milton of Buchanan *Stirling*	202
Minard *Argyll*	38
Moffat *D & G*	77
Monifieth *Angus*	26
Monikie *Angus*	26
Monkton *Ayrshire*	51
Montrose *Angus*	26
Morar *Highland*	131
Morningside	
Edinburgh, Lothian	169
Muir of Ord *Highland*	131
Muirend *Glasgow*	98
Muirshearlich *Highland*	131
Mull, Isle of *Inn Heb*	144
Munlochy *Highland*	131
Musselburgh *Lothian*	174

N

Nairn *Highland*	132
Nethermill *D & G*	78
Nethy Bridge *Highland*	132
New Cumnock *Ayrshire*	51
Newbigging *Lanarks*	159
Newcastleton *Borders*	63
Newington	
Edinburgh, Lothian	169
Newmarket *Lewis, W Isles*	210
Newmilns *Ayrshire*	51
Newton (Elgin) *Aberdeen*	17
Newton Stewart *D & G*	79
Newtonhill *Aberdeen*	17
Newtonmore *Highland*	133
Nigg *Highland*	133
North Bay *Barra, W Isles*	207

North Berwick *Lothian*	174
North Kessock *Highland*	133
North Queensferry *Fife*	90
North Ronaldsay *Orkney*	179
North Uist, Isle of *W Isles*	210
Northfield *Edinburgh, Lothian*	170
Northton *Harris, W Isles*	208

O

Oban *Argyll*	39
Ochiltree *Ayrshire*	52
Ochtertyre *Stirling*	202
Onich *Highland*	134
Ord *Skye, Inn Heb*	151
Oyne *Aberdeen*	17

P

Paisley *Glasgow*	99
Papa Stour *Shetland*	193
Parkgate *D & G*	79
Parton *D & G*	79
Pathhead *Lothian*	175
Peebles *Borders*	63
Penicuik *Lothian*	175
Perth *Perth*	187
Peterhead *Aberdeen*	17
Pilrig *Edinburgh, Lothian*	170
Piperhill *Highland*	134
Pitlochry *Perth*	188
Pitscottie *Fife*	90
Plockton *Highland*	134
Poolewe *Highland*	134
Port of Menteith *Stirling*	202
Port of Ness *Lewis, W Isles*	210
Portling *D & G*	79
Portmahomack *Highland*	134
Portnalong *Skye, Inn Heb*	151
Portobello *Edinburgh, Lothian*	171
Portpatrick *D & G*	79
Portree *Skye, Inn Heb*	152
Portsoy *Aberdeen*	18
Poyntzfield *Highland*	135
Prestonfield	
Edinburgh, Lothian	171
Prestwick *Ayrshire*	52

R

Ratagan *Highland*	135
Reston *Borders*	63
Rhynd *Perth*	190
Rockcliffe *D & G*	80
Rogart *Highland*	135
Rothes *Aberdeen*	18
Rothesay *Bute*	30
Rothiemurchus *Highland*	135
Rothienorman *Aberdeen*	18
Roundyhill *Angus*	26
Rowardennan *Stirling*	202
Ruthwell *D & G*	80

S

Salen *Mull, Inn Heb*	145
Sandwick *Mainld, Orkney*	178
Sanquhar *D & G*	80
Scadabay *Harris, W Isles*	208
Scalloway *Mainld, Shetland*	193
Scalpay, Isle of *Harris, W Isles*	208

Scaniport *Highland*	135	
Scourie *Highland*	135	
Scousburgh *Mainld, Shetland*	193	
Selkirk *Borders*	64	
Shandon *Argyll*	41	
Shieldaig (Loch Shieldaig)		
Highland	136	
Shiskine *Arran*	46	
Skelmorlie *Ayrshire*	52	
Skye, Isle of *Inn Heb*	146	
Slateford *Edinburgh, Lothian*	171	
Smithton *Highland*	136	
Sordale *Highland*	136	
South Laggan *Highland*	136	
South Queensferry *Lothian*	175	
South Uist, Isle of *W Isles*	210	
Southwick *D & G*	80	
Spean Bridge *Highland*	136	
Spey Bay *Aberdeen*	18	
St Abbs *Borders*	64	
St Andrews *Fife*	91	
St Boswells *Borders*	64	
St Catherines *Argyll*	41	
St Cyrus *Aberdeen*	18	
St Fillans *Perth*	190	
St Monans *Fife*	92	
Staffin *Skye, Inn Heb*	153	
Stair *Ayrshire*	52	
Stanley *Perth*	190	
Stenscholl *Skye, Inn Heb*	153	
Stepps *Glasgow*	99	
Stirling *Stirling*	202	
Stoer *Highland*	137	
Stonehaven *Aberdeen*	18	
Stoneyburn *Lothian*	175	
Stoneykirk *D & G*	81	
Stornoway *Lewis, W Isles*	210	
Straiton *Ayrshire*	52	
Stranraer *D & G*	81	
Strathaird *Skye, Inn Heb*	154	
Strathan (Lochinver)		
Highland	137	
Strathaven *Lanarks*	159	
Strathdon *Aberdeen*	19	
Strathkinness *Fife*	92	
Strathpeffer *Highland*	137	
Strathyre *Stirling*	204	
Stromeferry *Highland*	138	
Stromness *Mainld, Orkney*	178	
Strontian *Highland*	138	
Struan *Skye, Inn Heb*	154	
Swinton *Borders*	64	
Symington *Ayrshire*	52	
T		
Tain (Dornoch Firth) *Highland*	138	
Tarbert *Harris, W Isles*	208	
Tarbert (Kintyre) *Argyll*	41	
Tarbet *Argyll*	42	
Teviothead *Borders*	64	
The Braes *Skye, Inn Heb*	154	
Thornhill *Stirling*	204	
Thurso *Highland*	138	
Tighnabruaich *Argyll*	42	
Tillicoultry *Stirling*	205	
Tobermory *Mull, Inn Heb*	145	
Tomatin *Highland*	139	
Tomintoul *Aberdeen*	19	
Tomnavoulin *Aberdeen*	20	
Tongue *Highland*	139	
Tore *Highland*	140	
Torlundy *Highland*	140	
Torridon *Highland*	140	
Torthorwald *D & G*	82	
Town Yetholm *Borders*	65	
Trinity *Edinburgh, Lothian*	171	
Troon *Ayrshire*	53	
Turriff *Aberdeen*	20	
Twynholm *D & G*	82	
Tyndrum *Stirling*	205	
Tynron *D & G*	82	
U		
Uddingston *Lanarks*	159	
Uig (Uig Bay) *Skye, Inn Heb*	155	
Uigshader *Skye, Inn Heb*	155	
Ullapool *Highland*	140	
Uphall *Lothian*	175	
Urquhart *Aberdeen*	20	
V		
Vatten *Skye, Inn Heb*	155	
W		
Waternish *Skye, Inn Heb*	155	
Westhill *Highland*	141	
Whins of Milton *Stirling*	205	
Whithorn *D & G*	82	
Whiting Bay *Arran*	46	
Wick *Highland*	141	
Wigtown *D & G*	83	
Winchburgh *Lothian*	175	
Wishaw *Lanarks*	159	
Wiston *Lanarks*	159	
Wormit *Fife*	92	
Y		
Yarrow Feus *Borders*	65	